REVEREND
ADDIE WYATT

WOMEN, GENDER, AND SEXUALITY IN AMERICAN HISTORY

Editorial Advisors:
Susan K. Cahn
Wanda A. Hendricks
Deborah Gray White

Anne Firor Scott, Founding Editor Emerita

A list of books in the series appears at the end of this book.

REVEREND
ADDIE WYATT

FAITH AND THE FIGHT FOR LABOR, GENDER, AND RACIAL EQUALITY

MARCIA WALKER-MCWILLIAMS

UNIVERSITY OF ILLINOIS PRESS

URBANA, CHICAGO, AND SPRINGFIELD

CONTENTS

ACKNOWLEDGMENTS

There are many individuals and institutions whose time, energies, and resources have contributed to this book, and I want to convey my deepest gratitude to them. My intellectual journey and decision to become a historian emerged as an undergraduate at Northwestern University in the Department of African American Studies. I must acknowledge the two historians who helped shape my early exposure to the field, Nancy Maclean and Martha Biondi. Without Nancy's course, "Affirmative Action at Work," I may never have discovered Addie Wyatt and her remarkable life. And Martha's guidance and support expanded my knowledge and understanding of how to research, conceptualize, and write African American history. I am grateful that she agreed to serve as a mentor and model historian. Critical interviews, literature, and historical themes emerged from our conversations and her enthusiastic engagement with this book. At the University of Chicago, Adam Green and Thomas Holt provided consistent support for a biography on the life of Addie Wyatt, as well as thoughtful feedback and advice. Adam Green believed in the promise of this biography from the start. His faith and confidence in my ability to tell Addie Wyatt's story has inspired me to own my scholarly voice with greater authority. His comments on many drafts of the manuscript have consistently raised the conceptual and historical stakes of this book. And his help in navigating the sometimes turbulent waters of life in the academy has been invaluable. I am truly appreciative of the camaraderie that we share. Thomas Holt served as a model for how precision and clarity in writing can illuminate complex historical arguments about the nature of race, class, gender, and other categories of analysis in American history. His contributions to this biography are much appreciated. My sincerest gratitude goes to many University of Chicago faculty and staff for their support of this book and my future as a historian.

Special thanks must also be given to Jacqueline Goldsby for bringing me on as part of the Mapping the Stacks Project, funded by the Andrew Mellon Foundation; Commonwealth Edison; and the University of Chicago's Center for the Study of Race, Politics and Culture and the Division of Humanities. The Mapping the Stacks group camaraderie, delicious dinners, and collective commitment to making an intellectual contribution to African American history beyond the academy comprise some of the best memories and achievements from my graduate years. On the project, I worked out of the Vivian G. Harsh Research Collection of Afro-American Life of the Carter G. Woodson Branch of the Chicago Public Library. I met a wonderful archivist there, Michael Flug, and learned that the Harsh had recently acquired the Rev. Addie Wyatt and Rev. Claude Wyatt Papers. Over the years, his commitment to this book manuscript has been inspiring, encouraging, and limitless. Though I appreciate all of the Harsh Staff—Bob, Beverly, Denise, Cynthia, and Lucinda for making the Harsh a much-needed home, Michael took on the role of in loco parentis, friend, mentor, thoughtful critic, and champion. Thank you, Michael, for your work behind the scenes to make Addie Wyatt's story come to life.

Funding from the University of Chicago's Social Sciences Division, the History Department, Center for Gender Studies, and Center for the Study of Race, Politics and Culture assisted my early research and writing. A two-year Visiting Scholar appointment in the African American Studies Program at the University of Houston provided much-needed funding to complete the research and writing of this manuscript. Prairie View A&M University also provided key support in the final stages of this book. I must thank archivists at the Chicago Public Library, the Wisconsin Historical Society, Anderson University and Church of God Archives, the Mississippi Department of Archives and History, the Walter P. Reuther Library at Wayne State University, the Tamiment Library and Robert F. Wagner Labor Archives at New York University, the Schomburg Center for Research in Black Culture, the Martin Luther King Jr. Center for Non-Violent Social Change, the Robert W. Woodruff Library, Atlanta University Center, Dolph Briscoe Center for American History at the University of Texas, and the Schlesinger Library at Harvard University for their assistance.

This biography could not have been completed without those who were willing to share their voices. I must thank them for agreeing to sit down and talk with me. They include Addie Wyatt, Rev. Willie Barrow, Claude Wyatt III, Maude McKay, Timuel Black, Les Orear, Bennett Johnson, Rev. Calvin Morris, Mary Crayton, Katie Jordan, Sarah White, and Harold Rogers. René Wyatt-Hall, granddaughter of Claude and Addie Wyatt, provided thoughtful comments on chapters of the manuscript as well as support for this book. The grandchildren of Claude and Addie Wyatt—René Wyatt-Hall, Allen Wyatt, Brian Wyatt, Darren Montgomery, Claudea Wyatt-Ellis, and Sharron Wyatt—carry on the legacy of their grandparents. In addition, three interviews and oral histories of Addie Wyatt proved especially critical to reconstructing parts of her life. In 1977, Wyatt participated in a multipart interview with Elizabeth Balanoff as part of an Oral History Project in Labor History housed at Roosevelt University. A 2002 oral history conducted by Julieanna Richardson of The HistoryMakers provided particularly important insight on Addie Wyatt's childhood. Finally, an interview with the Chicago-based Working Women's History Project, conducted by Joan McGann Morris, also helped fill in important aspects of Wyatt's life in the labor, civil rights, and women's movements. Many thanks to the dedicated editors and staff of the University of Illinois Press for their support, enthusiasm, and hard work in literally bringing this work to life.

My family has been the greatest source of support throughout my life and I would not be who I am without you all—Mom, LaDonna, Nakesha, William, and the next generation of the circle, as well as the Jones and McWilliams clans. The life of an academic can be isolating, but I am thankful to the many friends who stuck by me and supported me and this book from near and afar. I must mention by name Traci, my partner in crime in the history department and without whom I might not have made it through graduate school. I also thank Jessica, whose friendship since college and willingness to travel the world have helped me connect to a broader world. You've always been a positive force in my life. Finally, I have to thank Leon, my husband, who has shared in all of my peaks and valleys during the writing of this biography. This process has not been easy, and when I've doubted my path, you were there to listen, encourage me and give unconditional love and support. Our relationship has been the greatest source of happiness for me.

REVEREND
ADDIE WYATT

TELL THE STORY

Hundreds of letters poured in to the headquarters of the Amalgamated Meat Cutters and Butcher Workmen of North America, and they were all addressed to Addie Wyatt, Director of Women's Affairs. The letters were from colleagues and friends congratulating Wyatt on her selection as one of *TIME Magazine*'s Twelve Women of the Year, which celebrated women who, in 1975, made significant contributions to American society.[1] Wyatt had mixed feelings about the honor. On one hand, she was grateful for the recognition, increased visibility, and clout that the article gave her; it made her "job of improving work conditions for women easier" by highlighting the need to have greater female participation in the membership, structure, and direction of the organized labor movement.[2] But Wyatt was also highly critical of the achievement and the *TIME* article featuring the honorees. In one of the many interviews she gave about the honor, Wyatt revealed: "Being one of the Women of the Year was really a surprise . . . and if I'd known what they were going to do, I don't know if I would have gone through with it. . . . They left out millions of faceless and nameless women who have made outstanding and inspiring contributions."[3] She stated her frustrations more pointedly in another interview: "That's 12 women in a year—you'd think they were trying to make up in one issue for all the neglect of women over the years."[4]

Wyatt's criticisms likely had as much to do with the article's content and characterization of the women's movement as they did with the neglect of women's contributions to society in the mainstream media. *TIME*'s "Women of the Year" article boldly announced and praised the women's movement and the entrance of more women into leadership positions—a change that bucked "the traditional relationships between the sexes." The article proclaimed that the change in American attitudes toward gender roles owed "much to the formal feminist

movement—the Friedans and Steinems and Abzugs. . . . [F]eminism has transcended the feminist movement. . . . and the women's drive penetrated every
layer of society, matured beyond ideology to a new status of general—and sometimes unconscious—acceptance."[5] *TIME* further attributed the beginnings of
the women's movement of the 1960s and 1970s to a handful of highly educated,
white middle-class women. Nonwhite, working-class, and poor women had
simply latched onto the feminist movement: "the belief that women are entitled
to truly equal social and professional rights has spread far and deep into the
country. Once the doctrine of well-educated middle-class women, often young
and single, it has taken hold among working-class women, farm wives, blacks,
Puerto Ricans, white 'ethnics.'"[6]

While the article revered Wyatt and the other honorees, it minimized the importance and contributions of women of color and working-class women in the
movement. The *TIME* article erroneously painted the women's movement of the
1960s and 1970s as an aberration, thereby divorcing it and its participants from
a lengthier history of women's rights activism over the course of the twentieth
century. Rather than passive recipients or belated participants, working-class
women and women of color played critical roles as leaders and activists in shaping the women's movement from within and challenging their marginalization
in the quest for women's equality. Working-class women and women of color
in the movement brought to it the importance of race, class, and gender as in-
terlocking lived identities that impacted the overall advancement of women in
all areas of society. More than anyone, Addie Wyatt—a black woman, a labor
leader and a feminist—transcended the barriers between the organized labor
and the women's movement in hopes of providing a stronger voice for women
in labor and for working-class women and black women in the women's movement. Though the article captured one of Wyatt's greatest passions, the pursuit of
women's equality, it did less to illuminate her long history of fighting for racial
equality within and outside of the organized labor movement and her role as a
civil rights activist in Chicago and the American South. Wyatt's credentials as
an ordained minister and the spirituality that was so essential to her activism
and leadership in social justice movements were also not featured.

Addie Wyatt believed in a universal, God-given human equality, inclusive
of freedom from racial oppression, discrimination, sexism, and poverty, which
denied human beings access to their full potential. Wyatt's personal struggles
with discrimination led to a lifetime of fighting against inequality through collective action, organizations, and social movements. From the 1940s through
the turn of the twenty-first century, Addie Wyatt blazed a trail of activism and
leadership in the American labor movement, the civil rights movement, the
women's movement, and the religious movement. Wyatt traversed the geo-
graphical, ideological, and demographic boundaries of these movements and

helped to broaden their scopes by pushing for even greater racial, gender, and class diversity within them. Addie Wyatt believed that progressive movements without a diversity of perspectives, representation, and solidarity in purpose, could not live up to their fullest potential and the highest goal of improving the quality of life for all people. It was the task of those who understood this dynamic to participate in and lead the fight against oppression, discrimination, and inequality. As someone who had firsthand experience with these isms and understood that any form of discrimination—racial, gender, or economic—were equally detrimental to humanity, Addie Wyatt was uniquely positioned to challenge and lead social justice movements.

Addie Wyatt (nee Cameron) was born on March 8, 1924, in Brookhaven, Mississippi, to Ambrose and Maggie Cameron, a presser and a part-time teacher, respectively. In 1930 during the Great Depression, the family fled Mississippi after Addie's father struck his white boss during an altercation. They relocated to Chicago where the family's financial struggles and abject poverty had an indelible effect on Addie Wyatt. However, it was also in Chicago that the family became members of the Church of God (Anderson, Indiana), which Wyatt would belong to throughout her lifetime. In 1940, at the age of sixteen Addie married her high-school sweetheart, Claude Wyatt, and the couple quickly added two sons, Renaldo and Claude III, to their family. After the passing of Wyatt's mother, Maggie, in 1944, Addie and Claude Wyatt assumed responsibility for Addie's six younger siblings whom they raised in the Altgeld Gardens Housing Project. The Wyatts were a part of the first generation of African Americans to live in public housing, which at the time in Chicago was some of the best housing available to blacks in terms of price and comfort. In need of work to help contribute to her growing household, Wyatt gained employment as a canner in Chicago's meatpacking district during World War II. She eventually became one of the city's most well-known and outspoken labor activists. Wyatt also became the first African American woman elected president of Local 56 of the United Packinghouse Workers of America (UPWA), one of the most racially progressive unions in the Congress of Industrial Organizations (CIO).

When the UPWA merged with the more conservative Amalgamated Meat Cutters and Butcher Workman of North America in 1968, Wyatt lobbied for and became head of the union's Women's Rights Department in 1974. In 1976, shortly after her *TIME* achievement, Wyatt became the first female international vice president in the history of the Amalgamated Meat Cutters. Three years later when her union merged yet again, Wyatt became international vice president and Director of Civil Rights and Women's Affairs of the 1.5 million member United Food and Commercial Workers (UFCW), one of the largest unions in the AFL-CIO at that time. Wyatt was one of the highest-ranked women in the organized labor movement when she retired from the UFCW in 1984. Though she was loyal to the labor movement and believed it to be the greatest resource for working people, Wyatt did not hesitate to participate in labor-based organizations that challenged workers and unions to acknowledge and ameliorate racism, sexism, and discrimination within the workplace and the organized labor movement. Wyatt belonged to three organizations that bridged a concern for black workers and working women's equity: the Negro American Labor Council (NALC), founded in 1961, the Coalition of Black Trade Unionists (CBTU), founded in 1972, and the Coalition of Labor Union Women (CLUW), which emerged in 1974.

While the labor movement and Wyatt's union served as organizational and political anchors, her activism and leadership consistently crossed over into other movements and struggles for economic, political, and social equality. An ardent supporter of the southern civil rights movement, Wyatt provided critical financial aid through her fund-raising in the UPWA's District One for the Montgomery Bus Boycott. In 1955, Claude and Addie Wyatt founded the Vernon Park Church of God, which contributed human and financial capital to demonstrations in the South including the Selma to Montgomery Marches. The Wyatts participated in and led local Chicago civil rights struggles around housing segregation, employment discrimination, health disparities, police brutality, and the need for black civic engagement and political power in the Windy City. They were founding members of Operation Breadbasket, initially the economic arm of the Southern Christian Leadership Conference (SCLC) in Chicago. Addie Wyatt was at the center of a progressive labor/civil rights/ religious coalition of black activists and leaders formed in the 1950s that made a lasting impact on independent and Democratic politics in Chicago. This same coalition, in conjunction with networks of independent progressives, Latinos, and women, elected Harold Washington as Chicago's first black mayor in 1983.

Addie Wyatt also remained a strident activist for women's rights, a commitment rooted in her religious background in the Church of God, which believed in and practiced, at least early on, equality in all facets of church leadership among men and women. Wyatt also found support for her belief in women's equality through the Bible and a belief that God created men and women as equal beings who must work together on equal footing to manage society. Wyatt began working for women's rights within organized labor. In 1962, she was appointed to President Kennedy's Commission on the Status of Women (PCSW) as a member of the Protective Labor Legislation Committee. Later she became one of the nation's most outspoken proponents of the Equal Rights Amendment (ERA) and began lobbying for its ratification in the early 1970s. Wyatt challenged the women's movement to incorporate the problems of working women and women of color into the agenda while seeking to motivate them to recognize their stake in women's issues and the women's movement. Wyatt even targeted sexism within the church by becoming ordained and preaching a theology of gender equality.

These developments remain, in a sense, Addie Wyatt's "greatest hits" and are held together by Wyatt's philosophy of liberation from inequality that infused her participation in the labor, civil rights, women's rights, and religious movements. By no means was her life a smooth, linear march toward greater personal fulfillment and collective victory against inequality. Wyatt's struggle for equality and the struggle of those in the fight with her was marred by crippling setbacks, pervasive and seemingly intractable discrimination, and the fracture of key coalitions and organizations needed to mount a formidable opposition to inequality. This book explores these ebbs and flows and is thus both a biography and a study of twentieth-century American history from Wyatt's vantage point, but written by a historian. As biographer Kenneth Silverman argues, "The biographer seeks what the subject's life meant *to the subject*, how the subject's experience registered on his or her consciousness, the satisfaction it supplied, the dilemmas it produced. This inwardness is what distinguishes biography from history."[7] Silverman sets biography apart from history, but biography can go beyond a focus on movement or event outcomes and shed greater light on the meanings of social movements to those who lived through them as they unfolded. Similarly, historian and biographer David Nasaw argues that "in the process of researching and writing about individual lives embedded in particular times and places, biographers discover and reveal ways in which their subjects assume, discard, reconfigure, merge and disassociate multiple identities and roles. . . . [I]t is the task of the biographer to disentangle, to prioritize, to attempt to understand how, in a given time and place, a 'self' is organized and performed."[8] This biographical study has at its core Addie Wyatt's own writings, recollections, and understandings of her life's work, combined with rich archival sources, movement histories, and interviews.

Addie Wyatt's theological understanding of Christianity and deep spiritualism resonated within her social justice movement activism. She had faith in the belief that an enduring and collective struggle for human equality and dignity will yield tangible results. Just as inequality endures, so must the struggle against it. In both cases, the biblical scripture from Hebrews 11:1, "Now faith is the substance of things hoped for, the evidence of things not seen" holds significance.[9] This is not a story of the death of racism, sexism, discrimination, and poverty, but rather a blueprint of a philosophy of equality that can provide an infrastructure for positive social change. Wyatt desired to break free from anything that oppressed the human spirit and its ability to not just survive, but thrive. This biography takes seriously, though not uncritically, the roles of faith and spirituality as motivating foundations for Addie Wyatt's movement activism. By virtue of her particular brand of spirituality rooted in the social gospel and gender equality, as well as her experiences as a black woman affected by race, gender, and class, Wyatt had direct insight into multiple dimensions of the human struggle, which manifested itself in the various movements she embraced. This insight allowed Wyatt to craft a philosophy of equality rooted in solidarity or a belief in a common set of values and struggles. Thus organizing, educating, and building community within and across groups were essential strategies that Wyatt used to advance her philosophy into action.

Taken in this light, it becomes even clearer why Wyatt remained so wedded to the organized labor movement, a movement whose lifeline is solidarity and collective action. Wyatt believed that the labor movement was the best possible vehicle through which working people could achieve a better way of life. But just because she believed that it was the best vehicle, did not mean that it was perfect and could not be made better. Thus Wyatt endeavored with others to push the labor movement beyond its limits in search of greater representation, participation, and leadership by women and workers of color. The shortcomings and limits of the labor movement in the way of racism and sexism warranted organization and change from within. But Wyatt also saw the utility of working beyond labor in the civil rights movement and the women's movement, both of which included working-class activists, women activists, and activists of color in pursuit of greater equality.

Wyatt's life holds historical significance because it illuminates new insight into the rich ties within and between the organized labor, civil rights, women's rights, and religious movements. This book ultimately argues for and supports a much more varied and expansive portrait of social activists whose commitments to equality traverse the rigid boundaries of social movement scholarship. Addie Wyatt's life history opens up a space for exploring the real complexities of the relationships between faith, race, class, and gender and the pursuit of liberation and equality. This book also explores important dimensions of the African American freedom struggle, such as a greater appreciation for the black working class and black labor organizing, both of which remain significant to African Americans and American labor history but remain understudied. Wyatt and progressive black trade unionists placed the concerns of working-class African Americans at the center of civil rights struggles and the quest for political empowerment. While scholars have questioned the relative silence of unionized and working-class women's voices within the labor movement and the women's movement, the role of black women as trade unionists and active members of the labor movement and their communities likewise remains woefully understudied. This book puts the struggles of black and women workers for inclusion and representation at the center of the American labor movement from World War II through the turn of the twenty-first century.

Addie Wyatt was indeed a feminist who believed in the social, political, and economic equality of men and women. The lack of black women's voices and experiences in second-wave feminism, as well as the lack of attention and recognition given to black women's voices in the civil rights movement and black power politics, prompted a core group of black feminists to articulate the theory of intersectionality in the 1970s and 1980s. As an analytical and theoretical tool, intersectionality refers to the ways in which social and political categories such as race, class, and gender converge as systems of oppression that contribute to black women's inequality.[10] Black feminist scholars such as Kimberle Crenshaw, bell hooks, and Patricia Hill Collins have been at the forefront of intersectionality theory, black feminist theory, and revisionist feminist scholarship since the late 1960s and early 1970s. Yet long before Collins, hooks, or Crenshaw articulated the theoretical underpinnings of black women's oppression, Addie Wyatt, and many women before her, were experiencing, calling out, challenging, and attempting to change the practices of discrimination, degradation, and assaults to their dignity as women. Wyatt and other black feminists of her generation need to be placed in the conversation about black feminism—what it is, what it looks like, and how it has been articulated over time. They need to be seen as viable constituents of the women's movement and all that it encompassed over the course of the 1960s, 1970s, and 1980s. As a black female trade unionist and Christian minister, Wyatt could appear to be an outlier in the feminist movement, but was in fact one of its leaders.

Because so much of Wyatt's development as an activist and leader took place within Chicago, the city plays a major role in her biography. Scholarship on Black Chicago has grown immensely within the past few decades and has been invaluable in providing a wider context for Addie Wyatt's life.[11] But her life also brings to light new or understudied dimensions of Black Chicago. Through a study of Wyatt's life, one sees how critical progressive black trade unionists, progressive women, and activist churches were to the city's economic and racial politics through the Harold Washington years. Labor activists allied with civil rights organizations and progressive religious leaders in a coalition against racial and economic inequalities that also served as a base for Democratic and independent black politics in the city.

Over the years, hundreds of journalists, scholars, writers, professionals, and students have interviewed Addie Wyatt about her life's work and legacy in social justice movements. Yet despite the interest her life has garnered over the years, very little has been written about Addie Wyatt in the historical record and there remains no full-length, in-depth scholarly study of her work as an organizer, activist, and leader.[12] I first met Addie Wyatt in February 2008 at her home in the Chatham neighborhood on the South Side of Chicago. She was eighty-four years old at the time and confined to a wheelchair due to a prolonged battle with arthritis and a debilitating stroke she suffered a few years prior. The stroke affected her endurance for interviews, so we briefly discussed her years of activism and leadership that spanned much of the twentieth century. While it became clear during the course of the interview that Addie Wyatt's ability to recall the details of certain moments in her life, such as the circumstances of her appointment to the PCSW and the extent of her involvement in the NALC, was not as sharp, she was able to recount with greater precision how her faith in God served as the very foundation for her participation and effective leadership in social justice movements.

It was not until two years after I first met Addie Wyatt that I believe she began to understand my desire to place her story and her voice—which binds together the often disparate ideological narratives of organized labor, civil rights, women's rights, and religious movements—in the historical record. I visited Addie Wyatt again on her birthday, March 8, 2010, also the date of International Women's Day. When I told her about a recent research trip that I had made to her birthplace, Brookhaven, Mississippi, she stopped short, reared back in her chair and looked at me in disbelief. "You went to Brookhaven?" she asked. "Yes," I replied and began to tell her how I visited the plot of land where her family's home used to be and watched the train pass through the depot that her family passed through eighty years earlier in 1930 as they left the South during the Great Migration. I told her that I had already made plans to return again that summer to learn more about her family's history—a history that she herself confessed to not fully know. I believe she began to understand that I wanted to write about more than just what she did. I wanted to better understand who she was and how the experiences of her life contributed to the public activist and leader she became. Near the end of our talk, she simply said to me, "Tell the story."

Using interviews, documents, sermons, and speeches, this biography tells the story of Wyatt's life in labor, civil rights, women's rights, and religious movements. Chapter 1 explores the centrality of family, faith, and experiences of racism and economic poverty during Wyatt's childhood and early teenage years. Chapter 2 continues an exploration of these themes, but within the context of Wyatt's nascent marriage to her high-school sweetheart, Claude Wyatt Jr., and her subsequent motherhood. The need to find employment in order to contribute to her household drove Wyatt to ultimately seek employment in the Chicago stockyards during World War II, thus introducing her to the gendered and racialized environment of meatpacking plants as well as the labor movement through the UPWA. This chapter also brings to light an important era of community and faith-based activism for Wyatt in the Altgeld Gardens housing project where she and her family resided from 1944 through 1955. In chapter 3, Wyatt's ascent in the UPWA from member to "activated" unionist, organizer, and leader over the course of the 1950s and 1960s is highlighted. During the same time span, chapter 4 specifically engages Wyatt's participation and leadership in civil rights struggles in Chicago and in the South, including campaigns for fair housing and access to medical care as well as the voting rights struggle in Selma. This chapter also surveys Wyatt's growing commitment to working-women's issues in the UPWA as well as her tenure with the PCSW from 1962 to 1963.

By the 1970s, Wyatt was a well-known and outspoken leader in the labor movement. Chapter 5 explores her ascent within the newly merged Amalgamated Meat Cutters and Butcher Workmen of North America as well as the birth of CBTU and CLUW. Wyatt's strategies for addressing the problems of working women and minorities during an era of increased discord between union leadership and members on the ground are also explored here. Chapter 6 explicitly engages the relationship between Addie Wyatt's faith and activism, most notably her work as a women's rights activist anod fierce proponent of the Equal Rights Amendment. Chapter 7 examines the tense last years of Wyatt's formal leadership in the United Food and Commercial Workers (UFCW) from 1979 to 1984 and looks at the promises and perils of black political and economic empowerment over the course of the 1980s and 1990s. The epilogue explores Wyatt's final years before her passing in 2012 and the lasting significance of legacy as an activist, leader, and believer in the freedom and equality of all people.

1

A CHILD OF
THE GREAT MIGRATION

If a Black Chicagoan has southern roots, chances are those roots trace back to Mississippi. One of the most well known and documented streams of the Great Migration is the path that African Americans took along the Illinois Central Railroad from the Magnolia State to the Windy City. Some migrants boarded the trains as far south as New Orleans while others boarded further north in Memphis. But the section of the Illinois Central Railroad that was most popular for migrants was the 250-mile stretch of railroad running from southern Mississippi up through the Delta, also known as the Mississippi Central Railroad. In 1930, six-year-old Addie Wyatt boarded a train and departed from the depot in Brookhaven, Mississippi, alongside her pregnant mother, grandmother, and three siblings. Born Addie Lorraine Cameron to Maggie and Ambrose Cameron on March 8, 1924, Addie spent the first six years of her life in Brookhaven. She was the second of what would ultimately be a large family of eight children born in both Mississippi and Chicago. Named after her maternal grandmother, Addie May Stubbs, and her paternal grandmother, Adeline Cameron, Addie was the first daughter born to Ambrose and Maggie.

When Addie and her family boarded the train at the Brookhaven depot, they were bound for Chicago to join Ambrose, who had made the journey months earlier under the cover of night, fleeing for his life after a physical altercation with his white employer. The Camerons left behind the ties of heritage and the familiar stabilities and instabilities of a southern life that was full of both comfort and injustice. The human lessons of black life in Mississippi taught the Camerons—and Addie in particular—about the struggle for humanity, dignity, and a life free from racism. Chicago would provide many of the same difficult human lessons but, in addition, the struggle for economic survival amid debilitating poverty. Deeply personal experiences with racism, poverty, and the desire for a better life dominated Addie's formative years. The importance of family, faith, and struggle as central aspects of her childhood and adolescence shed important light on the activist and leader she would become.

MISSISSIPPI

Anyone researching the history of black life in Mississippi will inevitably find an abundance of sources on the Mississippi Delta. Located between the Mississippi River on the west and the Yazoo River on the east, the Delta sits in the northwest region of the state. With its fertile soil, the area became of interest to planters seeking to cultivate its lands after Mississippi's organization as a territory in 1798 and subsequent statehood in 1817.[1] Historians and scholars of Mississippi have long focused on the Mississippi Delta when examining the history of blacks in the state—and for good reasons. As the center of cotton and agricultural production along the Mississippi River, the Delta furnished the means by which hundreds of plantations flourished in the nineteenth century. The population of enslaved blacks increased drastically, so much so that by the Civil War enslaved blacks represented the majority of Mississippi's population. In the Delta, labor opportunities for blacks were circumscribed by enslavement and its twin, sharecropping, which emerged all across the South during Reconstruction. By 1930, over 80 percent of blacks in the Yazoo Delta were sharecroppers or cash tenants and it was not uncommon for blacks in the Delta to live in predominantly black towns and rural communities.

The social, political, and economic relations between the races in the Delta and in the state as a whole remained dominated by whites, as evidenced in the title of historian Nan Woodruff's work, *American Congo: the African American Freedom Struggle in the Delta* (2003). Woodruff's analogy of the Mississippi River Valley as an American Congo connoted the extreme racial violence and political persecution faced by blacks in early-twentieth-century lumber, timber, and textile industries. Woodruff argues that the wholesale imperial economy of the New South came as a result of the seizure of black farmlands and a monopoly on black labor. In essence, racial hierarchies, along with racial violence, remained entrenched as Mississippians embraced the mantra of the New South and economic modernization. The state of Mississippi led the nation in lynchings from 1889 to 1918. The Delta had 43 percent of the 582 lynching victims in the state from 1889 to 1966, the vast majority of whom were African American.[2] Finally, the number of blacks who emerged from the conditions of the Delta as pioneers of later civil rights struggles, such as Fannie Lou Hamer and Amzie Moore, have sustained historians' interest in the region.

While these historians and others have provided important insight into aspects of black life in the Delta, the experiences of African Americans like the

Camerons potentially give us an alternative narrative. The Camerons and a number of black Mississippians lived outside of the Delta, in bustling towns as opposed to rural communities, and/or in areas with a white majority. Blacks outside of the Delta also engaged in a wide variety of economic enterprises as opposed to primarily agricultural work. Taken individually and collectively, these characteristics give a slightly different perspective on the possibilities of black life in Mississippi. In order to better understand the Camerons' experience outside of the Delta and Addie's childhood, one must piece together the complex history and racial mores of Brookhaven.

Located some fifty miles south of Jackson, Mississippi, and just over forty miles north of the Louisiana state line, by today's standards Brookhaven would be considered a small town with a population of less than 10,000—50 percent of which is African American. But at the turn of the twentieth century, Brookhaven, founded in 1835, was one of the largest and most important cities in southern Mississippi. Its location along the Illinois Central Railroad, which connects New Orleans and Chicago, and the Mississippi Central Railroad, which connects Natchez and Hattiesburg, placed the city in a prime position to advance its commercial interests in lumbering, manufacturing, and agriculture. As a transportation hub and the seat of Lincoln County, Brookhaven's commercial and economic opportunities attracted a number of residents from southern Mississippi and Louisiana. Established in April 1870 during Reconstruction, Lincoln County was controversially named for President Abraham Lincoln under the administration of Republican Governor James L. Alcorn and a Republican-dominated state legislature. It was the first county established in Mississippi after the end of the Civil War and after the state reentered the Union in February of 1870. Unlike many counties and cities in the Delta, both Lincoln County and Brookhaven held majority white populations well into the early decades of the twentieth century.

Suffering little physical damage as a result of the Civil War, Brookhaven grew rapidly during and after Reconstruction. The city had its first banks, telephones, electricity, and water plant operations all before the turn of the century.[3] Two major newspapers, the *Semi-Weekly Leader* and the *Lincoln County Times*, supplied the city's residents with local, state, national and occasionally international news. Freight and express trains going north passed through Brookhaven daily. Fifteen passenger trains headed north from Brookhaven to cities such as Memphis and Chicago on a daily basis, providing a direct passage for many blacks who would leave Mississippi for Chicago during the Great Migration.[4] By 1919, Brookhaven boasted two banks with deposits of two million dollars, and some ninety stores including a wholesale grocery store and two large department stores. Citizens patronized and utilized eleven garages, a $75,000 post office building, a county courthouse, a public library, twenty miles of graveled streets, two graded public schools, a convent, Whitworth Female College, a hospital, churches of all denominations, a Masonic temple, and a municipal light and water plant.⁵ These amenities certainly added credence to the city's claim of being the metropolis of southwest Mississippi.

The rise of Brookhaven's lumber and timber industries around the turn of the twentieth century and possibilities for employment outside of agriculture may have attracted the Cameron family to the area. They first appear in federal census and local county records in the Brookhaven area around 1910. Frank Cameron, Addie's paternal grandfather, was born in the antebellum era sometime around 1860. He was likely born into slavery, though it is not known for certain if he was born in Mississippi. His second wife, Adeline, was born sometime around 1870 and the two married about 1890. By 1910, Frank and Adeline had eight children ranging in ages from three to eighteen. Ambrose was the couple's youngest son, born sometime around 1904.⁶ Frank and his eldest son, Charles (Chas), both worked at the local planning mill in Bogue Chitto, a village just ten miles south of Brookhaven. As early as the mid-1850s with the coming of the railroads, sawmill towns emerged in and around Brookhaven in nearby villages like Bogue Chitto. Sawmill and mill towns were often constructed by lumber companies to keep their workforce nearby and stationary. Dry goods and grocery stores, post offices, small hotels, barbershops, jails, churches, schools, and retail and service industries, along with small homes were constructed near mills, almost always on a segregated basis.⁷ However, these services allowed men like Frank Cameron, who worked in the mills, to have their families and homes close to their place of work. While black and white men alike were hired to work in the mills, work was often on a segregated basis with black men performing the more dangerous and "less-skilled" tasks, often in groups and under the supervision of a white leader. Despite its plantation hierarchy, work in the timber industry supplied many African American men with greater economic means and, on average, more money than work in agriculture. Black women whose husbands, fathers, and sons worked at the local mills often hired themselves out as cooks, laundresses, and servants for private employers, presumably local white families.⁸

Over the course of the 1910s, the Camerons relocated to Brookhaven proper where the small black community had its own barbershops, pressing shops, eating houses, retailers, printers, shoemakers, schools, churches, and other businesses and institutions.⁹ Some blacks, including the Camerons, owned small homes in racially segregated neighborhoods. The economic, political, and social progress of blacks was heavily proscribed by racial differences and ideas of black vice, respectability, and place. White ideals of culture and entertainment manifested themselves in Brookhaven in the form of minstrel shows and special performances, such as the showing of D. W. Griffith's 1915 film, *The Birth of a Nation*. The film glorified the founding of the Ku Klux Klan and depicted the nation during Reconstruction as under attack by sexually aggressive, intellectually inferior African American men. When Brookhaven played host to the annual Convention of Confederate Veterans in 1915, the city showed the film at its opera house: "Accompanying the picture was a large orchestra which played background music as the film unrolled. Brookhaven became the talk of South Mississippi because of the ability of its citizens to bring its cultural and entertainment levels up to the highest standards."[10]

But it was more than just cultural demonstrations of racial ignorance and distinction that kept blacks and whites largely separated. The realities of Jim Crow in Brookhaven, and across the South severely proscribed black political power by disenfranchising blacks. Blacks in Brookhaven rarely registered to vote due to intimidation and the steep two-dollar poll tax levied against all who sought to vote. Blacks were further circumscribed by their minority status in Mississippi, where Democratic leadership dominated state politics since the end of Reconstruction in 1876. Educated blacks were often considered "uppity" by whites in Brookhaven, and attempts to breach Jim Crow through occupation and social standing were not tolerated. Sam Jones, a longtime white resident of Brookhaven whose father, P. Z. Jones, served as Brookhaven's mayor in the late 1920s, recalled the racial tensions of the time. While P. Z. Jones was in office, Burl Jackson, a black man, applied for the vacant office of Brookhaven postmaster. Sam Jones recalled the aftermath of Jackson's attempt to become postmaster and his relationship with his father:

> Burl applied for that position [postmaster], which made a lot of people in town very angry. They thought that was just too much. He didn't receive the appointment, but people didn't forget it. And it was rumored that on one occasion that he might be, that something might be done to him by the whites. He came down to our house to talk to my father about it and my father said, "Well, we can't have anything like that. You go home, get your wife and bring her down here." And he put them in one of the upstairs bedrooms for a couple of days. The whole thing blew over, nothing ever came of it, but that was very highly unusual for a white man to take in Negroes like that. And incidentally, my father would not shake hands with a Negro, wouldn't be intimate at all in any way, although he was very good to them. A lot of his clients were Negroes who couldn't afford to pay and it was all right, he would represent them without any pay but he wouldn't have any familiarity with them.[11]

This story reveals not only the ways in which blacks who dared to step out of their place lived in fear for their physical safety. At the same time, the relationship between Jones and Jackson illustrates how lapses in the conventional narrative of southern race relations played out, as it was men (not women), who temporarily blurred the color line. Such spaces for interracial intervention and interaction did exist, but they were often narrowly confined and in the end managed to uphold the racial status quo. In this case, the threat of racial violence by whites in Brookhaven precipitated an act of protection, both paternalist and moralist, by a white man on behalf of a black man. Nevertheless, P. Z. Jones, who might have been seen as a racial liberal in his time, constructed clear physical and personal boundaries between himself and blacks in order to maintain the dominant social and political order.

Despite black institutions and businesses in Brookhaven, blacks had no sustained newspaper or print voice through which to articulate their lives and concerns. Their presence in Brookhaven's two newspapers, The *Semi-Weekly Leader* and the *Lincoln County Times*, reveals an era in which whites labeled blacks as "colored" and "negroes" or more pejoratively as "darkies" and "pickaninnies." More often than not, *Leader* and *Times* articles focusing on blacks highlighted their criminality, stupidity, inferiority, and dependence in the face of white morality, intelligence, and dominance. Occasionally, black marriages, births, deaths, and articles on black racial uplift projects were featured, but seldom were they authored by blacks themselves and unmediated by white editors and authors.

This was the context in which the Cameron family lived in Brookhaven in the 1910s and early 1920s. This was also the world Addie's father, Ambrose, had to navigate. As an adult, Wyatt spoke about her father's frustrations with racism and believed that racial discrimination and inequalities hampered Ambrose, who did not complete high school but was characterized as a very smart and capable man. By 1916, the Camerons lived in a small home near downtown Brookhaven on South Second Street. Whether or not Frank Cameron, Addie's grandfather, died or simply left the family, Adeline Cameron was by then listed as the sole head of household, though she would continue to list her marital status as married on official records.[12] Not only had she "lost" her husband, but many of her children, including Ambrose's older sisters Mary and Martha, left Mississippi for a chance at better employment opportunities, some measure of racial dignity and respect, and the chance to make a life for themselves apart from their family. Martha eventually settled in Chicago, having made the journey during the first wave of the Great Migration, or the exodus of blacks from the South to northern urban centers from about 1910 to 1930.[13]

Why Adeline chose to stay behind in Brookhaven is unknown. Perhaps it was the fact that she had at least three young school-aged children, including Ambrose, still in her care and did not want to leave. Despite being unable to read and write, Adeline was a licensed and busy midwife who delivered black and white babies in and around Brookhaven.[14] To leave behind her steady clientele for an unpredictable life elsewhere may not have been desirable or feasible at the time. Ambrose, on the other hand, experienced a number of growing pains during his adolescence, including troubles with the law. He attended grade school at the Brookhaven Colored School, the first public school for blacks in the city founded in the 1880s, but he left to begin working for a local pressing shop as a delivery boy. In March of 1920 he made the front-page news of the *Semi-Weekly Leader*. Having gotten into an altercation with another young black man, Julius Braxton, Ambrose reportedly stabbed and critically wounded Braxton. The *Leader* did not report any of the details of the altercation or what led Ambrose to stab Braxton. However, Ambrose was temporarily jailed. Should Braxton die, Ambrose would be tried for murder. The *Leader* failed to follow up on the story, indicating that Braxton likely lived. While crimes committed by blacks against blacks generally received less-harsh punishments than crimes committed by blacks against whites, any brush with the law for a black man was sure to be trouble. However, the next time that Ambrose would find himself in the courthouse, it would be for an entirely different reason. A little more than a year after his bout with Julius Braxton, Ambrose was set to marry.

Perhaps it was his marriage to Maggie Mae Green,[15] by all accounts a beautiful young woman from Vicksburg, Mississippi, that helped Ambrose to settle down. Maggie was born sometime around 1905 and came from a small family including her mother, Addie Mae, and stepfather, Tyree, who were farmers. Maggie was a high-school graduate and secured a job teaching at the Brookhaven Colored School during summers.[16] This was no small feat as few black youths compared to whites graduated, let alone attended high school during this era in Mississippi. The majority of Mississippi's student population enrolled in the first through eighth grades. Out of the 291,229 black children enrolled in schools across the state, 112,918 were enrolled in the first grade alone and only 9,263 were enrolled in the eighth grade, demonstrating that educational attainment and literacy for black children two generations removed from slavery was incredibly difficult to obtain. This was especially the case in poorer rural and farming communities where schools were even less equipped with teachers and books and where crop schedules dictated student attendance.[17] As a black teacher, Maggie would have been paid much less than her white counterparts and as a part-time summer teacher, her pay likely was not more than twenty dollars for the entire summer.

Sometime during her summers spent in Brookhaven, Maggie met and fell in love with Ambrose. The couple married in May of 1921 and welcomed their first child, Ambrose Jr., the following year. Two years later in March of 1924, they welcomed their second child, Addie. At the time of Addie's birth, the family still resided on South Second Street in a small home just south of the Illinois Central Railroad depot. The family consisted of Ambrose, Maggie, their two children, and Addie's paternal grandmother, Adeline, who lived with the family intermittently throughout the 1920s. On the Cameron's block lived several other black families, all of whom owned their small homes and engaged in a variety of occupations, including washerwoman, cook, porter, sawmill laborer, teacher, clergymen, and carpenter. All possessed some level of home ownership, which was less common for blacks in other parts of Brookhaven. White families lived two blocks in the opposite direction on South Second Street with Whitworth Avenue as the dividing line between black and white households.[18]

Much of what is known about Addie Wyatt's childhood in Brookhaven comes from interviews and oral histories she participated in from the 1970s through the early 2000s.[19] In these interviews, Wyatt frequently spoke of her fondness for Brookhaven and the home that she shared with her family. She recalled the beautiful trees and flowers on her block as well as the cattle, chickens, pigs, and vegetables that the Camerons kept and cultivated and said that there was always plenty to eat because they produced so much of their own food. Though she hated having to walk in the hot summer mud, Addie loved when it rained because she and her siblings would get to go inside and sit with the older people who would tell stories, sing spirituals, and pray. Religion and a belief in Christian teachings were a part of Addie's world very early on, instilled by the adults in her life. She recalled feeling loved by her parents and by Jesus as a little girl.[20] Maggie and Adeline maintained a very close relationship, bonded by their strong faith. According to Addie, the family regularly attended a Baptist church in Brookhaven where she gave her first religious speech at the age of three. Adeline sometimes held prayer meetings, and Addie remembered that their home was a meeting spot where neighbors would come to listen to the Camerons' Victrola phonograph or to hear Ambrose play guitar with his friends in the backyard while everyone sang along, danced, and ate.[21]

Two childhood memories illustrate Addie's precociousness and outspoken nature as a child before the move to Chicago, which would force her to grow up quickly and take on the role of surrogate caretaker for her younger siblings. When Maggie was in labor with Addie's younger sister, Edna, two-year-old Addie protested against the neighbors who were taking care of her. They made the fatal mistake of braiding Addie's hair instead of maintaining the pageboy style with bangs that her mother gave her daily. Addie was not used to the painful braiding or the drastic change in her daily routine. Unaware at the time that her mother was in labor and therefore unable to spend time with her, Addie ran out into the street and began protesting at the top of her lungs, yelling, screaming, and crying. Neighbors came out from their homes and told Addie to get "her little black self" back home, but she sassed each one, telling them to mind their own business and leave hers alone.[22] Determined to speak out about her frustrations, Addie did not let her neighbors' taunts deter her from finishing her rant.

In another act of defiance, Addie disobeyed her parent's rules governing her play activities. Playing house was a popular game for children in Addie's neighborhood and more often than not, she played the coveted role of "mother." What set Addie apart was that she served *real* food at the makeshift dinner table she and her siblings set up and *not* mud-cakes, which was the typical sort of fare served in a southern Mississippi game of house. It wasn't that her family was financially better off than the other black families on the block. Addie simply did not like making, serving, or "eating" mud-cakes. She preferred real food and had the means to get it. Ambrose and Maggie occasionally tasked Addie with picking up the family's groceries from a nearby store. In her early tenure as "mother," Addie placed butter rolls, pig feet, sardines, and crackers for her game of house on her parents' tab, at first unaware of the costs added by her luxurious menu. Not heeding her parents' initial reprimands for her purchases, Addie continued to add her own groceries to the family's tab whenever it was again time to play house. Eventually, her insubordination came with consequences. Wyatt recalled hiding under her bed at the end of the week when she knew her parents would be on their way home after settling the grocery bill. Hearing the sound of their hurried steps on the wooden porch and the knowing pause as her father reached to pull a switch from the tree, Addie braced herself for the whipping to come. Her pursuits cost her dearly, but her defiance also cost the family financially.[23] These recollections from her childhood reveal something of Addie's precocious, defiant, and outspoken nature as a child.

While it would take her years to gain a full understanding of some of the more negative circumstances that surrounded her childhood in Brookhaven, Addie also recalled several memories about the discrimination and fears of racial violence that blacks experienced. As a midwife, Adeline Cameron delivered her grandchildren and the babies of black and white families in Brookhaven. Sometimes Addie was permitted to accompany her. On one occasion, Addie walked up to the front door and tried to enter but her grandmother quickly snatched her back and told her that they had to go through the back door because they were at the home of a white family. Addie recalled the significance of this incident in a 2002 interview with Julieanna Richardson, founder and executive director of The HistoryMakers: "I remember how she [Adeline] loved those babies and how she treated their mothers and their fathers, you know. She was a very, very popular person in town. And she could go almost anywhere, but she could not go in the front door."[24] As a midwife, Adeline possessed a certain level of access and intimacy with whites whose children she helped to birth, feed, and take care of. But social customs demanded that she respect the racial status quo and impart that burden onto her young granddaughter.

Addie had vague memories of lynchings and racial terror in Brookhaven:

> Sometimes we had very difficult situations when you had lynchings, you know. You'd hear the older people—now they wouldn't talk to us [children] about those things. But you'd hear them praying and if you were a sensitive child like I was, you'd be listening to what they'd say to try to determine what was going on. And

sometimes they were grieving about the neighbor's children. I can remember on one occasion and I don't know the name of the incident. One of the neighbor's son was lynched. . . . And it was frightening to us because you always had a feeling that they were going to lynch you too, you know.[25]

The older people would protest their treatment among one another, but never in front of whites, and Addie began to pick up on the fact that something was very wrong with the way whites in Brookhaven treated blacks. The lessons of racial mores and the assaults on black humanity that Addie became exposed to in Mississippi at such a young age stayed with her and helped to fuel her activism decades later in the labor and civil rights movements.

While it is difficult to be certain, the incident that Addie recollected was likely the 1928 lynching of the Bearden brothers in Brookhaven, which began just a short distance from the Cameron family home at the county jail and courthouse. On Friday, June 29, 1928, when Addie would have been just over four years old, mob violence struck Brookhaven and two black men were lynched.[26] The *Semi-Weekly Leader* covered the brutal murders extensively. In a front-page article, "Two Negroes Are Mobbed Here Last Night," the newspaper estimated that some 5,000 looked on while a mob kicked down the doors of the jail to get at the Beardens. Stanley Bearden reportedly got into an altercation with Caby Byrne after refusing to pay for services rendered to his car, allegedly pulling a gun on Byrne and shooting him twice. Nearby citizens, officers, and Byrne's brother, Claude, came to the rescue of Caby and shot at Bearden as he fled, shooting him five times in the back. Bearden was captured, attended to by a "physician who pronounced him as not dangerously wounded," and sent to the county jail along with another black man captured at the scene, who was apparently identified as Pluge Bearden, brother of Stanley, though sources dispute whether or not the two were brothers and if Pluge was in fact a part of the crime. A third man, brother-in-law of Stanley Bearden, was also taken to jail by the sheriff on suspicion that he had incited the argument, but when the mob broke through the steel doors after one hour of beating at them, they turned the man loose, "satisfied about his actions in the matter, and did not want him. The mob, as a body, were cool, collected and methodical about what they did. They knew what they wanted and intended to do and they did it. They did not brook any interference and were determined in their actions." The mob seized the prisoners and "just as mechanically as if they were soldiers on drill duty the two negroes were marched into two separate cars." The mob proceeded toward Old Brook about two miles south of Highway 51, which cut diagonally through the city. Pluge Bearden was strung from a tree and lynched while the mob and Stanley Bearden watched. After Pluge was declared dead, those in the mob and the crowd were allowed to shoot him.

Once back inside the city proper, Stanley Bearden was tied to the back axle of a car and dragged through the streets of Brookhaven for over half an hour, and then he was lynched in a tree in a small area just north of the city before his body was riddled with bullets. The *Leader* went on to state, "The mob had been very particular and sure to get only the two negroes they wanted, having certain identification made by those who knew the prisoners. Several other negro prisoners were not molested at all and were told not to be afraid as no harm was coming to them. Other than the dragging through the streets of Stanley Bearden the double lynching was what is classed as 'an orderly lynching.'" In the aftermath of the lynching, folks from surrounding areas went to view the bodies.[27] Hours later when the last of the lynching souvenirs had been collected by visiting whites, black family and community members collected the bodies to bury their mutilated dead. What took place in Brookhaven that day was not an anomaly as blacks across the South, Midwest, and some areas of the North fell victim to lynching and vigilante violence in the early twentieth century. The danger that befell blacks arrested or even suspected of committing any real or perceived crimes against whites—including murder, assault, rape, and even nonviolent transgressions such as an uppity disposition or economic prosperity—could spell death at the hands of violent white mobs.[28] Brookhaven, the pride of Lincoln County and the southwestern metropolis of Mississippi, struggled to promote an image of the New South—southern progress and racial cohabitation—amid the lynching of the Bearden brothers, the denial of Burl Jackson for the postmaster position, and countless other assaults on the dignity of its black citizens. While living in Brookhaven enabled its black citizens to partake in greater economic opportunities and have access to greater social and cultural resources, the boundaries and limits of racial progress in the context of Jim Crow severely proscribed black life.

The threat of racial violence, lynching, and death undoubtedly crossed Ambrose Cameron's mind just two years after the Bearden lynching when, in 1930, a physical altercation with his white boss at the pressing shop where he worked necessitated that he leave town almost immediately.[29] The exact details of the altercation are unknown. However, developments just prior to the family's relocation may shed additional light on Ambrose's troubles. In January of 1930 Ambrose was accused of writing a bad check, and two months later the Cameron family house was in danger of being sold due to the failure to pay taxes on the land in 1929. The couple had four small children—Ambrose Jr. (8), Addie (6), Edna (4), Emmett (2)—and Maggie was pregnant with their fifth child. Perhaps the dispute between Ambrose and his employer was over wages or a compensation discrepancy of some kind. Unlike Ambrose's altercation with Julius Braxton ten years prior, the repercussions for striking a white man could end his life and shatter the family. With little alternative, Ambrose boarded a train for Chicago the night of the altercation, leaving behind his family and the life he had known in Mississippi.

Whatever plans Ambrose had for his life in the South were quickly dashed and replaced by new questions of what life would be like in the North. How and when would he be able to send for his family? What would come of them and his home in the meantime? How would he locate his sister, Martha, and other relatives in a city far larger, more complex, and much faster than Brookhaven? Would he be able to provide for his family the kind of life they had in Brookhaven? Would they be better off in the North? Ambrose's dilemmas reveal that perhaps for many more migrants than just himself, migration was less a choice than a necessity. Migration was a process fraught with more mystery, tension, anxiety, haste, and caution than historians and scholars have paid heed to. Many more migrants than perhaps we will ever know were less willing participants and brazen trailblazers than apprehensive refugees moving forward but looking back at a home that was once theirs, however imperfect a home it may have been. Life for the Camerons was not ideal in Mississippi, but Ambrose and Maggie, with the help of Adeline, had begun to lay the foundation for a family strong in its faith, character, unity, and ties to community, despite the racial prejudices and injustices they faced. The Camerons would continue to try to cultivate these traits in Chicago, faced with a world of new opportunities and new adversities.

COMING OF AGE IN BLACK CHICAGO

Between April and October of 1930, Ambrose was able to send for his family. Shortly thereafter, Maggie gave birth to their fifth child, Willie. Willie, whom the family called Mickey, was the first of the Cameron children born in Chicago. While waiting for Ambrose to send for them, Maggie apparently did her best to persuade the children that life would be better in Chicago. However, when they arrived at their new home with their Aunt Martha, at 44th and Calumet, Addie was disappointed. She recalled her early reactions to Chicago in a 2002 interview with Joan McGann Morris of the Chicago-based Working Women's History Project:

> I was told that we were going to a place where we would be so much better off. I thought it meant the land of the free. But when we came to Chicago, I was shocked that we did not have fruit trees in the yard. We did not have vegetables. We did not have cattle or chickens and all of this we had in Brookhaven, Mississippi. During the years that we were struggling for survival as a family, we almost starved because it was so difficult getting work and providing for your families. So I had mixed emotions about coming to Chicago.[30]

Addie's statement reveals the dire straits in which many southern families found themselves upon arriving in Chicago. They were unprepared for the extremely cramped living conditions and kitchenette quarters of the city's concentrated black South Side population. Whereas the Camerons once had their own home, their large family had to adjust to sharing tight quarters with Ambrose's sister, Martha, her husband, son, and nephew. The confined nature of kitchenette living, shared tenant bathrooms, and overcrowding must have been a shock to new migrants like the Camerons. Families used to growing food in gardens and raising livestock on their own property in the South, faced new economic hardships as they were unable to rely upon farming to sustain their families. Moreover, the Camerons were a large family and they continued to grow throughout the 1930s. In 1932, Ambrose and Maggie welcomed another son, Bluett. A daughter, Audrey, came along in 1934 followed by their youngest, Maude, in 1937. The family struggled to survive in Chicago but attempted to reconstruct and maintain the bonds of kinship and worship that structured their lives in the South. The relative stability of their life in Brookhaven was replaced in a number of critical ways by economic instability and urban poverty.

No small part of the Camerons' circumstances was due to the fact that they migrated during the Great Depression, which compounded an already bleak picture for black migrants in Chicago. The dramatic growth of blacks residing in cramped and segregated spaces of the city altered Chicago's residential and demographic landscape. Between 1920 and 1930, the black population of the city more than doubled from 109,594 to 233,903.[31] By 1930, Chicago had the second largest urban black population in the country. During the first wave of the Great Migration from about 1910 to 1930, one and a half million African Americans left the conditions of the South for opportunities in northern urban industrial centers such as Chicago, New York City, and Philadelphia. They left Jim Crow conditions in the South including the threat and reality of racial and sexual violence, disenfranchisement, a lack of legal rights, underfunded and segregated schools, daily public and private assaults on their dignity and humanity, as well as a struggling southern agricultural economy. They journeyed north in search of greater opportunities and higher wages in a wider array of industries. Migrants sought out the attractions of urban life: freedom from racial terrorism, enfranchisement, civic and political participation, and the chance to live one's life with greater freedom from racial subordination.

Historical and popular scholarship on the first wave of the Great Migration to Chicago has supplied much of this narrative, documenting and engaging the factors that literary icon Richard Wright argued "pushed and pounded" migrants "driven and pursued" by the "extremes of possibility, death and hope" in their search for a new life.[32] Ultimately, the combination of factors that pushed and pulled black migrants north was incredibly complex and often difficult to disentangle. Each migrant journeyed north with a slightly different experience of southern life and from various precipitating events that triggered the act of migration. The Camerons followed in the footsteps of many families who journeyed separately north, usually behind a father, mother, or other principle wage earner. Once the initial family member found employment and housing, he or she would later send for the rest of the family.[33]

Once in Chicago, restrictive covenants and installment contracts to purchase homes outside of the black South Side kept the vast majority of blacks confined to Bronzeville, an area roughly forty blocks long stretching from 21st to 63rd streets and from Cottage Grove on the east to Wentworth on the west. Financial exploitation dominated blacks' experiences with housing in Chicago. Journalist Nicholas Lemann aptly described the process by which housing opportunities for blacks were created: "As migrants from the South crowded into the Black Belt, landlords converted more and more apartment buildings into kitchenettes to accommodate them. The neighborhoods became poorer and denser."[34] Too many blacks were forced to live in kitchenettes—dark, damp, vermin-infested apartments in disrepair—and suffered from higher rates of sicknesses such as tuberculosis and higher infant mortality rates. Worse yet, others made homes "in basements, alleys, garages, coal bins, storerooms, or other places never meant to house anyone."[35]

On one hand, being confined to the black South Side meant incredibly crowded, overpriced, and substandard housing with few options for those who could not afford to purchase a decent home. But exclusion from white neighborhoods and establishments enabled blacks from a variety of class backgrounds to construct a world that included a host of institutions, businesses, and organizations that provided the black community with valuable services and facilitated economic, political, and social solidarity.[36] Black Chicago had its own newspapers like the *Chicago Defender*, the *Chicago Bee*, *News-Ledger*, *Metropolitan News*, and several others.[37] The Binga and Douglass banks were in full operation prior to the Depression, and theaters, dance halls, pharmacies, small grocers, and churches prospered alongside other black-owned and black-operated institutions in Bronzeville. The Depression dealt an incredible blow to many of these institutions as residents and new migrants felt the burden of unemployment. Nearly 40 percent of Chicago's workforce was unemployed in 1932. Just prior to the Depression, about 20 percent of blacks held occupations classified as more professional "clean work," 41 percent engaged in manual labor, and about 34 percent were servants.[38] But by 1933, blacks represented over one-fifth of the city's total relief load even though they were only 8 percent of the population.[39] Many African Americans hoped that the administration of President Franklin Delano Roosevelt would enact a square and fair deal that would include them in the plan to lift the country from economic depression. They also hoped that they would be able to enjoy some of the fruits of a new American liberalism and advance in society economically, politically, and socially.

This was largely the context and the circumstances under which Ambrose and Maggie sought to gain employment to secure a place for themselves and their family in Chicago. Ambrose faced considerable difficulty finding steady employment as a tailor and Maggie was unable to teach in Chicago. While a high-school diploma could qualify one for a teaching position in the South, Chicago required a teaching degree of its black and white teachers and placed significant informal barriers for blacks seeking a teaching degree or position in the city's largely segregated public schools. In Brookhaven, both Ambrose and Maggie often supplemented their incomes by making and tailoring clothes for their children and neighbors.[40] In Chicago, where they knew so few people and where constant migration and relocation rendered the term "neighbor" somewhat specious, building up a clientele was difficult. Combined with an inability to grow their own food and manage livestock, the Camerons suffered greatly. Moreover, Adeline, who lived with the family until her death in the late 1930s, was by this time in her early sixties, and it is unknown whether or not she was still able to operate as a midwife or secure alternative employment. Times were hard not only for the Camerons, but for many other blacks in the city. Chicagoan Tim Ellis remembered trying to find a job during the Depression: "Well '29 and up until '35, '36 was rough. There wasn't anything like jobs. You didn't even have to worry about trying to find jobs because there weren't no jobs to be found."[41]

Piecing together inconsistent employment with relief and intermittent help from extended family, the Camerons barely eked out a living. Maggie eventually took on work as a domestic, one of the most common occupations for black women. Ambrose worked off and on at different tailors across the South Side. For a period beginning in 1935, he gained employment as a foreman on a New Deal Works Progress Administration (WPA) Project placing rocks against the lakeshore. Ambrose and Maggie dealt with the dehumanizing experience of joblessness and the family's financial struggles differently. While Addie loved and appreciated the efforts of both her parents, she revealed in a 1977 interview with Elizabeth Balanoff of the Oral History Project in Labor History that she did not fully understand her father in the same ways that she understood her mother and grandmother:

> I think he just barely finished elementary school but he was a very brilliant man, a great mathematician, a great spokesperson. He was aggressive but very frustrated. . . . My father would work 50 and 60 hours a week when he could get it and he still could not make enough money to take care of his family. It was always embarrassing to him when he came home and there was my mother and his children and he didn't have the rent or he didn't have food money or money needed for other things.[42]

Perhaps as a result of his inability to provide for his family, Ambrose became an alcoholic. Looking back, Addie supposed that "[h]e found this a means of escape. When I matured and grew up myself I began to understand that more than ever and it was one of the things that made me very, very determined to do what I could to help poverty stricken people and to help wage earners to earn a decent and livable wage."[43] The Cameron family's circumstances in Chicago revealed quite a bit to Addie as a young girl. The decline in their standard of living, the cramped spaces, her father's anger, and the uncertainty of life in Chicago revealed new aspects of her parents' characters that both troubled and inspired her. While her father's frustrations, bitterness, and alcoholism no doubt cast a dark shadow on the family, Addie still loved him and eventually came to admire and respect his desire to provide for his family. It was likely her own background and understanding of the effects of poverty on families that led her to support the labor movement and adequate employment, wages, and benefits for working men and women.

As for Maggie, Addie remembered that prayer was her mother's preferred route for dealing with the family's troubles: "My dear mother, who was a God-fearing woman used to wake up sometimes in the morning, pray for us, and send us to school without any breakfast at all, with the confidence that God was going to provide something. And when we'd come home in the evening, she'd say, 'God has answered our prayer.' We'd have a little hoecake that they'd make together with a little meal and a little water, and put some of that homemade sugar-and-water syrup over it, and we would eat that, sing, pray, thank God, and then go to bed."[44] Both Maggie and Ambrose instilled in their children a love for God and Christian faith, but it was Maggie and Adeline who took the children to church and were the spiritual anchors of the household. Maggie and Adeline focused on loving and trusting in God to guide the family through their difficulties. Wallace Best, a historian of African American urban religion, positions religion at the heart of the migration experience, especially for women who comprised the majority of church congregations across denominations during this period. Best argues that "the process of migration was about both change and continuity"[45] and that black Chicagoans crafted religious experiences that confronted and helped them cope with "the structural forces of racial oppression, economic deprivation, and spatial limitation that were at work."[46]

Addie struggled with the family's economic decline. Throughout the early 1930s, the Camerons moved several times in the Grand Boulevard and Douglas neighborhoods, and even lived on the West Side for a short time. In detailing her life for The HistoryMakers, Wyatt revealed the extent to which the family's constant moving affected her. On one occasion, when leaving school, Addie panicked, not remembering where her home was: "It was a very interesting experience in that because of our economic condition, it almost looked like every month we were moving again because when you can't pay the rent, you got to move. And I—I remember coming out of the school one afternoon asking the

Lord to help me to determine which house we lived in because I couldn't figure out which one to go back to. . . . It was an agonizing experience as a child."[47] It is probable that such an experience contributed to Wyatt's desire to have a stable home and sense of economic security in her adult life. Eventually, in the mid-1930s, the family settled into an apartment at 4243 S. Calumet and Addie enrolled in Felsenthal elementary school.

Addie learned several difficult lessons growing up young, poor, and black in Chicago. Her experiences being bullied and on relief (charity) tested and strengthened the Christian faith her mother and grandmother instilled in her. Cognizant that her mother did not allow fighting in their home and taught her children to never strike anyone, Addie did nothing when one day she was bullied by a group of girls who took her books and coat. She was angry and wanted to fight back, but did not because she knew her mother had a strict rule against violence and cautioned her children that they had to solve disputes without fighting, as taught to them through the Bible and reinforced through prayer. While Addie followed her mother's teachings by not fighting with bullies, she did not necessarily agree with Maggie that she should not fight back and stand up for herself. Maggie had an unshakable faith, and it was incredibly difficult for Addie to argue with the lessons of dignity, obedience, and faith in themselves, others, and God that Maggie preached.[48] Addie still had much to learn and experience in terms of the development of her own faith, but her mother's words and instilling of Christian principles remained with Addie as she sought to develop and practice her own Christian faith that actively questioned and rejected injustices.

The Camerons were among the 50 percent of Chicago's black residents who received some form of charity during the Great Depression,[49] and Addie despised the invasiveness and assumptions bred by being on relief. Many decades later, in an interview with The HistoryMakers, Wyatt recalled that "no child wanted to be on charity or wanted it known. And, of course, once a month the secret was out because these big trucks would come and stop in the middle of the block. And they had your food boxes. And the man would call the names so loud that everybody would know that Brown and Cameron and Williams and Jones was on charity. And that was so embarrassing to children, you know . . . we didn't have sense enough to really see that most of the people in the block was running out to get the boxes to take them back into their house."[50] She also received charity dresses and clothing once a month and remembered immediately tearing off the buttons and bows on the dress, desperately trying to make herself look different from the other little girls in class who wore the same charity dresses and shoes.[51]

Even worse, according to Addie, were the occasional visits of relief workers. Whenever the relief worker was scheduled to come to the home, Maggie scrubbed the children, put them in their best clothes, and cautioned them to behave and keep themselves clean. One day, Maggie asked the relief worker for a pair of shoes for Addie. On the surface, Addie's shoes looked almost new as they had been scrubbed and shined to accompany the starched dress she wore. But while her shoes were shined on top, the cardboard soles had long fallen out and she was barefoot underneath. When the relief worker asked her to pick up her feet in order to see proof that Addie really needed new shoes, Addie began to cry from shame and embarrassment, not wanting the worker to see her dirty feet: "it was so humiliating for me to have to pick my foot up to prove to her that the request of my mother was a legitimate one."[52]

The degradations and assaults on the Camerons' dignity bred anger, shame, and frustration from Addie, much like the feelings she experienced in Brookhaven witnessing her family and neighbors cope with racial violence. Embarrassed, frustrated, and upset at her family's poverty and the invasive and somewhat demeaning predicaments it put them in, Addie eventually learned to use these experiences to fuel her fight against poverty and racism. The strengthening and development of her Christian faith would be central to that endeavor: "It [poverty] instilled within me a fight against a system that would badger the poor, those who are underprivileged to the point that they just didn't want to respond to life. But there was something inside of us, and I thank God for my Christian rearing that gave courage and determination so that I could rebound and I could respond, but it breaks so many people down. And I've spent my life trying to help those people to standup, not because of, but in spite of what you have to face and what you have to go through."[53]

Other formative memories that Wyatt revealed in interviews include the changed nature of her role in the family after the move to Chicago. As the eldest female child in the family, Addie became responsible for cooking, cleaning, and looking after her younger siblings. This was another marked difference from her childhood in Brookhaven. No longer was she just playing house, she had to actively maintain the household. From the age of eight, Addie took on the care of her siblings and the housework while her mother and father were at work or out looking for work. Even though she often questioned why her parents continued to have children in light of their economic circumstances, each day after school, she tended to the children—cleaned them up for dinner, prepared dinner, and set the table by the time Maggie got home from work. After dinner, Addie headed off to the family's church, the Langley Avenue Church of God, where she played piano and sang in the choir. By the age of twelve, she was chief musician for Langley's youth choir and earned one dollar a week. Rehearsals took place on Monday and Wednesday evenings and often lasted until eleven o'clock at night. They continued on Saturdays, and performances for church services ran all day Sunday. After rehearsals during the week, she returned home to finish her homework and start the next day all over again. In addition to going to school, taking care of her siblings, and working at Langley, Addie made paper and fiberglass flowers as well as candy to sell, which often brought in an additional fifty cents a week. She passed her weekly earnings along to her mother for the household, which contributed greatly, given the family's poverty.[54]

But things did not always run as smoothly as Addie hoped, and juggling all of these responsibilities as an adolescent proved difficult. On one occasion while she was cleaning and cooking, the children remained outside long past the time that they were supposed to be inside and cleaned up. When her mother returned home from work, she asked Addie where the children were. Addie realized her grave mistake and ran downstairs and called the children by name: "When I saw them running down the streets and saw the condition that they were in, I did not know whether to take them and keep going down the streets, or whether to bring them into the house and face the discipline. But thank God for judgment. That judgment prevailed. Since I had no better place to take them, I brought them all in just as they were, and presented them to my mother. She was always so calm and considerate in her actions. She gave me a thump on the head, and a shaking and a reminder that I will never forget: 'Addie, when I tell you to take care of the children, I mean for you to do just that—be responsible for them and know where they are.'"[55] This was a valuable lesson that Addie would remember when, in 1944, her mother died from heart failure at the age of thirty-nine and Addie assumed care of her six younger siblings.

With her adolescence dominated by the responsibility of caring for her siblings and contributing to the family's economic survival, Addie's inlets and outlets for creative spiritual and social expression came from two different black institutions: her church—the Langley Avenue Church of God—and DuSable High School. The Camerons became members of the Church of God (Anderson, Indiana), upon moving to Chicago.[56] The Church of God emerged during the Third Great Awakening with the birth of Holiness-Pentecostal denominations such as the Church of God in Christ. Founded by Daniel Sidney (D. S.) Warner in the 1880s, the Church of God Reformation Movement is defined by a belief in the Holy Spirit, the personal experience of salvation that delivers one from bondage to sin, a belief in a spiritual unity with all other believers, and a fairly strict adherence to scripture and Biblical doctrine.[57] The belief in unity of the Church of God Reformation Movement translated into early churches that were interracial. James Earl Massey, an ordained minister in the Church of God and academic theologian, believes that blacks were attracted to the movement because of its message of unity among believers, focus on scriptural holiness and social cohesion. The fact that blacks were largely accepted into the movement in its earliest stages put credence and weight behind the teachings of the church. Denied social, economic, and political opportunities in the post-Reconstruction

South, the message of unity and the ability to actually worship in unity was a sign of acceptance. Massey writes, "Unlike other and older church groups, with their spirit of separateness and a built-in system to identify themselves as separate, the Church of God reform movement differed in that its doctrinal emphasis on the unity of all believers argued for social openness and a visible togetherness."[58]

Langley Avenue Church of God emerged in 1910, founded by a group of men and women who previously worshipped at the Church of God at 306 West 74th street where Elder E. A. Reardon was pastor. The group "were separated and found it necessary to establish a place where others could come and hear the full gospel preached uncompromisingly, free from fanaticism, regardless of race or color."[59] This suggests that perhaps this group of black men and women had worshipped in a largely white congregation, and issues of race and religious interpretation precipitated a split. The increased number of blacks in the Church of God Reformation Movement and at its international conventions began to draw charges from whites that there were too many blacks present.[60] Whites complained that blacks' style of worship was too demonstrative and time-consuming and filled with overly aggressive testimonies of faith and salvation, and that the movement would be best served by having separate congregations so as to make all members more comfortable.[61] Some blacks speculated that this was because of fears of interracial marriages and fears that whites would lose a certain level of prestige and status in society if they worshipped alongside blacks and violated "the social pattern of segregation."[62] Essentially, the unity and tradition of interracialism in the church succumbed to the prevailing segregation of the larger secular society. This resulted in the formation of the National Association of the Church of God in 1916 at West Middlesex, Pennsylvania, an organization of African Americans in the Church of God Reformation Movement that would have its own structure and camp meetings and be financially and administratively independent from the larger, national white bodies of the Church of God.

In its earliest years, Langley had its share of female pastors including Sister Lena Nelson and Elders Mary E. Ashley and Pearl L. M. Hall, not often the case in the more established Baptist and Methodist churches.[63] In 1920, Elder Sethard P. (S. P.) Dunn of Monroe, Louisiana, became pastor and ushered in a period of growth and prosperity for the church. Holiness churches like Langley exploded in growth and number during the Great Migration, catering to the unchurched and to migrants from the South who were used to more emotional forms of worship. Langley expanded rapidly under Pastor Dunn, and by 1924 the congregation grew to several hundred and worshipped in a modern building at 4338 Prairie Avenue.[64] In 1929, additional growth in membership necessitated more space. An addition to the church built that same year could accommodate an additional two hundred members and included a library, ladies lounge, print shop, and other offices. The church experienced astonishing growth and ranked second, nationally, in its membership in the Reformation Movement in the early 1930s. In 1932, Langley was by far the largest black Church of God congregation in Chicago and the nation, boasting some 565 registered members.[65] Under Dunn and with a growing black population in Chicago, the church developed an aggressive outreach ministry characteristic of independent Holiness churches that relied upon prayer bands to go out into the community and evangelize.

In 1932, the church opened a relief station in its basement and fed over two hundred people a day. In 1935, Pastor Dunn founded and became chairman of the City Pastor's Association of the Church of God, an organization of lay ministers charged with covering parts of the city to evangelize and grow the Church of God Reformation Movement. Dunn helped usher in a new "pulpit" for black spiritual leaders when he put Langley Avenue Church of God on a national scale through his radio programs, "Sending out the Gospel News" and the "Radio Shepherd," which aired Sunday mornings and evenings on stations WIND and WSBC. The Langley Avenue Church of God choir performed at the International Camp Meeting in Anderson, Indiana, in 1936. Its youth department carried out a special service for young people on the subject, "Jesus Christ, the Panacea for the Worlds Ills." This was the first time services had been arranged for and by blacks at the International Camp Meeting.[66]

It was during this period of expansion that the Cameron family joined Langley Avenue Church of God and became part of a dynamic movement of black Protestant Christians in Chicago. There were keen lessons that Addie learned while at Langley Church of God, one of which was the gender egalitarianism practiced within the church, a detail she frequently noted when speaking about the vast possibilities for women's leadership. Addie told an audience of veteran women civil rights activists in 1991 that she always saw women in powerful roles in the church and in her home and saw women leaders all around her as role models: "In our church women played roles equal to men. . . . We were always encouraged to accept leadership roles. The women were ministers. The women were directors of our choir. They were ushers, they were musicians, secretaries and trustees. They filled the roles in the church. I never thought it was unusual until I was older and found out that this was not true in all churches or in other institutions and organizations."[67]

It was certainly the case that during this time period very few black women held ordained pastoral, ministerial, and higher leadership roles in the mainline Baptist and Methodist denominations. It was in the spaces of more independent and newly established churches that women like Mary Evans, pastor of Cosmopolitan Community Church, and Elder Lucy Smith, pastor of All Nations Pentecostal, were able to lead Christian congregations in Chicago.[68] Susie

Staley, a scholar on women in the Church of God, supports Addie's observation of female leadership in the Church of God. In *Called to Minister, Empowered to Serve*, Staley writes that from its inception through the first three decades of the twentieth century, the Church of God upheld the place of women in ministry in the reformation movement, a stance that would decline sharply in the late 1940s and 1950s. The Church of God's roots were in the Holiness movement, which upheld the doctrine of sanctification as the second distinct work of grace following the first work of grace, conversion. Sanctification destroyed the sinful nature of the individual and lead to a purity of the heart. All of those who came before God in the Church of God were to undergo the experience of sanctification, an event which had to be publicly professed. Therefore, women's participation and witness to sanctification were also public, as women had to profess to others that they had converted and received salvation and sanctification. The notion that women should not speak in public or in religious spaces was challenged, as one needed to testify publicly about her sanctification experience or else it would be lost.[69]

Holiness movements vested their authority in the Holy Spirit as opposed to that of a priestly or pastoral office, which opened up space for women to hold prominent positions in the church. The Holy Spirit dispensed gifts of ministry to both men and women alike, and worship took place in a variety of settings from fields to camp meetings to class meetings, and were led by lay ministers and preachers. As the Church of God Reformation Movement was rooted in biblical scripture, early leaders preached the passage from Galatians 3:28, "There is neither Jew nor Greek, there is neither bond nor free, there is neither male or female: for ye are all one in Christ Jesus."[70] To those in the Church of God, this meant that men and women were to be equal partners in God's kingdom. Members also followed the prophecy of Joel in Acts 2:17–18, which suggests that both the sons and the daughters of the Lord shall pray, preach, and prophesy in the last days of the Earth. All of these factors added up to a movement that was ripe for women's participation and leadership.[71]

Decades later as an adult, Addie Wyatt would craft her own theology of gender equality informed by her early experiences in the Church of God. As a young girl in the church, women role models were visible all around her, instructing and illustrating to her what it meant to be a child of God and, ultimately, a woman of God. Two women in particular were instrumental in shaping Addie's experiences at Langley. One was the choir director, Laura Pitts. "We always thought she was mean," Addie remembered. "She would bang on the table with her baton and I had mixed emotions about her behavior. There were some things that I liked about it and some things that I protested. She used to shake my shoulders because I was aggressive too. I exerted leadership among the young people and they would follow me. As I got older, she and

I would laugh and talk about it."[72] Sometimes Mrs. Pitts refused to let Addie sing (Addie was also a lead singer in the choir) or play piano. When Addie protested this treatment, Mrs. Pitts whipped her for being sassy. Though she did not always agree with her methods, Addie admired Mrs. Pitts for her musical skill, dedication to the church, and tough attitude.[73] Still outspoken as she had been as a young girl in Brookhaven, Addie saw in Mrs. Pitts a match for herself and an image of a strong woman whose toughness, skill, and faith would not be undermined.

Addie also developed a friendship with another woman in the church, Elizabeth Brooks—a young, single black woman. "She would take me out and expose some cultural events I never would have been exposed to, being a member of a big family and poverty stricken . . . to be able to share good meals and events that we normally couldn't have because of the need to share with so many other brothers and sisters—she [Elizabeth] would take me to concerts and other places."[74] Addie saw Elizabeth as a different kind of role model, unlike her mother, grandmother, and Mrs. Pitts. Elizabeth was a single woman who used her resources and time to mentor Addie and expose her to a world that was larger than the confines of Bronzeville and the limitations imposed by her family's economic poverty. Similarly, Addie would embark upon a path of mentoring younger women in her church and in the labor and women's movements, believing in the power of building positive and supportive relationships with other women.

In addition to her family and church, the other important institution of Addie's youth was DuSable High School, which she began attending in 1936 at the age of twelve.[75] DuSable opened in the winter of 1936 after a fire destroyed a portion of Wendell Phillips High School. Primarily black since the mid-1920s, Wendell Phillips was one of the few high schools on the South Side of Chicago that blacks were freely able to attend and, as such, was extremely overcrowded. DuSable High School, located at 49th and Wabash, "was originally being constructed as a separate high school designed to keep the rapidly growing black high school population," recalled Lillie Lodge Brantley, founder of the Phillips/DuSable Alumni Council. The new school was originally given the name New Wendell Phillips High School. But the school's name was changed in 1936 to DuSable High School to honor the first known nonindigenous settler in the area, Jean Baptiste Pointe DeSaible (DuSable), of Haitian descent.[76]

DuSable boasted a 2,000-seat auditorium, swimming pool, two cafeterias, a rooftop conservatory, and an animal sanctuary where students could learn about zoology. The school had its own newspaper, *The DuSable Recorder*, and students could participate in a variety of activities—the Drama Club, the DuSable Hi-Y Club for Christian fellowship, the Negro History Club, the Spanish Club, the French Club, and the choir. The school had a thriving athletics program, which included fencing, swimming, track and field, baseball, basketball, and volleyball.[77] Addie was a member of the Beta Club, a group of girls who worked in the school's library. Musically inclined, she also played first clarinet in DuSable's Concert Band,[78] which was under the direction of the legendary Captain Walter Dyett. Over the course of his career, Dyett trained and directed thousands of students, including musical greats Dorothy Donegan, Gene Ammons, Fred Hopkins, and Dinah Washington. Dyett also created and directed the Hi-Jinks shows, which were student musical reviews composed of students. The Hi-Jinks shows were incredibly popular and tickets sold out fast.[79]

Instructors like Dyett were tough on their students and instilled within them a sense of pride, discipline, and perseverance. The school produced some of Chicago's and the country's greatest politicians, entrepreneurs, and activists, including first African American mayor of the city of Chicago, Harold Washington; publishing giant John H. Johnson; Olympic athlete and U.S. Representative Ralph Metcalfe; singer Nat King Cole; jazz pianist Dorothy Donegan; comedian and actor Redd Foxx, and many others. DuSable became a crown jewel of the South Side's black community and a symbol of black academic achievement and pride. Though known for its high academic achievement and stellar roster of attendees and graduates, many considered the school to be cliquish and sharply divided along lines of class and skin color.[80] Timuel Black, however, offers a different viewpoint of student relations at DuSable: "The black community was always moving as a group but at DuSable you had a concentration of talent where the rich and the poor, all on the south side had the opportunity to become friends and later in adulthood could benefit from associations with one another."[81] Black believed that the associations and friendships formed with classmates who had money and with classmates who had very little were long-term. Black also surmised that the successes and failures of alumni were collectively shared. Black, however, did admit that if there was some prejudice in DuSable, it came from older students against younger students because the upperclassmen were somewhat snobbish.

This was not the case between underclassman Addie Cameron and upperclassman Claude Wyatt Jr. Many of Addie's memories of her high-school years and time at DuSable involve her romance with Claude. Nicknamed "Pretty Boy," Claude was said to be extremely handsome, popular, and liked by many of the girls at DuSable. The courtship between Claude and Addie began in 1938 and was a significant experience for Addie, a young woman who had often questioned her own physical beauty because of the darkness of her skin and who dated little, if at all. Too busy with her responsibilities at home and at church, Addie never paid much attention to boys. But she became smitten with Claude Wyatt Jr., and their courtship led to a marriage that would last for sixty-nine years until Claude's passing in 2009.

Claude Wyatt Jr. was born in Dallas, Texas, in November of 1921 to Claude and Anna (Annie) Wyatt. Later that year, the Wyatts migrated to Chicago. Claude Sr. worked as a general laborer and skilled tailor, while Annie was a housewife. Much like the Camerons, the Wyatts struggled with poverty. The Wyatt home was frequently poorly furnished as the family had few possessions and moved around just as much as the Camerons. Many times when the family sat down to eat at the table, Claude's parents would caution the children to save some of their small meal just in case they had no food for the next day. The badges of poverty that angered and humiliated Addie were not escaped by Claude, and the two shared aspirations for economic stability and a better life. At school, low-income children like Claude who received a free carton of milk and a sandwich felt stigmatized. Claude believed that some teachers even discriminated against the poorer children who came to school every day wearing the same clothes. Some little boys wore girls' clothing and vice versa out of necessity. In order to avoid being picked on and getting into a fight before school, many children who wore these badges of poverty purposely arrived late in hopes that they would be free from the ridicule and taunts of their schoolmates. Claude remembered even having to fight at church during Sunday school because other children made fun of his clothes, the same clothes he wore each and every Sunday.[82]

Claude, like Addie, sought to turn his frustration with impoverishment into an opportunity to help improve his family's situation as well as his own. By the time he was fourteen, Claude spent nearly all of his free time working for money—on vegetable wagons, cleaning basements and backyards, running errands, selling *Defenders*, searching alleys for jugs and milk bottles to return to local stores, and washing windows. He also worked part-time at a dry cleaners. He became recognizable among street hustlers because of how much time he spent on the street looking to make extra money. Claude's dedication to finding work helped his family financially, but it did not help his grades. Because his moneymaking endeavors dominated most of his time, he spent little time studying and focusing on school. As a result, he received grades that were just above passing. Whatever he lacked in academic zeal, Claude sought to make up for in his physical appearance. He and his best friend, Raymond Dudley, were known around school and the community as "Pretty Boy" and "Dutch," respectively. "Pretty Boy" was the name given to Claude by his friend, neighbor, and classmate, Nat King Cole. Both used some of the proceeds from their jobs toward the creation of a stylish and impressive wardrobe that—according to Claude—when combined with his charm and easy personality, was the envy of their male peers and the key to the attraction of their female classmates.[83] His rise in social status as a result of working and being able to afford nicer clothing was no doubt a psychological feat for Claude, who had been bullied because his poverty was so visible. Thus, dress was more than just the evidence of his ability to acquire money; it was a symbol and a manifestation of upward social mobility, at least among some of his peers. Both he and Addie, who wore homemade clothes that her mother made from scraps of the unwanted clothing of her domestic employers, developed a taste and affinity for dressing well and fashionably.[84]

Claude recalled his first attempt to talk to Addie: "A friend and I were walking to school one day and I saw her." Addie was dressed uniquely and Claude, who had a love for clothes, was intrigued: "I liked her, and my friend called and told her I wanted to meet her."[85] Addie, however, was not interested. Petite and attractive, Addie had not had any boyfriends and was not looking for one at that time. But Claude persisted and showed up unannounced at the Cameron family's home some days later. In a 1977 interview with Elizabeth Balanoff, Addie recalled how Claude began to court her: "I opened the door and there he stood. I was shocked, I didn't know whether to welcome him in or excuse myself, so I welcomed him in. I introduced him to my mother who liked him because he was very attractive in manners as well as appearance. That's how I met him."[86] The two began dating. They stole time to talk with one another in the halls of DuSable between classes, and Claude carried Addie's clarinet on their walk home. Reared in the Methodist church, Claude began attending and eventually joined Addie's church, Langley Avenue Church of God. Addie was incredibly drawn to Claude: "He was a senior and I thought that he was the most handsome man I had ever seen. He was such a wonderful young man. My mother loved him. My family loved him and I did too."[87]

Claude graduated from DuSable in February of 1940. He and Addie were in love and began to contemplate their future. Maggie desperately wanted Addie to attend college because education had been an important facet of her own life. Ambrose, however, refused to send Addie to college, for reasons unknown. Perhaps he could not afford the cost of college or did not want to part with his oldest daughter who contributed so much to their home. Addie was just sixteen years old and Ambrose may have also feared the autonomy she would gain attending college. Addie often heard her parents arguing about her education, a contentious issue in the Cameron household.[88] Young and in love, Addie and Claude made the decision to get married: "He [Claude] was a member of a very poverty-stricken family, too, and we thought we could better our own lives by getting married and going on our own. I felt that this would not create difficulty for my parents. They were not going to send me to college anyway."[89]

With support from both sets of parents, the two were married in May 1940 by Pastor S. P. Dunn at the Langley Avenue Church of God. According to Addie, Claude was young, charming, and hardworking and showed a loyalty toward his family, believed in God, and had a desire to be successful in life. She was an intelligent and resourceful young woman, having spent her childhood largely within the confines of her home, church, and school. Love, a mutual attraction, and a deep desire to rise above poverty and make a new life for themselves united the two as a couple. They hoped to build a home free from the frustrations and humiliations of poverty and the constant relocation and instability of their childhoods. Having born witness to the perils, perhaps more so than the promise of the Great Migration, Addie hoped that she and Claude would fare better on their own as a young family.

Escaping the cycle of poverty became the primary objective for Addie and Claude Wyatt. Addie Wyatt's experiences of racism and poverty in the South and in the North played critical roles in the formation of her youth and early adulthood. Both racism and poverty altered the dynamics of her family life and created instabilities common among this generation of blacks born in the South, but who came of age in the North. Still, there were indigenous black political, social, and cultural institutions born out of black urban experiences with racial segregation, like Langley Avenue Church of God and DuSable High School, that served as beacons of stability, which instilled faith, dignity, community, and a desire for racial progress and upward mobility in blacks. Growing up in abject poverty, Addie Wyatt developed a nascent perspective, or philosophy, that was very much aware of the humiliation, frustrations, and destructive consequences of poverty for individuals, even if she was not altogether versed on the specific structural causes of economic inequality and exploitation. Wyatt's perspective was also shaped by her engagement with female leadership and power in the church and the importance of faith in moving through obstacles. Her perspective was likely influenced by peers and teachers at DuSable where academic and civic engagement were encouraged as a means of upholding and dignifying black potential for success. These experiences and others would ultimately aid Addie Wyatt in defining and sharpening a universal philosophy of freedom from poverty, racism, and sexism and a commitment to struggling against inequality with others in social justice movements.

2

IN SEARCH OF WORK
AND COMMUNITY

Waiting in line impatiently, Addie hoped that she would get her turn to use the telephone before the whistle sounded, calling the women back to work. If not, she would have to wait a few more hours until her lunch break to check in on her baby boy, Renaldo, who was just a few months old. Annie Wyatt, her mother-in-law, usually kept Renaldo but had been unable to do so, forcing Addie to leave him with a neighbor in hopes that he would be okay. As a young first-time mother, Addie couldn't stand being away from her baby. Was he being fed? Was he being changed? Had he been crying? These questions ran through her mind over and over again. She was not alone in her worries. In line for the telephone were a number of her coworkers, more young black women hoping to check in on their children before returning to the relentless pace of the canning line in an Armour & Company meatpacking plant in the Chicago stockyards.

The year was 1941 and Addie Wyatt was just seventeen years old. She was one of the youngest on the line canning stew for the U.S. Army in the dawn of America's direct involvement in World War II. Having been a part of the Great Migration a decade prior, Addie found herself in yet another massive movement of people—that of women and African Americans into the industrial wartime workforce. The exodus of men from manufacturing and industrial jobs who were either drafted into service or volunteered to fight in the war, created a vacuum of workers as increased wartime production necessitated an uneven yet sizable demand for workers. Many women, African Americans and other workers of color, sought to fill this gap and take advantage of the wartime economy.

Yet ideally, Addie Wyatt would have been miles away from the stockyards, at home caring for her baby. Her every intention upon marrying Claude was to become a housewife and raise a family. Struck by Claude's charm, talents, desire for economic comfort, and ability to bring in money on a consistent basis, Addie was sure that combined with her own talents and will to rise above poverty, they would fare better together rather than under the separate households of their large and impoverished families. In her mind, Claude would be the breadwinner and she would be the housewife. Such an arrangement had not been possible between her parents due to the size of their family, her father's inability to find steady work, and the inability of his earnings to support the family on a consistent basis. For working class and impoverished black families, the income of an African American principle wage earner (regardless of sex) was often not enough to support a family, making it imperative that those in the household who could contribute financially did so. After having worked for money outside of the home as a young girl for years, combined with her reverence for motherhood, it was Addie's desire to assume a more traditional role of housewife as opposed to the role of mother/wife/worker that black working-class women like her mother Maggie often assumed.

But just months after giving birth to her first child, Renaldo, in November of 1940, Addie realized that she would have to contribute financially to her home:

> I had to go to work to help my husband make a life for our family at an early age. And I was somewhat embarrassed because I thought that I ought to be able to stay at home and to raise our children, and that my husband would be able to do all of those wonderful things, but I discovered very early that, if we were to have a home to make, I would have to work with my husband outside of the home for pay, as well as work inside of the home to do those home chores.[1]

Claude's wages alone were not enough to support their growing family. The eight dollars per week that Claude made working at the dry cleaners had barely been enough to take care of him and Addie. The expenses brought on by the birth of their first child and a second son, Claude III, soon after made it imperative that Addie find work. To make matters worse, finding adequate housing was nearly impossible. The couple's youth was a strike against them because landlords feared they would be financially incapable or too irresponsible to pay the rent on time. An already racially constricted wartime housing market, a housing shortage in Bronzeville, and their financial shortcomings left Claude and Addie with few alternatives other than to live with Claude's parents until their conditions could improve. The life that the young Wyatts were living little resembled the life Addie had envisioned.

The search for adequate employment and housing, while navigating the challenges of marriage at such a young age, were the paramount concerns of the Wyatts during the early 1940s. As much as they hoped their union would pave the way for a better, more stable life, the early years of their marriage were wrought with instability, as were their prospects for upward economic mobility. Addie Wyatt's entrance into the workforce opened her eyes to the realities of racial and gender discrimination as structural and institutional barriers not only to employment in meatpacking, but to job promotions and job security once hired. Despite the opening of wartime industrial employment to greater numbers of blacks, Hispanics, and women, racial and gender discrimination were not forgone during the wartime economy. For Addie Wyatt, the United Packinghouse Workers of America (UPWA) became an important ally and powerful resource for working men and women in the stockyards.

IN SEARCH OF WORK

When it became imperative that Addie seek employment outside of the home, she relied upon a set of skills she gained at DuSable High School. As a part of her studies, she took typing classes and could type a commendable 60 to 70 words per minute. Needing employment, she set out to find clerical work and searched the newspapers for available typist positions. But she was consistently turned down, often told that a position just posted had already been filled.[2] The fact that she was only seventeen but appeared much younger may have been a factor in the rejections. Moreover, she had not finished high school due to the birth of her first child. But racial discrimination likely served as a formidable barrier to her attempts to secure clerical work, as such work was more often than not the domain of white women. Black workers, especially black women, were largely confined to semiskilled and unskilled domestic service and, to a lesser extent, manufacturing jobs. Black women were largely excluded from clerical and technical positions such as telephone operators, typists, and secretaries in white companies.[3] Desperate for work, Addie answered an advertisement for butchers at an Armour & Company meatpacking plant in Chicago's stockyards, located between 39th and 47th streets and bounded by Halsted to the east and Ashland to the west. Claude had worked briefly at Armour & Company for a short time between graduating high school and working full-time at the dry cleaners. He encouraged Addie to apply because many of the positions at Armour and in meatpacking were unionized and, as a result, paid good wages. His urging would ultimately prove life-changing for Addie.

Although significant barriers remained, by 1941 a number of crucial changes opened the doors of the big five Chicago meatpackers (Armour & Company, Swift, Cudahy, Morris and Wilson) to female and African American workers, making Wyatt's chances for gaining employment more favorable. Some 50,000 Chicagoans worked in the Second City's meatpacking plants during World War II, of which nearly 40 percent were African American and 20 percent were women.[4] African Americans, particularly in Chicago and other large cities with diverse economies, saw an increase in the number of job opportunities available in sectors outside of domestic and service work: "[B]lack workers found employment in the food processing industry (including meatpacking), the iron and steel industry, and wholesale and retail establishments."[5] One-quarter of Chicago's black workers were employed in the city's packinghouses by the end of World War II.[6] And the number of black women working in packinghouses increased more than fivefold between 1940 and 1950.[7]

In the early years of the twentieth century, African Americans comprised the vast minority of meatpacking workers and had a history of serving as strike-breakers when white workers walked off the yards in 1894, 1904, and 1921. A strikebreaker was one of the only ways African Americans could break into meatpacking. Blacks were subject to discrimination by their white coworkers, employers, and employee unions. They were seen as antiunion not only because of employer propensity to employ them as strikebreakers but because their presence often threatened white organized workers. In light of the dynamics between black and white workers, blacks were wary of a union's ability to represent them equally. Intense racial animosities on the shop floor, combined with intense racial violence in the city leading up to and following the 1919 Chicago Race Riot, worked to limit the presence of black workers in meatpacking and the overall power of existing unions such as the Amalgamated Meat Cutters and Butcher Workmen of North America.[8] In the 1930s, the proportion of black workers in Chicago's meatpacking plants increased to 30 percent, giving blacks a more viable presence on the shop floor.[9] A number of these black laborers were at the helm of a new workers' association—the Packinghouse Workers Organizing Committee (PWOC), which was in part responsible for improved working conditions in the plants, more minority and women workers in the plants, and better wages.

Since its inception in 1937 under the Congress of Industrial Organizations (CIO), the PWOC had been anchored by a multiracial coalition of workers, including African Americans, Irish, Poles, Greeks, Italians, Portuguese, and Mexicans. The PWOC and other workers' organizations and unions founded under the CIO differed in organizing style, structure—and to varying extents—ideologically from the older, more established, craft-based, and mostly white unions of the American Federation of Labor (AFL) founded by Samuel Gompers in 1886. The most noted exception to the AFL's lily-white unions would be A. Phillip Randolph's Brotherhood of Sleeping Car Porters, founded in 1925 and chartered by the AFL. Perhaps the most vital difference between the AFL and the CIO, established in 1935, was that the latter chose to organize "skilled" and "unskilled" workers alike, across racial and gender boundaries. The AFL had an official policy of egalitarianism and antidiscrimination, but its focus on organizing workers with only "skilled" job classifications led to an organization that was largely the domain of white men. Black workers and women workers were often systematically denied "skilled" job classifications, resulting not only in a lack of union representation but lower pay and greater difficulty securing promotions on the job. The AFL likewise failed to sanction its affiliates that did discriminate against workers of color, turning a blind eye to segregated and lily-white locals, even though such policies divided workers and thereby weakened labor's strength.[10] CIO affiliates would not be free from racism, sexism, and discrimination on the shop floor and in the union, but the CIO's efforts to organize greater numbers of women and workers of color permanently altered the demographic and ideological landscape of the American labor movement.[11]

The PWOC operated nationwide. Herbert March, a young white communist, was the notable leader of the Chicago PWOC. Like other CIO affiliates, the PWOC embodied the spirit of working-class militancy born in the 1930s during the crucible of the Great Depression. The PWOC aggressively embarked on a campaign to win representation for workers, gaining ground at smaller meatpacking plants while eventually securing wins at the large packers such as Armour and Swift. The PWOC "perfected the art of the slowdown and the departmental stoppage around grassroots issues, thus creating both confidence in the power of worker unity and reliance on a rank-and-file style of leadership."[12] The PWOC's commitment to improving working conditions, standardizing a grievance process that was both fair and timely for worker issues, and commitment to interracial unionism drew in younger generations of black workers new to meatpacking. Blacks migrating to northern industrial centers like Chicago increased the numbers of black workers in meatpacking plants and the membership of more progressive groups like the PWOC, which argued against discrimination in hiring and on the shop floor.

The PWOC saw discrimination as undermining efforts to strengthen unionism by dividing workers and creating divisions in pay, benefits, seniority, promotions, and working conditions. The increase of black workers in the packinghouses provided support for all workers' increased wages and better working conditions and later offered black workers the chance to use their growing numbers, strength and influence to protest racial segregation and discrimination on the job, in their unions, and in their communities. Labor historian Rick Halpern argues that whereas they were once wary of organizing and unions, black workers in the 1930s "provided the backbone and dynamism to a powerful interracial, interethnic alliance" and "supplied the leadership behind the new unions."[13] While the PWOC helped in organizing black workers, black workers in turn supported, bolstered, and helped direct the PWOC's policies and practices.[14] In fact, many local leaders of PWOC campaigns were black workers, such as Swift employee Phillip Weightman of Local 28. When the PWOC dissolved in 1943 to become the United Packinghouse Workers of America (UPWA), the union remained committed to its social and interracial unionism, even if it struggled at times to put its philosophy into practice and transmit that philosophy to its members.

It was in this milieu of growing worker influence and the increased number of African American and women workers in the industry that Wyatt applied for the open butcher position at Armour. Unfortunately, she possessed no real skills as a butcher. Barely one hundred pounds and just over five feet tall, Addie had trouble maneuvering the pig carcass and, according to the butcher foreman assessing her, had no real knife skills. She was quickly thrown off the line. Before leaving, however, Wyatt spotted six white women waiting outside of the front office and inquired as to what they were doing. She learned that they were applying for clerical positions as typists in Armour's front offices. Sensing a perfect fit given her typing skills, Wyatt waited with the women until all were called in to take the typing test. Everyone, including Addie, passed the test and were told to report to work the following Monday. But when Wyatt arrived the following week to begin her job as a typist, she was immediately put to work canning stew for the army with other black women:

> I told them [the other black women] that I was there to type but I was packing stew there temporarily, but they knew better. I began to look around and observe certain things and I felt that I was going to go into the office soon. But they knew that I wasn't going into that office. And I was waiting for them [management] to invite me into the office and they never did.[15]

Bewildered and frustrated, the realization of why she had not been asked into the front office sunk in. Black women were not hired in Armour's front offices, even if they did possess the qualifications for clerical work. Throughout the 1940s, African American women were routinely turned away from a variety of positions in the front office and in the plants that were deemed the domain of white women, while white women were encouraged to apply for these same positions deemed "women's work."[16] While the PWOC and later the UPWA bolstered interracial unionism in the plants, many of the departments within the plants remained heavily segregated by race and sex, and black women often felt the sting of both.

The world of the meatpacking plant and the shop floor was vastly different from the front office. Meatpacking plants were quite dangerous even though a number of measures had been taken to improve their conditions since the turn of the century. Spurred in part by Upton Sinclair's scathing exposé of the industry in *The Jungle*, progressive-era activists determined to clean up the industry and make it more efficient. Workers and union officials also demanded and negotiated for improvements in the plants. Job classifications and plant departments were structured in such a way that white men mainly held jobs in the skilled trades and mechanical units. Black men were relegated to the physically arduous departments for less-skilled laborers, such as the killing floor where carcasses were first sent for butchering. Men on the killing floor dealt with respiratory illnesses, suffered from cuts and bruises, were subject to severe fluctuations in temperature, operated dangerous machinery, and worked daily around knives and cleavers that more than once caused critical injuries to fellow workers and occasionally death. Women rarely worked directly alongside men during this period in the packinghouses. Instead of butchering the meat, women tended to hold jobs processing the meat once it had already been butchered, working in slicing, canning, and casing departments. Black women were most often found in the offal and casing rooms that were hot, unsanitary, and had floors slippery with meat byproducts while white women worked in cleaner departments such as bacon slicing or in the front offices performing clerical work.[17] In some regions of the country, the only way that black women could even enter into meatpacking and other industries was by first becoming janitors and then later through promotion to production jobs.[18] On occasion, black, white, and Hispanic women would work in the same department alongside one another. This complex matrix of racial and gender discrimination ultimately worked to proscribe the opportunities for job advancement and promotion for all except white men.

Wyatt, initially angry as a result of being barred from the front office typist position, soon learned that her job canning stew paid more than what the typists earned. She would receive sixty-two cents an hour, which averaged out to about twenty-four dollars per week. White women typists made only about nineteen dollars per week. This was because the canning department was unionized and had a strict wage scale in its contract, whereas the typists were not unionized. For "dirty work," Wyatt received much more per week than for clean, white women's work. Wyatt later estimated that black women typists, if they had existed in any measurable numbers, would have earned about twelve dollars per week if they were fairer in complexion and even less, around eight dollars per week, if they were darker in complexion like herself.[19] Jobs in the meatpacking industry overall paid wages much higher than work in the domestic and service-related sectors in which African Americans tended to dominate. Thus, despite its disadvantages, employment in meatpacking often garnered respect and praise among blacks in Chicago. For Wyatt, whose chief concern was earning a decent wage to help improve the financial and living conditions of her family, this was an unexpected benefit in light of the racial and gender discrimination she encountered. In her first few months of employment on the job, Wyatt signed a union card and joined the PWOC, which in 1943 became the United Packinghouse Workers of America. Her union dues were two dollars per month.

Wyatt did not fight for her job as a typist, which she had rightfully earned, principally because she would make more money in the segregated yet organized canning department. Though the work was not difficult to learn, Wyatt remarked, "It was fast work. You were in motion the whole eight hours. You were constantly moving, taking cans off a conveyer to weigh the cans for accurate weight and putting the cans back on the line. You had to do that for eight hours."[20] The monotony of work on the line, the fast pace, and having to stand for hours on end made "women's work" difficult in its own right. But the pay was good and the tangible benefits of organized work in the canning department (despite its drawbacks) were initially what drew Wyatt into the union. It would be over a decade before Wyatt would begin to utilize her direct experiences with racial and gender discrimination to act, organize, and lead others against the front-office discrimination of black women. Nonetheless, Wyatt encountered further episodes that clearly illustrated the resources and benefits of union representation.

Wyatt filed her first grievance several months after she began working at Armour & Company. Promoted to an interracial (though still female) department because of her good work record, Wyatt's new position entailed putting lids on cans of stew. The job was much cleaner and came with a slight increase in pay. After a few weeks in her new post, a white foreman pulled her off the line and placed a white woman at her post instead, effectively overriding Wyatt's seniority and bumping her down to a lower department and pay grade. Addie protested and argued with the foreman, questioning why she had been removed. Another young black woman, Van Johnson, a union steward, witnessed the commotion and went over to mediate. Johnson asked Addie if she would like to file a grievance on the grounds that the actions of the foreman went against the union's collective bargaining agreement with Armour. Addie said yes and Johnson filed a formal grievance against Armour officials.[21] Being in a racially mixed department in the plant did come with certain benefits, such as an increase in pay and a cleaner work environment, but Wyatt's job was at risk because as a black woman, she could be demoted or disposed of by the company if management sought to employ a white woman in her place.

Days later when Wyatt and Johnson walked into the front office to meet with two white male Armour officials to discuss Addie's grievance, Wyatt was afraid that they could not win. Sitting across from the Armour officials, she felt her gender and racial identity acutely and was amazed that she and Johnson could sit across from two powerful white men and voice their opinions and complaints on equal footing.[22] Johnson did much of the talking as the union representative, but at one point during the meeting, Addie spoke up and began to voice her outrage. She told officials just what she thought about being unfairly replaced. Before she could launch into a discussion of other shop floor concerns not directly related to her grievance, Wyatt felt Van Johnson tugging on her uniform—a signal to be quiet. Wyatt was disappointed as she was just revving up. After the meeting,

Johnson explained her actions: "Listen, whenever you win a grievance, don't keep arguing." Addie was stunned. She had been so caught up in the moment and preoccupied with voicing her outrage that she hadn't even noticed they had won the grievance and that she would be allowed to go right back to the line putting lids on cans.[23] Again, Addie witnessed the power of the union at work. Not only was her job protected, but the union provided workers, regardless of race or sex, the ability to fight against discrimination on the job and to even lead one another in representing the union and fellow workers.[24]

Soon after, about ten months into her employment at Armour, Addie discovered that she was pregnant with her second child. Afraid she might lose her job, Addie discussed her pregnancy with coworkers and union representatives. She found out that as a member of her union local, she was eligible for pregnancy leave. Organized women at Armour & Company had successfully bargained in their contract to get up to one year's leave of absence for pregnancy without the loss of their jobs or demotions to lower job classifications. Such contract clauses were some of the earliest acts of organized women to push for concessions solely based on "women's issues" and would not become standard or widespread in UPWA contracts until the 1950s.[25] Wyatt was spared the fate that many working women fell victim to while pregnant. Mary Salinas, a Mexican American woman who worked at an Armour plant in Fort Worth, Texas, recalled how she and other women were laid off when pregnant and that some managers would wait until a woman was in the hospital giving birth to fire her.[26] Addie was spared such a fate and given up to one year off, meaning that she could return to work when her child reached three months of age. This was a significant boon for women in the union. Their leave policy was ahead of its time for women in meatpacking and in other industries that saw female expansion as a result of World War II and the wartime economy.[27] In the 1960s and 1970s, pregnancy leave would be a major demand of the women's movement, and Addie Wyatt was at the forefront of campaigns for maternal and child-care legislation for working women.

Wyatt took advantage of the leave and left work to have her second son, Claude Wyatt III. Three months after his birth, Wyatt returned to work for Armour & Company and was reassigned to her old job, eager to get back to earning decent wages for her family.[28] She recalled in an interview with The HistoryMakers, "I then had a great, greater amount of appreciation for the union. And I wanted to do something to help build it. But I didn't want to be a leader in the union. I just wanted to help build it. And I began to inquire, what I can do to make a difference."[29] Grateful to the union for her wages, promotion, and pregnancy leave, Wyatt recognized its importance and the need to sustain and grow the movement. But she was reluctant to seek any sort of union leadership. While her reasons for this remain elusive, a number of factors in her personal life likely played into her unwillingness to do much more beyond maintaining membership in the union, utilizing its benefits and praising its worth.

One important factor was Wyatt's increasingly unstable hold on regular packinghouse employment, reflecting the variable pace of production and the demands of the wartime economy. When wartime production slowed and during postwar reconversion, meatpacking plants, like many companies, reduced their workforces in the name of efficiency and profit maintenance. Thus Addie, who was relatively new to the plants, lacked the seniority to secure her job when production slowed or when the company reduced its workforce. Many women, but especially black women who found industrial employment during the war, fell victim to the practice of last-hired, first-fired. Some 60 percent of black women found themselves taking up work in private household and institutional service positions, despite the increasing numbers of women overall who continued to enter the industrial labor force in the postwar period.[30] While Addie Wyatt did not blame the union for her predicament, it seems likely that her perilous employment situation exposed some of the limits of the union's capacity to stabilize her circumstances. As much as the union could do in the way of providing benefits and resources for its members during the war, unions like the UPWA struggled to resist concessions and maintain gains made prior to postwar reconversion. Yet overall, Wyatt's early exposure to the UPWA planted an appreciation for the tangible benefits of the union and its interracial roots.

Laid off and rehired multiple times between 1942 and 1944, Addie continued to struggle to help Claude make ends meet. Cycling in and out of meatpacking, Addie eventually found stable employment in meatpacking in 1947. In the meantime, the couple dealt with the difficulties of caring for two small children. Child care was a constant concern during the times that Addie worked. When she was not working, she could take care of the children but in turn was unable to bring in much income. She was, however, able to finish her high-school requirements by taking courses at an adult education center in the city.[31]

Personal crises occupied much of Wyatt's life in the years between 1940 and 1945. The problems of finance, housing, and raising two small children when she and Claude were practically still teenagers themselves, led to her marriage being on shaky ground. According to Addie, the young couple left Langley Avenue Church of God and strayed away from the teachings of the church. As a young girl, Maggie, Adeline, and the Church of God taught Addie to read the Bible and the scripture as an illustration of how to conduct herself as a Christian and practice her faith. For years she attended church services at Langley every Sunday and led choir rehearsals sometimes two to three times a week. She prayed daily, and her mother and grandmother constantly sought to instill the principles of Christianity in Addie and her siblings. Thus, her break from the church was a drastic departure from her youth.

What exactly precipitated the Wyatts' temporary departure from the Church of God is unknown, as are many of the details surrounding the exact circumstances of their early marital struggles. In a 1979 interview with Sarah Anderson, a graduate student at Anderson University, Wyatt disclosed the fact that she had left the church and that her marriage experienced troubles beyond the realm of finances and housing. In the early years of her marriage, Wyatt found herself frequenting nightclubs and "living the life" in an effort to keep up with her husband, who was often away from home at night. Even though she did not like the nightclub atmosphere, Addie's friends advised her that she too would have to spend her nights out if she wanted to keep her husband. Addie turned to her mother and mother-in-law for counsel. Maggie gave Addie a powerful piece of advice that she herself had likely come to rely upon, having married Ambrose as a teenager and then dealing with the consequences of his alcoholism. She told Addie, "If God cannot keep him, you cannot keep him."[32] Addie would have to have faith in God, in the bonds and covenant of her marriage, and in Claude and his relationship with the Lord, however far both of them had strayed.

It took time and an epiphany for Wyatt to actually begin transforming her outlook on her marriage and faith. After one particular night out in a club, Wyatt decided that it would be her last. Fearful of what her actions in the nightclub might mean for the salvation of her soul, Wyatt prayed "that if God spared her to get out of there He would not encounter her sharing in that experience again. So she went home."[33] By her own admission, Addie did not go to another nightclub, but she also did not immediately return to the church. And it took time for her relationship with Claude to improve. She and the children left Claude's parents' home to live with the Camerons, overwhelmed and frustrated by the duties of marriage, motherhood, and work. Eventually, she alternated between living with her family on the South Side of Chicago and with the Wyatts who relocated to Robbins, Illinois, an African American suburb south of Chicago.[34]

We cannot know with certainty how Addie and Claude resolved the tensions and problems in their marriage. A series of trying familial crises, a chance at decent housing, and a renewal of faith may well have compelled needed stability and reconciliation. In March of 1944, Maggie Cameron fell seriously ill and was bedridden for a week before passing away from hypertensive heart disease caused by chronically high blood pressure. She was only thirty-nine years old. Whether hereditary or the result of stress and an inability to properly care for herself while caring for a large family, Maggie's death dealt a significant blow to the Cameron children. She was the center of the Cameron household and the children's anchor. Her illness was sudden and her death came as a shock to Addie and Claude: "We were really surprised. We didn't know that she was going to pass away and when we got there the doctor told us that there was no hope for her."[35] On her deathbed, Maggie begged Addie and Claude to take her children and raise them. If it was not possible to take all of the children, she requested that they at least take her youngest two, Audrey and Maude.[36] Unable to refuse her mother's dying request and fearful that her siblings might be separated and put in foster care, Addie and Claude agreed that they would care for the six younger Cameron children—Edna, Emmett, Bluett, Mickey, Audrey, and Maude—who at the time of Maggie's death ranged in age from seven to eighteen. Addie's older brother Ambrose Jr. was abroad fighting in the war.

Taking in her siblings promised a new set of challenges for Addie. She was a young mother trying to put her marriage on track and provide for her own young sons. Financially, she and Claude would no doubt struggle to feed six additional mouths, but the couple made a promise to Maggie and committed themselves to taking the children in as soon as possible. Addie recalled how the apartment the Camerons lived in was deplorable: "At the time, we lived in a terrible rat-infested apartment with rats as big as cats. Sometimes we'd have to fight them off the children. I was trying to get out of that place, not knowing where to go. I tried to rent various places, but I was young and my husband was young and they would not rent to us because of our youth. So we kept praying and trying."[37] In addition to the constant layoffs and rehires at Armour, which complicated taking care of their children and Addie's siblings, Claude was drafted into the U.S. Navy in July of 1944, just four months after Maggie's death. He would spend the following year at the Great Lakes Naval Base in North Chicago, Illinois. Addie kept up a relentless schedule trying to keep her family together while Claude was away in the Navy. She would turn the bulk of her attention toward securing adequate housing for her growing family.

ALTGELD GARDENS

One day in 1944, Addie Wyatt spotted an advertisement for Altgeld Gardens, a new housing project on the far south side of Chicago for defense workers. Addie went to the nearest Chicago Housing Authority (CHA) housing office and applied for housing at Altgeld, only to find that her name would be added to a lengthy waiting list. In order to qualify for housing at Altgeld, both she and Claude would need to be employed in defense work. Claude's service in the Navy fulfilled that requirement, but Addie's employment at Armour did not. She left the stockyards and applied for a series of jobs, often working just long enough to see if the position would meet the CHA's employment requirements for Altgeld Gardens. Eventually she found employment working at an ammunition container company in Harvey, Illinois, in a plant whose production was geared 100 percent toward defense.[38]

At this time, she and her two young boys, Renaldo and Claude III, lived with Claude's parents in nearby Robbins, Illinois. Each day, Wyatt commuted to and from work in Harvey to spend time with her children in Robbins. Several times per week she made the commute from Robbins into the city to 42nd and Calumet where her siblings were still residing. Most of the time, they were left unattended as Ambrose, grieving Maggie's death and still battling alcoholism, was rarely there. Occasionally one of Ambrose's older sisters, likely Martha, checked in on the children and stayed with them. When Addie made her trips to check on the children, she would cook enough food for them to last for a few days or at least until her next visit.[39] She also commuted to the northern suburbs of Chicago to the Great Lakes Naval Base in order to see Claude. At just twenty years old, Addie shouldered an immense amount of responsibility for her family.

After gaining defense employment in Harvey and thereby meeting the CHA's preliminary requirements for Altgeld, Addie and Claude were selected for an entrance interview. Claude received leave from the naval base and the two interviewed with a CHA housing agent. Addie Wyatt explained their plight and the grueling pace she maintained to keep her family intact. As Addie saw it, she had to "recapture and recover and revive them [her siblings] to keep them surviving and to keep them going" after the death of their mother.[40] Finding decent, affordable, and safe housing was paramount to this endeavor. Compelled by their story, the housing agent agreed, and the Wyatts were cleared to move into Altgeld the very next week, sometime in the fall of 1944.[41]

While Addie convinced the housing authority that the situation with her family was dire, the process of actually taking her siblings from the family's home and bringing them to live with her was much more fraught. Ambrose was initially unwilling to give up his children even though his addiction, intermittent illnesses, and incredible grief disabled him from taking care of them properly. In some ways, the events that led to his fleeing Mississippi and the difficulties he experienced in finding steady work in Chicago had broken him. His frustrations and anger with the shortcomings of his life and his experiences with racism and economic poverty created distance between his family and him, despite the love that he felt for his children and the love they felt for him in return. Yet at the same time, his children were all he had and he likely feared losing them. His mother, Adeline, passed away in 1938 and then Maggie, his beloved wife, died in 1944. He may have wanted to keep his children in hopes that one day he would be able to consistently provide for them as their father. In the end, Ambrose allowed the children to live with his sister temporarily in Bronzeville before they relocated to the far south side to live with Claude, Addie, and the boys in Altgeld Gardens.

The Wyatts were part of a vanguard generation of black Chicagoans and Americans who were "the firsts" to live in government-funded public housing, much of which was constructed beginning in the late 1930s as a solution to housing crises sweeping the nation. For African Americans in Chicago, the housing crisis was due to a number of factors. Large numbers of blacks continued to migrate from the South to northern industrial cities in the 1930s and 1940s, swelling the populations of cities like Chicago, exacerbating and exposing the high levels of residential segregation, inadequate slum housing, and high rents that plagued Black Chicagoans. By 1940, 78 percent of all blacks in Chicago lived in Bronzeville.[42] And between 1940 and 1950, Chicago's black population grew by over 215,000 and created a dramatic housing shortage. Moreover, the growing numbers of poor and low-income families needed to be housed. Veterans returning from the war and defense workers contributing to the war effort demanded housing for themselves and their families. They believed that service for the nation, regardless of race, should reciprocate access to better housing among other rights and benefits.

Government-funded public housing emerged as the nation's and Chicago's solution to the housing crisis. Created in 1937, the Chicago Housing Authority sought "to provide decent, safe, sanitary housing to the poor and to remove slums and blighted areas." The CHA, under its first executive director, Elizabeth Wood, had its hands full navigating the city's racial politics and administering housing.[43] Very few of the city's early housing projects were racially integrated. Many of the CHA's earliest housing projects like the Cabrini Homes and Trumbull Park were built to house white families. The opening of the Ida B. Wells Homes in 1941 on the city's South Side was the first housing project primarily for African Americans and was considered a beacon of pride for blacks in its early years. Altgeld Gardens, which opened three years later, was modeled after the Ida B. Wells Homes and constructed primarily for African American families engaged in defense work.[44]

But as much as we know about the history of race and the development of public housing in Chicago, much of the literature has focused on what went wrong with public housing. With the exception of a few scholars like J. S. Fuerst, former research director for the CHA, most have chosen to look at public housing as a problem, rather than for its possibilities. To critics, public housing was and is a world constructed and constricted by policy makers as opposed to a world in which residents could conceive and sustain communities enjoying unique resources and opportunities for engagement and vitality.[45] It is important not to lose sight of the ways in which public housing, in Chicago and elsewhere, was a mixed blessing for midcentury African Americans, much like the Great Migration and industrial wartime employment. For the Wyatts and other black families forming the first generation of public housing residents in Altgeld, the uncertainty and cruelty of the housing market and the cramped, slum conditions of tenement life in Bronzeville were left behind. But also left behind was community: the close proximity to family members, social networks, schools, churches, jobs, and aspects of black cultural engagement that were not readily available in the industrial surroundings of Altgeld and nearby white communities inhospitable to the presence of blacks. Racially and geographically isolated, Altgeld's residents and attentive CHA managers had to do much of the work of fashioning a cohesive and enhancing community with its own social, political, and communal opportunities.

The construction of Altgeld began in November of 1943 on vacant lands between 130th and 133rd streets, bounded by Langley Avenue on the west and Greenwood Avenue on the east, just southwest of Lake Calumet. Altgeld Gardens was named after John Peter Altgeld, Illinois governor from 1893 to 1897, who resided in Chicago's remote Riverdale community. Dating back to the early nineteenth century, Riverdale had been a heavily industrialized area comprised of working-class Dutch, Swedish, Irish, German, and Russian immigrant families. Some African Americans worked in industrial and manufacturing plants in Riverdale, but very few resided in the immediate area. White residents of Riverdale protested the construction of Altgeld, aware that the housing project was intended for African Americans. Their protests and African American demonstrations in support of the construction of Altgeld would be nowhere near the scale of the riots that took place as a result of the CHA's attempts to integrate veteran housing projects like Airport Homes and Fernwood Park in 1946 and 1947, respectively.[46] Nor would the level of protest be near that of the housing riots in Cicero in 1951 or the Trumbull Park disturbances from 1952 through 1954. Despite the protests, construction on Altgeld reached completion in 1944. The population of Riverdale grew more than sixfold between 1940 and 1950 due to an increase in the number of African Americans in the community. Whereas decades before European immigrants and second-generation families dominated the area, African Americans represented 84 percent of Riverdale's population by 1950—an increase that took place in the span of six years since the opening of Altgeld. The increase was also due to the outmigration or flight of whites from the community.[47]

Altgeld Gardens officially opened on September 18, 1944, though some families had already moved in over the summer. With an estimated cost of nine million dollars, the housing project sat on 157 acres of land and consisted of 162 groups of two-story row houses with 1,500 apartments; the vast majority of the residents were African American war defense workers and their families.[48] Each housing unit had a front and back yard, bathroom, kitchen, living room, and storage space, and ranged in size from three to six rooms.[49] All had central heating, automatic hot water heaters, gas ovens, ice boxes, and double sinks in the kitchens, private bathrooms with built-in modern tubs, windows with screens, storm doors, and incinerators.[50] Residents paid rent on a sliding income scale depending on the overall size of their family and the size of the unit they were renting. Owned by the federal government but administered locally by the Chicago Housing Authority, Altgeld was one of CHA's largest housing communities.[51]

Two of the initial requirements for housing at Altgeld were that heads of household have employment in government war defense work and that families have at least one child, seventeen years of age or younger. Many of the CHA housing projects were built for families with children, and the safe upbringing of children was considered a primary concern for contractors and the architects. Of the original 7,000 Altgeld residents, 61 percent were under the age of nineteen.[52] Altgeld Gardens' homes were built in blocks arranged in the shape of a letter "u" that faced out toward the street, leaving the interior of the blocks fenced in as play areas for children. That way, women presumably working in the home could easily keep an eye on their children at play.[53] The construction of communities like Altgeld were markedly different from the later construction of Chicago's State Street high-rise public housing communities like the Robert Taylor Homes and Stateway Gardens, both of which were criticized for the inability of parents to keep watch over their children during playtime and lack of suitable, safe, and visible play spaces.

Shortly after opening, the CHA added a nursery to Altgeld. Addie Wyatt was appreciative of the CHA's efforts to provide child care for families. As employment in war defense industries was a prerequisite to eligibility for housing at Altgeld Gardens, providing child care was also a way to keep women and men employed. Prior to Altgeld, Addie remembered arranging child care: "Child care at the community center did so much for our children. Before that, they went from one neighbor's house and one friend's house to another. Every morning, you had to find somebody to keep the child. You'd leave screaming children and never know if the kid got his lunch."[54] The nursery at Altgeld, built partly due to the demand of its residents, filled a void for black workers and took adequate child care off their long list of concerns. It also helped to make Altgeld a more self-contained, self-serving, and autonomous community.

Altgeld's row houses were quite a step up in terms of their quality and spaciousness, something many residents were not used to but had longed for in their previous housing. Claude Wyatt, who referred to Altgeld as "the baby doll of all the projects" and "a real showplace" enjoyed the fact that he and his family had three bedrooms, a living room, kitchen, and utility room all for themselves. They shared wall space with only two apartments directly to the left and the right. There was no one above or below them and no cavernous building to enter into. In short, public housing and Altgeld gave the Wyatts their first real home in Chicago. Claude remembered, "I was so excited when I first moved in there. I would put my key in the front door, go out through the back door, come around to the front door again, and walk in and go through—again. I couldn't believe it."[55] Feelings of pride and ownership translated far for black families seeking upward mobility and decent living conditions. Those feelings, along with CHA staff rules and expectations, led residents of Altgeld to organize themselves, their blocks, and their community around issues important to them.

In its early years, the vast majority of households in Altgeld Gardens were composed of working two-parent families, and the views of these families toward Altgeld were quite favorable. Andrew Greenlee, a retired superintendent of the Chicago Police Department who spent his early childhood years in central Mississippi, recalled moving into Altgeld as a young boy with his family in 1944. His father had come up to Chicago the prior year and, after finding work, was able to send for his family of ten. They moved into a three-bedroom, one-bathroom apartment in Altgeld. The homes at Altgeld were by no means mansions and many large families still felt crowded, but the quality of housing offered much more than what they were able to find elsewhere in the city's designated areas for blacks. Finally and most importantly, Altgeld was more affordable than existing inflated housing prices for the working-class families that dominated Altgeld. Greenlee remembered Altgeld fondly as a "wholesome place" where the homes and atmosphere of congeniality reminded him of the South.[56] Erman and Dorothy Sing, who met and married in Altgeld, remembered the fines levied against residents who did not cut their grass or littered on the property and the high regard they shared for their community. Hortense Irwin Bright, retired principal of Lucy Flower High School, relocated to Altgeld with her family in the mid-1940s. Bright's father left the family to serve in the army in France during World War II and abandoned the family after his tour of duty. Bright and her mother and three sisters were living in the back of an old mattress factory on 31st street in Chicago when her mother learned of Altgeld Gardens. The family was able to move into Altgeld, and though her mother traveled each day from the far South Side to the West Side for work, Bright appreciated how much Altgeld had improved their lives.

For many in this early generation of Altgeld residents, public housing brought people and families together, rather than causing them to grow apart. William Shaw, a retired Deputy Chief of the Chicago Police Department, moved into Altgeld in 1945 with his mother and father and four siblings. He recalled, "When we moved to Altgeld, it's almost like I died and went to heaven. For so many years, as long as I had been living, we were always bundled up, we never had rooms of our own. Altgeld Gardens afforded us the opportunity to spread out, to have some form of privacy, and to live as a family, truly as a family."[57] Shaw felt, as did many other public housing residents across the city at the time, that the administration of the CHA "gave out a feeling of caring for what happened to each apartment and the family in it. I recall, every once in a while, someone from the development came by and talked to the family and inspected the apartment. We didn't consider this any invasion in our privacy. . . . The administration during that period of time wasn't the enemy."[58]

Altgeld residents took ownership and advantage of the community's resources and institutions to create services for its residents that were not already in place. On its opening day, "there were no school buildings, stores, or places for worship services"[59] in Altgeld. In order to educate the many children of Altgeld, school rooms were set up in a row of apartments in the property's 800 block where they would remain until school buildings could be constructed. Over the next ten years, Altgeld grew immensely and was described by former resident Willie Black McShane as "a town within itself" equipped with schools, Catholic and Protestant churches, and "a currency exchange, 5 and 10 cent store . . . shoe repair shops, shoe stores, clothing stores, a drug store, laundry mats, jewelry stores, cleaners, restaurants, and practically any kind of business you can name."[60] A shopping center at 131st and Ellis housed many of these stores along with the Altgeld Gardens Co-op store where residents purchased and owned shares of stock. In a 1953 article in the *Altgeld Beacon*, resident Lucius Evans celebrated, "nine years of hard work by all the residents cooperating together to achieve one of the most attractive communities in the city of Chicago."[61] Residents of Altgeld were by and large proud of the community they constructed.

Social activities and community organizing were a major part of life for both children and adults in Altgeld. Altgeld residents formed their own baseball, softball, and basketball teams and had annual tournaments and championship games. Brownie troops and sewing and embroidery clubs were run by women in the community for young girls.[62] On Halloween, children trick-or-treated within Altgeld Gardens and enjoyed a special bonfire, apple cider, and candy at the Children's Building.[63] On weekends, films were shown at the Children's Building. For youth especially, there were skating nights, dances, social clubs, and the Wyatt Choral Ensemble (WCE), a singing chorus for youth founded by Addie and Claude Wyatt in 1947. A Pythagorus Lodge, Citizens Committee, and Employment Guild all operated in Altgeld. The community newspaper, the *Altgeld Beacon*, featured regular updates on the activities of its residents and the CHA. The newspaper even maintained a regular beauty column and featured event and activity listings for the Children's Building and the Altgeld Library. Altgeld residents elected one another to representative positions on the community's Coordinating Council. All elections passed through a Board of Election Commissioners of Altgeld Gardens, composed of residents and staff. Overall, residents were active in pushing for and supporting additional services deemed necessary for the operation, sustainment, and growth of their community. Programs were held to raise money for school sports teams, block recreational teams, a nursery, a preschool dental clinic, and other resident-initiated endeavors. Isolated from these services elsewhere and unable to access those in the area because of racial discrimination, Altgeld residents fought for and established these institutions in their community.

The efforts of Altgeld Gardens residents along with the early support of the CHA to create a cohesive, progressive, and model community did not go un-noticed. Paul Robeson made a special appearance at the dedication of George Washington Carver High School in 1948, a brand new facility built to educate Altgeld's youth. Altgeld's Administration Building, also known as the Children's Building or Carver Park, provided more communal space for residents and their children in addition to the recreational rooms housed on each block. Joe Louis, heavyweight boxing champion of the world, appeared at the building's dedication. Louis would make other appearances at Altgeld Gardens, includ-ing attending the first annual talent show of Altgeld from which proceeds went toward the purchase of musical instruments for the Corliss High School band.[64]

When the CHA hosted its annual flower festivals and Altgeld's anniversary program, the accomplishments of Altgeld Gardens residents were prominently featured alongside the achievements of residents from the Dearborn Homes, Francis Cabrini Homes, Wentworth Gardens, Lathrop Homes, Ida B. Wells Homes, and other early CHA communities. The 1951, 1953, and 1954 editions of the *Altgeld Beacon* covered the annual festivals and featured congratulatory notes from prominent public officials, including notable black political scientist Ralph Bunche, who wished the residents of Altgeld success in their "outstand-ing housing project"; former first lady Eleanor Roosevelt; Vice President of the United States Alben Barkley; and U.S. Senator from Illinois Paul Douglas.[65] Illinois Governor Adlai Stevenson also sent his congratulations, calling public housing "one of the most socially significant enterprises of our times." Residents were given beautification awards for the homes with the best yards and flower displays as well as awards for outstanding community leadership. The annual festival marked a time, according to Robert Fairfax, editor and publisher of the *Altgeld Beacon*, to "let those who have gathered here at Altgeld today carry back to all parts of our city the message that public low-rent housing benefits—not depreciates—communities. Let the beautiful flowers, the green lawns, the many demonstrations of good citizenship which the project residents have shown strike down the great lie put out by the enemies of the program—namely, that public housing and its residents will destroy a good community."[66]

Combating this image and sustaining a model community were early priori-ties for residents at Altgeld, well before public housing movements in the 1960s and on sought to combat such perceptions of their communities as pathological spaces of urban blight. Building a good community was a primary concern for many residents of Altgeld. Each block of Altgeld had a Block Committee that was responsible for block morale and keeping up the appearance of the block:

> To the tune of "America the Beautiful" coming over the public address system, the residents rush to their windows, door and side-walks to listen. Having their attention, the Block Committee members remind them of the importance of home and property care, cutting the grass, planting flowers for yard beautification, cleaning areas around the incinerators, proper disposal of garbage . . . [and] clean homes inside and out, which means washing walls and floors, keeping clean and attractive windows, correct care of sinks, cooking stoves and toilet facilities. They are also reminded of their responsibility for their children's conduct—for teaching them to appreciate beautiful surroundings and to respect their own and their neighbors' property. Observance of all these factors will contribute to making and keeping Altgeld Gardens a beautiful and a pleasant community in which to live.[67]

The statement above illustrates that there was a socializing process at Altgeld. The belief was that these residents had to be tutored in the art of modern living, keeping a clean beautiful home, and minding their children. The thrust for improvement was not lost on the Wyatts: "People on our block were striving to improve themselves. I don't know how many were striving to get out of there, because we weren't. We had just found this heavenly place. We loved it and wanted to stay."[68]

One of the critical organizing committees for residents was the Altgeld Tenants League, which fought hard to raise the income ceilings for tenants in order to keep higher-income families in the community and stave off tenant turnover. In the postwar era, the policies of the CHA shifted toward providing housing solely for low-income and poor families and the agency began evicting higher-income families. Under the Federal Housing Act of 1949, the city of Chicago and the CHA embarked on an ambitious project to secure federal housing monies for the creation of low-rent housing on slum and vacant sites, thereby increasing the amount of housing overall and decreasing the number of slums.[69] Whereas during the war, residents who worked in defense jobs were able to apply for and receive housing at Altgeld, during the postwar era income restrictions began to alter the composition of Altgeld's residents. In 1953, an addition to Altgeld, the Philip Murray homes, expanded the community. The addition was part of a 10,000-dwelling, $100 million project, backed by federal money to house growing numbers of poor and low-income families. The Philip Murray homes included sixty-three two-story row house buildings along with a new wing to the existing Altgeld community building and additional space for administrative services.[70] Named for labor leader Philip Murray, who died in November of 1952, the Murray homes were completed in 1954 and housed low-income families as opposed to the working-class families that had dominated Altgeld in the prior decade.

More and more of the early residents of Altgeld who were employed and earned decent wages were pushed out because their incomes exceeded CHA guidelines.[71] In the late 1940s and early 1950s, nearly 500 families left the CHA, either evicted or under threat of eviction because of their higher incomes.[72]

> The "up and out" theory was that as tenants' incomes rose above the maximum eligibility limits, they would then move to private housing. This turnover would make a large number of units regularly available for new applicants. By 1950, however, 27 percent of CHA families received public aid, and about one-third had one parent missing from the home. CHA was becoming the landlord for hard-core poverty families, who had suffered from long-term deprivation and discrimination.[73]

It is understandable that the CHA would focus on providing housing for impoverished families in need. But its new policies had a number of negative effects on longtime working-class black residents of public housing, especially in highly autonomous and organized communities like Altgeld. Perhaps most important to the community as a whole, these individuals were invaluable members of Altgeld who contributed to its social, economic, and civic dynamism. The "up and out" theory may have worked for white families in the 1940s who were able to utilize their economic upward mobility to take advantage of expanded housing opportunities in the Chicagoland area, but residential segregation made it difficult for black families to seek and gain access to those same opportunities.

The Altgeld Tenants League had its work cut out as higher-income families were slated for eviction. The Washington family's four members, who had resided in Altgeld since 1944, were evicted once Mr. Washington's income as a steelworker reached $5,000 per year. The Johnson family searched in vain for alternative affordable and decent housing for over a year, but with an estimated annual income of $5,584, they too were slated for eviction. The Savage family, headed by Thomas Savage, a fitter for a railroad car manufacturer, believed the eviction to be unjust in light of the difficulties black families faced with discrimination, high rents, and poor housing outside of Altgeld. The Savage family income was estimated to top over $7,000 per year. The Bell, Allen, Gilmore, Pettis, and Minor families all found themselves in a similar bind, either recently evicted or slated for eviction.[74] After Addie Wyatt joined the staff of the UPWA as an organizer and staff representative in 1954, her salary along with Claude's, who worked as a finance clerk for the U.S. Postal Service, exceeded income limits. They too had to leave Altgeld in 1955 after eleven years of residence. The Wyatts and many other families uprooted by the CHA's income limits did not want to leave public housing. A number of Addie and Claude's relatives had relocated to Altgeld Gardens or started their own families there, and the feelings of belonging and community cultivated at Altgeld during that first decade were difficult to leave behind.

Yet as much as Altgeld residents hoped to engineer, nurture, and maintain the "paradise" they constructed during its first decade, Altgeld was not devoid of significant problems both known and unknown to its residents at the time. A major factor behind the organizing of resources and self-autonomy of Altgeld was its geographic and racial isolation. Public transportation to and from Altgeld was unusually expensive, infrequent, and difficult to navigate for adults who traveled across the city and surrounding suburbs for work. Even though they were within the city limits, Altgeld residents paid suburban rates and were ineligible to transfer to other routes once in the city unless they paid full fares instead of transfer rates.

Racism in nearby communities also worked to tarnish the experiences of Altgeld residents when they were in need of medical attention or emergency resources. Blacks were not admitted to the nearest hospital, Roseland Community Hospital, unless they were on their deathbed. Located just northwest of Altgeld, Roseland was an all-white neighborhood. Addie and Claude Wyatt recalled two instances in which family members or neighbors were refused adequate treatment or admittance at Roseland. When the Wyatts' niece, Diane, was pregnant and near delivery, the family had no choice but to take her to Roseland because of its close proximity. It was New Year's Eve, bitter cold, and the baby's head was crowning by the time the family got to the hospital. Hospital staff delivered the baby and then pushed mother and child out into the hallway of the hospital without adequate clothing and care. It was not until a police officer was able to take the family into the city to Cook County hospital, which treated blacks, some sixteen miles away, that mother and child could receive additional medical attention. Claude Wyatt drove a chronically ill neighbor back and forth for an entire year to Cook County Hospital in the Wyatt's car. Barred from admittance to Roseland Community Hospital, staff there would only ask him about his ailments, give him a prescription for medication, and send him home.[75]

Making the connection between the segregation of Altgeld and racial discrimination in the surrounding communities and Chicago was secondary to the Wyatts. Years later, the pair remarked, "We never really thought at the time in terms of being discriminated against. Because it was all black folks. We weren't even sensitive to that. Just give me decent housing, give me decent health, give me a decent job and give a good education for my kids and don't worry about it. We were only sensitive to having a comfortable place to live, you know. Whereas today we are a little wiser."[76] The Wyatts' reasoning illustrates the ways in which the consciousness of Addie and Claude Wyatt was not yet oriented toward recognizing and fighting racial discrimination on a structural level. Just as Addie joined the union because of the very real, tangible, and coveted resources that it could give her, the Wyatts focused on the benefits of Altgeld, rather than its shortcomings. The immediate concerns of housing, child care, employment, and education were foremost in the minds of this young couple. Their ethos of upward mobility at this early stage in their lives was rooted in their ability to access these resources without necessarily understanding how racial discrimination on a structural level could limit access to those same resources, regardless of their best individual efforts to overcome. This is not to denigrate the Wyatts, for they certainly played a crucial role in Altgeld Gardens through the formation of the WCE, but it is important to note that their shift toward activism and leadership was not immediate or innate; rather, it developed over time.

One of the most serious issues to emerge out of Altgeld Gardens was that of environmental hazards. Altgeld was "constructed on a former garbage dump owned by the Pullman Company" and "located in the heart of the Calumet Industrial District" where its neighbors included "at least fifty landfills and toxic waste sites, a sewage treatment plant, and a range of industries that utilized coke ovens, blast furnaces, refineries, scrap yards, and chemical plants."[77] Founded in June of 1979 by Altgeld resident Hazel Johnson, People for Community Recovery (PCR) sought to educate Altgeld's citizens about environmental problems in their community and to mobilize against hazardous toxins in low-income and minority communities. Johnson, known as the "black mother of the environmental movement," would eventually travel all the way to Washington, D.C., for PCR's recognition as one of the nation's top environmental activist organizations. PCR was one of nine 1992 recipients of the President's Environmental and Conservation Challenge Awards. President Barack Obama would spend some of his early years as a community activist and organizer in Chicago working with People for Community Recovery.[78]

Environmental problems were a concern for early Altgeld residents. A petition signed by 1,200 residents was sent to the city of Chicago and the Chicago Housing Authority asking that something be done to cover a large drainage ditch running south from 133rd Street to the Calumet River. Some fifteen feet across and often filled five to six feet high with raw sewage during heavy rains, the petitioners argued that the drainage ditch was a menace to Carver schoolchildren whose play area was near the ditch, and also to Altgeld residents who had to smell its noxious fumes. Moreover, the ditch was a breeding ground for insects, a disease risk, and an eyesore. The petitioners hoped to have an additional 1,800 signatures in order to prove the seriousness of their case and the worthiness of their cause.[79] But none of the residents seemed to be aware of the extent to which the environment would affect the wellness and livelihood of the community because many of these problems remained to be seen in the mid- and late 1950s. Over the years, residents would complain of the high instances of cancer among current and former residents of Altgeld Gardens.

The homes at Altgeld were built with asbestos in them, which was not removed until sometime in the 1990s. PCB transformers, a harmful pollutant, were also utilized in the construction of Altgeld homes. Former Altgeld resident Roscoe King named more than twenty people who had died as a result of some form of cancer, all of them having lived in Altgeld Gardens, including two of Addie's siblings, her sister Edna and brother Mickey (Willie Cameron).[80] Addie Wyatt would fall ill with several illnesses throughout her lifetime, including breast cancer in the 1990s. Congressman Charles Hayes, a neighbor of the Wyatts on Block Three for several years, died from complications with lung cancer. Hazel Johnson, PCR's founder, lost her husband to lung cancer in 1969, just seven years after they moved to Altgeld. Multiple members of several families died as a result of complications with lung (according to Johnson, many of whom did not smoke) and breast cancer, which many former residents believe is directly attributable to the toxic environment around Altgeld. That environment included the dump and wasteland on which it was built and the numerous factories and sanitation plants that maintained their presence in the area or were built in the years following the construction of Altgeld. Miscarriages and asthma were also common in Altgeld, and Johnson estimated that some 60 percent of Altgeld residents had either survived or died from some form of cancer.[81] The environmental threats posed by Altgeld's location became a chief concern for later residents of the community. Whether or not Addie Wyatt aligned herself with the cause for environmental justice during and after her time at Altgeld is unknown.

WYATT CHORAL ENSEMBLE

Early residents of Altgeld have worked hard to recount a different trajectory and reality of black life in the early years of public housing that has been one of progress, upward mobility, and community shared by both public housing residents and housing authority administrators alike, perhaps more than they have highlighted the ongoing problems that Altgeld residents face. For some who left Altgeld, their memories of its earliest years continue to play a role in their perceptions of public housing, especially those who were members of the Wyatt Choral Ensemble, founded by Addie and Claude Wyatt in 1947. For the Wyatts, the formation of the ensemble marked a turning point in the development of their faith and leadership abilities. The Wyatts had a hand in the dynamism of community organizing and feeling of black autonomy in Altgeld by injecting an element of spiritual renewal and evangelism into Altgeld's youth. For Addie in particular, the founding of the Wyatt Choral Ensemble (WCE) coincided with a spiritual journey that brought her closer to her Christian faith and continued her connection to gospel music. Though she left Langley Avenue Church of God in the 1940s, Addie continued to grow as a gospel pianist, earning a reputation singing and playing for religious services and funerals, which helped her earn additional income. While living in Robbins, Illinois, with Claude's parents, Addie attended services at Great Hope Missionary Baptist Church under Reverend E. R. Williams and became director of Great Hope's choir. In 1947, Rev. Williams became pastor of Ward Chapel Baptist Church in Chicago at 37th and King Drive. The church changed its name to South Park Baptist Church and its Sunday services were broadcast over WHFC-AM radio every Sunday afternoon.[82] Wyatt continued to direct the choir under Rev. Williams.

The gospel music scene in Chicago in the 1940s and 1950s grew rapidly and Chicago gospel artists such as Thomas Dorsey, Mahalia Jackson, Roberta Martin, and others rose to national prominence.[83] In the late 1940s, Addie and Claude formed their own gospel group, the Wyatt Singers, who performed at South Park Baptist Church and various music festivals and events across the city. Addie sang and conducted the group, which included Claude, brother Emmett Cameron, son Renaldo Wyatt, Ora Lattimore, Louise King, and others throughout the short tenure of the ensemble. They recorded several songs with Decca Records including "Someday I'll Bow before Him," "He Is Able," and Thomas A. Dorsey's "What Could I Do if It Wasn't for the Lord?" When Elder Lucy Smith, founder and pastor of All Nations Pentecostal Church, lost her star musician and granddaughter, "Little Lucy," who left to tour with the famous Roberta Martin Singers, Addie Wyatt replaced her. This was a supreme honor given the prominence of All Nations' music ministry and the skill of Little Lucy as a gospel pianist. Wyatt reportedly accompanied the great Mahalia Jackson on several occasions. Both experiences put Wyatt back in the company of strong and talented women of faith. Much of the Wyatts' world in the late 1940s revolved around gospel music, but it was the WCE that started them down a path of ministry and religious leadership culminating in the formation of the Vernon Park Church of God in 1955.

Their presence and visibility in Chicago's golden age of gospel music helped to further make a name for the Wyatts, a respected and well-known young couple in Altgeld Gardens. The Wyatts were one of the first families on their block to have a television and after the neighborhood children learned this, their home was rarely empty. Televisions were a rarity in Altgeld and even though it was only a small twelve-inch General Electric Brand monitor, it was much more than many of the other families had.[84] And while the Wyatts were by no means rich, Claude's stable employment with the postal service and Addie's stable employment with Illinois Meat greatly improved the family's finances.

The purpose of the WCE was "to help decrease delinquency among [the] youth in Altgeld Gardens and to create a better understanding in the minds of the youth toward Christ."[85] As much as Altgeld residents provided positive activities for their youth, not all young people who grew up in Altgeld or who arrived at the housing project engaged in these activities. Combating juvenile drug and alcohol abuse was a concern for many adults in the community. Addie Wyatt, who rededicated her life to God after attending a revival near Altgeld Gardens, directed the ensemble, which at its highest point included nearly one hundred members. Most of the singers were teenagers; the Wyatt boys, Renaldo and Claude III, were not. The ensemble frequently performed at Calvary Baptist Church in Chicago along with other gospel groups such as the Wooten Choral Ensemble and the Maceo Woods Singers.[86] The WCE sang carols in Altgeld at Christmas, held concerts at the Children's Building, and presented a musical at Altgeld's Progressive Missionary Baptist Church.

Performances were extremely important to members of the ensemble. They were a source of pride, but it was the group itself—its sense of purpose, discipline, and belonging—that really made an impact on its members and made the group remarkable. Ensemble members considered themselves a part of something grand, which helped many to feel as if they were truly a part of the Altgeld community. Much of the group's focus was also on bringing members closer to God, therefore preaching, prayer, and scripture readings were a regular part of rehearsals and gatherings. The Wyatts started the ensemble because they felt that the geographic isolation of Altgeld led many youth astray and resulted in their involvement in illegal activities such as drug and alcohol abuse, prostitution, and gang violence. Sensing the need to provide more positive alternatives for Altgeld teens, the Wyatts created the ensemble and opened up their home:

> We'd take the living room furniture and move it into the kitchen, and the young people would sit all over the floor, up the stairs, and in the courtyard—and we would sing together. They would come over, sometimes every day. They'd come over at night—sometimes until midnight. Those who were in trouble, you know, they would come over and we would pray with them and talk with them. We would take anybody in—didn't care who you were—but you had to change.[87]

The open-door policy of the Wyatts reflected a desire and willingness to minister to youth, regardless of what their troubles were. However, in return, the young couple wanted to see measurable change in their behaviors. Much like the religious process of conversion and sanctification through which one changes and becomes a Christian, the Wyatts applied the same principle to youth who came to them and wanted to be a part of their spiritual community.

Alvin Lewis was one such member of the WCE who was troubled prior to joining. According to the Wyatts, they found the teen, a school dropout, lying on a sidewalk of Altgeld Gardens, drunk and cursing. They began to talk with him and encouraged him to turn his life around by getting back into school and turning his life over to God.[88] Lewis recalled his introduction to the WCE differently. He and his family moved to Altgeld in 1951 from the West Side of Chicago when he was a teenager. He was the fourth of ten children and his father was in and out of the workforce due to a heart condition, which left the family reliant on public aid. The family went from sleeping in a two-bedroom apartment, sleeping wherever they could including in the kitchen, to Altgeld where the children were only two to a room and the family had hot water, a nice bathroom, and a shower. To make money, Alvin "hustled" by gathering scrap metal and paper. He detested school and ended up in a reform school for truancy and rebellion; he later dropped out of it also. One of Lewis's friends, Roosevelt Wilson, turned his life around and became "saved" by "good people that helped [him] out and took [him] in." Those good people were the Wyatts. One day, Roosevelt told Alvin that he was taking him to a party, but really it was a prayer meeting held at the Wyatt home. Lewis felt that the resulting "conversion experience was the keystone experience" of his life.[89] The Wyatts opened up their choir to Roosevelt, Alvin, and other young men and women who were considered thugs by the wider community, a move that prompted some of the more "respectable" residents of Altgeld to pull their children from the choral ensemble and chastise the Wyatts for their lack of ministerial qualifications.[90]

Roscoe King, who lived in Altgeld Gardens from 1945 until 1952, remembered joining the choral ensemble for two reasons: he had a huge crush on Addie's younger sister, Audrey, and because he was a "gang-banging, reefer-selling" thug in trouble with the law who had no choice but to turn his life around or end up in jail. King and his friends in Altgeld drank wine and smoked marijuana, causing many in the community to give up on them. But Addie insisted that King and his friends join the choral ensemble, over the objection of Claude and other Altgeld parents who threatened to pull their children from the chorus. Refusing to back down to the parents, Addie's response was, "Well, you'll just have to take the children out."[91] Her determination to win over the souls of these wayward youth and do what she felt was right outweighed whatever actions the parents might take in response. King spoke fondly of Wyatt and the ensemble: "Addie Wyatt came into our lives, and she had us involved in church and good things that took all that other stuff away. Addie and Claude Wyatt were the biggest influence on young people that came out of Altgeld. I used to go to their house and sit there until twelve or one at night, and they would read the Bible to me, trying to straighten me out."[92] Addie and Claude put their experiences and faith to use, trying to guide other youth toward the Christian faith. Moreover, growing stronger in her Christian faith and taking seriously her mother's words that she would have to "look for the good in people," Addie refused to turn troubled youth away from the WCE. According to Wyatt, these youth were "physically hungry and spiritually hungry."[93] Evangelizing and winning people over to the cause of a greater good would become a lifelong commitment for the Wyatts.

Praise for the Wyatts' efforts came from the editors of the *Altgeld Beacon* and the CHA's leadership. The *Altgeld Beacon* featured a short piece on the Wyatts in 1953: "The Wyatt family who are well known in Altgeld, Chicago and the suburbs . . . have trained the teen-agers of Altgeld and have promoted them in various recitals, programs for churches, school affairs and radio. They are the leading citizens of Altgeld for their outstanding efforts and the interest they have taken in our young people. Everyone has heard the beautiful Wyatt chorus sing. They are considered the finest in Chicago."[94] The WCE became a staple at CHA events after director Elizabeth Wood heard the chorus rehearsing in the Wyatt's home. She was so impressed with the group that she regularly invited the chorus all over the city to perform at CHA functions and programs and gave the group several awards, which, according to Claude Wyatt, "made the young people feel like they were somebody."[95] Addie Wyatt and Elizabeth Wood developed a friendly relationship and in 1951 or 1952, Wood presented Wyatt with her first "Woman of the Year" award for community leadership at Altgeld.

The WCE operated for eight years until disbanding in 1955 when the Wyatts left Altgeld due to their excess income. It became too difficult for the Wyatts after relocating to the Hyde Park neighborhood to continue to direct and manage the group. The ensemble touched the lives of many youth at Altgeld and turned many lives around for the better. The group was a crowning achievement and a personal boost for the Wyatts whose understandings of themselves as Christians began to translate outward beyond the realm of personal salvation into evangelizing. More importantly, the WCE was a family affair. Wyatt's siblings and sons, who had beautiful voices, were a part of the chorus. For Addie, who feared that she would lose her siblings to foster care, those fears were eased at Altgeld and through the Wyatt Choral Ensemble. She and Claude were able to provide for her siblings, especially the younger ones, with a sense of security and stability. A number of Addie's siblings met and married their spouses in Altgeld and a few even remained in the community to raise their children. For eleven years, Altgeld Gardens provided the sense of stability and a consistent home that the Wyatts had desired for years.

The Wyatts made a number of close friends in Altgeld Gardens. Charles Hayes, a leader in the UPWA and later the first trade unionist elected to the U.S. Congress, lived alongside the Wyatts in Altgeld Gardens on Block Three in the 1940s and early 1950s. In a 1993 interview with The HistoryMakers, Hayes remarked that he, Claude and Addie "grew up together out in Altgeld Gardens" and that the "first decent apartment [he] ever had in this city, was public housing."[96] The friendship and working relationship in the organized labor and civil rights movements between Hayes and the Wyatts would last for five decades until the passing of Hayes in 1997. A resident of Altgeld in its early years, Wyatt was again part of an institution and a community that would produce some of black Chicago's most politically active citizens and produce among them a shared sense of community, purpose, and civic responsibility similar to DuSable High School. The Wyatts, Charles Hayes, Gus Savage, Oscar Brown Sr., Oscar Brown Jr., and other notable black Chicagoans emerged out of this generation of Altgeld residents.

The 1940s were ultimately a period of internal struggle and progress for the Wyatts. They were concerned with the magnitude of the problems before them— the instability of their marriage, economic poverty, a lack of adequate housing, crises of faith, the death of Maggie Cameron, and the future of their family. Glimpses of the activist and leader that Wyatt was to become were visible in an era ripe with black organizing around issues of racial discrimination, civil rights, and political rights across the nation. The Wyatts engaged in organizing in their own way, through the Wyatt Choral Ensemble and Altgeld Gardens, which sparked a greater desire to minister and bear witness to the ways in which religious faith and spirituality could aid in bringing about positive change and community cohesion. That desire manifested itself in their founding of the Vernon Park Church of God in 1955. Moreover, Addie Wyatt's skill and ability to minister and lead in Altgeld became an important asset in her career as a successful and effective labor organizer in the UPWA.

3

FOR THE UNION
MAKES US STRONG

In 1953, the UPWA's first National Anti-Discrimination and Women's Conference called on its 300 local unions and 125,000 members to elect delegates who would attend the meeting and "discuss and formulate plans to completely eliminate segregation and discrimination in [the] plants" and establish "activities to achieve equal rights in our local plant towns and in the national community."[1] Addie Wyatt's level of union participation changed when she became the sole delegate from her local, UPWA Local 56, to attend the conference, held in Chicago. It was her first large union meeting, and Wyatt began to see the greater value of the union for its workers, especially its female and minority workers. She began to believe more than ever that the union could win important gains for working people if they worked together collectively:

> When I walked into the room and I saw white workers, black workers, Hispanic workers, women and men, and when I heard the discussion that went on, how they were championing the cause of all these groups, and how they were talking about unity and togetherness, I knew then that this was the wonderful force . . . that we need to have to bring about the change that I was looking forward to. They also inspired us and encouraged us to fight for male and female, black, white, Hispanic leadership.[2]

The scene before Wyatt was entirely new to her. Rarely in her day-to-day life outside of work did she interact with whites and Hispanics on a significant basis, much less discuss the problems of racism, sexism, and workers' rights. Her community, Altgeld Gardens, was entirely black, and only once a year during the Church of God's Brotherhood Sunday did her congregation even worship with whites.[3] Through the union, Wyatt began to see the possibility of a multiracial movement of people dedicated to equality on the job and improving one another's lives. This appealed to Wyatt because it meant that she would not have to struggle for job security, fair treatment, and a better way of life alone. A true believer in the social gospel and a growing convert to the idea that people could make their lives better by taking action together, what Wyatt witnessed at the conference made her an even bigger believer in the UPWA as the vehicle for collective struggle.

It was Addie Wyatt's participation in the UPWA and the organized labor movement that helped to elevate and deepen her understandings of racism, poverty, sexism, and discrimination as structural problems that affected collective groups, not just individuals. Wyatt's experiences in meatpacking as a union activist and leader, combined with her religious faith and community organizing, ultimately led to a worldview or philosophy in which poverty, racism, sexism, and those they affected were inextricably linked. Therefore, the fight against discrimination and oppression in any form was collective, and solidarity in collective action would be fundamental to overcoming those struggles. In the UPWA, Wyatt saw the promise of workers banding together despite differences in race, gender, and national origin to demand fair and equitable treatment on the job. What began as an appreciation for the union and the tangible benefits it provided for its members soon translated into a vested interest in seeing the movement grow as a vehicle for progressive social change and economic and political empowerment.

Addie Wyatt's path to greater union activism and leadership is exemplary of a key turning point in the history of the UPWA and other progressive unions that began to recognize the need for greater worker solidarity in a challenging postwar environment. Wyatt's rise to leadership coincided with a powerful push in the UPWA to attack and eradicate discrimination within its ranks, by company management, and ultimately outside of the workplace. Propelled by leadership at the highest ranks of the UPWA and progressive rank-and-file members, the union created a solid antidiscrimination program that proved to be fairly, though not entirely, successful in dismantling racial discrimination on the shop floor and in the union. At the same time, women in the UPWA had to constantly articulate the sex discrimination and isolation they experienced at work and the union as equally worthy of dismantlement. The leadership of black union women like Addie Wyatt ultimately proved crucial to bridging the concerns of working women with antidiscrimination. Black women faced difficulties in trying to break past Jim Crow in lily-white, female departments and past Jane Crow in the largely white- and male-dominated union leadership. Though reluctant at first to become a union organizer and leader due to the overwhelming responsibilities of work, home, and community, Wyatt's faith and sense of social gospel ultimately fueled her capacity to give much to the labor movement.

ADDIE WYATT'S PATH TO UNION LEADERSHIP

After experiencing intermittent layoffs throughout the early 1940s, Wyatt gained full-time employment in 1947 at Illinois Meat Company, a small independent packinghouse of about 300 workers, later purchased by meat processing giant, John Morrell & Co. Wyatt worked in the potato canning department peeling potatoes by hand before subsequently moving on to the sliced bacon department. It was difficult and tedious piecework but she earned a decent pay and relished having steady employment for the first time since she entered the work force in 1941. Workers at the plant were organized into Local 56 of District One of the UPWA. Headquartered in Chicago, along with the international leadership of the union, District One covered five midwestern states including Illinois, Indiana, Michigan, Ohio, and Wisconsin. While there were a number of blacks at Illinois Meat, white men formed the majority of the plant's workforce, and Wyatt recalled that the UPWA held a significance presence in the plant where she personally witnessed little visible discrimination.[4]

Wyatt was a member of Local 56, but not much is known about her activities within the union between 1947 and 1953, other than that she lent support to pivotal UPWA strike actions and rallies. For much of this period, Wyatt characterized herself as an average union member, and the lack of mention of her in the archives of the UPWA and in her own papers in terms of union activities corroborate this fact. In the infamous 1948 national strike that the UPWA lost after a bitter and dangerous months-long battle, Wyatt's plant was not one of the 65 to 100 struck plants shut down nationwide. Wyatt remembered participating in some of the rallies and demonstrations to support the strikers, but she had no direct involvement in the strike that claimed three deaths and over 700 arrests. The strike began on March 16, 1948, after the UPWA and other packing unions failed to reach an agreement with the packing companies on pay increases for workers. The packers offered a wage increase of nine cents per hour, much lower than the wage increase of fifteen cents per hour that organized workers in the auto and steel industries reaped.[5] Through contract negotiations, slowdowns, demonstrations, and ultimately strikes, postwar workers expected adequate wage increases and their share of postwar economic prosperity to deal with the rising cost of living. Postwar labor-management-government relations were tense with the passing of the 1947 Taft-Hartley Act. The act constricted the power and liberties of labor unions, effectively peeling back important legal measures put in place to bolster unions and workers since the 1930s. The prevalence of McCarthyism and anticommunism in the United States undergirded portions of the Taft-Hartley Act, which effectively considered unions and worker militancy to be communist fronts.

While the UPWA continued to grow in membership through the mid-1950s, the challenges of the postwar era were evident in the failed nature and outcome of the 1948 strike. For starters, Ralph Helstein, international president of the UPWA since 1946, did not agree with the strike. Helstein believed the correct plan of action should include breaking down the packers one at a time through negotiation in conjunction with the UPWA's chief rival union, the Amalgamated Meat Cutters and Butcher Workman. Others feared that if the UPWA did strike and shut down plants, the Amalgamated and other unions would agree to the nine-cent wage increase, cross the picket line, and put UPWA workers out of jobs in key plants. Nevertheless, militant rank-and-file UPWA workers and leaders put pressure on the international to send out a strike order against the big four meatpackers whom they argued could and should provide workers with more.[6]

Very early on, the UPWA received little public support for the strike, and as many skeptics of the strike feared, the Amalgamated settled for the nine cents an hour contract and worked through the strike, undermining the UPWA's efforts at seeking a better contract. For over two months, as many as 100,000 UPWA packinghouse workers across the country were out of work.[7] As a measure of solidarity, staff members of the international took no pay during the strike. Some packing companies brought in nonunionized labor to work in the struck plants. As striking workers demonstrated on the picket lines, fights between workers, strikebreakers, and police led to three deaths and hundreds of arrests. With no headway made through negotiations, growing worker frustration, and near destitution, the UPWA ended the strike. Workers accepted the original proposed wage increase of nine cents an hour.[8] The most militant workers and strike leaders were fired upon returning to work and the amount of worker grievances UPWA staff had to handle as a result of these terminations kept the union busy while it tried to recuperate financially from the strike.

A period of internal strife due to the fallout of the 1948 strike marred the UPWA and its relationship with the CIO. During this time, Helstein's leadership as president was tested but ultimately left intact. He would remain president of the UPWA until its merger with the Amalgamated in 1968. Despite the failure of the strike, UPWA members continued to push for wage increases, better working conditions, and fair treatment on the job. Though she did not participate in the 1948 strike, Wyatt did recall participating in a noontime demonstration in the stockyards in the winter of 1950 where over 15,000 workers braved a temperature of ten degrees below zero to hold a rally for wage increases, better working conditions, and worker solidarity. Wyatt remembered freezing half to death at the demonstration as she held a sign that read "Equal Pay for Women."[9] Even before her period of heightened unionism, Wyatt's actions suggest that she may have been aware of certain inequities in the plants, not only racism and discrimination stemming from her own experiences at Armour, but also discrimination toward women. Indeed, in the poststrike years, antidiscrimination became a key strategic and ideological course that the UPWA embarked upon to foster worker solidarity and union strength.

In the 1948 strike, African Americans played critical and consistent roles as supporters of the strike. In turn, they hoped to see their status within the union elevated not only in terms of greater attention to plant discrimination but also in union participation and leadership. Their interests dovetailed with those of Helstein and the UPWA's top leadership. Both were determined to create a union that could withstand the packers' attempts to divide workers on the basis of race and weaken the overall bargaining power of the UPWA.[10] According to Cyril Robinson, biographer of Ralph Helstein, the UPWA needed a way to galvanize and reenergize its workforce after the failure of the 1948 strike. Likewise, Helstein, a social democrat of Jewish ancestry, supported civil rights measures and pressed for antidiscrimination resolutions and the means to enforce them. UPWA leaders and a cadre of rank-and-file workers who believed in interracial social unionism hoped to rid it of internal racial discrimination in order to create a union that could stand together and demand better contracts, fair and equitable job opportunities, and decent working conditions. Thus, it was not only discrimination and racism by employers, but the prevalence of discrimination and racism among union members that required attention and remediation through aggressive antidiscrimination policies, programs, and sanctions. The union would have to put its platform into action and ensure that the composition of its leadership reflected the growing diversity of its membership.

Since its inception, the UPWA had a strong civil rights clause in its constitution and put similar clauses against discrimination in its agreements with employers. After the 1948 strike, the UPWA pursued antidiscrimination with new life. President Helstein partnered with John Hope II of Fisk University on a study of discrimination in the union. Commissioned over the course of 1950, the Fisk Race Relations Study collected survey data from UPWA locals and districts to determine the level of discrimination at play in the union and in the plants. The survey asked locals to detail the demographics of their membership and plants, the level of African American and minority participation in local unions, the prevalence of discrimination in pay and promotions, local community discrimination, and a number of other factors relating to the overall extent of racism in the union and in the plants. While the survey uncovered locals that worked hard to minimize discrimination in the plants, signaling that the union's commitment to antidiscrimination was not just a top-down mandate but an initiative taken by the more progressive locals, the survey also exposed locals who actively discriminated against its members or left discrimination unchecked. The survey revealed the prevalence of segregated locker rooms, lunchrooms, and pay lines along with skilled job classifications closed to black workers. Incidents of racial prejudice among union members revealed the need for greater diversity on the staff of the union and firm antidiscrimination education and programming.[11]

The UPWA created an International Anti-Discrimination (A-D) Department in 1950 with International Vice President Russell Lasley as its first director, who was also the highest-ranked African American in the union. The A-D department had the task of implementing the union's antidiscrimination platform and programs. The department mandated the creation of antidiscrimination committees at the district and local level. It also produced pamphlets, educational workshops, and other resources for members so that they would be equipped in policing and reporting discrimination. Curiously, discrimination against women and sexism was not a top item for the department. In 1950, Jaruthea Coleman and other black women from Local 28 of Chicago took notice of the lack of black women being hired in the female pork-trim department at their Swift plant. They contacted Lasley and the A-D department, having recorded the number of white versus black women who applied and were hired. The A-D department sent in a white woman to apply for a position in the pork-trim department. She was reportedly told that she should encourage some of her white female friends to apply since the company was looking to replace blacks brought into the plants during WWII.[12] Lasley filed a formal complaint with the federal government and labor authorities and Swift was found guilty of violating its labor agreement with the UPWA, which barred discrimination in employment. The company was ordered to hire twelve to thirteen qualified black women in the pork-trim department with seniority and back pay.[13]

The Swift ruling prompted the UPWA to take a more active role in seeking justice for black women workers. The union embarked on a campaign to see greater numbers of black and Mexican women hired in lily-white women's departments in packing plants across the country. As labor scholar Dennis Deslippe argues, discrimination against black women was often considered race discrimination and not discrimination that was gender based as well: "UPWA leaders judged their progress in batting this discrimination by assessing the improvement of minority women's status compared to that of white women—but not to that of white men or African American men."[14] The UPWA did not seek to dismantle sex-segregated departments and job classifications but rather to racially integrate women's departments. There was no consistent working women's platform or agenda that the union pursued. There were no female union executives, no female district directors, and no female field representatives in the union heading into the 1950s. Women had broken through to achieve vice president and secretary positions at the local level and were shop stewards handling grievances in some plants, but they were unable to establish spaces for higher-level leadership and power at the regional and international levels, which contributed to the union's inability to adequately address gender discrimination.

Black women, whose issues stood at the intersection of race and gender-based discrimination, took active roles in illuminating the special problems that women workers faced. At the 1950 UPWA Constitutional Convention in Minnesota, women raised the issue of when the union would fully embrace the sizable portion of their membership, which happened to be female. Women like Jaruthea Coleman of Swift Local 28 and Annie Alexander of Armour Local 347, both of Chicago, took to the floor to demand that the UPWA give more consideration to the wage gap between men and women and pursue equal pay for equal work in contracts. They argued for the establishment of an international women's activity committee composed of women *and* men, the creation of women's activities committees at the district and local level, and special training for women seeking leadership in the unions. Women had already started forming women's activities committees at the local level, but by and large they were only in locals that had active female union participants, as opposed to those locals lacking female participation and where sex discrimination went unchecked. Female activists argued for more women in the executive offices of the union and believed that since women represented one-third of the union's membership, there should be at least one female field representative per district.[15] The pace of change for the increased status of women in the UPWA would be painstakingly slow. The UPWA worked best in securing equal pay for equal work and eliminating wage differentials for men and women by the late 1950s, but similar outcomes in terms of leadership and a broader working women's platform remained elusive.

This was the context in which the A-D Department held its inaugural conference in 1953. The major goal of the three-day meeting was a call for greater leadership opportunities for minority and women workers in the UPWA. The message resonated with Wyatt and she went back to her local, urging that more women and minorities needed to run for and get elected to leadership positions throughout the union. She became convinced that working side by side in positions of leadership and influence, rather than as subordinates, minority and women workers could play a much greater role in the union and increase its likelihood for improving the lives of working people. Wyatt's call for greater representation resonated with elder female members. Women like Hattie Gardner, Bessie McCauley, Rose Wright, and Sophie Kosciolowski, had all argued for greater women's leadership and participation in the UPWA for over a decade. As veteran female leaders, they were looking to pass the torch to a younger generation of female unionists. Gardner and McCauley began asking Addie to run for an open vice president position in the local. She turned them down, not willing to be the one to answer her own call for more women's leadership. But the elder trade union women persisted, perhaps seeing in Wyatt key leadership qualities. Eventually, they won her over. Addie concluded, "No one wanted those jobs. This was a job that required quite a bit for a young person to assume those jobs. And nobody really wanted to step out. . . . I told them I would take it not really knowing what I was doing."[16]

Wyatt reluctantly cast her name for the position, still unsure about possibly becoming a union leader: "[L]ike most people, I appreciated the union, but I was not willing to lend my time and my talent. I was involved in the church. I was very involved in the community working with youth, and I just didn't see that this was the place where I wanted to contribute."[17] Already working a full-time job and prioritizing her work in the church, the Wyatt Choral Ensemble, and Altgeld over the union, Addie Wyatt hesitated to run in the election, fearful of what the additional responsibilities would require of her already busy life. She was a wife, mother to her two sons, full-time worker, community youth organizer, and gospel pianist, and she was active in the church. Wyatt's reluctance to become a leader of her local reveal important concerns of working mothers and wives during this period, and specifically black women who had worked outside of the home for pay for decades. More than just the "double duty" dilemma of working outside of the home for pay while taking on the duties of a homemaker that labor and feminist scholars have popularized, women like Wyatt who engaged in community or faith-based activities maintained a triple duty to work, home, *and* community.[18]

Although some black churches and black women's clubs welcomed black women positions of leadership,[19] union leadership was still held predominantly by white men. This presented an entirely new environment that Wyatt likely perceived as inhospitable to the presence of a woman, much less a black woman. It was only after Wyatt came to the realization that "though active in the church and that made you feel good, the church had no way of effecting your economic conditions," did she truly understand how critical the union was to working people. If the union was to sustain itself and grow, she and others would need to play a greater role in serving it. Persuaded by union women who had paid their dues, Wyatt decided to run. She vowed that if she won she would never sacrifice her work in the church because that was the spiritual foundation of her survival.[20] But sacrifices would surely come as a result of her rapid ascension in the labor movement and her growing commitment to labor and equal rights.

On the day of the election, Addie recalled leaving for home right after work, unable to even cast a vote for herself. Perhaps she was nervous and forgot to do so, or doubts got the best of her and she feared that her race, sex, and inexperience were obstacles too great to overcome in the election. But her fears were unfounded and despite her self-sabotage, Wyatt found out the next morning that she had in fact won the election. She was the new elected vice president of Local 56 at just thirty years old. Many of the members congratulated her, but some of the men were skeptical of her ability to do the job. Wyatt remembered them taunting her: "You're a woman. This is a man's job. And you're a Christian. What do you do when you get a room full of tough-talking men? How can you negotiate a contract or arbitrate a dispute? You don't even swear!"[21] Addie Wyatt was a petite and attractive young woman—a feminine, Christian lady who spoke softly but with confidence and conviction. Union work had the reputation of being rough-and-tumble men's work—no place for a woman such as herself.[22] The men may have legitimately questioned Wyatt's ability to effectively represent them in light of the challenging economic changes in meatpacking, such as the automation and relocation that imperiled the futures of many workers. But it is also likely that Wyatt fell victim to a catch 22 when it came to the question of women and leadership in the UPWA. Some male members argued that women were content to sit and reap the benefits of union membership while not doing anything to contribute to the day-to-day operation of the union beyond paying dues. Some women argued that their lack of participation in union activities was due to the inhospitable nature of union meetings, including the use of foul language, drinking, long meetings that cut into the time women had to spend at home taking care of their families, dirty union halls, and men's unwillingness to train women as leaders. At the same time, when women voiced a desire to become more active and actually ran in elections, many lost and were ridiculed for wanting to take on the male job of union leadership or were told they were too inexperienced to lead.[23]

Wyatt assured the men that she would be able to do the job and that her Christian faith was an asset, not a liability. She believed that with faith in God, in herself and in the principles of the union, she and her fellow workers would prevail. Wyatt's mental toughness and fortitude in the face of criticism rested on an unshakable faith in God and the abilities and talents she believed God instilled in her. Her spiritual upbringing, reclamation of her faith as an adult, personal history with strong female leadership, organizing success in Altgeld, and belief in the interracial unionism of the UPWA all contributed to Wyatt's belief that she could advocate effectively for her fellow workers.

Addie may have been able to effectively respond to the male critics in her local, but telling her husband about her new post was not as easy. It took her three months to tell Claude that she was a union officer. Claude had a full-time job working as a finance clerk for the post office and was also involved in the Church of God and with the Wyatt Choral Ensemble. The couple's lives were heavily intertwined in their faith and youth ministry. One evening at dinner, Addie finally revealed to Claude that she was vice president of her local. She explained to him that the union was important and crucial to the survival of their family and that she had to do all that she could to contribute to it. According to Wyatt, she went on and on before Claude finally stopped her. He would support her, but cautioned that things at home still had to run smoothly and familial responsibilities could not be neglected.[24] In the end, Claude, the couple's two sons and Addie's younger siblings took on more responsibilities like cooking, cleaning, and laundering when Addie was unable to do so.[25]

Still working full time, Wyatt stepped into her role as vice president and negotiated contracts and served on the Local 56 grievance committee. Her first grievance involved a coworker with a spotless twenty-year record at Illinois Meat who had allegedly been caught by the plant superintendent stealing meat off the line. He was fired on the spot and appealed to the union, desperate to have his job back. UPWA local grievance committees were normally headed by the president of the local but on the day of the grievance meeting Local 56's president, Frank Shock, happened to be sick. As vice president, Wyatt had to assume leadership of the grievance committee. Having never served as a local union steward whose job would be to lead grievances on a regular basis, Addie found herself in uncharted territory and prayed to God for guidance before entering the meeting. She asked God to help her "make the best possible contribution to this meeting." The case was difficult and Addie wondered how she could argue against the superintendent who claimed to witness the theft and company officials who were dead set on maintaining company policy and sending a no-tolerance message to workers.

In a rare published manuscript, Wyatt wrote about the grievance meeting some twenty years later. She recalled that, "a sense of God's presence reassured me":

> Since I was on the bacon line at the time of the incident, I can't say whether or not this member is guilty as charged. But I know this man, just like you do. We all know that he has a large family and that he had been credited as a good employee up until this time. *If* he stole the meat, he probably did it to feed his family. I know that doesn't right a wrong, but haven't we all made one mistake in our lives? The man needs another chance. On the basis of his past record he should be given it."[26]

Relying on the worker's favorable history of employment, Wyatt argued on his behalf for a second chance. Her argument proved persuasive and the plant officials allowed the worker to return to his job after one week's suspension. Grievance committee members congratulated Wyatt on a job well done in a tough grievance. The win helped her to become more confident, comfortable, and respected by her fellow members as a leader. Wyatt credited her faith in God and strategy of seeking common ground with others as key to winning the grievance and saving a man's job. Wyatt believed in a sense of fairness and humanity in everyone and that if you can reach them on that basic level, the chances of a favorable outcome increased.[27] Her approach as a labor leader was to tap into the humanity of those involved. No doubt influenced by her faith and spirituality, Wyatt's approach was also informed by a lesson her mother taught her as a child, which was to always look for the best in others. Even though the worker was culpable, Wyatt chose to focus on his past work record as a measure of his worth on the job, undergirded by an appreciation and compassion for the man's humanity.

Addie served as vice president for about six months before Frank Shock, Local 56 president and a white man, resigned for familial reasons. As his successor, Wyatt became the first woman president of Local 56. She continued to negotiate contracts and handle grievances with top-level management. One of Wyatt's most important responsibilities was to enforce antidiscrimination policies and ensure that they were not violated by companies or the local.[28] She utilized the international UPWA policies to question discriminatory plant practices, place antidiscrimination clauses in contracts, and monitor company hiring and treatment of minority and women workers. Union leaders constantly struggled against discrimination in hiring and employment practices and faced opposition not only from company management but from many of their own members who ultimately disagreed with some of the union's more progressive policies in regards to women and minority workers.[29]

The UPWA's 1954 Constitutional Convention in Sioux City, Iowa, illustrates just how contentious antidiscrimination and working women's rights programs were within the union. Addie Wyatt served as secretary of the UPWA's Anti-Discrimination Committee and gave the committee's report, which called for the institution of antidiscrimination committees at the local level and the protesting of segregated facilities by union members. It also called upon locals and the international union to support the efforts of the National Association for the Advancement of Colored People (NAACP) in eliminating segregation and discrimination in employment and public institutions.[30] The report caused a stir among the membership. At the convention, Wyatt participated in a grievance between a UPWA minority field representative and a local that had separate dressing facilities for whites and blacks and separate pay lines that allowed whites to stand under a canopy when it rained while blacks stood out in the open under no cover. The local was instructed to eliminate the segregated dressing rooms and pay lines, but rather than comply, its delegates walked out of the convention.[31] Rather than capitulate to the new program of the UPWA, some locals disaffiliated with the union.

The UPWA experienced important victories and defeats in its heightened commitment to antidiscrimination. Though the aforementioned local retained its commitment to segregation, other locals from Minnesota to Baltimore to Louisiana dismantled physical Jim Crow walls that served to divide black workers from white workers in locker rooms, bathrooms, break rooms, lunchrooms and pay lines.[32] At Local 25's Wilson plant in Chicago, a white foreman was fired after striking a Mexican worker, and an interracial campaign propelled the mechanic department in the plant to hire its first black tinsmith in its fifty-year existence.[33] Rath, an Iowa packing company, was notorious for its refusal to hire black women beyond janitorial positions. Anna Mae Weems, a worker in Local 46, finally got hired into the company's all-white sliced-bacon department in

1954, prompting a walkout, or "hate strike," from the white women. When the predominantly black male hog-kill department threatened a work stoppage if the plant fired Weems, the white women were told that they could either return to work or be fired.[34] They returned and Weems eventually became a shop steward in the department for the very women who initially refused to work with her. Similar cases of hate strikes and successful integration of departments took place across the UPWA's districts, due to the implementation of aggressive antidiscrimination campaigns by workers at the local level and international support for such actions. In parts of the South and Midwest, UPWA local support for antidiscrimination broke down along racial lines. Black and Mexican workers supported the international antidiscrimination program while whites were more reticent to embrace the program entirely or feared reprisal from coworkers and management should they step out against the status quo. As Swift worker and organizer Frank Wallace argued of his local in Fort Worth, Texas, "Whites were skeptical; they had a greater fear of their bosses than blacks or minorities. They may have seen the need for changes, but they were not the ones who wanted to step out in front and begin a program, or begin an organizing drive that's going to help the situation."[35]

A year after the 1953 Anti-Discrimination and Women's Conferences, women and men still had complaints about the lack of gender diversity in the union's leadership. These complaints boiled over at the 1954 Constitutional Convention in Sioux City, Iowa. Some men complained that women failed to participate in or care about the union, wanting only the benefits of it, while other men believed that women really had no place in the union's leadership. Women, on the other hand, raised a number of arguments about why in 1954, when they comprised 30,000 or one-quarter of the UPWA's membership, they still lacked representation at the top international and district levels of leadership. Even at the local level, they were very few women presidents or vice presidents. Prior to the conference, a campaign began to challenge the lack of women's leadership. Stella Geesaman, a white woman and president of Local 58 in Missouri, planned to enter a bid for the elected position of international vice president. Prior to the convention Geesaman had the backing of a number of women and men in the UPWA who pledged to vote for her, including Addie Wyatt. Wyatt was to nominate Geesaman on the floor but she never got the opportunity to do so. Rumors were circulated around the convention that if the women nominated Geesaman, then black International Vice President Russell Lasley would lose his spot rather than unpopular white International Vice President, A. T. Stephens. The signal was sent that there was only one spot for women and blacks to share on the international board. The women were advised to withdraw Geesaman's candidacy and wait for another year to push for a woman international vice president.

As the men started to pull their support from Geesaman, so did a number of women; according to Wyatt, they did not want to divide themselves from the men, according to Wyatt. With a sinking campaign and not enough time to find a way to save it, Geesaman withdrew her name.[36] Whether or not there was any truth to the rumor that a female vice presidential candidate would cost the union a black vice presidential candidate is unknown, as is the source of the rumors. But there was a concerted effort to ensure that a female candidate would not be considered for a position on the union's executive board, revealing that however much the union backed antidiscrimination in terms of greater racial diversity in its leadership, the same consideration did not fully apply to women in the union. It would take twenty years, well after the merger between the UPWA and the Amalgamated, before women would sit on the International executive board as international vice presidents, one of whom was Addie Wyatt.

More than anything, the 1954 constitutional convention revealed the deep fissures that underlay the UPWA's efforts to enforce its antidiscrimination policies and to make way for greater female and nonwhite leadership in the union. Nonwhite and female workers committed to the UPWA's interracial social unionism were eager to see their desires for greater leadership, unity, and power within the union accepted and respected. The push for antidiscrimination, civil rights, and women's rights within the UPWA coincided with changes in the meatpacking industry that were disproportionately detrimental to nonwhite and women workers. While its membership had grown throughout the 1940s and early 1950s, the UPWA witnessed a steady decline beginning in the mid-1950s, largely as a result of automation in the industry and what unions called "run-away shops." Between 1954 and 1959, the UPWA lost over 24,000 members, close to one quarter of its total membership.[37] As early as 1955, large companies like Wilson, Armour, and Swift began to cut whole departments out of their operation and shut down entire plants. When the first big Wilson plant closed in 1955, over 2,500 workers from Local 25 were affected. The packers moved their operations to rural areas and to the South where worker populations were less likely to unionize, keeping worker costs down and profits at a steady or higher rate.

Smaller plants like Illinois Meat were also affected by changes in the meatpacking industry—particularly automation, the mechanization of labor or tasks traditionally performed by people. Throughout the 1950s and 1960s, government regulations, increased demand for meat products, and technological innovations altered the ways in which meat products were processed. Because women were largely confined either by choice or by discrimination to working with processed meat, they lost their jobs at a disproportionate rate. Women typically worked in the casing, slicing, and curing departments in meatpacking—areas subject to automation sooner than butchering and slaughtering. Charles Hayes, District One director, addressed the issue of rising unemployment in the union in a 1962 article in the *District One Champion*:

The top nine packers reported a whopping 16.49% overall increase in their profits this year over last year. Swift's 1962 profits of $16,313,927, a 33.3. percent increase over 1961 was modest compared to Hygrades' increase of 800 percent. But still they cry that they are suffering from a profit squeeze and cruel competition from the smaller houses. They demand we take cuts in wages and benefits we have won for the workers in our union. Between 1956 and 1962, one out of every six workers in the packing industry has lost his job—permanently. Over 28,000 men and women have been the victims of automation and plant closing. . . . The jobs of our members are at the heart of the matter. . . . The growth of our union is the answer to those who would destroy us.[38]

Under Wyatt's tenure as president of Local 56, a major layoff took place in Illinois Meat. The all-female dry beef department was entirely dismantled due to automation. The women who were laid off assumed that after their unemployment compensation ended, their seniority, or time spent on the job, would entitle them to other jobs within the plant and that they would be rehired. Seniority was a contentious issue. Dual seniority lines based on sex placed men and women in different tracts. Women who lost their jobs had to wait for other "female" jobs to open up and were unable to apply for "men's" jobs that might be open. The heavy layoffs in predominantly female departments prompted calls for a single seniority line for all workers regardless of race or sex.

The plan that UPWA union leaders devised in order to address the controversy between layoffs, seniority, and rehiring, was the ABC system. Category A corresponded to the jobs primarily held by men, category B corresponded to jobs primarily held by women, and category C designated jobs that could be performed by either men or women. The ABC system of job categorization did provide some middle ground for work that men or women could perform, but it mostly left sex-based job classification intact. Male workers were afraid of losing their jobs and any hold they might have on seniority and thus resisted calls for single seniority lines. It did not help that one of the prevailing stereotypes about working women was that they worked for pin, or spending money, and did not need to work in order to support their families. Breaking down the pin money stereotype and other gender biases that worked to keep male and female workers at odds with one another remained a significant problem for working women for decades to come.

The struggle was that much more difficult in the meatpacking industry where all jobs were at risk. In the end, there were some women who protested having to do some of the only available jobs on the killing floor considered "men's work." Wyatt remembered having to work with the women in order to ease their fears and challenge their beliefs about the differences between men's and women's work. Men's work was not always more physically arduous and beyond the capabilities of women, and it often paid more money. Slowly but surely, Wyatt saw more women willing to take on these jobs.[39] If women were to maintain a foothold in the industry, the divisions between men's and women's work had to be challenged, and union staff, including Wyatt, would need to move beyond the ABC system to question the presence of sex-based job classifications, the discriminatory practices of employers, and the protectionism held onto by both men and women. Men wanted to keep their advantages, arguing that their higher-paid, more skilled status in the workforce was due to the fact that they needed to provide for their families, not realizing or acknowledging women were breadwinners too, and that the whole-scale dismissal of women's departments dealt them a short hand in the way of increasing pressure on their production, speedups without an increase in pay, and the loss of union members. Women, on the other hand, had to be willing to embrace a wider array of jobs in order to maintain a presence in the plants. They had to recognize that the "protections" afforded to some women really did more to protect the company's profit margin than it did women's jobs and their ability to contribute to their households. Education about changes in the industry and the adverse effects that racial and sexual divisions of labor had on workers was where the UPWA needed to focus its energy in order to overcome the gender- and race-based biases of its membership.

As president of Local 56, Wyatt honed her skills as a negotiator and mediator to implement the union's antidiscrimination policies and to save the jobs of working men and women in a rapidly changing workplace. Implementing and enforcing antidiscrimination policies involved working not only with company officials and plant managers but also with workers who knowingly and inadvertently served as some of the most formidable opponents to change. These skills and experiences would prove crucial for Wyatt as she moved from leadership in the local to leadership in District One. Charles Hayes, newly elected District One director, friend, and Altgeld neighbor, appointed Wyatt to the position of international field representative in 1954. Hayes was the first black director of District One, elected earlier that year. The union's international headquarters were in Chicago, and Hayes, as district director, automatically held a seat on the UPWA's International Executive Board. The union had nine districts and nine total district directors, two of whom were black.

During his tenure as district director, Hayes launched a successful campaign to move the District One headquarters from the area around the meatpacking district on the near west side to the predominantly black South Side of Chicago. The headquarters were relocated to the former Bacon's Casino at 49th and Wabash. In 1958 a new building, the Packinghouse Labor and Community Center, was erected on the same site. The move forced nonblack workers to journey to the South Side for union meetings and social functions. Hayes and others hoped that this would facilitate a greater sense of solidarity and understanding between black and nonblack workers and it also served the interests of the district, which had a growing African American population that largely resided on the South Side. Though its primary purpose was for UPWA meetings, conventions, social functions, and day-to-day administration, the center became a community institution. Black civic, political, and religious organizations met in the building and community members were frequently invited to attend UPWA events and learn more about the problems facing working people and the benefits of organized labor. Blacks in other labor unions used the center as well. Ellwood Flowers, a member of the Amalgamated Transit Workers Union Local 308 who worked for the Chicago Transit Authority (CTA), first learned of Hayes and District One of the packinghouse workers in the late 1950s. Flowers rose to leadership in the union and remembered calling on Hayes for favors, including use of the new headquarters, support in labor demonstrations, and general solidarity for the efforts of black transit workers employed by the CTA. Moreover, Flowers recalled that he and other blacks in the labor movement in Chicago tried to model and fashion themselves after Hayes, who was an eloquent speaker and a stalwart fighter for civil rights.[40]

Hayes and Wyatt first developed a friendship as neighbors in the Altgeld Gardens housing project. Charles Hayes arrived in Chicago sometime during 1942 or 1943 and quickly found work in a Wilson meatpacking plant where he became a member of the UPWA's Local 25. Hayes had been instrumental in organized labor in his birth town of Cairo, Illinois, helping to organize fellow workers at a hardwood flooring company under the Carpenter's International Union, and subsequently served as president of its newly formed local.[41] He led the local for two years before seeking more stable work and better pay in Chicago to support his small family. In the late 1940s, Hayes served as chairman of Local 25's grievance committee, working on behalf of thousands of workers in the plant. He became an international field representative and made a name for himself as a brilliant speaker, labor man, and powerful voice for antidiscrimination and civil rights in the UPWA.[42]

Hayes also made a name for himself as a nuisance among the meatpackers. He was a leader in the UPWA's 1948 strike and was fired for his work as a strike leader. He was unemployed for nearly a year before a favorable ruling by the National Labor Relations Board overturned his termination. Hayes rose to union leadership from the bottom up, elected to various positions because of his dedication to the union and his fearlessness in negotiating with companies. He became the "gentle giant" of the UPWA and rose to leadership in District One in the early 1950s, backed by a growing and more influential African American membership.

While not singlehandedly responsible for the district's reputation as an ally for civil rights, Hayes was a key driving force, actively involving the district and the union in ongoing antidiscrimination efforts. During his first years as director of District One, Hayes appointed two black women to posts as international field representatives—Jaruthea (Coleman) Thrasher and Addie Wyatt. The post was one of the highest that a woman could achieve at the time.[43] Thrasher and Wyatt were also the union's first black female international field representatives.[44] Thrasher was a steward and recording secretary of Local 28 and worked at a Swift. She developed a reputation as a leader and activist in District One and established a dynamic and well-attended women's activities committee in her local. She also spearheaded the investigation into Swift's refusal to hire black women into its pork-trim department. While Thrasher remained an international representative for a short time, Wyatt remained in the post for twenty years.

Charles Hayes and Addie Wyatt developed a special friendship founded on their mutual respect for one another and their commitments to labor and civil rights. Hayes appointed Wyatt to the position of international field representative because he felt that she was articulate and talented enough to get the job done. And she was committed to the labor movement. Hayes also tapped Wyatt for the position because of her strong faith and ability to speak to people in terms of what was morally right.[45] Addie had gained a reputation both in Altgeld and in the union as a capable leader and powerful persuasive voice. In her short time as leader of Local 56, Addie accomplished major feats, including restructuring of job classifications to allow women whose departments were automated to continue to have employment. She won grievances and saved jobs, successfully negotiated contracts, and won the confidence of her coworkers. Hayes knew that outside of the Chicago area, where Addie would do much of her work as a field rep for the district, many of the workers and employers had never really encountered a black woman union representative. Such dynamics would surely pose a challenge, but Hayes had full confidence in Addie's ability to represent the union and its workers. She was also direct and knew how to effectively take the position that civil rights and women's rights were important to the livelihood of all workers and that the labor movement had to be at the forefront of the defense of those rights. Wyatt rarely won everyone over to the deeper ideological mission of the UPWA, but few could argue with her ability to produce measurable improvements for workers across the board.

Wyatt was grateful to Hayes for his faith in her. Not all men in organized labor were sympathetic to the concerns of working women, nor were they eager to make a space for women, especially black women, to represent and serve as a face and voice of authority in the union. Wyatt was inspired and encouraged by the working relationship she and Hayes developed: "Together we shared many difficult moments because he was a black male with a predominantly white, male membership and I was a black female with a predominantly white male leadership, and here we were two top leaders in the district."[46] Just as white support was crucial to the success of antidiscrimination campaigns and increased minority leadership, male support was central to the fight against sexism and workplace discrimination. Hayes and Wyatt were able to lean on one another for support in the movement, but they were also both attuned to the fact that they needed to be able to reach all workers, despite differences in race, sex, and geographic location. Women needed male support to seize some of the power that accompanied union leadership and to fight unequal pay, lack of job opportunities, and lack of adequate medical care among other key problems. Hayes's mentorship and the support of men in the movement were important to Wyatt's path to leadership. She often stated, "I never could have gotten the opportunity that I have had these many years had there not been some men who were willing to share with me."[47]

After her tenure as president of Local 56 ended, Wyatt assumed her duties as an international field representative full time—a position that took her out of working in the plant and into the field as a union official. International field representatives worked under district directors and traveled extensively throughout their districts to negotiate major contracts; handle large complex grievances; organize unorganized workers; run district-level educational programs, leadership training schools, and conventions; and represent the union in community and political affairs.[48] Wyatt performed all of these functions and took on added responsibilities. She edited the district's monthly newspaper, the *District One Champion*, and assumed the duties of the district's program coordinator, a position previously held by African American musician, playwright, poet, and actor Oscar Brown Jr.[49]

As program coordinator, Wyatt was in charge of special programming and fund-raising for civil rights organizations and initiatives across the district. She organized the district's Leadership Training Schools, which taught staff and elected officers about the structure of the union, the art of contract bargaining and negotiations, methods for handling grievances, and how to establish women's nation committees and other key programs to promote worker solidarity. The UPWA's district leadership schools took place in Ottawa, Illinois, at a United Auto Workers (UAW) training facility and consisted of one to three days of training for groups ranging from 50 to 100 members. Wyatt publicized consumer boycotts and awareness rallies against meatpackers who refused to hire Spanish-speaking and black workers. In addition to these other duties, Wyatt continued to work with women. Unlike the United Autoworkers of America (UAW), the UPWA did not have a women's department. Wyatt led District One's Women's Activities Committee and served as a resource for existing local women's activities committees and those struggling to get off the ground.

Because she held several staff positions, Wyatt did not receive as many organizing assignments as her counterparts. However, she experienced her fair share of wins and losses in the ongoing battle to organize the unorganized and expand the UPWA's membership. The very first plant Wyatt was assigned to organize was the Berth Levy plant in Chicago. Organizing operations began after a period of surveying plant operations and conducting background information on the company, the composition of the workforce, and the history of organizing drives within the plant. Often, there was an initial plant contact, a worker who contacted union officials seeking representation or a worker whom union officials perceived as receptive to UPWA representation who could serve as an inside contact. Organizers attempted to build relationships with key workers who maintained some sort of formal or informal leadership and camaraderie with the other workers. At Berth Levy, Wyatt's inside contact was reportedly fired after the third week of the organizing campaign. Either through worker gossip, the keen observation of management and company officials, or workers who alerted the company of the organizing campaign, inside contacts and any worker accused of or proven to be signing union representation cards could be dismissed. Such dismissals were against the collective bargaining rights that workers enjoyed under the National Labor Relations Board (NLRB), but company officials routinely violated these rights, sending a message of fear and intimidation to workers that efforts to organize could mean the loss of their jobs.

Organizing at Berth Levy initially took place at a slow pace due to workers' fears of management reprisal. At the time that her inside contact was fired, Wyatt had only five workers out of 300 who had signed representation cards. So she put her energies toward getting the inside contact, a woman, rehired on the basis that she should be able to return to her job as part of her right as a worker to organize. When the worker returned to the plant and told her coworkers that she was able to return to work—not in spite of, but because of—her organizing efforts, more workers signed cards. Still Wyatt faced significant opposition. She, along with other UPWA members, stood outside of the plant in the early mornings and late afternoons handing out leaflets and representation cards to workers. Some would hand the cards and leaflets over to management, signaling their loyalty to the company, while others took a more direct and inflammatory approach of actually slapping the materials out of Wyatt's hands.[50] On the day of the election, Wyatt stayed with the NLRB election official and watched as he counted each and every single vote. Ultimately, the campaign was successful and the UPWA won the right to bargain for Berth Levy employees.

Some of Wyatt's organizing assignments involved fairly small operations such as the Barney Manufacturing Company in Chicago, which she organized in 1958. Barney operated a small workforce of forty workers, 95 percent of whom were black and 90 percent of whom were women. It was customary for the UPWA to assign whenever possible black field representatives to organize primarily black plants, white field representatives to primarily white plants, and Hispanic or Spanish-speaking field representatives to primarily Hispanic plants. Though it espoused the approach of worker solidarity and antidiscrimination, the UPWA was not immune to the bonds of race and culture that existed among workers. At Barney, Wyatt again encountered fear and trepidation on the part of workers who feared company reprisal for their efforts to secure union representation. But in talking with workers and making home visits to discuss the benefits of unionization, Wyatt was able to get thirty-seven of the forty workers to sign UPWA representation cards. Eventually, the UPWA won the election.[51] Campaigns to organize workers could range from fairly straightforward and short like Wyatt's campaign at Barney, to monthslong and even yearlong attempts to organize workers or take over representation from other unions.

Perhaps the most difficult company that Wyatt attempted to organize was the Curtiss Candy Company, her second major assignment. Family owned and a fixture in Chicago since its founding by Otto Schnering in 1916, Curtiss Candy Company operated a large workforce in several plants across the Chicagoland area. The company manufactured popular candy bars like Baby Ruth and Butterfinger, and also produced and packaged peanuts, popcorn, cookies, and soft drinks. District One leader Charles Hayes assigned a team of field representatives—including Wyatt, Sam Parks, Rachel Guajardo, and Joe Zabitski—to organize workers in the company's ten Chicago area plants. The particular plant that Wyatt was assigned to organize had about 1,500 workers. She later described the organizing campaign at Curtiss as the one she "would love to forget forever." Wyatt recalled pulling out all the stops to try and persuade workers to sign up for representation, including arriving at the plant as early as 4:30 in the morning, making fried chicken and potato salad to serve to the workers, and making home visits. Organizing at Curtiss called for fourteen-hour—sometimes eighteen-hour—days of educating workers about the union and what it could do for them.

Before the election at one Curtiss plant, a portion of the plant that housed worker union cards was destroyed in a fire. Subversive tactics by company officials during the campaign and on the day of election also jeopardized organizing efforts. Election notices were not posted until the day of the election, even though this was a violation of NLRB election rules that required employers to give adequate advanced notice of representation elections. Some workers were reportedly told that they would have only half an hour, as opposed to having the entire workday, to place their vote. Workers who were active in the organizing campaign were fired or laid off prior to the election, and management even voted in the election against unionization to outweigh those in favor of UPWA representation.[52] Wyatt ultimately lost the election at her Curtiss plant by 300 workers, 545 in favor and 811 against. The loss at Curtiss was a devastating blow to the UPWA, which—after several unsuccessful attempts to organize the plants—gave up its organizing drive at Curtiss. Eventually, the company unionized, but not with the UPWA.[53] Organizing was difficult work. Overnight, Wyatt would go from a promising meeting with company workers signaling a possible successful campaign to having not one worker commit to sign a UPWA representation card. Workers would lose interest in unionization, become undone by company intimidation, seek representation with other unions, balk at paying union dues, or become wary of the day-to-day commitment needed to keep the union running.

Organizing and serving as the district's program coordinator occupied much of Wyatt's time as a field representative, but she was also able to engage in ongoing districtwide antidiscrimination efforts. Director Hayes, Wyatt, and other district leaders embarked on a campaign to finally end discrimination against black women in the front offices of Armour & Company. In the early 1950s, dozens of qualified African American women repeatedly found themselves locked out of lily-white front offices, just as Wyatt had been in 1941. District leaders capitalized on support from Chicago's black community and religious leaders to aid their efforts to get black women hired. They "tested" company officials by repeatedly sending in black and white women for front-office positions and, without fail, the white women were hired while the black women were dismissed or offered positions elsewhere in the packinghouse.[54]

District leaders took their campaign for front-office integration to the federal government. Wyatt and a cadre of UPWA leaders traveled to Washington, D.C., in 1955 to demand enforcement of Executive Order 10557, which prohibited employment discrimination among government contractors. Armour & Company and other meatpacking giants had contracts with the federal government. The D.C. delegation included Director Sam Parks of the Anti-Discrimination Committee, President Leon Beverly of Armour Local 347, International Vice President Russell Lasley, International Officer Cathie Drosnan, District One Director Charles Hayes, and Joseph Benzenhoffer, a member of Local 347's Grievance Committee, which spearheaded the three-year campaign against Armour for not hiring black female office workers.[55] The UPWA, utilizing Executive Order 10557, successfully fought for the hiring of black secretaries and office personnel, pledging that they would soon turn their fight to the other big plants, Swift and Wilson. By the end of the year, black women were working in front offices as typists, office clerks, and secretaries.

The geographic sphere of Wyatt's labor activism and leadership continued to expand over the course of the 1950s and 1960s. Her position as a field representative came with a substantial pay increase and required traveling all over District One into downstate Illinois, Indiana, Michigan, Ohio, and Wisconsin. The international union could draft an antidiscrimination clause and decree that districts and locals abide by it, but in reality it was up to workers on the ground to educate one another and recognize discriminatory practices where they existed and challenge them. Addie Wyatt carried this commitment to educating workers on the ground with her across District One in her role as a field representative, but she was often tested. A number of assignments required that

Wyatt travel to downstate Illinois to organize unorganized workers and negotiate major contracts. Sometimes Charles Hayes or other field representatives accompanied her, but frequently she traveled alone and faced a considerable amount of racism. Most hotels and restaurants would not serve her. Often she ate dinners of cheese and crackers and even slept in her car because she had no lodging. On one particular occasion, Wyatt was sent to lead an organizing campaign at a sausage-packing plant downstate. She recalled how the workers grabbed the leaflets from her and some even spat in her face when she tried to get their attention. Wyatt remembered, "I smiled and gave them leaflets anyway. After the plant was organized, we held a meeting. And when I walked in, those workers stood and applauded."[56]

Despite the undeniable presence of antiunion attitudes, and racist and sexist views, Wyatt had to persuade workers that the benefits of the union outweighed their lack of collective bargaining rights and would place all of them in a better economic position. And she had to do so within a black female body, trying to appeal to predominantly white males who initially refused to see her as their ally, much less their equal. But the proof was in the outcome, and in the end the workers at least recognized Wyatt as a capable organizer and negotiator if not their equal. Much like in her local, Wyatt had to prove her competency, commitment, and ability to get things done for workers. Her approach to contract negotiations and union business in these hostile environments remained to find a common human ground with workers and company representatives. Wyatt argued, "My approach and manner of dealing with people helps them to understand that I am not asking for any special favors, that I came to do a job that I'm capable and qualified to do. I don't want to be a threat to anyone, but at the same time I am not going to cut myself short. Neither am I going to cut the workers short and so I just proceed to do what I have to do. In time I have found that there's a part of all of us that's touchable if you can get beyond the veneer."[57] Wyatt did not seek to win her detractors over by belittling them, fearing that such an approach would foreclose on any opportunities for fostering solidarity and a shared sense of commitment to the principles of the UPWA.

Wyatt faced a considerable amount of doubt as to her organizing and negotiating skills because of her physical appearance and pronounced femininity. Petite and attractive, Wyatt wore sophisticated, unique, and flattering clothing and accessories not common for women workers and union organizers in meatpacking. In an industry often identified with the slaughtering of meat and seen as wholly unfeminine, Wyatt stood out with her penchant for the latest fashions. Soft-spoken, well-mannered and transparent about her Christian faith, Wyatt radiated a kind of femininity that mirrored 1950s-style images of domesticity. This led some to question the strength of her intellectual abilities and skills as a union representative. Others believed that Wyatt might rely on her looks to achieve favorable outcomes for herself and workers. One of her first union bosses, Sam

Parks, gave Addie a serious piece of advice early in her union career: "You're a nice-lookin' woman, but your looks won't get you no place around here. Your production is your greatest defense and security."[58] Parks was known for his frankness, but also for his commitment to workers and the UPWA. Wyatt carried his advice with her through the remainder of her career in the labor movement, focusing on productivity and favorable outcomes for workers above all else.

Company officials who were not used to dealing with female union representatives, much less black women representatives, frequently made reference to Wyatt's looks when she arrived for negotiation and grievance meetings. On one occasion, Wyatt recalled company men taunting her, "Now, we're going to have beauty," to which she responded, "Brains as well. Dumbness isn't necessarily an ingredient of femininity."[59] In an era when adult women were commonly called "girls" and treated as such, Wyatt worked hard to demand respect and urged women to demand respect from male employers and coworkers. Many female union leaders had to battle against stereotypes about where their priorities lay, the degree of their loyalty to the movement, and their competency in union organizing and leadership. Women in the UPWA had a difficult terrain to map in terms of getting male unionists to understand the complex ways in which they were considered outsiders within the movement they supported and in getting respect from company management as union representatives.

Wyatt consistently sought to prove that she was a competent and effective union leader. She worked to increase the power of the union through its membership but also to increase the power and resonance of its ideology of worker solidarity across differences in race and sex. These experiences did not deter Wyatt from her work as a union leader; rather, they made her commitment to the labor movement and equality even stronger. If the UPWA were to become a powerhouse for working people and a force against race and sex discrimination, it would need its workers to support those ideals. Wyatt became determined to keep herself and the union in that struggle regardless of the real barriers and denials of respect and dignity she routinely faced by the very workers she represented. She maintained a sense of duty and responsibility to working people that ultimately went beyond the shop floor and out into society. The UPWA provided an invaluable training ground for attacking racial discrimination and raising the issue of sexism in the labor movement. Just as her status within the UPWA began to rise as she became further entrenched in the world of labor organizing and leadership, Wyatt's status as an advocate and fighter for civil rights and women's rights gained greater prominence and recognition outside of the labor movement. Over the course of the 1950s and 1960s, Wyatt began to build strong networks and coalitions of black faith, civil rights, and women's rights activists determined to fight racial and gender inequality.

4

CIVIL RIGHTS AND WOMEN'S RIGHTS UNIONISM

Members of the UPWA's District One found themselves in a unique position. They were poised on the *other* side of the picket line, ready to cross it in order to pick up a small group of black families who had specifically sought their help. A meeting at the Parkway Dining Room in Chicago had been planned for the families, residents of Trumbull Park who recently "integrated" the housing project and were at the center of one of the city's most prolonged, infamous, and violent housing riots from 1952 to 1955. Clashes over the integration of public housing erupted in the city between 1946 and 1953 in what historian Arnold Hirsch has termed "an era of hidden violence" when racial tensions over community space and residential rights to housing reached a boiling point.[1] Addie Wyatt, who was among the group of interracial trade unionists, agreed to provide safe transportation for the families who were under daily assault from violent mobs of neighboring whites and even Hispanics protesting the presence of blacks in their community. Wyatt and her fellow trade unionists braved stone throwing, angry taunts, threats, and damage to their vehicles upon entering the housing project and subsequently leaving with the families.

At the meeting, District One director Charles Hayes took the time to assure the families that the union was behind them, ready to defend their rights to public housing and assist them financially from a $4,000 Defense Fund for Trumbull Park Families collected from union members. Some of the families included UPWA members, like Frank London Brown, who would go on to write a novel about his experiences, *Trumbull Park*. Hayes, ever ready to mobilize the power of the union, addressed the residents: "We know that sometimes you have to fight fire with fire. We will come to your rescue when you need help. If a race riot breaks out, unity between Negro and white workers in our union will be shot to the devil."[2] Sam Parks, antidiscrimination director for the district, also spoke to the residents: "[S]omebody had to be on the front line in Trumbull Park and you are it. You are in the forefront of the fight for the rights of the Negro people of America."[3] Joseph Benzenhoffer, a white trade unionist who played a significant role in antidiscrimination and civil rights efforts in the union, also addressed the families at the meeting: "As a white trade unionist, I know the conditions that exist in the stock yards. I know the situation we will be faced with if Trumbull Park isn't brought under control. We have resolved, regardless of the cost and consequences, that we must support the families in Trumbull Park. . . . We are ready to battle and do everything possible for Trumbull Park."

Though each man acknowledged the bitter struggle of individual families for the right to live in Trumbull Park, their focus was on the collective aspects of the struggle, its significance to the fight for civil rights, and the role that the UPWA with its "commitment to interracial unionism"[4] would play in aiding and overcoming the struggle for fair and open housing. Addie Wyatt, international representative for the union, also focused on the collective aspects of the struggle, but believed its foundations were spiritual: "Your families have our sympathy, as well as our support. . . . We say fight, fight, fight. The race is not to the swift and not to the slow but to the one who endureth to the end. We have not achieved anything without struggle. We are sure that the victory will come because more and more we are feeling it and we are interested in sharing whatever problems you have."[5] Blending biblical passages from the Book of Ecclesiastes and the Book of Matthew, Wyatt lent moral and religious credence to Trumbull Park's black families and labor's role in aiding them. She went on to link the righteousness of the families in the face of great hostility to that of Jesus Christ, who in the face of doubt, opposition, and ultimately crucifixion remained steadfast to his principles and mission. Forever melding her spiritual faith with her secular activism, Wyatt contended that God was on the side of the dispossessed and the righteous—in this case those seeking their God-given right to fair and open housing.

It was the summer of 1954 and while the rioting, terror, and racial violence at Trumbull Park received national news coverage, the nation was still reeling from the U.S. Supreme Court's decision in the landmark case, *Brown vs. Board of Education*, which deemed state-sponsored segregation in public schools unconstitutional. The case thrust the issue of civil rights and the illegality of segregation onto a national scale. The widespread prevalence of residential segregation in Chicago made open neighborhoods and housing one of the most pressing civil rights issues in the city. The 1950s were turbulent times for labor activists like Wyatt seeking to overturn widespread and long-held patterns of segregation, racial violence, and political suppression. Progressive labor activists were at the forefront of Chicago's civil rights struggles, drawing upon their ongoing fight for workplace equality and organizing power to address inequality beyond the workplace.

Over the course of the 1950s and 1960s, the UPWA's most radical contingency, which included Addie Wyatt, initiated or enlisted in local and national civil rights campaigns around open housing, adequate healthcare, voting rights, and employment. In the process, labor activists like Wyatt blurred the often stark dividing lines between the civil rights movement and the labor movement. In forming alliances with key civil rights and community organizations in Chicago and in the South, the UPWA's commitment to antidiscrimination translated into much-needed financial and human capital for civil rights initiatives. The UPWA became a recognizable progressive force in the newly formed AFL-CIO, working both within and beyond the workplace to improve the total lives of working men and women. Both missions did not come easy and the UPWA was by no means a multiracial paradise where differences in race, ethnicity, class, gender, religion, and politics melted away against calls for worker solidarity. As a rising leader and committed grassroots mobilizer in the labor movement, Addie Wyatt became a veritable bridge, linking the fate of working men and women in labor to the burgeoning civil rights and women's rights movements.

BUILDING A BRIDGE BETWEEN THE LABOR MOVEMENT AND THE CIVIL RIGHTS MOVEMENT

Labor scholars Rick Halpern and Roger Horowitz have argued that "although issues of economic equality remained paramount, UPWA local unions in the postwar period forged dynamic alliances with the black community and spearheaded efforts to attack discrimination in housing and schools, protest police brutality, open up new avenues of black employment, and mobilize the black vote. Significantly, these activities occurred with at least the tacit, and often the active, support of white packinghouse workers."[6] Throughout the 1950s and 1960s, the UPWA continued to work against racism and discrimination in its locals, which was an ongoing struggle. In the UPWA, that commitment went beyond the workplace out into the greater Chicago community to the American South. Wyatt applauded the UPWA's efforts to support civil rights causes and believed that because of its efforts, progressive UPWA members had faith in the union and its impact on the labor movement. Wyatt asserts that the UPWA stood out in its pursuance of fairness, equity, and antidiscrimination, but it was not the only union in the AFL-CIO to support civil rights. Unions with sizable and active black members and strong pro–civil rights leadership like the United Auto Workers (UAW), District 65 of the Retail, Wholesale and Department Store Union (RWDU), the International Union of Electrical Workers (IUE), the Amalgamated Clothing Workers of America (ACWA), and certain locals of the Food, Tobacco and Agricultural Workers (FTA) lent significant financial and human capital to the civil rights movement. But by and large, the labor movement was too often a perpetuator of racial inequality whose commitment to civil rights failed to go beyond verbal support, symbolic conference resolutions, and unenforced constitution and contract clauses. The 1955 merger of the more conservative craft unionism of the AFL, led by George Meany, and the more diverse, mass production–based CIO, led by Walter Reuther, resulted in an AFL-CIO that struggled to recognize and address its own racism. Though Meany took on the leadership of the AFL-CIO as its president, radical pro–civil rights forces from the former CIO unions continued to make noise and call out their fellow affiliates that allowed racism to thrive.

One of the most illustrative examples of the UPWA's commitment to equality was District One's Packinghouse Workers' Civic and Community Committee (PWCCC). Charged with enhancing union-community relations and attacking the problems that union members faced outside of the plant, the PWCCC, would "not rival the NAACP or the Back of the Yards Council," but instead "through the mediums of community action, political action and public relations . . . would organize and rally the people around issues prevailing in their community."[7] Members of the PWCCC offered their support to the families of Trumbull Park and protested outside of city hall and the mayor's office in favor of open housing. The union's programming department, led by Richard Durham, held numerous programs and ran several ads in local newspapers about the need for action and order in Trumbull Park. The PWCCC even reached out to the UPWA's rival union, the Amalgamated Meat Cutters and Butcher Workman, to form a support committee for black families in Trumbull Park. Pat Gorman, an international leader in the Amalgamated and civil rights supporter, responded affirmatively: "The Trumbull Park situation is unthinkable and yet in a supposedly free nation like ours the whole putrid program has the secret support of too many lily-whites who brazenly give lip service to intolerance of all character. Naturally we are more than willing to cooperate with your group."[8] Throughout the trouble at Trumbull Park, the PWCCC lent financial and moral support to the families.

Members of the PWCCC also embarked on an ambitious campaign to bring an end to discrimination in healthcare and open up facilities such as the Roseland Community Hospital to blacks. As with aid to Trumbull Park families, fighting discrimination at Roseland was personal for Addie Wyatt. Her niece was turned out into the cold just after giving birth at Roseland and forced to travel miles into the city to ensure that she and her baby were in sound health. The battles the PWCCC waged—no doubt influenced by Wyatt, Hayes, and others who lived near the Roseland area—offered the chance to take on discrimination outside of the stockyard that directly affected the day-to-day life of black packinghouse workers. The PWCCC lobbied for passage of the Harvey-Campbell Ordinance, which would forbid hospitals from denying admittance and care on the basis of race, creed, or color. The committee circulated several flyers around the Chicagoland area about the campaign to open up Roseland and other discriminating hospitals. One such flyer featured a mother carrying the lifeless body of her young son in reference to a case where a black mother was reportedly told that her child was not sick enough to be hospitalized and turned away. The child died soon thereafter. Aside from the moral and legal wrongs of discrimination in medical care, the PWCCC argued both in the case of Trumbull Park and Roseland Hospital that because workers, regardless of skin color or gender, paid taxes, they had a right to the resources and services those tax dollars provided.[9] UPWA president, Ralph Helstein, endorsed the efforts of the PWCCC and wrote to Illinois Governor William Stratton for his support: "Our union, representing 105,000 Packinghouse Workers, strongly urges that you approve Senate Bill No. 105, which denies tax exemption to hospitals practicing discrimination. After a long struggle, our union has won company-paid hospitalization plants, but our great number of Negro members have been cheated of their right to hospitals of their choice and deprived of medical care."[10]

The PWCCC stepped beyond the confines of the meatpacking district to help bring about positive change for its workers. In doing so, it was necessary for the UPWA on a local level to build bridges with civil rights organizations like the NAACP. Willoughby Abner, a prominent UAW leader in Chicago, headed the South Side chapter of the NAACP. During Abner's tenure as president of the Chicago branch in the mid-1950s, the UPWA worked closely with the branch in the way of shaping an independent black political voice that launched assaults on the city's discriminatory housing policies and employment practices.[11] Both groups worked together on "don't buy" product campaigns, boycotts, and sit-ins in stores and restaurants in the Chicago area that refused to serve blacks on an equal basis as whites. The PWCCC coordinated support for Trumbull Park families with the Chicago branch of the NAACP, and the two organizations teamed up for a mass rally to celebrate Negro History Week at Greater Bethesda Baptist Church in February of 1956. The rally featured Mississippian T. R. M. Howard. As the keynote, Howard spoke on "the mob terror of the South" while the other panelists, Hayes, Abner, Helstein, and A. Lincoln James, pastor of Greater Bethesda, spoke on the need for Chicagoans to support their southern brethren in the fight for civil rights.[12]

Many blacks in Chicago who were born or had roots in Mississippi still traveled there to see relatives and therefore had close ties to the racial violence unfolding in the state. The murder of fourteen-year-old Chicago teen, Emmett Till, in Mississippi in August of 1955 hit close to home for blacks all over the nation, but especially in Chicago.[13] The UPWA quickly galvanized its membership in support of justice for Emmett Till and his grief-stricken mother, Mamie Bradley. Together with Marie Alroth of District One's Local 100, Wyatt planned a Labor-Community Tea fund-raiser in which over 150 UPWA women from District One were in attendance. Over $300 was raised to support Bradley. Not soon after, Wyatt worked with Hayes and other District One staff to plan a mass protest rally with Mamie Bradley as the featured speaker.[14] Charles Hayes spoke out against the Till murder, racial violence in Chicago, and the inability of the city's political leaders to recognize the connection between racism in Mississippi and racism in Chicago. In a statement issued in response to Mayor Richard J. Daley's condemnation of Emmett Till's murder, Hayes argued that Chicago was not yet a haven of democracy:

> Our union heartily endorses and welcomes the statement of Mayor Richard J. Daley of Chicago urging that President Eisenhower act in securing justice in the Mississippi murder of young Till. We wish to point out to Mayor Daley, however, that Emmett Till was hardly less safe in Greenwood, Mississippi than he would have been in Trumbull Park, Chicago. We wish to point out to Mayor Daley that right in his own backyard in Trumbull Park, Negro men, women, and children have been besieged, stoned and threatened by the same kind of white supremacists as those who lynched Emmett Till in Mississippi.[15]

Ever critical of Daley and the city's unwillingness to acknowledge, address, and dismantle racism in Chicago, Hayes, Wyatt, and District One members would later become an important part of the Chicago Freedom Movement in the 1960s. Hayes went on to call upon women's organizations in America to "protest against the vicious use of white womanhood as an excuse for such murders."[16]

Local labor organizers fused their struggles for equality in the labor movement with their ongoing daily struggles against racism, segregation, and discrimination—problems that the civil rights movement sought to eradicate and redress. These were the same problems the UPWA had been addressing with moderate levels of success since the 1940s.[17] As Addie Wyatt often explained, the labor movement that she was a part of was the civil rights movement, and she had been engaged in civil rights struggles prior to Dr. King and the southern civil rights movement.[18] From the Till trial on, the UPWA would dispatch financial, legal, and human capital to the civil rights movement, and Addie Wyatt was consistently at the heart of those organizing efforts. She was the foot soldier behind fund-raising in District One for the Montgomery Bus Boycott and the Southern Christian Leadership Conference (SCLC). She collected food, clothing, and funds for "tent city" tenant farmers and their families who were kicked off their lands in Fayette County, Tennessee, in 1960 after registering to vote. And she helped organize a large contingency of UPWA members to attend the 1963 March on Washington.

Addie Wyatt helped make the UPWA an important source of financial support for the southern civil rights movement. In 1955, Charles Hayes called on
her to raise funds for Dr. Martin Luther King Jr. and the Montgomery Improvement Association's Bus Boycott. Wyatt drew upon her understanding of
the UPWA's antidiscrimination campaigns and her rhetorical skills to garner
financial support from workers. Some were eager to help with the effort while
others remained dead set against supporting civil rights, believing it to be outside of the purview and purpose of their union. Hayes believed that with her
strong commitment to the UPWA and religious background, Wyatt could appeal to workers on a moral basis.[19] But convincing workers to lend physical and
financial support to the Montgomery Bus Boycott and "to give credibility" to
the nascent civil rights movement was by no means an easy task.[20]

How King and the Montgomery Improvement Association (MIA) first came
to contact the UPWA for aid is unknown. Perhaps the UPWA reached out to
the boycott's leadership first. The union's Freedom Fund fund-raising campaign
began in earnest in 1955 to support southern civil rights initiatives. In February
of 1956, King journeyed to Chicago to meet with UPWA representatives. At the
meeting were Charles Hayes, Richard Durham, Russell Lasley, A. T. Stephens,
Catherine Brosnan, King, and Reverend Owen Pelt of Shiloh Missionary Baptist
Church. King discussed the background of the boycott, their demands, and the
strategy of challenging the constitutionality of bus seating. The possibility of
the UPWA spearheading efforts to put pressure on the Montgomery Bus Lines
parent company's headquarters in Chicago was also broached. King highlighted
the need for support from the UPWA and Chicago not just on a financial level,
but a moral level. The UPWA provided an immediate contribution of $1,000,
pledged the support of its Montgomery locals, Local 309 and Local 322, and assured King that more funds would be on the way.[21] In addition, the union helped
publicize the boycott in the North and offered its own legal team as resources
for the MIA and the SCLC.[22] The UPWA served as a valuable resource for the
movement, having greater disposable funds and access to a large rank-and-file
base. The union lent its knowledge of boycott tactics, legal strategies, and ways
to garner local community support. In turn, the union sought support from
King and the movement for worker struggles and organized labor.

Addie Wyatt helped District One raise $8,000 in support of the boycott, the
largest contribution of any district to the Freedom Fund. The international had
a goal of $20,000 but fell short. At the end of its eighteen-month fund-raising
campaign, the union collected a total of $11,000 (the majority from District One)
for the MIA. For her part, Wyatt credited her "faith in God, faith in the movement, and faith in the people, white and black, that [they] were serving." She
traveled throughout District One speaking at local union meetings and events
to collect funds in support of the boycott.[23] Wyatt's success proved that she was
capable and adept at securing crucial financial resources for labor/civil rights

initiatives. When Dr. King again journeyed to Chicago in 1957 to retrieve the funds and speak at the UPWA's Fourth Annual Wage and Contract Conference and Third National Anti-Discrimination and Women's Activities Conference, Wyatt was the representative elected to escort King to the conference. At the conference, King thanked the union for its financial contribution and acknowledged that the UPWA and the labor movement were fertile training grounds for black activists in the freedom struggle. The UPWA was the first union in the city of Chicago to host King and give support to the movement.

Wyatt and King developed a close relationship as spiritual leaders, civil rights activists, and proponents of working-class struggles. As a result of her experiences in the UPWA, Wyatt felt that the success of the civil rights movement and the labor movement ultimately depended on coalitions and building mass grassroots support for both movements. She recalled that Dr. King also believed in this approach: "He [King] clearly recognized that the most effective means for working people to achieve economic, social, and political justice was thru [*sic*] the organized labor movement. And so, from the very beginning, he involved the labor movement, along with the church and community, in a coalition which included black, brown, white, and ALL PEOPLES, raising a clarion call for freedom and equality which was heard around the world."[24] The UPWA, King, and the SCLC developed a working relationship wherein both supported one another's efforts in improving the lives of working people. And they did so over ten years prior to King's Open Housing Campaign and the 1966 Chicago Freedom Movement.[25]

Wyatt became a labor advisor to the SCLC and remembered working with Dr. King fondly: "He was a sincere person with great faith in God and great faith in people. He loved people. He had a great sense of humor. There were times when we'd meet together [and] it was so wonderful to see him relax and laugh heartily at things that would happen—some experiences we would go through, and he and I would pray from time to time."[26] Their relationship was deepened by their shared Christian faith. Although King was Baptist and Addie was a member of the Church of God, they both believed in the social gospel and the connection that must take place between saving souls and improving the day-to-day lives of the poor and working people.

In 1955, the Wyatts founded their own church, the Vernon Park Church of God, on the South Side of Chicago. While their congregation struggled to grow in its early years, by the mid-1960s Vernon Park grew to a respectable size and could be counted on to provide support for civil rights and labor-based campaigns across the city. The Wyatts, along with close personal friend and civil rights activist, Reverend Willie Barrow, later worked with a young Jesse Jackson at the request of Dr. King to start the SCLC's Operation Breadbasket in Chicago. Wyatt's relationship with King and the southern civil rights movement, originated from her work as a labor activist and organizer in the UPWA, but those ties were strengthened by a spiritual belief in the righteousness of civil rights struggles. Her dual affiliations with Chicago's progressive labor forces and activist ministries further cemented her place in the faith, labor, and civil rights network that contributed greatly to Chicago's black political culture.

On March 18, 1965, Wyatt and close friend and civil rights activist, Willie Barrow, arrived in Selma, Alabama, just over a week after "Bloody Sunday," in which voting rights demonstrators were brutally attacked by local law enforcement. Wyatt was there to aid in preparations for the next big march from Selma to Montgomery, scheduled for Sunday, March 21. Hundreds of clergy, civil rights activists, and other concerned supporters had also arrived. A cadre of UPWA leaders including Helstein, Lasley, and staff member Harry Alston were also in Selma. The UPWA was in the middle of a fund-raising drive for its Fund for Democracy to aid in ongoing civil rights struggles in the South, and wanted to show its support for the black residents of Selma and other disenfranchised citizens across the South.

Wyatt chronicled her journey in a short piece entitled, "My Sojourn to Selma, Alabama." She discussed the sacrifices of those in Selma for the procurement of their voting rights and of their hospitality in the face of such turbulent times. She wrote, "This is a tense battle of nerves, but the power of love and endurance is evident in their battle scarred and worn faces." Wyatt and Barrow's host family consisted of a mother who was a school teacher, and her three children. All, save the four-year-old son, were victims of "Bloody Sunday" and had been jailed multiple times in pursuit of voting rights. As a volunteer, Wyatt chose kitchen duty at one of the local black churches, but even this required a training and orientation session that instructed "what to do and what not to do" during her stay and how to protect herself against an attack. Nightly "mass meetings were held. Freedom songs were sung, speakers from different churches and other organizations addressed the crowd. Special financial contributions were made and individual offering received."[27] For Wyatt, the spirit of community among civil rights activists in Selma was invigorating and inspiring, as was their endurance to fight for "human dignity and justice," much like the families in Trumbull Park a decade earlier. The connection of civil rights struggles in the South and in Chicago was not lost on Addie Wyatt. Her trip to Selma was one of the defining moments of her career as a labor leader, civil rights activist, and religious figure because of the perseverance of the residents and the collective nature of their struggle.

While the UPWA worked well with the Chicago Branch of the NAACP, the SCLC, the Student Non-Violent Coordinating Committee (SNCC), and other civil rights groups during the 1950s and 1960s, not all civil rights organizations were hospitable to the UPWA and willing to work alongside the union. Sometime in the late 1950s, Wyatt and several UPWA members attempted to attend an NAACP meeting in Detroit where they were working with several locals on organizing campaigns, strikes, and contract negotiations and in need of greater support from the local community. According to Wyatt, her group was turned away from the NAACP meeting and the UPWA was accused of communist domination.[28] The perception of the UPWA as led by communists was a significant criticism hurled at the union by a number of organizations, including rival unions who hoped to gain greater representation in packinghouses. The UPWA did have some self-identified communists like Herbert March, the first director of District One, who were integral to the founding of the union in the late 1930s and early 1940s. At the same time, the UPWA's militancy could also be attributed to radical members like Wyatt who did not identify with communism.

Political red-baiting of progressive CIO unions like the UPWA was common during the McCarthy area. The anticommunist movement ripped apart the CIO. Red-baiting and the passage of the Taft-Hartley Act in 1947, which contained an anticommunist affidavit for representatives of American workers, put the spotlight on unions. Over the course of 1949 and 1950, eleven "leftist" unions, including the International Longshore and Warehouse Union, the United Public Workers of America, and the United Electrical, Radio and Machine Workers were purged from the CIO, constituting a loss of nearly one million members.[29] Despite its commitment to interracial social unionism and the presence of active communist members in the UPWA, the union escaped the CIO purge and even benefited from the purge by gaining workers from the expelled Food, Tobacco and Agricultural Workers Union. But it did not escape investigation by the House Un-American Activities Committee (HUAC) nearly a decade later. Former UPWA International Vice President A. T. Stephens left the UPWA after a bitter dispute with Helstein, Durham, Hayes, and others in 1959. He then wrote to George Meany, president of the AFL-CIO, telling him that there was a dangerous subversive element in the UPWA that needed containment. Several members of the union, including Charles Hayes, were brought before HUAC in Chicago and questioned about their membership in the Communist Party-USA. In the end, no action was taken by HUAC or the UPWA against the questioned activists.[30] Addie Wyatt was not questioned.

The UPWA had on its books a rule that no members of the CP-USA were to hold elective or appointed positions in the union and maintained its own Review Committee to investigate possible violations of its policy. The UPWA argued in its defense, "If there are in our ranks persons with a Communist past, their present adherence to the democratic principles of our union represents a symbol of the victory of democratic philosophy over totalitarianism, and we see no purpose in placing them in the public pillory."[31] Influential community leaders in Chicago also came to the defense of the UPWA during the HUAC investigations. Theodore Jones, then president of the Chicago branch of the NAACP, wrote Congressman Francis Walter, chairman of the HUAC committee, expressing "confidence in the integrity and loyalty of the incumbent officers and directors of the United Packinghouse Workers of America." Moreover, Jones felt that "because of its vigorous fight against segregation of races it [the UPWA] has attracted many enemies who overlook the corrective housecleaning the incumbent officers and directors have accomplished. The UPWA not only preaches adherence to human rights principles but practices them within its own organization."[32]

Similarly, Joseph Meegan, cofounder and executive secretary of the famed Back of the Yards Neighborhood Council, came to the defense of the UPWA as a beacon of democracy rather than its adversary: "Under the leadership of President Ralph Helstein, the United Packinghouse Workers of America AFL-CIO has made tremendous contributions to the welfare of the members of its union, and to their communities. We have been deeply impressed by the fearlessness and the courage the union has displayed in meeting the issue of race relations and discrimination, particularly concerning the Negro people. United Packinghouse Workers of America are certainly far in the forefront in the democracy and a bulwark against discrimination."[33] The comments of Jones and Meegan opposed the HUAC charges and championed the UPWA as the true keeper of democracy whose efforts on behalf of workers and minorities deserved praise rather than suspicion and vilification. Despite escaping relatively unscathed from the HUAC investigations, the UPWA was branded as an outsider organization in the AFL-CIO. When AFL-CIO Vice President Walter Reuther nominated Helstein to the body's executive council, President George Meany and southern white members of the council reportedly blocked Helstein on the grounds that he was "too controversial" and "not a team player."[34]

Addie Wyatt echoed the sentiments of UPWA supporters. She never saw the UPWA as anything but an organization trying to bring about a better life for working people. Moreover, Wyatt rejected attempts to divide progressive forces. She could not understand why the Detroit chapter of the NAACP would not want to associate itself with the UPWA, a union that had a history of proven support and action on behalf of better economic, political, and civil rights for working people. Wyatt believed that the communist label was nothing but a front for those unwilling to denounce racism and give the UPWA credit for its accomplishments. Furthermore, Wyatt believed that blacks who experienced racism and labeling had to resist such efforts against institutions, organizations, and others who spoke out against injustice.[35] Wyatt did not denounce the UPWA or deny her affiliation with the union because it had proved to be a labor organization dedicated to workers. The UPWA was first and foremost a union, but it was also a civil rights organization, a political organization, and, for a growing number of women, it held the possibility of becoming an organization through which they might push for greater rights. Wyatt came of age politically in the

UPWA, embracing, shaping and expanding its ideals and policies along the way. She would spend the rest of her life acting as a bridge between the labor, civil rights, women's rights, and even religious movements, always seeking for a way to uphold the equality of rights of minorities, women, and working people.

AN EMERGING NATIONAL PRESENCE

In the early 1960s, Wyatt became involved with the Negro American Labor Council (NALC), an organization that sought to address and alleviate the problems of black workers and their marginalization within the AFL-CIO. Formed in 1960 by A. Philip Randolph and others, the NALC was primarily composed of black workers and union leaders and was a membership organization. The NALC originated from black worker's concerns with racial discrimination in the AFL-CIO. Not a strong advocate of civil rights, the AFL remained steeped in charges of discrimination by black workers who were routinely barred from employment and membership in its union affiliates. Blacks in the AFL were sometimes forced to form separate locals apart from the locals that served their workplaces. Founded to challenge the AFL, the CIO was more radically oriented and racially progressive, though by no means perfect in its acceptance and treatment of black workers. While some were optimistic that the 1955 merger of the AFL and CIO would lead to a more welcoming and antiracist labor movement, others were skeptical and doubted the sincerity behind the AFL-CIO's tacit support for civil rights legislation and organizations.[36] A. Philip Randolph, leader of the International Brotherhood of Sleeping Car Porters and the 1941 March on Washington Movement, was by far the most recognizable and influential African American in the labor movement. Loyal to the AFL since 1937, A. Philip Randolph served as the only African American on the newly formed AFL-CIO's executive council. Randolph resisted membership and affiliation with what he saw as communist-led or communist-dominated organizations such as the National Negro Labor Council (NNLC) founded in the early 1950s.

Randolph became frustrated with continuing racism in AFL-CIO affiliates and the lack of progress in integrating black workers equally into the fabric of the organization. At the AFL-CIO's 1959 Convention in San Francisco, California, Randolph delivered a powerful speech indicting the organization for failing to sanction unions that maintained segregated locals or continued to bar African Americans from apprenticeships and equal representation. Randolph and other black labor leaders were also upset that the AFL-CIO lacked a formal antidiscrimination policy. An irate Meany confronted Randolph and asked, "Who the hell appointed you as guardian of all the Negroes in America?" Addie Wyatt attended that convention and felt the sting of racism and indignation at the heart of Meany's question as well as the disrespect shown to Randolph. Less than one year later, in 1960, the Negro American Labor Council was born.

The first national convention of the NALC took place in Detroit in 1960. Randolph defined the function of the new organization in a speech before the convention:

> The Negro American Labor Council will seek Negro trade unionists in every craft, class and industry to join its ranks. It will be pro-Negro but not anti-white. It will have no color bar. It will be non-partisan but not non-political. It will be anti-Communist, anti-Fascist, anti-racist and anti-colonialist. It will support pro-labor and pro–civil rights legislation but not the fortunes of the Democratic or Republican parties. Recognizing that only within the framework of a democratic society can a civil rights and labor's rights movement exist, the NALC will unequivocally support and defend the democracy and freedom at home and abroad.[37]

Randolph positioned the NALC as an organization firmly aligned with the democratic ideals of organized labor. The NALC would not be above criticizing the inability or unwillingness of labor leaders to enforce antidiscrimination policies and increase the number of black union members and leaders. Fuel was added to the NALC's fire with the publishing of NAACP labor secretary Herbert Hill's "Racism within Organized Labor: A Report Five Years after the AFL-CIO." Hill offered a scathing critique of the AFL-CIO for adopting antidiscrimination clauses in its constitution, but making little effort to actually enforce antidiscrimination in its affiliates. Hill argued that discrimination in the AFL-CIO took four forms: outright exclusion of Negroes, segregated locals, separate racial seniority lines in collective bargaining agreements, and exclusion of Negroes from apprenticeship training programs controlled by labor unions."[38] Racially segregated affiliates and local chapters of unions operated all over the South and in many northern industries as well.

Although the NALC was primarily concerned with labor rights and the economic well-being of black workers, local NALC chapters developed their own ways of targeting discrimination and racism in labor and in the community. The Chicago chapter of the NALC, led by Chicago Public School teacher Timuel Black, was particularly militant. The group met at the UPWA's District One headquarters at 49th and Wabash and addressed discrimination at all levels of labor from the shop floor to the lack of black workers in city government. The Chicago chapter also voiced its concern over discrimination within the Chicago Public Schools and played an important role in the boycotts against school superintendent Benjamin Willis. The Chicago chapter's Women's Division put on social functions, fund-raisers, and educational conferences and submitted resolutions to the City of Chicago in favor of better housing for workers and minorities.[39] The group, which included Addie Wyatt, also staged protests outside the churches of pastors like Rev. Joseph Jackson of Olivet Baptist Church, who was an outspoken critic of Martin Luther King Jr. Rev. Jackson spoke out against direct action as a tactic in the civil rights movement and refused to support the 1963 March on Washington.[40] Addie Wyatt believed strongly that churches and religious institutions needed to support civil rights action and commit financial and human resources to the civil rights movement. Her participation in the NALC's efforts to shame those who refused to support the struggle for civil rights aligned with that belief. A deep schism existed between leaders like Jackson and King about the role that churches should play in secular struggles and the degree to which those struggles were within the domain of Christian action. Many questioned King's tactics and the method of direct nonviolent protest that he adopted. Wyatt did not.

Tim Black was a fellow DuSable High School alumnus and good friend of Addie and Claude Wyatt. He recalled how close the two were as a couple, the level of support Claude showed Addie in her organizing activities, and how—as a minister—Claude did his own fair share of championing labor and civil rights. Black recalled that Addie was always someone he could count on in NALC demonstrations: "Addie was not loud but she was consistent and persistent in stating her point of view. She was very clear and an active participant in confrontations."[41] He also believed that Addie was "mission oriented and philosophically driven." If there was an issue near and dear to the cause of working people, women, or African Americans, Addie was sure to be at the forefront, organizing others and leading the cause. And she was able to move in many circles by virtue of her status in the local labor movement and her years of activity in religious circles in Chicago. Her organizing abilities, deep spiritual faith, and ability to relate to others the necessity of a cause lent Wyatt a certain kind of movement clout. She was respected as a local leader in the labor movement and outside of it as well.

In many ways, the mission and goals of the NALC bridged Wyatt's concerns with civil rights in the UPWA to the treatment of blacks throughout the labor movement. According to Wyatt, she joined the NALC because the organization and the union were "a part of the same movement." Wyatt continued: "There [were] some of us who would give leadership to go forward. We did it ourselves and some of our members when they saw us go forward would join us because they believed in what we believed in and they were willing to support what we supported."[42] Civil rights and women's rights organizations, labor leaders, and black trade unionists from across the country all attended NALC conventions.[43] The meeting of activists from labor, civil rights, and women's organizations fit within Wyatt's brand of coalition, grassroots, and rights-based activism. As a labor leader, Wyatt led by example and joined organizations and causes that championed the struggles of minority and women workers. She had been able to do much within the confines of the UPWA, but her participation in the NALC helped in many ways to expand the base of her activism and persuade members of her union to do the same. The NALC helped to extend her impact and visibility in the community. Work that could not be accomplished entirely through the UPWA had the possibility of being accomplished through the NALC. And in many cases, the UPWA's financial and human resources were crucial to the campaigns and victories of the NALC and the fight against racism in Chicago.

Wyatt's involvement in the NALC, in particular its Chicago chapter, further positioned her within the city's wide network of militant black labor activists as someone willing to step out from her union and engage in action against discrimination beyond the labor movement. The NALC and the UPWA both played important roles in the Chicago Freedom Movement, a partnership between Dr. King, the SCLC, and the Chicago-based Coordinating Council of Community Organizations (CCCO) in 1966. During one of Dr. King's planned marches against housing segregation in the Marquette Park neighborhood of Chicago, Wyatt was marching when she learned that her car had been burned by a mob of angry whites. According to Timuel Black, rather than leave the march to check on her car and file a police report, Addie paid the news little heed and continued to march.[44] The white mob was violent toward the group of about 700 marchers. At one point, King was struck with a stone. Wyatt was hit in the leg with a brick hurled from the mob. It took two weeks for her to recover enough to return to work.[45]

A WORKING WOMEN'S AGENDA AND THE PRESIDENT'S COMMISSION ON THE STATUS OF WOMEN

As much as Addie Wyatt embraced the cause of civil rights, she equally embraced the problems of working women and struggles against sex discrimination in the workplace. Scholars such as Dorothy Sue Cobble, Nancy Gabin, Diane Balser, Dennis Deslippe, Karen Pastorello, and Nancy MacLean have done excellent work to document the history and importance of working women in the development of second-wave feminism. A broad and diverse network of what Cobble terms "labor feminists" worked within their unions and on a national scale to bring about changes in the workplace and in employment legislation that they believed would favorably impact working women.[46] These labor feminists, including Addie Wyatt, held "a vision of equality that claimed justice on the basis of their humanity, not on the basis of their sameness with men."[47] Wyatt's counterparts in the labor movement were longtime and emerging union women leaders such as Bessie Hillman of the Amalgamated Clothing Workers of American (ACWA); Mary Callahan of the International Union of Electrical Workers (IUE); Millie Jeffrey, Caroline Davis, Dorothy Haener, and Olga Madar of the UAW; Myra Wolfgang of the Hotel and Restaurant Employees Union (HERE); Catherine Conroy of the Communication Workers of America (CWA); and Esther Peterson of the AFL-CIO.

In addition, Wyatt's network of black women leaders in the labor movement, whose activism straddled the realms of civil rights and working women's rights, grew to include women such as Clara Day of the International Brotherhood of Teamsters; Lillian Hatcher of the UAW; Gloria Johnson of the IUE; Maida Springer Kemp of the International Ladies and Garment Workers Union (ILGWU); Lillian Roberts of the American Federation of State, County and Municipal Employees (AFSCME); Ola Kennedy of the United Steelworkers of America (USWA); and Alzada Clark of the United Furniture Workers of America (UFW). The numbers of women in industrial, clerical, professional, and service sectors would increase as a result of legislation such as the 1964 Civil Rights Act and the creation of the Equal Employment Opportunity Commission (EEOC). Expanded access to higher education and the overall gains of the civil rights movement and second-wave feminism also aided the expansion of women's employment opportunities. But Wyatt and labor feminists of the 1950s and 1960s were less beneficiaries of these developments than they were active contributors to their formation and relative success. These black and white female unionists often worked together to push for equal pay, civil rights legislation, and labor law reform, although not without significant debate and at times debilitating fractures.[48] But their ability to work together challenges narratives of the women's movement or working-class women's labor activism as solely the domain of white women. The scope of Wyatt's engagement with the problems of working women over the course of the 1950s and 1960s included "unionizing" women on a regional level in her capacity as a UPWA field representative, as a union delegate to national labor women's conferences, and ultimately as a member of the PCSW.

As a field representative and perhaps the most visible woman in District One of the UPWA, Wyatt led the district's Women's Activities Committee. Unlike the UAW, the UPWA had no international or national women's bureau. Therefore, efforts to address the problems of working women were more decentralized and required a considerable amount of coordination across union locals and regional districts. UPWA women had pushed to have discrimination and sexism challenged with as much fervor as racial discrimination. Given the difficulties brought on by automation, run-away shops, and the debate over dual versus single seniority, the union would inevitably have to face the problem of job reclassification and sex-segregated work. The UPWA took steps to eliminate wage differentials among men and women in major contracts by 1953, but women at smaller, independent plants outside of the major contracts still received unequal pay for equal work. UPWA women's outstanding demands included adequate medical care, a consistent and well-defined procedure for pregnancy leaves, and equal access to promotions and new jobs within the plants.

As head of District One's Women's Activities Committee, Wyatt's approach to dealing with the problems of working women in the UPWA involved several strategies: "unionizing" women already in the union through the formation of women's activities committees, attending women's conferences nationwide to brainstorm with other female labor activists, advocating for protective labor legislation that would help working women, and using grievances to challenge the loss of women's jobs in the plants. The first and last of these strategies took place exclusively within the union, while the second and third took place on a broader national scale. Unionizing women already in the UPWA was one of Wyatt's main strategies to increase the roles and leadership opportunities for women in the union. She advised existing women's activities committees and encouraged the formation of such committees in locals where none existed. Women's activities committees had several goals: to motivate women to become more active in the union, to educate women on the structure of the union and to know how to use it when they encountered problems on the job, to have more women seek and be elected to leadership positions and as conference delegates, and to support one another.

Wyatt urged union women to take on more active roles in the union and seek leadership roles in order to increase their power to bring about change. This was no easy task because many of the women, according to Wyatt, did not want to become more active in the union for fear of losing their jobs or creating tension with men in the workplace. Some women were apathetic while others outright opposed women's committees and Wyatt's presence in their locals. They branded her a troublemaker out to disrupt whatever progress and privileges women had already gained. Concerned about creating divisions between themselves and men in the workplace, some female unionists resisted women's activities committees and any "feminist" activism in the workplace that they deemed divisive and detrimental. Others were concerned about what criticisms greater union activity might bring from their husbands, friends, and religious circles. Perhaps most paramount was the fear that women might lose their jobs if they became too vocal about sexism and discrimination. Before Wyatt could convince men to accept women's leadership and partnership in the activities of the union, she first had to convince women to accept those roles and see themselves as more than passive beneficiaries or powerless victims of the union. They had a right to work and care for their families, and sexism and discrimination only limited their earning potential. Women could not sit by and take whatever was given to them, which more and more consisted of layoffs and cutbacks. Women needed to see themselves as workers, leaders, and full-fledged members of the union with the capacity and responsibility to shape it for the benefit of themselves and the movement as a whole.

In any local that she helped establish a women's activities committee, Wyatt continued the union's focus on education as a means of empowering its workers to strengthen the overall movement. Wyatt—aided by UPWA women like Hattie Gardner, Bessie McCauley, and Emma Beck—distributed fliers and pamphlets about the history, contributions, and ongoing struggles of women in the UPWA. Women were tutored in the art of getting elected as a delegate to key conferences and conventions, how to study union contracts in order to know when their rights were being violated, and how to be confident in working with their union brothers. The need to volunteer for committee work in order to take part in the decision-making apparatus of the movement was also a key thrust of the women's activities committees. Women attending the committee meetings were provided child care, and the meetings were kept to a reasonable time so as not to interfere with many women's second job as a homemaker. Once a core leadership and membership took form, the new women's activities committees went about reaching out to and recruiting women in their locals. Thus, Wyatt's goal in unionizing was the democratization of the union apparatus. Only with women more involved in the day-to-day running and organization of the union could their problems be thrust to the forefront of the UPWA agenda.

Perhaps it was her commitment to the problems of working women that led UPWA President Ralph Helstein to select Addie Wyatt to serve as his replacement on President Kennedy's Commission on the Status of Women (PCSW) in 1962.[49] Pressured by a large constituency of labor feminists who had given him support during the 1960 presidential election, Kennedy established the PCSW on December 14, 1961, with Executive Order 10980. The commission would terminate on October 1, 1963. Its task was to produce a final report on the status of American women and the recommendations for alleviating prejudice and discrimination toward women in society. From the outset, the scope of the PCSW was limited to making recommendations on public policy and legislation affecting women.[50] By 1960, twenty-four million women were working, and that number was expected to grow to thirty million by 1970. The federal government was the largest employer of women. The average woman earned three-fifths of what the average man made, yet more women were taking on greater financial responsibilities within the home and providing for themselves and their families. And over one million women were unemployed despite employment shortages in traditionally female fields such as teaching and nursing.[51] These statistics provided a powerful impetus for the formation of the commission and displayed the Kennedy administration's commitment to at least recognizing the importance of women in society and understanding what barriers precluded them from obtaining full citizenship and employment opportunities. At the same time, the work of the PCSW and its final report were intended to aid federal legislatures in weighing the hundreds of pieces of legislation concerning American women that were brought before Congress in the early days of the women's rights movement of the 1960s and 1970s.

President Kennedy appointed former first lady Eleanor Roosevelt as head of the commission, but she passed away in 1962 before its conclusion in 1963.

Esther Peterson, assistant labor secretary to President Kennedy and head of the U.S. Women's Bureau, was officially second in command but ran the commission with the help of Kathy Ellickson. Commission members included Senator Robert F. Kennedy, Congresswoman Edith Green, National Council of Negro Women leader Dorothy Height, and other business executives, labor leaders, academics, and politicians. Commission members served as the heads of seven committees: Civil and Political Rights, Education, Federal Employment, Home and Community, Private Employment, Social Insurance and Taxes, and Protective Labor Legislation. Each consisted of twelve to fifteen members including community leaders, politicians, academics, social workers, trade unionists, and civil rights activists. In addition, four consultations on Private Employment Opportunities, New Patterns in Volunteer Work, Portrayal of Women by the Mass Media, and Problems of Negro Women were held. Wyatt was a member of the Protective Labor Legislation Committee.

The PSCW and its committees were carefully crafted to achieve a balance between women's rights advocates who supported protective labor legislation with some adjustments and those who were for ratification of the Equal Rights Amendment (ERA). A deep schism existed among labor feminists and working women as to whether equality or difference in the form of protectionism should be held as the standard for women in the workforce. Since women began working in industry, protective labor legislation offered separate working standards and conditions for women on the basis of their sex and slighter physical makeup. Protective labor legislation was intended to protect women wherever they worked, whether in the home or in the workforce, and often included maximum work hours for women, restrictions from unduly arduous work tasks, and a guaranteed minimum wage. These laws, often enforced at the state level, were designed to protect women and designated them as a distinct class of worker separate from men, largely based on consideration of women's social roles as well as perceived physical and intellectual limitations. In theory these laws would protect women, but in reality female domestic workers, many of whom were black, were not protected at all. On the other side of the divide were those who backed the ERA, which states: "Equality of rights under the law shall not be denied or abridged by the United States or by any state on account of sex." Shortly after women gained the right to vote in 1920, the ERA was introduced in Congress yearly to ensure that women would be full citizens. Proponents of the ERA argued that protective labor legislation served as a way for employers to discriminate against women and keep them marginalized economically within the workforce, if not out of it completely. This, in turn, limited women's earning power and their ability to support themselves and their families. Because women could work only limited hours and only in certain positions, employers could choose to hire men in the name of "greater productivity" rather than hire women.[52]

The Kennedy administration hoped that the PSCW would occupy a middle ground between the two positions, affirming the need for protective labor legislation but recognizing that certain laws would need to be altered in order to accommodate women who wanted or needed to work more hours and women whose employment opportunities had suffered as a result of protective labor legislation.[53] This was ultimately the stance taken by the Protective Labor Legislation Committee and the PCSW as it rejected the ERA, arguing that despite rampant discrimination against women in the workplace, constitutional change was not the proper course of action. Protective labor laws needed to be amended and evaluated on a case-by-case basis. Those that aided working women should be strengthened while those that hindered women or were obsolete should be eliminated. In forming the PCSW and its commissions, Esther Peterson and others involved in the early stages of its planning hoped to alter the course of the commission in such a way that those who were in favor of the ERA and who were feminists were not alienated from the commission, but they also were not in control of it. They were fearful that the PCSW may be categorized as another "minority discrimination project" and so sought to quell the presence of more radical and outspoken feminists and minority women who could co-opt the commission and limit its mainstream appeal.[54]

Addie Wyatt's appointment to the PCSW's Committee on Protective Labor Legislation was featured in the *District One Champion* and the *Chicago Defender*. She was praised as being one of a handful of African Americans on the committee along with Dorothy Height, Pauli Murray, and several others. Given the dynamics of the commission and its commitment to protective labor legislation, the discussions, findings, and recommendations of Wyatt's committee were of central import to the PCSW. The committee on Protective Labor Legislation was charged with reviewing the past fifty years of labor laws and delivering any recommended changes to wage and hour laws, regulation of housework, maternity benefits, hazards to health and safety, night work, workmen's compensation, collective bargaining, labor law administration, and the equalization of standards of labor legislation across the states.[55]

The committee met three times over the course of 1962 and 1963 in Washington, D.C. Its task was to determine whether or not protective labor legislation or equality between men and women should be the policy and practice toward women in the workplace. Though Wyatt was not yet a supporter of the ERA while on the commission, she questioned the extent to which her committee could adequately carry out its task and understand the benefits and drawbacks of protective labor legislation without actually talking to working women. For Wyatt, the committee was too far removed from understanding the various feelings of working women on protective labor legislation. At their first meeting, Wyatt asked the committee if they were "in the best position to really determine the attitude and the feelings of the millions of women who really feel very keen about this particular point, I mean just by asking it amongst ourselves—and I am sure most of us have a limited knowledge as to really what exists here, the problems that exist." Wyatt continued, wondering whether "in the absence of hearings . . . even if it is on a regional basis of some sort where we can get the expressed opinions of people or groups that are really involved in these particular problems, that we aren't in the best position to say that we ought to limit our recommendations."[56] Some members agreed with Wyatt, but the majority of the committee was skeptical of her proposal. They believed that too few women would attend the hearings and that logistical and financial undertakings of such an approach were too great for the committee to handle. They agreed, however, to reach out to large employers and labor union leadership for their perspectives on protective labor legislation.

Wyatt continued to offer her opinions during committee meetings. She drew upon her experiences as a local union president, field representative, and female worker in the UPWA when addressing the committee. On the issue of limited work hours for women, Wyatt linked women's unemployment to automation and its growing grip on industry in the nation:

> [E]mployers are considering many things when it comes to the employee that will be kept on the job. And I think that in trying to decide whether or not this one can perform the job best, whether they can get more service out of them, they take into consideration the woman and her ability to do the job plus her ability to be a regular employee, and also whether or not this woman can work the number of hours that might be required. . . . I think that when some of the employers take this into consideration that they are more likely to lay the women off or refuse to hire women and they will instead hire men. This has been some of our experiences, especially in the highly automated plants.[57]

Responses to Addie's comments ranged from agreement that the issue of limited work hours needed to be further researched to outright dismissal. Committee member and Associate Director of the Conference on Economic Progress Mary Keyserling acknowledged that limited work hours might be a limitation for women, but that it was a minor problem. The committee needed to stay on top of larger, bigger goals.[58] Wyatt also questioned whether the committee would pay specific attention to the marginalization and discrimination of older women and minority women in the workforce and what role, if any, current protective labor legislation played in their (un)employment.

Occasionally, Addie Wyatt's expertise as a leader in the UPWA was solicited, but more often than not she felt somewhat alienated from the committee and its approach. Karen Pastorello, biographer of Bessie Hillman, argues that the Protective Labor Legislation Committee deferred to Hillman as the senior labor woman on the committee and as a member of the Commission. Then vice president of the ACWA, Hillman sought to steer the committee toward what she saw as the most important issues before the committee: "minimum wages, maximum hours, and equal pay for equal work."[59] While on the commission, Wyatt continued to work as a field representative and was required to send regular reports back to the international about the work of the commission. In one letter to Russell Lasley, vice president and head of anti-discrimination, Wyatt detailed the happenings of a one-day Conference on Job Opportunities for Women sponsored by the PCSW in Washington, D.C., in September of 1962. She included a frank assessment of the PCSW: "My personal opinion is that there is still a wide gap between this group's understanding of what the problems of the total work force are and what some of the more realistic approaches to solving them are."[60] She was a part of a committee who believed, "it is not our job to try to revolutionize the world."[61] This was at odds with the philosophy Wyatt came to embrace as a member of the UPWA, which believed in working peoples' ability to eradicate discrimination from within and outside of the union. Wyatt was used to UPWA women's conferences where working women came together to discuss their status as workers and the unique problems they faced in the workplace and often outside of it. For Wyatt, functioning on a committee designed to recommend policies for working women when only a small minority of those on the committee were in fact working women must have been frustrating.

In the end, the Protective Labor Legislation Committee praised existing legislation, especially minimum wage laws, as instrumental "to the much improved status of women wage earners" and called for their extension where they did not exist, as well as premium pay for overtime work. The committee called for equal pay for comparable work regardless of an employee's sex, better regulation of night work and industrial house work for women, and the establishment of maternity benefits under social insurance and disability programs. The committee saw discrepancies in protective labor legislation enactment as an issue and argued that some laws, including minimum wage laws, overtime compensation, maximum hour laws, workmen's compensation, and collective bargaining rights should be equal and strengthened among male and female workers.[62]

In October of 1963, the PCSW issued its final report, *American Women*, including overall recommendations from the commission as well as individual committee findings and recommendations. According to scholar Dennis Deslippe, *American Women* was "a document wrought with paradoxes" that struggled to stake a place within the burgeoning women's movement and navigate the tension between calling out discrimination against women "without directly endorsing the ERA [equal rights amendment]."[63] The 86-page report explored the problems of American women in the areas of education and counseling, home and community, employment, labor standards, security of basic income, women under the law, and women as citizens. In truth, much of the report was about the problems of working women and inequalities that existed in women's access to decent and equal wages, adequate employment, and barriers to promotion and advancement beyond positions deemed as "women's work." The report also focused on the overall lack of unionized women. Women workers across industries were much less likely to be unionized as compared to men: 13 percent to 30 percent, respectively. Working in largely unorganized industries and in positions that were exempt from the federal minimum wage and hours laws, the commission recommended the extension of federal (protective) employment legislation to service, retail, agriculture, and nonprofit organizational jobs where women were likely to be employed.

In addition, *American Women* recommended paid maternity leaves, federal aid for adult education in order to help women build essential employment skills, state "equal pay for equal work" laws commensurate with the 1963 Equal Pay Law, the extension of unemployment benefits to workers in a wider variety of industries, increased Social Security benefits for widows comparable to the wages of their deceased husbands, and better child-care and community health services for families at all economic levels. Wyatt urged in the *District One Champion*, that the report was just the beginning of a movement that needed to begin: "Women's work must now begin in earnest. . . . Otherwise, the findings and recommendations will gather dust in the file-and-forget department of the Administration." Wyatt urged that UPWA locals study the report and decide which issues are most applicable and urgent for them and work with the community to lobby for legislation that will address the issues. She wrote, "We will implement this report only if we have a broad degree of participation. Both women and men must want to see it done."[64]

The PCSW became a model for state and local commissions across the country. It also helped to galvanize key pieces of legislation like the 1963 Equal Pay Act and Title VII of the 1964 Civil Rights Act prohibiting discrimination in employment. Both of these increased the visibility of working women's issues in the labor movement and boosted women's activism in a variety of sectors. The PCSW was not all that Addie hoped it would be, but her tenure with the commission increased her visibility and allowed her a greater platform from which to work on behalf of working women within both the UPWA and the organized labor movement. As much as Wyatt would have liked to see the PCSW engage itself more with working women on a grassroots level, the political, economic, and social debates that arose around the status of women, especially the debate over protective legislation versus equality, sparked in Wyatt a greater need to hone her own philosophical understandings of the basis for gender equality in the workplace and in society.

Wyatt went on to serve on the Illinois Commission on the Status of Women for three terms over the course of the 1960s and early 1970s. She became a widely sought after speaker for conferences and meetings on equal employment and working women—from the White House to unions across the country. She continued to champion women's issues in the UPWA, but was at a critical juncture in terms of which strategies and solutions could best solve working women's problems. In the debate over equality versus difference and whether protective labor legislation was a help or hindrance to working women, Wyatt believed that "equality is important, and some of the protective laws are obsolete, but they must not be abolished unless adequate substitutions are passed."[65] She recognized that in reality, women performed triple duty at work, in the home, and in their communities and needed protection against excessive work hours and dangerous working conditions. At the same time, protective legislation laws often impeded women's equality on the job and did nothing to remedy unequal pay, lack of promotions, and other drawbacks; therefore federal legislation in was still required in the form of Title VII of the Civil Rights Act and the creation of the EEOC. Taking a more nuanced approach, Wyatt cautioned against stripping away all protective legislation, but also seemed open to legislation that might better elevate the status of working women and alleviate discrimination. By the end of the next decade, Wyatt would become a staunch and very vocal supporter of the ERA.

The 1950s and the 1960s were the formative years of Addie Wyatt's labor activism and leadership. If the church was her sacred home, then the labor movement was certainly her secular home. The labor movement was by no means perfect, but Wyatt was proud that the UPWA stood at the forefront of fights against discrimination in labor. The UPWA was a leader in these efforts prior to the civil rights movement and waged a constant battle against discrimination, not only in the community and with employers but among its own membership.[66] Wyatt often stated that in Chicago the labor movement *was* the civil rights movement. If not *the* feminist movement, the labor movement was certainly the vehicle through which working women like Addie Wyatt fought against discrimination and sexism, even while embracing equality and difference as two sides of the same coin for women's advancement and fair treatment.

The UPWA served as a viable training ground for Wyatt and she began to develop a greater understanding of the need to fight against economic poverty, racism, and sexism collectively with others. She developed a deep commitment to the labor movement and believed it was the most effective vehicle to win that fight. Initially reluctant to take on a greater role in the union, by the end of the 1960s, Wyatt was one of the most recognizable figures in Chicago's labor movement and in the struggle for racial, gender, and economic equality. Elected and appointed to key positions of leadership, Wyatt relied upon her intellect and intuition, rhetorical skills, Christian faith, and knowledge of working people's struggles to aid in her work in Chicago, the southern civil rights movement, the NALC, and the PCSW. Though the NALC and PCSW were thoroughly different in their origins, orientation, and composition, each helped Wyatt to further understand the problems of racism, sexism, and economic equality on a national scale. Her participation in both endeavors also cemented her place in the organized labor movement as a leader willing to address and challenge race- and sex-based discrimination.

Wyatt's work with the PCSW also exposed her to the challenges of being a somewhat marginal voice on a national, large-scale commission. The PCSW was far removed from the kinds of grassroots activism and participation among working people and working women specifically, which Wyatt was accustomed to cultivating and utilizing. In many ways, the challenges that Wyatt faced in adjusting to the top-down approach of the PCSW and its limited policy-making abilities would become ever more salient as she rose to greater heights in the labor movement.

Wyatt's experiences as an organizer and leader during this period exposed her to the philosophical differences and commonalities among organizations that advocated for racial and gender equality and economic empowerment. Facing automation, runaway shops, falling membership, and tough union competitors, the UPWA would merge with the larger and more conservative Amalgamated Meat Cutters and Butcher Workmen in 1968. The merger dealt a significant blow to Chicago's progressive labor movement, but it did not spell the end of efforts to reform the house of labor. Addie Wyatt would find a way to continue to develop her own understanding of the ways in which inequality worked to delegitimize the bonds between human beings across race and sex and how best to combat that process.

5

CHALLENGES IN THE HOUSE OF LABOR

In the summer of 1971, a group of notable black Chicago women came together for a one day conference, "Power—What Is It, and How Do We Use It," held at Commonwealth Community Church on the city's South Side. The conference, moderated by Etta Moten Barnett, included a series of guest speakers and panelists from the Chicago Urban League, the National Organization for Women (NOW), and the University of Illinois. The luncheon speaker for the conference was none other than Addie Wyatt. In her address, Wyatt echoed the thrust of the conference, namely that black women already held access to numerous sources of power through their careers, civic participation, and spirituality. Greater power would come through harnessing these resources and tying them to organizations whose missions included increasing the quality of life for women and incorporating them into the decision-making bodies of society. Wyatt offered to the group, "Our country and our world face the darkest hour of the century, beset by many problems, many of them perilous—the vicious war in South Viet Nam in which our boys and husbands are being killed and maimed; environmental pollution, inflation and unemployment—the scarcity of jobs which should signal a warning to us that we are in a crucial period. . . . It is time for women to take a stand! It is time for us to speak out!"[1] Power was about harnessing resources already available but also utilizing those resources to create the kinds of collective organizations and institutions that could best respond to the economic, political, and social challenges of the day. Indeed, much of Wyatt's career during the late 1960s and through the 1970s would involve finding ways to increase her own power and voice in the labor movement in order to aid the cause of increasing the profile, representations, and leadership of minorities and women in the movement. Only by making unions and worker organizations more accountable and representative of their diverse memberships could such organizations thrive and meet labor's challenges.

Addie Wyatt's rise to national prominence in the labor movement continued throughout the 1970s during which she emerged as one of the staunchest voices for working women in the labor movement and in the women's movement. By the end of the decade, Wyatt became one of the highest-ranked women in the organized labor movement when she was appointed as an international Vice President and Director of Women's Affairs for the 550,000-member Amalgamated Meat Cutters and Butcher Workman of North America. Her dedication to the ratification of the highly controversial Equal Rights Amendment (ERA) pushed Wyatt even further to the fore as an outspoken voice for gender equality. In addition, she was a founding member of the Coalition of Black Trade Unionists (CBTU) in 1972 and founder of the Coalition of Labor Union Women (CLUW) in 1974. These events marked a central transformation of Wyatt's development as a nationally recognized labor leader and African American feminist at a time when labor, women's rights activists, and black workers faced challenges to the legitimacy of their struggles. High unemployment, antilabor sentiments and legislation, factionalism within organized labor, and the loss of manufacturing during the 1970s posed severe challenges to the labor movement. Trade union women like Addie Wyatt faced considerable male backlash toward the advancement of women's rights and women's greater participation in the workplace and in society. And while key pieces of civil rights legislation had been enacted to enforce the political and legal equality of blacks, a wide gulf remained between black workers and full equality and representation in the labor movement and society.

In this context, Wyatt becomes an important and compelling figure in our study of the relationships between race, gender, and the organized labor movement. Labor in the 1970s is often cast as a movement incapacitated and near death, hampered by structural economic forces and a widening gulf between its leadership and membership.[2] Yet Addie Wyatt was on the rise as a leader in her union and in the movement. By the end of the decade, her speaking engagements included some forty to fifty events per year before labor and nonlabor audiences eager to hear her prognosis and prescriptions for the organized labor movement and working people. She consistently included calls for greater leadership and representation for women and minority workers as well as a broad plank of state-sponsored economic, political, and social legislation designed to bring about equality in America. This chapter explores Wyatt's specific responses to the challenges of organized labor and the struggle for racial and gender equality within it. Ultimately, Addie Wyatt's commitment to working people, equality, and human dignity defined her roles in the organized labor movement, the women's movement, and the advancement of black Americans. These commitments were reflected in the organizations that she helped to found, participated in, and hoped to make more fully accountable to their constituencies. Her organizational memberships and belief in the righteousness of equality provide significant insight into the ways in which rank-and-file and progressive labor leadership in the 1970s helped to *sustain,* and in some instances grow, an increasingly diverse labor movement despite the real challenges the movement faced.

THE MERGER

In 1968, the UPWA merged with the Amalgamated Meat Cutters and Butcher Workman of North America (hereafter Amalgamated) after years of declining membership and contracts and difficulties navigating a rapidly changing meatpacking industry. Chartered in 1897 under the newly formed American Federation of Labor (AFL), the Amalgamated was originally a union of cattle slaughterers, sausage makers, and hog and sheep butchers. The Amalgamated had a primarily white male membership and struggled with racial tensions. During an unsuccessful six-week strike in 1904, meatpacking companies brought in African Americans from the South as scab labor and housed them in parts of the plant to shield them from striking workers.[3] The union lost 75,000 members as a result of the strike, which crippled its membership. In 1917, the union moved its international headquarters from New York to Chicago, the new center of the nation's meatpacking production. By 1919, the Amalgamated successfully increased its membership to 100,000.

The UPWA and the Amalgamated often competed in organizing workers in the meatpacking industry, and the actions of the Amalgamated in the 1948 strike left a bitter taste in the mouths of UPWA members and staff. Both unions encountered major challenges to their collective bargaining power and membership, one of which was automation. Automation resulted in the loss of thousands of jobs and contracts for meatpacking unions as early as 1949. In 1953, the UPWA and the Amalgamated entered into a pact to engage in joint negotiations with the packers, to disclose and exchange collective bargaining information with one another, to seek approval for contracts, and to respect each other's picket lines.[4] The pact intended to give each union a leg up in contract negotiations as well as stave off competition. The meatpacking industry was not the only industry to experience automation. A number of scholars have written about the effect of automation in American industry since the 1950s. Most notably, historian Thomas Sugrue argues that automation was attractive to automobile manufacturing companies because it provided the possibility of increasing output and production while reducing labor costs.[5] Ultimately, the reduction in labor costs entailed the loss of thousands of jobs for black and white workers in Detroit, as well as the flight of secure jobs from the city. This led to greater contestation over remaining jobs and more intense racial discrimination despite the efforts of blacks, labor unions, and community institutions against such practices. While

Sugrue focused primarily on race, women in the auto industry also faced greater discrimination as a result of the greater contestation over remaining jobs. Just as Wyatt worked with members of the UPWA to reallocate jobs for women whose entire departments had been automated, women in the auto industry similarly fell victim to automation of their entire departments and the loss of work.[6] In addition to the meatpacking and auto industries, steel, textile, and a number of other manufacturing industries faced similar challenges to their membership and bargaining power as a result of automation.

In the case of the UPWA, additional factors beyond automation led to its dissolution. The flight of jobs and industry, changes in government regulations in food production safety, a lack of plant modernization, an inability to respond to technological advancements, and the rise of meatpacking corporate conglomerates and greater antilabor sentiments all contributed to the merger with the Amalgamated. In the UPWA, the term "runaway shops" came to signify the flight of meatpacking giants like Swift, Wilson, Armour, and Cudahy from the Chicago stockyards, seemingly overnight, to rural areas of the South and Midwest. Combined with the rise of independent plants like Iowa Beef Processing, Inc. (IBP) in 1960, the terrain upon which unions needed to organize shifted sharply to populations of younger, rural, more transient, less union-oriented, and often immigrant workers. It was difficult for the UPWA to organize the unorganized with a shadow of the membership and finances it previously possessed for conducting long and difficult organizing campaigns. Les Orear, a founding UPWA member and an international staff member in both the UPWA and Amalgamated, believed that organizing efforts were made even more difficult by the union's responsibility to protect and renegotiate contracts for its current membership, which was growing older and more concerned with protecting job security and benefits they had struggled mightily to procure and maintain and less interested in organizing the unorganized.[7]

These factors and others dealt significant blows to the viability of the UPWA. A merger with the Amalgamated became an attractive option despite fears of becoming incorporated into a union not nearly as progressive, heterogeneous, or committed to training labor leaders from the bottom up. Many UPWA members saw the merger as necessary, but they feared the inevitable "clash of cultures" between the two unions and wondered if and how the UPWA's philosophy of interracial social unionism would fare among a much larger, more conservative membership and bureaucratic labor leadership.[8] The Amalgamated had broadened its reach beyond the shop floor into the grocery and retail markets. With the birth of chain stores during the Depression era, the Amalgamated expanded its organizing efforts to gain contracts with major chain retailers such as Kroger, Safeway, A&P, and the National Meat Dealers Association—a move that ultimately proved beneficial to the union.[9] As more and more plants closed in Chicago and in urban centers across the nation, the Amalgamated felt less of the blow because of its presence in an expanding grocery and retail market.

The merger agreement between the UPWA and the Amalgamated argued that a changing political and economic climate in the country, decreased numbers of organized workers, factions and divisions within organized labor, and a greater "concentration of corporate strength and economic power in the hands of great conglomerates of industry" contributed to an environment for labor that was more and more hostile. Therefore, unions needed to work together to increase their strength and bargain with more powerful and profitable employers. Workers needed "to bargain for their fair share of the proceeds of the great increases in man-hour productivity that new technology is producing daily." The new Amalgamated would represent a union with the strength of over half a million workers in meatpacking and "believed that with a single voice, they could fare better in the packing, food and grocery industries."[10]

ADDIE WYATT, THE AMALGAMATED, AND THE PUSH FOR A WOMEN'S AFFAIRS DEPARTMENT

For UPWA members, the dissolution of the union that they had worked to build and mold into an organization concerned about the total lives of workers within and outside of the plant, was devastating. But it did not spell the end of their loyalty to the labor movement or their union. Trade unionists like Addie Wyatt, Charles Hayes, and others remained committed to antidiscrimination in the Amalgamated, to greater participation and leadership opportunities of women and minorities in unions, and to organizing the unorganized. If endorsed and acted upon within labor, these commitments would increase the number of organized workers and strengthen the bargaining power and collective fate of workers in the Amalgamated. The core of the UPWA's progressive and radical contingency sought to spread their philosophies and strategies of interracial social unionism and greater participation, representation, and leadership on the part of women and minority workers in the Amalgamated. They would face considerable challenges, as UPWA members made up only about 10 percent of the newly merged union. The new Amalgamated represented much more than packinghouse workers, including workers in wholesale, retail, slaughtering, sausage, poultry, eggs, food, cannery, fur and leather, dehydrating, food processing, livestock care, fish, sugar, and agriculture. Twenty-one of the twenty-six seats on the Amalgamated's International Executive Board (IEB) were reserved for former Amalgamated leaders, leaving only five seats for former UPWA leaders. Moreover, Ralph Helstein, the dynamic leader of the UPWA, was relegated to the non–policy-making role of special counsel and became one of several international vice presidents on the IEB. He eventually retired in 1972 after just four years in the new union. The top leadership of the newly merged union included the Amalgamated's Thomas J. Lloyd as international president and Patrick Gorman as secretary-treasurer. Well-known for its strong, independent locals, the Amalgamated's international leadership operated in a more supervisory, bureaucratic role.[11] While the UPWA did have strong locals, the district leadership structure and high involvement of Helstein and other international staff in the daily operations, campaigns, and direction of the union stood apart from the structure and flow of the much larger Amalgamated. The new structure of the union and the relationship between rank-and-file members and union leadership would count for only some of the obstacles former UPWA members faced in the Amalgamated.

In the initial years after the merger, Wyatt continued to work under her close friend and mentor, Charles Hayes, as an international field representative and district program coordinator, which included planning conventions and running the district leadership training schools. Hayes remained director of his district (now District 12 under the Amalgamated), which secured him an automatic promotion to international vice president and a seat on the union's International Executive Board. He was one of two blacks on the IEB. Wyatt also coordinated the Committee on Political Education, or COPE, programming in the District. Her responsibilities included alerting District 12 members about important labor legislation as well as critical issues relevant to workers such as health care and civil rights legislation. Her efforts on behalf of COPE began with the UPWA and her role as a member of the PCSW and the Illinois Commission on the Status of Women cemented her status as a labor leader who frequently came into contact with policy makers, politicians, and lobbyists. As an Amalgamated staff member, Wyatt enjoyed a much larger salary and benefits package than she received with the UPWA and worked out of the Amalgamated's headquarters just north of downtown Chicago.

Absorbed into a much larger union, Wyatt spent the majority of her time in the 1970s attempting to raise the profile of working women in their unions and in society at large. This did not mean that she abandoned her commitments to community and interest in community organizing and empowerment. Both through her church, the Vernon Park Church of God, and as a member of Operation Breadbasket, Wyatt maintained a vested interest in the spiritual and economic well-being of black Chicagoans. Operation Breadbasket, an organization originally formed as the economic arm of the SCLC in Chicago, was led by local black ministers, including Addie's husband, Claude Wyatt. The organization targeted businesses in black communities that profited off of blacks but failed to employ them, sell black-owned and manufactured products, or patronize black financial institutions in the community. Breadbasket targeted companies in Chicago such as High-Low Foods, A&P Grocery and the Jewel

Tea Company, to name a few. Breadbasket recognized the economic power of blacks as consumers and producers of key products and sought to harness that power to counteract black unemployment and underemployment. Although led by ministers, the organization attracted a fair number of black trade unionists and labor activists in Chicago and would become an important conduit for organizations like Black Labor Leaders and the Coalition of Black Trade Unionists.

In Breadbasket, Wyatt found success in organizing consumer clubs among black women through churches and community organizations, harnessing the power that they already had as concerned citizens and activists. She also rallied union members and labor activists to demonstrate and, in some cases, boycott companies who refused to negotiate with Operation Breadbasket by providing more jobs for their consumers, placing black-owned and manufactured products on their shelves, hiring black contractors and service companies, or working with local black banks and credit unions, of which Chicago had several. Wyatt's participation in Operation Breadbasket was no doubt fueled by her interests in increasing economic opportunities for workers, especially those who could later be organized into unions, thereby expanding the rank-and-file base of the labor movement. For progressive labor activists like Wyatt, the possibility of increasing the membership and growing the labor movement through organizations like Breadbasket provided alternative ways of combating labor's slow death. But her participation in the organization also reflected the level of determination and organization she felt black communities needed to embrace in the post–civil rights era of black power: "Negroes must begin now to plan ahead—stop allowing Whites to plan for us, excluding us, in the future economics."[12]

Beyond economics, Wyatt worked with black political and civic leaders in Chicago on behalf of police reform in black communities. With Congressman Ralph Metcalfe and Reverend Jesse Jackson, Wyatt frequently spoke out against police brutality in rallies, demonstrations, and organizations founded to better protect and ensure the rights of black citizens vis-à-vis Chicago's notorious police force. She also participated in women's organizations such as the Chicago chapter of NOW and black women's community organizations like the League of Black Women, founded in Chicago by Arnita Boswell in 1971. The League was comprised of professional and nonprofessional black women who endeavored to improve the lives of black women and their communities through education, charity, political awareness, job placement, and health and wellness programming. Wyatt continued to work with other black labor leaders to improve the working conditions and power of blacks within the labor movement and to make the labor movement more inclusive and representative of its black workforce.

Ultimately, it was the plight and status of women workers within and outside of the organized labor movement that garnered the bulk of Addie Wyatt's attention and activism during the 1970s. Her primary goal was to increase her stature and the status of working women in the Amalgamated. In 1972, she decided to run for an open vice presidency position, which would ensure her a spot on the IEB. If elected, she would become the first female international vice president in the history of the Amalgamated. Charles Hayes gave Wyatt his support for her candidacy and understood that her primary goal would be to fight for a Women's Affairs Department for the 100,000 women workers in the Amalgamated who formed 20 percent of its membership but had no female representation on the IEB. International Secretary-Treasurer and former Amalgamated President Patrick Gorman supported Wyatt's candidacy but believed she would be an even better fit for a six-member Advisory Council to the Executive Board. Council members would attend IEB meetings but have no voting power.[13]

Gorman envisioned the Advisory Council as sort of an apprenticeship for those seeking board positions where they would be able to gain the experience needed to effectively serve as a board member in the future. Perhaps Gorman supported Wyatt's candidacy but feared that she would not be elected for lack of experience or name recognition in the union, having come from the UPWA. Gorman also hoped that the Advisory Council would be more multicultural and representative of the Amalgamated's ever more diverse membership. If positions on the council were a doorway into the IEB, perhaps Gorman hoped to shape the council in such a way that minority and women council members would have a better chance in representing the union *eventually*. Gorman wrote to Wyatt, "Mexican-Americans, of which we have many outstanding members, should be represented and they are not. Now, with just two Black members on the Board, in terms of numbers it is unthinkable with probably 145 to 150,000 Black members. Months ago, in 'The Butcher Workman,' I suggested that it was about time that women in the organization, numbering over 100,000 should also have representation."[14]

Perhaps Gorman really did believe that the Advisory Council was a necessary stepping stone or gateway for potential executive board candidates like Wyatt who might not have the votes, name recognition, or unspoken physical requirements, such as the proper race and gender. Gorman was respected and trusted in Chicago by black labor leaders because of his support for civil rights, blacks in the movement, and strong labor solidarity. Born in Kentucky in 1892, Gorman joined the Socialist Party at the age of seventeen in Louisville. As a young labor organizer, he broke social conventions and organized interracial chapters of the Amalgamated at a Swift plant in Moultrie, Georgia.[15] He served as president of the international from 1923 to 1942 and then as its international secretary-treasurer until his retirement in the late 1970s. Gorman stood out as an ally for blacks who had come from the UPWA, and he and Wyatt developed a friendship that, although not as close as her friendship with Charles Hayes, was indicative of the female *and* male networks of support that helped Wyatt emerge as a respected voice in the movement. He shared his penchant for writing poetry and music with Wyatt, who was a gifted gospel musician. When Gorman fell ill and was hospitalized in May of 1972, Wyatt visited him with flowers and an ice cream soda. Likewise, Gorman visited Wyatt when she was hospitalized for hypertension in 1974 and 1976. Gorman gave Wyatt his utmost condolences upon the passing of her older brother, Ambrose Cameron Jr., to heart disease in 1971; her younger sister, Edna Turner, in 1973; and a younger brother, Bluett Cameron, to lung cancer in 1977.

Gorman respected Wyatt as a charismatic and exacting trade unionist. In urging Wyatt to consider an appointment to the Advisory Council, he wrote to her, "I have listened to you as a chairlady and have heard you talk to large gatherings and you equal any. Don't consider this an absolute pledge, but a frank expression of your ability. You have a natural desire, and I have known it for a long time, to serve in a larger capacity and, if I can, I want to be helpful."[16] Gorman acknowledged Wyatt's interests in working on behalf of women in the union, but did not appear to fully grasp or yet support the scope of Wyatt's interests in the creation of a Women's Affairs Department over a reboot of old-school women's auxiliaries. Gorman wrote, "[A]t one time, we had as many as 30 to 40 Ladies Auxiliaries operating quite successfully, chartered by our International Union. I don't believe there is one left. There is a responsibility, I feel, for getting the women, the wives and daughters of our membership, more interested in our organization and more interested in the problems that affect the people—more interested, frankly in the trade union movement, a good portion of which is almost dead."[17] But what of the women *in* the Amalgamated who needed to be unionized or whose participation in their unions needed to be validated and recognized?

Gorman thought highly of Wyatt and sought to persuade her to consider an appointment to the Council, but Wyatt was determined to seek the vice presidency position and push forward a resolution for the creation of a Women's Affairs Department. This was risky for Wyatt. She had the support of Charles Hayes and some rank-and-file members, but Gorman, other leaders, and the larger constituency of the Amalgamated could not be counted on to vote for her. Moreover, in order to run for an open vice presidency position and to push a women's affairs resolution, Wyatt would have to tender her resignation as a staff member and international representative in order to be a delegate to the Amalgamated's 1972 International Convention in Miami. Gorman indicated that a position on the Advisory Council combined with working to reboot the women's auxiliaries would allow her to keep her twenty years of seniority and salary, but she would still need to formally resign from the General Organizing Assembly or GOA, the structural body within the union for its staff.[18]

Correspondence between Wyatt, Gorman, and Hayes over the summer and early fall of 1972 indicates that Wyatt continued to push for election to the IEB and a Women's Affairs Department over a position on the Advisory Council.

Charles Hayes supported her and wrote to Gorman on Wyatt's behalf. Hayes argued that Wyatt's main concern was for women's affairs and that a spot on the Advisory Council "wouldn't do it in terms of women's issues." He supported the creation of a Women's Affairs Department with Wyatt as its head and even offered the names of others who could be nominated to the Advisory Council in her stead. Hayes felt that as a black woman, Wyatt would do well in heading the department and representing the union.[19] Gorman's response was that he still preferred for Addie to sit on the Advisory Council: "She has all the intelligence that a council member should have. She can make as good a speech as anyone of us; perhaps better. She receives invitations from all over the country to address gatherings of national importance and above all, she is a woman—and a Black woman."[20] Gorman likewise noted Wyatt's race and sex and believed that both would serve in the interests of the union by diversifying its leadership or at least its pathways to leadership. In short, Wyatt had support from the top leadership of the union who wanted to see her advance, but in measured steps that were not in her control.

It is likely that the leadership of the Amalgamated had their own candidate for the open vice president position already slated. Unfortunately for Wyatt, she did not receive enough votes at the International Convention and lost the election bid. Rather than lose everything, Wyatt accepted the appointment to the Advisory Council. She and Doris Crane, an Amalgamated woman from Portland, Oregon, were the sole female appointments to the twelve-member council. In an effort to preserve Wyatt's seniority and salary, Gorman gave Wyatt a new title, exempt from the rules concerning staff members, appointments, and elections, as assistant director of the Civil Rights Department under Harry Alston, an African American man and former UPWA staffer. The Civil Rights Department fielded EEOC complaints made by workers against companies for discrimination and against locals for discrimination and lack of representation.[21] Dismayed but not undone by the happenings at the convention, Wyatt was successful in introducing a key resolution calling for the creation of a women's affairs department in the union, one that she hoped to lead. In a letter to Patrick Gorman, Wyatt continued to push for the new department: "Brother Gorman, I have suggested to Brother Hayes and others who have mentioned it to me that since we failed to elect a woman to our Executive Board it would be a step in the right direction to establish a department on women's affairs. This action would certainly be regarded by many of our women as being much more productive in bringing forward future women leaders than the appointment of any woman to the Advisory Council which only meets twice a year."[22]

For Wyatt, the appointment to the Advisory Council was not enough, so she pursued, with a dogged determination, the creation of a women's affairs department. The union needed to create such a program in order to make a much larger, more significant commitment to addressing the problems of women workers in the Amalgamated. She believed that "a program of such depth would not be designed to divide or destroy our present union programs but rather to unify and strengthen them by bringing forth much of our underutilized woman power. If only our leaders of our union could envision the value of such a new thrust—the rewards of dynamic and devoted Amalgamated women would be greater than the investments."[23] According to Wyatt, women were an untapped resource within the union and the labor movement as a whole, whose livelihoods and talents were critical to the survival and growth of the movement. Her mission was twofold: to inspire women to take on a greater role in the function, operation, and leadership of the union by educating them on its processes; and to make the leadership of the union more responsive and accountable to its women workers by supporting key legislation in the way of working women and women's rights on the job and in society.

Wyatt lobbied Amalgamated men and women at conferences, conventions, and meetings for their support of a Women's Affairs Department. Her efforts eventually paid off. Two years after her resolution at the 1972 International Convention, the Women's Affairs Department was established in 1974 with Wyatt as director. Few predominantly male unions like the Amalgamated had autonomous, staffed women's affairs departments during this period. Most had no such department or had too few women members to push for such an entity. Other predominantly male unions folded women's issues into the duties of regular departmental staff or maintained decentralized women's committees at the local union level.[24] With a small office space and one assistant, Wyatt's work to increase the participation, unionization, and representation of over 100,000 women in the union began. The direction and mission of the department was to "establish a positive, relevant and meaningful women's program emanating from the International Union."[25] The department focused on three major areas: getting women involved in unions from the local to the international level, helping them to resolve their in-plant problems through the union structure (as opposed to outside legal action), and training and encouraging women to organize the unorganized and be effective union spokespersons in their communities and in the political arena.[26] Special seminars, workshops, local conferences and the creation of local and district level women's affairs committees were the vehicles through which Wyatt hoped to achieve these goals.

The Amalgamated's District 12, which encompassed the old UPWA's District One, was where women's activities committees flourished. Many were led by active former UPWA members, which made Wyatt's work in expanding the committees to include Amalgamated women somewhat easier. Between 1974 and 1977, Wyatt oversaw the creation and maintenance of twenty-one local women's activities committees and three district-level women's activities committees. About one-third of these committees were in the Midwest, mainly in

Illinois, Indiana. and Michigan. The majority of the rest of the committees were spread out across the East Coast. Just two were located in the South. Wyatt also spoke at local, district, and international meetings about the need for working women's issues and women's rights. She served as a resource for women who had questions about the union's organization and resources as well as the level of its commitment to bringing more women into the fold of the Amalgamated. Wyatt traveled extensively throughout the country helping to organize local committees and educate women on the structure and function of the union and how to integrate pay equity, promotions, child care and health care into bargaining contracts. Wyatt had a considerable amount of autonomy in terms of how she would structure programming and organizing for women through her department but needed International approval for conferences and endeavors that required significant contributions from the Amalgamated.

Requests for Wyatt to address union and nonunion engagements ballooned during the 1970s and were fielded through both the Women's Affairs Department and International Secretary-Treasurer Gorman's office. When Wyatt appeared before Amalgamated's Local 342, International Safety Director Nikolas Abondolo, a member of the local, sang her praises: "I want to extend my own appreciation to you for permitting me to participate in what I considered one of the greatest teaching and learning experiences I ever had. It must be said and will be said, that if Amalgamated would look for someone to do the work that you have been assigned to do, they could find no one better to do it. We have heard nothing but praise from every person leaving our conference and the climax of our day, which was the high point for everyone was the joining of the hands and the reading of the 'gospel,' yes! Sister Wyatt solidarity for everyone." Abondolo also sent a letter to Patrick Gorman, lauding Wyatt's speech: "You will note by the content that over a hundred women, senior citizens and men were overwhelmed with Sister Wyatt's speech and the message she had to bring. I have attended many conferences, rallies and meetings, but I have never been inspired by anyone as I was today by Sister Wyatt."[27]

Gorman believed in Wyatt's charismatic, devoted, and thorough approach to labor unity and the problems of women and minority workers in the movement. In a letter to leaders of a Tel-Aviv labor conference, Gorman conveyed his regret that Wyatt would be unable to attend due to the union's financial constraints. These constraints were due to significant membership losses resulting from high unemployment and a recession in the early 1970s. Gorman gave his regrets to the organizers of the conference: "You pay a wonderful complement [sic] to our Women's Affairs Department Director, Addie Wyatt. There is no doubt she would add something to the meeting in Israel that will be lacking without her. . . . I have the feeling that without her presence something will be missing because she, in my opinion, is the most articulate representative of the trade union movement in the United States so far as knowing her subject and discussing it in a manner that holds the listeners from the beginning to the end."[28] Gorman was typically supportive of Wyatt speaking at non-Amalgamated functions as long as her hosts could contribute financially to her travel and Wyatt remained in the service of her union and the labor movement. Director of Women's Affairs Wyatt became the face of women in the union and her visibility in the Amalgamated and the labor movement increased overall. When international labor leaders and representatives traveled to the United States to better understand the American labor movement or, more specifically, women in the American labor movement, Wyatt's office at the Amalgamated headquarters in Chicago was a stop on their American tour. Wyatt hosted trade union leaders from Japan, Sweden, Italy, Ghana, Senegal, Zaire, the Soviet Union, and many other countries.

As high-profile as the Amalgamated's Women's Affairs Department and Wyatt's appointment as its director were, not all union members saw the new department as necessary. Eugene Utecht, a fellow Advisory Council member, claimed that the Women's Affairs Department created unnecessary divisions in the Amalgamated. In a candid letter to Patrick Gorman, Utecht expressed his concerns ranging from the financial burdens of the new department to whether or not women's programming would be mandatory at all levels of the union. He doubted the department was even needed. Utecht argued that there was no discrimination in his Minnesota local and that workers were treated equally. He wrote, "The very inference of women needing a special group indicates to me there may be an underlying want to break away and to be in a position where they can demand from fellow workers rather than mutually solving problems with both sides receiving equal opportunities. If there is a social fight that needs doing, the women and men in our local pitch in and do it together." Utecht went on to say, "I think that Addie Wyatt is a very energetic, zealous person, who could be a great asset to any International Union if she directed that drive within herself to organizing the unorganized or the concentration of bettering industries within our own International where rates are substandard and conditions are below par without reference to sex. I personally have felt that our civil rights department covered all aspects of the problems dealing with color, creed, sex, etc."[29]

Utecht's criticisms of Wyatt and the formation of the Women's Affairs department appear to be rooted in a number of beliefs. The first was that workers' primary identities and experiences on the job were as laborers and that race, gender, and other identities were secondary. What differences existed between workers paled in significance compared to their similarities and the need to fight as one unit against threats to labor. There was no need to divide men and women by creating local women's committees because men and women in Utecht's local worked well together. To Utecht's knowledge, there were no complaints from the women in his local about discrimination; had there been, the Civil Rights Department would be the appropriate entity to handle such a problem. Utecht believed that Wyatt's vision of the Women's Affairs Department would create problems between men and women, usurp the powers and scope of the locals, and draw much needed resources away from improving the working and economic conditions of all workers in the Amalgamated. Much like criticisms waged against the women's movement, Utecht implied that the Women's Affairs Department did not provide solutions to sexism and discrimination, but was rather an instigator and aggravator of gender strife. For Utecht, the problems faced by women workers were the problems faced by all workers in the Amalgamated as a result of poor working conditions, wages and increased numbers of unorganized workers who needed to be incorporated into the labor movement.

Whether or not Wyatt responded directly to Utecht's criticisms is unknown, but she routinely had to defend and explain the need for the department. In May 1975, Wyatt became the first woman to grace the cover of the Amalgamated's publication, *The Butcher Workman*. In the article featuring her work as Director of Women's Affairs, Wyatt discussed the letters and calls she received from women in Amalgamated locals who supported the department and the creation of specific programming to bring about greater equality and participation of women in the union. Perhaps these were not the women in Utecht's local, but many women in the union craved greater institutional resources to deal with discrimination, sexism, and a lack of attention to women's issues, such as health and medical care, pregnancy leaves, child care, and proper working conditions. These specific issues often applied to women workers in a more direct way, especially pregnancy or women's health issues, and therefore were at the forefront of women's concerns on the job but far too often not at the forefront of the local union's agenda. Women were also seeking ways to become active participants in the movement and not just dues-paying members.

Wyatt stated: "Amalgamated women know that they have made progress because of the union. They know too that banding together in true trade union solidarity will attain for them improved benefits. They know that the men in the union cannot and should not be asked to do the job of achieving progress for all alone. Women are ready to become full partners in the struggle for a decent way of life. Their skills and talents are needed and they are willing to contribute to the union cause."[30] Thus, Wyatt saw the department and her work as director of the department as in line with the goals of labor solidarity. It was her hope that if women played a greater role in the labor movement, they would strengthen its bargaining and staying power and make the movement more accountable to all of its workers. Men could certainly be, and at times served as, allies of women in the labor movement, but the ongoing presence of sexism and discrimination in many locals as well as the workplace rendered women's activities committees and the Women's Affairs Department necessary. Wyatt believed that women needed these spaces to voice their concerns and share with other women. They needed them to gain the skills necessary to become confident leaders. These committees did not have to preclude their participation in the locals but could certainly enhance it.

The union did experience its fair share of discrimination charges brought by women workers, giving credence to the idea that all was not well in the Amalgamated. As head of the Women's Affairs Department, Wyatt was frequently called upon by top Amalgamated leaders to mediate disagreements between women, their employers, and local unions. Though she did not oversee EEOC claims that came to the union, Wyatt worked with Civil Rights Department head Harry Alston on cases that specifically involved women's claims of sex discrimination and harassment. In the late 1970s, she worked on two tough cases. A group of Amalgamated women in Pittsburgh, Pennsylvania, who worked at A&P Grocery chose to partner with an outside organization, Committee to End Sex Exploitation at A&P (CEASE) because they felt that their local unions were not doing enough to address women's discrimination in pay and promotions, inadequate working conditions, and sexual harassment. Working with CEASE, the women filed EEOC charges against A&P and the Amalgamated. Wyatt was brought in to try and convince the women to work within the union to find solutions to their problems and to offer the women the support of the Women's Affairs Department in the future. The case was eventually settled.

Wyatt also traveled to a Swift plant in Dumas, Texas, where she worked alongside Local 775 president, Selestino Morales, and women in the plant to investigate rampant sexual harassment by company officials.[31] Wyatt was eager to serve as an ally and resource for women and local union leaders seeking her support and the support of the union's top leadership. But Wyatt was also frustrated that her two-person office lacked the real administrative and financial resources it needed to be more effective. She wanted to be aware of issues of sex discrimination and sexual harassment *before* they escalated, not after. And the union had to *defend* women's rights, not aid in their abuse. Wyatt was less interested in cleaning up the union's messes than preempting sex discrimination and harassment through education, tough contract clauses, and women's leadership. In this sense, the expansion of women's activities committees and women's representation in the union could only aid in ensuring that women felt they had a voice in the union and could count on the union to give proper address to their issues, thus truly representing their safety and equality before employers.

The Women's Affairs Department received its share of praise and skepticism in the Amalgamated, but Wyatt continued to push forward in pursuing her goals for the department. Expanding the number of women's activities committees at the local and district level did not happen as quickly as Wyatt anticipated, but she experienced relatively more success in this area than with her other goals for the department. One of her most elusive goals included holding a biennial International Women's Convention for the Amalgamated with district-level women's conferences in alternating years. She also called for the creation of an International Women's Advisory Committee comprised of a male and female leader from each district to help implement policies favorable to union women and their increased participation in the union. Wyatt urged better communication between her department and the IEB as well as district and local level leaders whose aid she needed to help form and sustain women's activities committees. Wyatt also requested assurance that the Women's Affairs Department would remain a separate department and not become absorbed into another division. Most of her recommendations were tabled, especially as the Amalgamated contemplated yet another union merger in the late 1970s.

Despite the work that Wyatt felt the Women's Affairs Department still needed to undertake, her efforts on behalf of Amalgamated women and her growing stature in the organized labor movement did not go unnoticed. In 1976, eight years after the merger, two years after the creation of the Women's Affairs Department, and months after being selected as one of *TIME Magazine*'s Women of the Year, Wyatt was elected as an international vice president to the Executive Board of the Amalgamated, its first ever female member and only black woman. She continued to head the Women's Affairs Department, but her spot on the IEB increased her bureaucratic functions. It simultaneously offered Wyatt the opportunity to directly reach the top leadership of the union about pressing women's concerns and roles in the union. For the first time, she held the same position of international vice president as her friend and mentor Charles Hayes and had a seat at the Amalgamated's decision-making table.

Outside of the Amalgamated, Wyatt did not shy away from founding and supporting independent movements of labor constituencies who sought to transform labor beyond their individual unions to make the movement more inclusive and representative of workers of color and women. Expanding the base of economic and political power for working people was paramount, but increasing the access of minority and women workers as important assets to that base was just as critical. Wyatt was a central figure in both the formation of the Coalition of Black Trade Unionists and the Coalition of Labor Union Women movements, which criticized organized labor's lack of enforcement and support of antidiscrimination toward minorities and women but believed that unions held the key to improving the lives of all working people. In many ways, Wyatt's commitment to CBTU and CLUW were not secondary to her work in the Amalgamated but necessary to ensuring democratization and diversification in organized labor, a process that she hoped could make her job of organizing and leading women and men trade unionists less difficult.

THE COALITION OF BLACK TRADE UNIONISTS

In September of 1972, twelve hundred black trade unionists from thirty-seven different AFL-CIO affiliates across the country journeyed to Chicago to discuss their grievances with the leadership of organized labor. The grievances of black trade unionists were many and included a desire for greater black leadership on the AFL-CIO's executive board and at the international, state, and local levels of their affiliates. Black trade unionists also demanded an end to lily-white unions and discrimination in hiring, pay, promotions, and seniority lines. Additionally, they called for better working conditions and a commitment by organized labor to a broader social justice platform. But what precipitated the call for the founding of CBTU was that the AFL-CIO, led by George Meany, chose to remain neutral in the 1972 Presidential election and refused to support Democratic candidate Senator George McGovern. Though the AFL-CIO stopped short of outright endorsing the incumbent President Richard Nixon, black trade unionists interpreted their neutrality as a slap in the face and reasoned that a failure to endorse Senator McGovern was a vote for President Nixon's continued presence in the White House.[32]

The political divide between black trade unionists and the larger labor movement was a major theme at the founding convention of CBTU. Five men—William Lucy (AFSCME), Charles Hayes (Meatcutters), Nelson Edwards (UAW), Cleveland Robinson (District 65), and William Simons (AFT)—formed the executive leadership of CBTU. William "Bill" Lucy, president of CBTU, delivered a pointed speech indicting President Nixon on his record toward African Americans, working people, and organized labor. Lucy argued that black trade unionists could not afford to support a presidential candidate who degraded the poor and unemployed, slowed the progress of civil rights, froze wages, and offered a policy of "benign neglect." Lucy believed in a two-party political system and understood the argument of AFL-CIO leadership and some black trade unionists that neither labor nor blacks should "be in the hip pocket of any single political party." But in this particular presidential election, Lucy and CBTU supporters saw the choice as a clear one for Senator McGovern. McGovern opposed the Vietnam War and denounced "big labor" bosses whose focus remained oriented toward big business and not rank-and-file workers. While McGovern's critique of labor gained the ire of George Meany, it also garnered support from unions like AFSCME, the IUE, UAW, and Retail Clerks who broke with the AFL-CIO and endorsed McGovern over Nixon.[33] Lucy argued that those in the labor movement should particularly be against President Nixon because of his opposition to the 1972 Minimum Wage Bill, his proposed anti-strike legislation for the transportation industry, and his opposition to collective bargaining rights for public employees.[34] Politically, CBTU and the ALF-CIO were at odds.

During this period, black labor leaders (still predominantly male), wrestled for a seat at labor's decision-making table (still predominantly white males). Black labor leaders like Lucy, Hayes, Edwards, Robinson, and Simons held leadership in AFL-CIO affiliates but had no real power to shape the decisions made by George Meany and other top officials. These were decisions that bore heavily upon the livelihood of working-class trade unionists, many of whom were African American. Black trade unionists felt as if their voices had not been heard because they were not adequately represented at the decision-making table. A 1974 study by the *Chicago Reporter* documented the plight of black workers in a multipage feature, "Numbers, but No Clout: Minorities in the Chicago Labor Movement—Many in the Ranks, Few in Leadership."[35] The feature interviewed influential Chicago labor leaders, including Charles Hayes, Addie Wyatt, Timuel Black, Jim Wright, Clara Day, Harry Alston, James Kemp, and Miguel Arias. These leaders cited everything from racism in labor leadership to apathy among black trade unionists to the inability to see civil rights as central to union survival, as problems that minority labor leaders faced.

Harold Rogers, longtime Chicago labor activist, influential CBTU member and close friend of Charles Hayes, recalled the high racial tensions in the AFL-CIO during this period that led to the formation of CBTU. Political differences, continued discrimination in employment and job promotions, and a lack of leadership opportunities in unions helped to fuel blacks' discontent with the AFL-CIO. As Rogers argues, black trade unionists approached racism within the organized labor movement as institutional racism demonstrated by the AFL-CIO's nearly lily-white board. AFL-CIO affiliates continued to discriminate against blacks, Hispanics, and Asians in employment and unionization without the sanction of the AFL-CIO even though such actions were in direct violation of its antidiscrimination policies.[36] As blacks in the movement saw it, organized labor had failed in incorporating black workers into the movement and was not at all concerned with the fate of the 15 percent of its membership who happened to be black.

CBTU was not, however, the first gathering of black trade unionists at odds with the direction of the AFL-CIO on political and discriminatory practices. Twelve years prior in 1960, A. Philip Randolph and other black trade unionists formed the Negro American Labor Council (NALC), discussed previously. The founding mission of the NALC was "to fight and work for the implementation and strengthening of civil rights in the AFL-CIO and all other bona fide unions" along with increasing the numbers of blacks in unions, opening up lily-white unions to blacks, increasing opportunities for employment and promotion on the job, and encouraging blacks to become more active in all levels and areas of the union.[37] Local NALC chapters dictated the direction and scope of the organization. Militant chapters like the Chicago chapter waged a public war against racism and discrimination in organized labor by staging demonstrations against racist employers and locals, which gained the ire of George Meany. He denounced the NALC as a "form of dual unionism, black separatism and black nationalism."[38] Ultimately, Randolph resigned his presidency in the NALC, citing that the organization had become infiltrated by Communist separatists. The work of the NALC was delegitimized and the internal struggles within the organization, combined with declining membership and funds, led to an organization that was but a shadow of its former self. Randolph went on to found another organization in 1965 with friend and movement activist, Bayard Rustin, called the A. Philip Randolph Institute (APRI) which then took on the role of civil rights watchdog in the labor movement.[39] Later, the APRI and the CBTU would bump heads over CBTU's militantism and perceived antagonism toward the AFL-CIO.

Left with the legacy of a militant NALC chapter, black trade unionists in Chicago, the founding site of the CBTU, continued to fight for labor while fighting against discrimination within its ranks. In hotly contested elections in the city in the 1960s and 1970s, militant black trade unionists like Addie Wyatt, Charles Hayes, and Harold Rogers supported and endorsed the candidacies of black, prolabor congressional candidates, including Gus Savage, Harold Washington, and Ralph Metcalfe, while the predominantly white Chicago trade union movement refused to endorse prolabor black candidates. Politically, black trade unionists in Chicago found themselves at odds with their white counterparts, a division that would lay the foundations for an organization like CBTU. Thus the crux of the formation of CBTU was not just about racism and discrimination in the trade union movement but also divergent politics between black and white unionists. Black trade unionists were unwilling to support or remain neutral toward candidates whose labor and racial politics were questionable. One of Wyatt's close friends, former Olympic medalist and politician Congressman Ralph Metcalfe, addressed unionists at the first annual conference of CBTU: "There is a new black man, and there is a new black woman . . . [and] no longer are we content to be taken for granted. No longer are you to tell us what to do, but you are to discuss with us and we will make our own agreements."[40] Black trade unionists in Chicago also did not wait for labor leadership at the city and state levels to address growing unemployment and the need to expand organizing efforts, especially among blacks.

CBTU's Chicago roots were also born out of Black Labor Leaders, a group that worked closely with Operation Breadbasket as it transitioned to Operation

PUSH in 1971 under the direction of Reverend Jesse Jackson. Hayes was Black Labor Leaders' first president, and the group—including Addie Wyatt, Bob Simpson, and Clara Day of Teamsters, and Jackie Vaughn of the Chicago Teachers Union—aided Breadbasket in its product boycotts and demonstrations across the city. According to Rev. Calvin Morris, who began working as a Breadbasket staff member in 1967, "Labor often came to the rescue of Breadbasket and the SCLC, especially because labor had money. They had membership and they had the money. They had a critical mass, particularly of black laborers. Black laborers supported us because we helped to provide jobs. . . . [T]hey also understood the experience of solidarity that we were trying to build in the community and on the picket line. Through strikes and other organizing, they had the experience and shared that experience and expertise with us."[41] Wyatt's husband, Rev. Claude Wyatt, was a key minister in Breadbasket and the couple often used their church as the headquarters for organizing campaigns. Addie Wyatt, Charles Hayes, and others were influential in encouraging their fellow union members and leadership to lend financial strength to Breadbasket, which helped mobilize blacks around issues of labor and employment in their communities.

The CBTU functioned as an umbrella organization and allowed for blacks from various unions to meet and support each other on common struggles against racism and discrimination in their unions. It also allowed for older, more experienced leaders in the movement to mentor and work with younger blacks who sought leadership roles but lacked the support and training to take on those roles. The organization also helped to bring more blacks into the labor movement and increase the participation of organized black workers. Inherent in the scope of CBTU were ways to sustain and grow the labor movement by training younger blacks, who frequently made up larger proportions of the labor movement, in the art of trade unionism. In many ways, CBTU reflected the kinds of goals that Wyatt and other packinghouse workers had pursued in the UPWA in terms of dismantling discrimination in unions and opening up the doors of equality. CBTU waged a fight against federal and labor budget cuts and for better health services, education, and social service programs for the poor. At the time of its founding, there were nearly three million unorganized black workers. Black youth unemployment hovered around 42 percent and black male unemployment stood at 23 percent.[42] CBTU believed that organized labor could do more to tackle the staggering unemployment in black communities and be more aggressive in organizing unorganized black workers and sought to fill some of that role, believing that unorganized populations formed a vital source of untapped power for a movement under significant assault. This stance often put CBTU in the position of challenging the AFL-CIO and its affiliates to live up to the ideals of solidarity and inclusivity as core labor values. CBTU went on record in support of affirmative action in the labor movement, a move which Wyatt applauded and argued should extend not only to blacks and people of color, but to women as well.

Wyatt was a staunch supporter of affirmative action and believed that in such dire economic times with daily assaults on the labor movement, unions had to be more proactive in fighting unemployment and organizing workers. Wyatt supported the seniority system, but she argued that as long as seniority functioned as a barrier to black and female advancement, the system served as a potential legal and financial liability that could ruin the integrity and longevity of unions:

> What the labor movement is learning today is that it is not enough to adopt a sound and principled policy and to be willing to act against any violation of the policy brought to the attention of the union. It is not even enough that the union itself practiced no discrimination and that its contracts on their face are non-discriminatory. The labor movement today faces a far more affirmative responsibility, a responsibility to engage in active examination of the factual situation that actually exists in each plant the union represents, in each department of the plant, to examine not merely what its contracts say but how they have operated in practice.[43]

Beyond a systematic investigation into the practice and presence of discrimination in plants and unions, employers and organized labor still had to do more. Wyatt went on to argue:

> The unions today are confronted with the responsibility not only to oppose discrimination, but to demand that the employer join with the union in action to remedy the results of past discrimination, in action to invite and encourage the entry of the victims of past discrimination into plants and departments from which they have been barred in the past, and to demand training and promotional programs which will enable them to move upward into positions from which they have been barred in the past. . . . [T]hese actions are not only right as a matter of principle, they are essential as a matter of protection of the integrity of our seniority systems.[44]

For Wyatt, organized labor could not afford to continue its benign neglect of minority and women workers, nor could it actively stand by and endorse its seniority, placement, and promotion programs which systematically barred and overlooked capable workers who happened to be minorities and/or women. Across the country, as a result of EEOC and other antidiscrimination legislation, women and minority workers were filing suits against companies and unions calling into question the legality of longstanding lily-white and "lily-male" lines of seniority.

In addition to affirmative action in the workplace, the right to assert their leadership and have their voices heard was a principle concern and organizing point for CBTU. Similar to the defunct NALC, the CBTU saw itself as an organization for the improvement of black workers within organized labor as well as an organization that kept the well-being of the black community in mind. While CBTU actively distanced itself from the role of a civil rights organization, the organization made its attempts to bridge the plight of black workers in the labor movement to broader concerns about the economic and political struggles of black and poor families. Black trade unionists in CBTU saw unions as largely responsible for the creation and sustainment of a strong black middle class.[45] Therefore, black unionists played integral roles in their communities. CBTU sought to "work cooperatively and actively with church, social, civic, education and civil rights organizations to improve the living conditions of black and poor families, and that black trade unionists seek out opportunities to serve on local boards and commissions in order to maximize the participation and influence of black and poor workers in community decision-making."[46]

Not all blacks in labor applauded the formation of CBTU and accepted its calls for collaboration and cooperation. The CBTU became known as a militant black labor organization, and was viewed by some as a threat to organized labor. When CBTU leadership reached out to Bayard Rustin and APRI to work on several initiatives in 1976, Rustin declined, citing differences in the missions and strategies of the two organizations. Rustin wrote, "we see our public role as one of defense and support of organized labor. . . . If there is a problem with a union that requires our attention, we deal directly with that union; we do not air our disagreements in the press or in the public . . . [and] we are most careful to abstain from publicly criticizing any black trade union leaders whether they be members of the AFL-CIO executive council or members of the CBTU." Rustin continued to lay out the differences between the two organizations: "You have taken the position that it is the responsibility of CBTU to be a vocal and public critic of the established trade union movement and its leadership on issues on which you disagree. You furthermore have taken the position that—at least in the past—that you have the obligation to criticize other blacks who are members of or associated with the established labor movement including the A. Philip Randolph Institute."[47] Rustin believed that although both organizations wanted to make labor more inclusive of African Americans, their strategies and approaches were irrevocably at odds. Rustin charged that CBTU lacked a certain level of discretion and loyalty to the AFL-CIO.

CBTU President William Lucy responded to Rustin and decided to set the record straight on CBTU's role in the labor movement: "The impulse for the formation of CBTU was provided when the AFL-CIO Executive Council voted for a position of neutrality in the last presidential election. CBTU firmly believes that the black worker has and must exercise the right of choice." He went on to argue, "The CBTU has no intention whatsoever of weakening the labor movement, to the contrary, the more success we have the stronger the labor movement. The major difference being that the black worker will have a greater and more effective voice."[48] Lucy cast CBTU as an organization that was loyal to organized labor but willing to do whatever it took to strengthen the movement and the conditions for African Americans within it. Sometimes, this meant justly criticizing the AFL-CIO. Unlike the APRI, the CBTU operated independently and received no financial support from the AFL-CIO in its early years.

Despite critiques of its relationship to the overall labor movement and the fact that the AFL-CIO and many of its affiliates failed to recognize CBTU, local and statewide chapters of CBTU emerged across the country after its founding convention. Politically, these chapters sought favorable labor legislation and lobbied for passage of the ERA and an expanded minimum wage. The organization successfully backed Charles Hayes's candidacy for U.S. Congress in which he became the first trade unionist elected to Congress. CBTU also supported Alexis Herman's efforts to become the first African American labor secretary. Local CBTU chapters pushed for the election of minority and prolabor politicians, judges, and other elected officials. Organizing, voter registration, and political education by CBTU and black trade unionists in their unions and communities were key to these successful outcomes. At its conventions and local meetings, CBTU members also educated themselves about the benefits and problems of technological innovations, high unemployment, the flight of industry from urban to rural areas, and the rise of huge multinational and transnational corporate conglomerates and their effect on workers.[49] CBTU endeavored to stay ahead of these trends as much as possible by continuing to push for the organizing of unorganized workers, greater attention to the service sector dominated by people of color and women, and an attention and focus to international labor issues. CBTU opposed the Vietnam War, was a major entity behind the economic boycott of South African Apartheid regimes, and went on record in support of African trade unionists.

Few scholars have looked at the formation of CBTU in depth and the organized response to the conditions of black workers in the organized labor movement in the post–civil rights era. Moreover, the presence of active black women trade unionists cannot be discounted as crucial to the early and ongoing success of CBTU. Wyatt credits herself with inspiring CBTU: "The Coalition of Black Trade Unionists, to tell the truth, was started by me, . . . Every Wednesday we met at the Packinghouse. On Wednesday we met together and that was to try to encourage the brothers. The brothers had a hard time because they didn't have [the] strength and support that they needed. We had to build that strength and support and to encourage them to hold on."[50] These were men who were employed and served as local leaders in various AFL-CIO affiliates: "They didn't have pull through the leadership and they were leaders, most of them were leaders but could not take hold of the leadership. Most of the leadership was by white leaders. But we would encourage them that we had the right to leadership."[51] Bob Simpson of the Teamsters and later president of CBTU's Chicago chapter, recalled that Addie Wyatt was a persistent and consistent voice of strength and encouragement at the Wednesday morning meetings of black laborers and the early days of CBTU. Simpson and other black union leaders looked up to Wyatt, Charles Hayes, and blacks who came out of the packinghouse union.[52]

Harold Rogers's impressions of Addie Wyatt were that she had a strong union background but also a strong religious faith and a faith in humanity that inspired people. Having a strong plant background, Wyatt's primary concerns were the day-to-day struggles of working people. Rogers remembered Wyatt to be very calm but also one whose spiritual faith and social consciousness were quite potent and crucial to the trade union movement. Others who brought a similar spiritual foundation and support to CBTU and movement activism were Rev. Willie Barrow, Rev. Jesse Jackson, and Rev. Clay Evans, longtime pastor of Fellowship Missionary Baptist Church in Chicago. CBTU even recognized the important role that faith played in the lives and day-to-day struggles of its membership. From the very start, CBTU implemented a Sunday morning worship service into its conventions, which became, according to Rogers, one of the most well-attended and important components of its annual meeting.

Addie Wyatt was one of the earliest women's rights activists and leaders in Chicago's labor movement. Wyatt was instrumental in pushing for greater numbers of women in such positions as well as pushing for greater female representation on CBTU's executive board and within the organization.[53] In its early years, Rogers remembered CBTU events and conventions being majority male. It was only later in the 1970s and early 1980s that more black women joined CBTU. Black women trade unionists like Wyatt, Clara Day (Teamsters), Ola Kennedy (USWA), Alzada Clark (UFW), Lillian Roberts (AFSCME), Agnes Willis (IUE), and Constance Woodruff (ILGWU) either sat on the organization's leadership council or played pivotal roles in beginning and sustaining local CBTU chapters. Wyatt, along with Anita Patterson, led CBTU's Women's Board for several years and sustained a women's program that included regular women panelists at CBTU conventions as well as workshops on the history and concerns of black women in the labor movement. The organization eventually established an award in Wyatt's name given to dynamic black women trade unionists.

For Wyatt, women had to be actively involved in any movement or organization promoting the interests of working people, including CBTU. The proportion of women and minority workers in the labor movement increased over the course of the 1970s, the exact moment which many scholars have labeled the period of labor's death and demise. Progressive labor activists like Wyatt were no doubt aware of the challenges that labor faced, but they also saw untapped potential with the increase of women and minority workers. An increase that could be key to sustaining and growing the labor movement by unionizing organized workers and increasing the appeal of unions as true democratic entities to new workers. Both CBTU and CLUW held the capacity to function in these critical roles. Their constituencies wanted to see themselves and their concerns better reflected in the leadership and representation of the labor movement. Necessarily, the fight for equality and fairness in the workplace and in the unions required workers to respond with strategies and solutions for procuring a more equitable movement. For Wyatt, the creation of a Women's Affairs Department in the Amalgamated, the founding and early success of CBTU and the birth of CLUW as an organization for labor union women served as her responses to the challenges within organized labor.

THE COALITION OF LABOR UNION WOMEN

The mission and purpose of the Coalition of Labor Union Women in many ways mirrored that of CBTU. Both organizations demonstrated a belief in the idea that unions could and should be the best avenues through which to overcome discrimination and neglect. Both CBTU and CLUW remained loyal to organized labor while criticizing its lack of inclusivity and equality among women workers and workers of color. As such, the missions of both organizations spoke to Wyatt's own beliefs about the potential power of the labor movement and the promise of equality and solidarity among its rank-and-file members. Many trade union women felt as if their concerns were not being fully addressed within the labor movement. More unorganized women needed to be organized, and organized women needed to become more visible and increase their participation in unions. While there were two black members on the AFL-CIO's Executive Council, there were no women, and the demographics of the council closely resembled the demographics of many AFL-CIO affiliates where women had difficulty rising to leadership positions beyond the local level. According to Wyatt, "We did not have women at the table in the labor movement speaking for women on the economic issues. We had to get them there, to train them and to be sure that they were inspired and willing to be a part of the struggle for better jobs and working conditions."[54] Moreover, few trade union women were visible in the burgeoning feminist movement. In addition to the problems of representation and leadership, too often organized (and unorganized) women were placed in sex-segregated jobs categorized as semi- or unskilled work, resulting in less pay and fewer opportunities for promotion. In addition, dual seniority lists and structures like the UPWA's defunct ABC system allowed for the continued segregation and lack of opportunities for women in the workplace. A lack of paid and unpaid maternity leave, sexual harassment, and inadequate health and medical benefits also fueled the need for a stronger voice for union women.

While CBTU had predecessor organizations like the NALC, there had never been a national organization devoted to the issues of working women in the organized labor movement. Regional women's organizations such as WAGE on the West Coast, the short-lived United Union Women out of the Midwest, and various women's caucuses formed in local and international unions represented women in labor at one time or another. Women leaders in the UAW, Amalgamated Meat Cutters, Amalgamated Clothing Workers of America, Teamsters, and other unions began corresponding about such an organization as early as 1971. The core group of union women leaders involved in these exchanges had been active in their unions since the 1940s and 1950s and included women like Addie Wyatt, Olga Madar, Clara Day, Edith Van Horn, Gloria Johnson, Myra Wolfgang, and Dorothy Haener. Wyatt captured the aspirations of CLUW's founders: "There were women's political caucuses, NOW [National Organization for Women], and church women's groups that were formed, but we had no trade union women's group. We thought it was time for one. We could see the women's movement moving and surfacing as it had never done before and we knew that we had to be a part of it."[55] CLUW's organizers envisioned a coalition that would connect and mobilize women from different unions across the country and give voice to the problems of working women in the labor movement while providing a voice for organized working women in the feminist movement.

Beginning in the summer of 1973, CLUW's founders organized a series of regional conferences for trade union women in order to gauge their interest in such an organization. Addie Wyatt and Edith Van Horn served as the cochairs of the Midwest Conference of Trade Union Women Leaders in Chicago in June of 1973. The conference included sessions on economic security, upgrading women in unions, and on-the-job, legislative action around the ERA, minimum wage, child care, and national health insurance. One of the most well-known feminists of the time, Gloria Steinem, attended the conference as a special guest. The women in attendance revealed their frustrations with the lack of union interest in negotiating women's issues as part of the collective bargaining process, including child care, paid pregnancy leave, and contraception as a medical benefit. Betty Robinson, a UAW member from Indiana, revealed that even though her local had a women's activities committee, women still needed to get permission from the men to put on programming. In her opinion, women needed their own organization, run by women. Mollie West of the Chicago Typographical Union stated, "Our union has a small minority of women, and active women have a hard time. You start out by being a joke, graduate to being a nuisance, then a pain in the neck, and then if you get elected, a threat."[56] The experiences of Robinson and West were eerily similar to the experiences of women seeking to become active in the UPWA in the 1940s and 1950s, revealing that while strides had been made in incorporating women into the union structure, unions were still dominated by a male culture and power structure. Other women at the Midwest regional meeting agreed with conference organizers that the problems and concerns of working women needed to be addressed within the labor movement, as opposed to within "women's lib groups." Trade union women had to become more involved in their local union meetings and conferences and attempt to gain policy-making posts in order to address their problems. A national organization could go a long way in providing resources and training for union women seeking to become more active.

The women in attendance at the Midwest Conference were overwhelmingly in support of a national organization, but Wyatt warned them that the road ahead would not be easy. Drawing from her own experiences as a female leader in the UPWA and the Amalgamated, Wyatt assured the women that they would be labeled troublemakers, separatists, and supporters of dual unionism for their efforts. But they had to remain steadfast in their commitments to women's issues and not be persuaded to give up the fight once they returned to their locals. At the New York Trade Union Women Conference in January of 1974, Wyatt gave the keynote address where she declared that a national organization would not be a threat to the labor movement. She stated, "I am one that is in total support of the labor movement and I want the record to show it. . . . [L]et the record show that our intent and our goals are to build a labor movement stronger than we ever had before. Our objectives must be to build it and not destroy it, to unify it where it has been divided, and to strengthen the participation of women members at all levels of the trade union movement. That's really what we're about." She went on to reveal, "I would be the first to say that I have not always been happy and satisfied with the things the union did. But I've never been so dissatisfied that I thought I would desert it. In spite of the weaknesses of the labor movement, its strength is much greater. It is the strongest instrument working people have to achieve their economic, political and social goals."[57] Wyatt encouraged those in attendance to attend the CLUW's first national conference in downtown Chicago that spring.

CLUW's leadership had little to no funds for the conference and relied on personal friends and contacts for meeting space at the Pick Hotel and refreshments for attendees. Addie Wyatt and Edith Van Horn again served as conference cochairs. In addition to her day-to-day responsibilities with the Amalgamated, Wyatt worked tirelessly, corresponding with the other organizers and planning the conference agenda. CLUW's organizers expected 1,500 women to attend the conference based on registrations, but twice as many women showed up on the first day of the conference. Three thousand women represented fifty-eight different unions. Over half were attending a conference for women or trade union women for the first time and nearly one quarter were African American.[58] The conference included sessions on the structure of unions, the problems of working women in the organized labor movement, and how women could gain the training needed to take on greater responsibilities and leadership in the union. Wyatt believed that women were good organizers in many areas of society including in their communities and churches and that those organizational skills needed to be translated to the art of trade unionism.[59] Only with greater visibility, stake and say in the direction of the union could women bring their concerns to the fore and push for solutions.

CLUW's organizational structure included a National Executive Board with Olga Madar of the UAW as founding president, Addie Wyatt as national executive vice president, Linda Tarr of AFSCME as secretary, and Gloria Johnson of the International Union of Electrical Workers as treasurer. The executive board also included four regional vice presidents: Joyce Miller (East Coast), Clara Day (Midwest), Dana Dunham (South), and Elinor Glenn (West Coast).[60] As scholar Silke Roth argues, many of CLUW's top officers were full-time union officers in their labor unions, which gave CLUW some clout as a bona fide women's group within the labor movement. A 200-member National Officers Council helped democratize the organization and determine its direction. Local chapters, elected state officers, standing committees, and special task forces rounded out CLUW's structure. Eventually, the organization would hire its own staff and develop a research and education center as well as a regular newsletter.

The organization had four main areas of concern that comprised its mission: to organize the unorganized; to seek and support affirmative action in the workplace and obtain equal rights for women in hiring, promotion, classification and pay; to encourage women to play a more active role in legislative and political processes; and to increase the participation of women within their unions. CLUW lobbied for better child-care facilities funded at the state and federal level, an adequate minimum wage, better health care for women, updated OSHA standards for women, and full employment legislation. CLUW also supported abortion rights, an end to sexual harassment in the workplace, better services and support for victims of domestic violence, and a shorter work week with no reduction in pay. Some of these initiatives would better the working conditions of all workers irrespective of gender, while others were geared toward specific problems that women faced. But all were framed as issues critical to improving the lives of working women in the organized labor movement.

CLUW served as a bridging organization that connected the issues of working women within the feminist movement to gender bias and gender discrimination within the organized labor movement.[61] But tensions within CLUW began as soon as the coalition got off of the ground. While 3,000 had attended the founding convention, three years later the organization had a membership of only 3,500. Difficulties in keeping track of membership at the local, state, and national level were cited as part of the reason, but ideological divisions within CLUW were surely a culprit. CLUW was not founded as an independent collective bargaining entity for women that would rival other unions. It was founded as a mobilizing coalition for women and a watchdog for discrimination and gender inequality in organized labor.

CLUW's loyalty to the AFL-CIO and resistance to forming a separate women's entity drew the ire of more radical women in organized labor who saw CLUW as a tool for high-ranking women in the movement to advance themselves. These women criticized CLUW's leadership as being out of touch and not invested in the true needs of rank-and-file women.[62] A power struggle ensued in its early years between members who wanted CLUW to become a women's union and CLUW's leadership who disagreed with such a move. Wyatt recalled:

> Even though the unions had not given the kind of recognition and support that women required, still the union was the best channel through which we could win our objectives and we were content to remain within the structure. Therefore we denied those who thought we could serve our best interest by forming women's unions. Some of us had come through that already. There were those who thought that blacks ought to form black unions and we strongly took a position that blacks had to remain within the mainstream of the labor movement and whatever problems they had would be dealt with by labor.[63]

CLUW faced a serious dilemma. While it wanted to be an organization for all trade union women, its unwillingness to completely break away from the AFL-CIO resulted in the loss of more radical women who possessed the very leadership skills and conviction CLUW needed to bring its many goals to fruition.

The fact that the organization already had a set structure and mission did not sit well with some attendees at the first national conference. Ceil Poirier, a member of the Office and Professional Employees International Union (OPEIU) was disappointed with CLUW from the start. She expected to see only organized women in the labor movement at the conference, but was dismayed to see a number of men, women on welfare, and nonunionized workers in attendance.[64] CLUW leaders later determined that unorganized women could not hold membership in the organization. Only organized women and women in the middle of organizing campaigns could become a part of the organization. Poirier seemed to take less issue with the narrow scope of CLUW than she did with the structure of the conference. She felt as if rank-and-file women in the organization had been railroaded and their voices subsumed under the agenda of the conference leaders who dominated the podium and made the final say on important motions and resolutions. In short, she felt as if "CLUW leaders conducted the entire conference exactly as the stereotype union bosses would have conducted it."[65] While some women were turned off by the organization in its early years, many rallied around the organization and accepted both its limits and possibilities. By the late 1970s, membership began to increase significantly and by the end of the 1980s, reached well over 10,000.

As national executive vice president of CLUW and as a vocal advocate for women's empowerment in organized labor, Wyatt had a vested stake in the organization and the policies it advocated. She became involved in membership drives and labor education for union women through local and state chapters. In building women's affairs committees in the Amalgamated and speaking to union and labor groups throughout the country, Wyatt never hesitated to discuss CLUW and always had CLUW membership applications on hand. Along with other CLUW officers, Wyatt met with AFL-CIO head George Meany in 1975 to discuss the scope of CLUW and the concerns of labor women, and to campaign for a woman's seat on the AFL-CIO's Executive Council. It would take five years before a woman, Joyce Miller, a member of the ACWA and CLUW's president at the time, would be appointed to the council in 1980. Beyond these efforts to make CLUW a recognized and bona fide organization for labor women, Wyatt lobbied and campaigned for ratification of the ERA and expanded child care for working women and families.

Wyatt's own views on the ERA had changed since her tenure with the President's Commission of the Status of Women (PCSW). While on the PCSW, Wyatt agreed with the majority of her committee members that the ERA might eradicate protective labor legislation already in place for women. Protective labor laws at the state level capped women's work and overtime hours, considered their physical and in some cases intellectual limitations on the job, and monitored their working conditions, supposedly in consideration of their roles as mothers, wives, and homemakers. The debate between working women over the ERA centered in part around whether or not equality and identical treatment of men and women on the job would lead women to lose whatever gains they felt protective labor legislation provided. The catalyst for Wyatt's change in opinion on the ERA was a ruling by the Southern Federal District Court of Illinois, which held that an Illinois law on the books that regulated women to eight hours per day, forty-eight hours per work-week conflicted with the watershed 1964 Civil Rights Act.[66] All across the country, protective labor legislation that targeted women and created gendered legal laws came under fire. The 1964 Civil Rights Act opened up the space for pro-ERA groups who believed that the amendment would finally solidify women's rights under the nation's foremost political document—the U.S. Constitution.

The subsequent dismantling of a number of protective labor laws targeting women due to the laws' violation of Title VII of the 1964 Civil Rights Act rendered such laws moot. Title VII of the 1964 Civil Rights Act prohibits employment discrimination on the basis of race, sex, religion, color, or national origin. Women who believed that they had been discriminated against on the basis of their sex and/or race, challenged that discrimination using the Civil Rights Act. Even under protective labor laws, women faced considerable discrimination in terms of hiring, pay, and promotions as well as inadequate working conditions. With those laws challenged and dismantled under Title VII, some who had been hesitant to support the ERA, like Addie Wyatt, now had less of a reason to oppose it. Others believed that with the dismantling of protective labor laws for women at the state level, federal legislation in the form of a constitutional amendment like the ERA could provide the necessary framework for equal opportunity and treatment in the workplace and beyond. A growing number of lawsuits challenged dual and discriminatory seniority systems, further supporting the move toward equality rather than protectionism in the workplace. While Wyatt did not believe that the ERA would eradicate all forms of discrimination toward women any more than laws banning racial discrimination had done, she believed that passage of the ERA would "at least be a step in the right direction in that it will announce to the nation and to the world that the United States of America has reaffirmed its belief not merely that all men are created equal, but that all PEOPLE are created equal."[67]

Two of Wyatt's close friends reflected the stark divisions among labor women on the ERA and its perceived effects on workplace equality. Olga Madar of the UAW and first president of CLUW supported the ERA and Myra Wolfgang, vice president of the Hotel and Restaurant Employees and Bartenders International Union as well as a founding CLUW member, opposed the ERA. Madar and pro-ERA advocates in the UAW were behind the union's endorsement of the proposed amendment in 1970. That same year, both Madar and Wolfgang testified before the U.S. Senate in support of and against the ERA, respectively. Madar worked in a male-dominated industry where protective labor legislation was perceived as hampering women's abilities to compete with men for jobs and promotion opportunities. Wolfgang worked in a female-dominated service industry where protective labor legislation was perceived as operating in a more beneficial manner by protecting the majority of the workforce. While some scholars have argued that working-class women and women in organized labor were generally against the ERA, the advocacy of CLUW and a number of labor unions illustrate that who supported and opposed the amendment was much more complex and cut across lines of class and socioeconomic status. The divide on the ERA had more to do with whether or not one interpreted equality and identity of treatment as beneficial or detrimental to women and men in the workplace and in everyday life.[68]

In her testimony before the United States Senate, Olga Madar likened the struggle of women to that of blacks for equality and paralleled how the ERA might function as a legal tool for women in the same ways that civil rights leg-islation had for blacks:

> [T]he struggle for women's rights is not unlike the struggle of black Americans for equal rights and opportunity: both are part of the larger struggle for human dignity and the general enhancement of the quality of life; and both are at the mercy of attitudes, values, assumptions and habits of mind—many of them, in the case of women, held unconsciously by many men—which have been taken in, so to speak, with the air people breathe and which cannot be taken out or legislated out of existence by the mere passage of laws. Nevertheless, laws have a considerable influence on behavior, when they are administered well and vig-orously enforced.[69]

From Madar's perspective, the ERA was necessary to begin a transformation in society toward viewing women as having the right to equal opportunity and power, not only as workers but as citizens and, most important, human beings. Madar believed that the ERA was less a threat to American democracy and society than it was an essential element of a democratic nation. Madar argued that the ERA sought not to do away with the fact that men and women were different beings, but to do away with the idea that those differences necessitated the superiority of one group above the other.

Myra Wolfgang testified that the ERA would in fact further jeopardize pro-tective labor legislation, which she believed gave women the greatest chance at equality. Protective labor legislation laws needed only to be strengthened and enforced more consistently in order to advance working women. Wolfgang believed it would be difficult to enforce an amendment like the ERA, which did not "require promotion of women to better or 'decision-making jobs.' It does not elect more women to public office. It does not convince men to help with the housework" but would more likely have the effect of making women responsibility for contributing half of all financial responsibilities in the home and for the family.[70] Wolfgang believed that feminists and women's liberation groups had unduly influenced Congress to pass the amendment. She argued that women achieved greater equality through the recognition of gender differ-ences that protective labor legislation acknowledged. A law mandating equality between men and women would threaten gender difference and the positive benefits of difference for women.

Despite the ongoing debate over the ERA, between 1970 and 1973, twenty-one unions endorsed the proposed amendment, including the Amalgamated in 1973. The AFL-CIO reversed a long tradition of opposing the ERA and en-dorsed the proposed amendment in 1973 as well, in part due to the strident lobbying of pro-ERA forces, but also because the House and Senate passed the Amendment in 1972 and sent the legislation on to the states for ratification by March 22, 1979. Twenty-two states immediately ratified the amendment in 1972. By 1978, a total of thirty-five states had ratified the ERA, three short of the thirty-eight states needed to ensure its addition to the Constitution. Though dissent on the ERA remained among labor women in CLUW, the organization worked with its state and local chapters to lobby for passage, held labor rallies for the ERA, and produced literature helping to dispel myths about its passage. By 1973, but perhaps even sooner, Wyatt began giving speeches about the need to ratify the proposed amendment in her home state of Illinois where ERA opposition forces were well-organized. She even testified before the Illinois State Senate Executive Committee in 1973 in support of the ERA and worked closely with the Chicago chapter of CLUW to secure more support. Wyatt came to see the ERA as a human right designed to protect both women *and* men from the harmful effects of discrimination. She often told men that as long as women could be hired to perform a job for fewer wages, their own jobs would not be secure and their households would suffer because women were unable to contribute as much economically.[71] If ratified, the ERA could serve to support the legal equality of men and women on the job. At the same time, Wyatt did not abandon her pursuit and support of legislation and policies attentive to men and women's differences, specifically women's status as potential mothers and the very real problems working pregnant women and mothers faced on the job.

In addition to lobbying for the ERA, CLUW took on an active role in lobbying the federal government, employers, and unions to expand access to affordable child care. Wyatt knew that many women entering the workforce in the 1970s did so because they were either the sole providers for their families or essential economic partners in the home. Even those women who worked because they desired to do so might eventually need access to safe, affordable, and convenient child care. The importance of an issue like child care allowed CLUW to gain an even greater support base. An ongoing battle persisted to have maternity-related medical care and leave covered by employer health and benefit plans. Beyond birth, working mothers were often responsible for securing child care. In addition to pushing for maternity and child care as a provision in collective bargaining, Wyatt worked with organizations like Citizens for Day Care, Inc., and the Day Care Crisis Council of the Chicago Area to expand access to child care, ensure the proper conditions of child-care facilities, lobby for child-care legislation and funding, and assist in adult job training for families in need.

For Wyatt, child care was a familial and societal obligation with profound implications: "I think the responsibility of rearing children should be placed upon the shoulders of the man and the woman and the society in which we live, because after a few years if we are productive and successful in the rearing of our children, they can go out in the world and make their own contribution to society."[72] Similar to her stance on ERA, Wyatt saw improvements in child care as equalizing the liberties men and women could enjoy. If a child entered into a productive or unproductive life, society experienced both the rewards and the negative consequences and therefore needed to take a greater role in the rearing of children. Expanded, affordable, and adequate child care was one of the ways in which society could do so. CLUW believed that a nation's investment in child care was a direct indication of that nation's commitment to children and families. In 1977, Wyatt was given paid leave by the Amalgamated to attend a three-week CLUW Childcare Seminar funded by the German Marshall Fund of the United States. Wyatt, along with twenty-three other women including CLUW President Joyce Miller, Millie Jeffrey, Clara Day, Lois Felder, Dorothy Haener, Gloria Johnson, Consuelo Nieto, Muriel Tuteur, and Louise Smothers, traveled to Sweden, Israel, and France to survey each nation's extensive set of child-care policies and programs.

In each nation the women found a "strong national commitment to child-care programs," especially early-childhood education. In contrast to the United States and its heavy focus on individualism, industrial nations with growing female workforces like Sweden, Israel, and France maintained networks of government, private, employer, health, and community-based organizations to provide child care. A combination of taxes, employer benefits, social service funding, and a sliding payment scale on the part of families contributed to the comprehensive child-care programs of each nation. In a perfect world, CLUW would have liked to see universal free child care but its final report from the seminar urged the United States to adopt a national comprehensive child-care policy with a sliding pay scale. The seminar abroad was enlightening for Wyatt. Wyatt's understanding of issues ranging from racism to sexism to family policy planning were no doubt influenced by her international travels and awareness of organized labor on a world scale, an awareness that expanded over the course of the 1970s through her work for the Amalgamated and her participation in CBTU and CLUW. Wyatt continued to learn and then argue that complex problems required complex and comprehensive sets of solutions in order to enhance the quality of human life.

Addie Wyatt believed that without input from, representation for, and leadership by workers across race and gender, the movement with the greatest potential for improving the lives of working people could manifest and harness only a fraction of the power needed to get the job done. Both CBTU and CLUW maintained ties with the AFL-CIO, but this did not mean that both groups were officially accepted within the movement. It would not be until the mid-1990s, and the changing of AFL-CIO leadership with the election of John Sweeney as president, that constituency labor groups like CLUW and CBTU were officially recognized and endorsed by the AFL-CIO. Throughout the 1970s and even into the 1980s, many unions refused to financially support CBTU and CLUW and refused to fund their members' attendance at CBTU and CLUW conventions, conferences, and events. Nevertheless, ground support from rank-and-file union members indicated that there was a need for such organizations and networks of support to combat racism, sexism, and discrimination in the workplace and the AFL-CIO. Despite their limitations, these organizations played essential roles in training generations of black and women trade union leaders, encouraging them to initiate change and claim stakes in a movement that was supposedly near death. The result was tangible benefits to organized labor.

Katie Jordan and Mary Crayton, two African American female unionists, spoke of the ways in which CBTU, CLUW, and Wyatt's contributions and status in labor helped them to better navigate the movement. Jordan worked as a fitter-tailor in a Chicago clothing company beginning in the 1960s. She recalled:

> Becoming a fitter as a Black person was unheard of, one of the executives said it would be over his dead body that a Black person would become a fitter. . . . There were a lot of things going on in that company that did not get straightened out until CLUW came along. They wanted to name all women assistant fitters so that they could pay women less. We said, no, that's not going to work.[73]

Jordan, originally a member of the Amalgamated Clothing Workers of America (later UNITE-HERE), had been active in her workplace fighting for workers' fair pay and promotions through the union. But she felt somewhat alienated at her first few union meetings because there were so few blacks and so few women in attendance and in leadership positions. It was only once she joined CLUW, where she met Addie Wyatt, Clara Day, Barbara Merrill, and other black women, that she even learned about CBTU and its role in bringing together black trade unionists. Jordan "learned what was going on through these women—she didn't get it from her union."[74] For Jordan, organizations like CBTU and CLUW were instrumental in providing a platform and foundation for blacks and women to address grievances. But even more so they created a sense of solidarity for those in the labor movement who felt isolated in their struggles against racism and sexism.

Mary Crayton worked as a staff member and organizer for several different unions beginning in the early 1970s including AFSCME, Service Employees International Union (SEIU), and the Communication Workers of America (CWA), mainly in the South. Crayton became a local president in her own union, the Office of Professional Employees International Union (OPEIU). She was the only African American in her local, and when members learned that she was the sole candidate running against an incumbent who did not want to run again, members called the international headquarters and requested a merger with another local in order to put a halt to the election. It was only when they learned that their union dues would be doubled as a result of the merger that they agreed to have a black woman as their president.[75] Crayton recalled that still in the late 1970s and early 1980s, there were few black women trade union leaders, especially in smaller unions and in the leadership of the AFL-CIO. She first learned of Wyatt through the formation of CLUW:

I had never met her, but I would hear about her all the time. People would talk about her leadership abilities and the work that she was doing with the meatpackers. I would just, any chance I would get to read an article or talk to somebody that knew her, I would take advantage of that. And while I was in New Orleans, because I was the president of the local, I made sure that we were part of the Coalition of Labor Union Women. So I then was able to go to the CLUW conventions and I became a state vice president.[76]

Crayton did not become close to Wyatt; rather, she looked to Wyatt as a mentor from afar, one that she sorely needed as an emerging black female leader in the trade union movement.

It was at a national CLUW conference in the early 1980s when Crayton first met Wyatt. She recalled, "She was so articulate. She was polite. You could tell that she had control of the situation when she would speak and I went to a workshop with her. Like so many others . . . there were so many people wanting to meet her. It wasn't like I was somebody that she knew personally, but she impacted my life so much because I could see the strength in her. She really embodied social justice and economic justice for workers, especially for women."[77] Eventually Crayton was hired as a field representative for the national AFL-CIO's Chicago region in 1987. Three years later, Crayton was appointed by AFL-CIO President Lane Kirkland as its first female region director (Region 7), which comprised New York, New Jersey, Puerto Rico, and the Virgin Islands. Wyatt's struggle and the struggle of other black women in organized labor to become respected voices helped Crayton to deal with her own experiences of isolation, sexism and racism in the movement.

The ongoing presence and growth of CBTU and CLUW attests to the faith and loyalty of thousands of black and women workers to the principles of organized labor. Both organizations arose in the years that many have cast as the period of labor's postwar demise, which requires a reconsideration of labor's modern history inclusive of the legacies of organizations like CBTU and CLUW and the contributions of labor leaders like Addie Wyatt. Both CBTU and CLUW became powerful organizing forces in the labor movement and members believed in the idea that workers should band together in unions in order to improve their lives and sustain the movement. In this respect, their want to transform the union from within is understandable. As an emerging leader in the organized labor movement and the women's movement, Addie Wyatt captured the admiration of up-and-coming trade unionists who were inspired by her commitment to social and economic justice. Trade unions and organized labor ultimately provided a significant and somewhat constant realm of activism and leadership for those who sought a movement with the potential to adequately address the problems of racism, sexism, and economic poverty.

6

A BLACK CHRISTIAN FEMINIST

Addie Wyatt breathed a sigh of relief. After a grueling eight-hour ordination examination by some of the toughest leaders in the Northern Illinois Ministerial Assembly (NIMA) of the Church of God (Anderson, Indiana), she was now an ordained minister. The NIMA credentials committee included prominent African American male ministers Rev. Marcus Morgan, Rev. Charles McLeod, Rev. Willie Wright, and several others. Each grilled Wyatt on everything from the specifics of her call to the ministry to her knowledge of the Bible. Her grasp and understanding of the principles of the Church of God were evaluated. Also scrutinized were Wyatt's letter of ministerial intent, personal testimonial statement, thorough background check, and ministerial endorsements illustrating that she lived a true, clean Christian life adhering and providing witness to the word of God. The examination tested Wyatt's ethical, spiritual, intellectual, and theological fitness for the ministry. Although she successfully passed the formal ordination examination, there was still one final question on the table. Rev. Willie Wright questioned Wyatt: "Do you obey your husband?" To which she pointedly replied, "That has never been a problem with us, we were both obeying the Lord and that took care of that."[1]

The year was 1968 and Wyatt was one of few women nationwide who sought and successfully achieved ordination in the Church of God.[2] Regardless of Rev. Wright's intent behind questioning Wyatt's submission and obedience to her husband, the fact that he felt compelled to raise the question at the examination says much about the state of women's ordination and ideas about the proper role of women in the church and in society. One could argue that Rev. Wright's question was colored by the women's movement gripping the nation in the 1960s, which called for women to protest discrimination; limited economic, political, and social opportunities for advancement; and second-class citizenship as a result of their sex. Wyatt was firmly embedded in this movement. Fears that the women's movement would turn traditional roles between the sexes on their heads and negatively alter gender relations within the family fueled some of the harshest opposition and criticisms of the movement by religious conservatives. But questions about the obedience and submission of women to men had been regularly encountered by women of faith seeking ordination, particularly black women, since the growth of independent black Christian churches in the nineteenth century. Black women of faith such as Maria Stewart, Jarena Lee, Julia Foote, and others faced questions about the veracity and authenticity of their "call" to the ministry and whether they possessed the spiritual, theological, and intellectual ability to minister and lead Christian congregations.[3] The questioning of women's call to the ministry often resulted in the outright denial of their ordination, and in those cases where women were ordained, opportunities to serve as pastor and preach to a congregation were slim.

Perhaps Wright's question about Wyatt's obedience toward her spouse would have been asked of a male candidate for ordination as well. But Wyatt's response to Rev. Wright illustrates a different theological understanding of the role of women in the church and in society.[4] Her response signified to Rev. Wright that both she *and* her husband, Rev. Claude Wyatt Jr., were dually and equally accountable to God above one another and that in following and obeying God's will they were able to perform their roles as husband and wife. Essentially, both were directly accountable to God as individuals and were equal partners in their marriage. Ironically, Wyatt had in a sense "obeyed" her husband, for it was he who convinced her to seek ordination in hopes that ministerial credentials would give her greater authority to speak out and organize against sexism, racism and economic injustice from within the church.[5] Wyatt's response to Rev. Wright sheds light on her theological understanding of women as equal partners in their marriages, families, churches, and society, which became more explicit in her ministry and activism over the course of the 1970s and early 1980s.

Addie Wyatt addressed hundreds of audiences across the nation on the rights and responsibilities of women in the church and in society—as Christians, workers, wives, mothers, voters, leaders, and equal participants in the running of society. Beyond supporting bread-and-butter issues like the ERA and an end to workplace sex and race discrimination, Wyatt believed in the need for a transformation of societal thought on gender roles and the equality of men and women. Likewise, her strong religious faith fueled Wyatt's activism against discrimination and oppression in the labor, civil rights, and women's rights movements because she believed in the humanity and dignity of all people—women included. Wyatt combined a tradition of black Christian women's community and faith-based activism with elements of a liberation theology that she fashioned and honed from not only her religious upbringing, but her experiences as a black woman with racism, sexism, and poverty.

Addie Wyatt believed that all women needed to join in the fight for equality because God commissioned them to be equal partners in society. But she also believed that because black women acutely felt the burdens of sex, race, and class, they needed to be at the forefront of shaping sacred and secular movements for social justice that could aid in the liberation of themselves, their families, and their communities. Wyatt embodied these commitments in her own life, and her ministry offered an alternative to conservative, antifeminist interpretations of the Bible popular among the religious right and opponents of the women's movement. Addie Wyatt's ministry opened up religious spaces and engaged biblical, feminist, racial, and economic conceptualizations of justice and fairness in an attempt to bridge the sacred and secular through the language of equality.

SITUATING REV. ADDIE WYATT WITHIN AFRICAN AMERICAN RELIGIOUS SCHOLARSHIP

The centrality of Wyatt's religious belief to her leadership and activism in social justice movements cannot be overstated. Black women's religiosity and faith-based activism have played critical roles in the formation, sustainment, and structure of freedom movements, community struggles, and black church history. Charles Payne, a historian of the civil rights movement, found that African American women's spirituality fueled their participation in civil rights struggles in Mississippi: "Faith in the Lord made it easier to have faith in the possibility of social change."[6] And in her groundbreaking work *Witnessing and Testifying: Black Women, Religion and Civil Rights*, scholar and theologian Rosetta Ross recovers the extent to which religious faith infused the activism of noted women civil rights activists and leaders like Fannie Lou Hamer, Septima Clark, Ella Baker, and Diane Nash. Elements of both Hamer's and Nash's faiths closely resemble that of Wyatt. Fannie Lou Hamer's practice of infusing prayer, biblical passages and gospel music into civil rights struggles and ability to see the "congruence between civil rights practices and her belief that being Christian meant helping others" became well-known in the movement in much the same way that Wyatt's faith and religiosity were identifiable parts of her labor and community-based activism.[7] Similarly, Diane Nash adapted Rev. James Lawson's principles of nonviolent civil disobedience and consideration of racism and segregation as social sins. Nash viewed her civil rights activism and the movement as the "church" that needed to reach out and redeem the souls of those who chose to discriminate and disrespect the humanity of others.[8]

Wyatt, who was active in some southern civil rights struggles alongside her lifelong friend and fellow preacher, Rev. Willie Barrow, would have had knowledge of these women and the degree to which their beliefs in human dignity bestowed by God influenced their civil rights activism. As a woman operating in male-dominated institutions like the union and the church, Wyatt likely would have identified with Hamer and Nash's struggles to be recognized as leaders in the civil rights movement. However, Wyatt's life has the capacity to reveal the intersections between black women's faith and their participation in other movements, such as the labor movement and the women's movement, which have been far less studied than the relationship between black women, faith, and the civil rights movement. Though scholarship on black women's faith and faith-based activism has increased within recent years,[9] more work needs to be done in order to understand how black women have accepted, questioned, balanced, or attempted to subvert patriarchal notions of power seemingly inherent in Christian ideology and in the leadership of black churches. Moreover, how black women like Wyatt achieve and negotiate spiritual leadership and authority against racism and sexism beyond the church warrants greater study.

Also key to understanding the context of Wyatt's religiosity and theological perspective is the development of three strands of liberation theology—black liberation theology, Christian feminist theology, and womanist theology—all of which emerged beginning in the late 1960s, right around the time of Wyatt's ordination. Although the term was not actually coined until the early 1970s, *liberation theology* originated in the 1950s and 1960s in Catholic churches in Latin America as a result of national political and economic developments across the continent that ignored, displaced, and further impoverished the poorest of society. A push to return to the true meaning and teachings of Christianity as a religion of liberation from poverty and social and economic oppression became fuel for social justice movements.[10] In the United States, liberation theology melded with the social gospel tradition in Christianity that dated back to the nineteenth century. Believers in the social gospel argued that Christianity held the tools for dealing with society's moral, political, and social problems including poverty, corruption, and injustice. The social gospel tradition was perhaps best organized in churches in the late nineteenth and early twentieth centuries but arguably best articulated by civil rights leaders such as Martin Luther King Jr. and Fannie Lou Hamer, whose Christian faith and belief in the social gospel infused their fights against racial injustice and economic poverty.

James Cone, a black seminarian and theologian, was the first to interpret liberation theology from a black Christian perspective as black liberation theology in the late 1960s. For black Americans experiencing racial oppression (often in conjunction with economic poverty), the theme of liberation through the story of the Exodus in the Old Testament and Jesus Christ as liberator of the oppressed in the New Testament lent moral credence to their personal and collective struggles. A black theology of liberation grew "from an identification with the oppressed blacks of America, seeking to interpret the gospel of Jesus in the light of the black condition. It believes that the liberation of the black community *is* God's liberation."[11] Cone believed that prevailing racism in Christian teachings, churches, theological seminaries, and throughout America society went against the social and liberation gospel of Jesus Christ who ministered to and sought to liberate the poor and the oppressed. Cone perceived the silence of white theologians on the issue of racial injustice and their lack of involvement with black liberation struggles as a betrayal to Christianity's core teachings, echoing the sentiments of Martin Luther King Jr. in his "Letter from Birmingham Jail." Black liberation theology, a theology of relevance, utilized the theme of liberation for the historical and contemporary context black Americans found themselves in. Cone hoped that his indictment of white theologians would bring about some change within the seminaries and mainstream Christianity, but he also hoped that black churches and black clergy would embrace black liberation theology and become more involved with the plight of black communities in the post–civil rights era.[12]

Feminist theologians, most notably Rosemary Ruether and Mary Daly, emerged during the same era in which the women's liberation movement and second-wave feminism permeated every area of society. Feminist theologians interpreted liberation theology from a gendered, feminist perspective, and they questioned if and how one could situate women's equality and feminism within the teachings of Christianity. Both Ruether and Daly pointed to the long history of women's subordination in the church and the church's abject silence or biblical defense of women's oppression as proof of long-standing patriarchy. Some feminist theologians sought to appropriate Jesus Christ as a true feminist for his recognition of women in the Bible as persons of faith worthy of recognition, praise, and the privilege of witnessing his ministry and resurrection. Others questioned passages in the Bible utilized to corroborate women's subordination in the church and society and lambasted the relative lack of women in the Bible. But they still viewed Jesus Christ as a liberator on the side of the oppressed and, in identifying women as an oppressed group, believed that Jesus Christ would be on the side of women's liberation from all oppression.[13] Feminist theologians posed the question: If Jesus Christ recognized women as Christians and as full human beings, what was holding back the twentieth-century church and American society from doing so?[14]

Black Christian feminist and womanist theologians criticized the liberatory viability of both black liberation theology and feminist theology.[15] Womanist theologians challenged black theologians for failing to realize that sexism was a force of oppression against black women, a charge levied against the black power movement. Without an adequate recognition and prescription for dealing with sexism within and outside of churches and communities, black liberation was bound to fail. Womanist theologians also criticized white feminist theologians for neglecting to challenge racism as a force of oppression against black women, a charge also raised against the women's movement. Similarly, feminist theology would fail to make a meaningful impact if the racial oppression facing black women and other sisters of color was to remain unchallenged and intact. With neither black liberation nor feminist theologies able to adequately speak to black women of faith and provide a path for acknowledgment and liberation, womanist theologians such as Jacquelyn Grant, Katie Cannon, Cheryl Townsend Gilkes, Delores Williams, Kelly Brown-Douglass, and many others articulated a theology rooted in the Bible but interpreted through the lens of black women's intersectionality and struggles to overcome oppression.[16] Thus black women's experiences with racism, sexism, and economic injustice constituted the basis for the creation of a womanist theological perspective above and beyond their early exclusion from black liberation and feminist theologies. In addition, womanist theologians bemoaned the severe shortage of black women in seminaries and in formal ministerial roles within black churches.

The depth of scholarship on black Christian women's faith and various manifestations of liberation theology has not been exhausted in this brief summary. Rev. Addie Wyatt's life and work as a religious figure offers a theological outlook concerned not only with gender inequalities in the church, but in the political and social movements that she and many other black women frequented, including the labor movement and the women's movement. With religious authority, Wyatt spoke from the pulpit about the evils of sexism, racism, and poverty and implored women, especially black Christian women, to understand that their true calling as Christian women was to step up and grab a hold of their God-given equality and fair share in managing the affairs and problems of the world. As a labor leader and feminist who believed in the equality of men and women, Wyatt's theology of equality and humanity influenced her work as an activist and her activism likely influenced her faith as well. While Wyatt's articulation of the role of theology and religion in social movements often predated articulations of black, feminist, and womanist theologies, her presence in progressive religious and civil rights circles indicates that these concepts of liberation theology would not have been foreign to her. What shaped Wyatt's theology was the combination or intersectionality of her life's experiences—her faith and family history in the Church of God; her personal experiences with poverty, racism, and sexism: and her movement activism and leadership.

VERNON PARK CHURCH OF GOD

The seeds of Addie and Claude Wyatt's partnership in ministry were sown in the Altgeld Gardens Housing Project and in their founding of the Wyatt Choral

Ensemble for teenage youths in their community. The ensemble gained notoriety for the high quality of the singing and musicianship under the direction of Addie Wyatt, who had years of experience as a gospel pianist and chorus conductor. The Wyatts held prayer and bible study sessions with chorus members while teaching them the value of pride, dignity, and responsibility and the power of belonging to a collective. Soon they were called to the ministry. The Wyatts were asked to assume the leadership of Mt. Zion Baptist Church, a congregation brought down from within by internal struggles. Left without any leadership, some of the remaining members of Mt. Zion heard the Wyatts preaching at a revival and contacted the couple to see if they would take on leadership of their troubled flock. The Wyatts prayed about the request and decided that it would be feasible as long as the members were willing to convert to the Church of God Reformation Movement. The membership agreed and, in 1955, the Vernon Park Church of God gained its official charter and corporation. The Wyatts were in their early thirties, with two young teenage boys and two full-time jobs. In its first few years, Vernon Park struggled with a small membership of about twenty and had no real edifice. The congregation initially worshipped in the garage of one of its members on 93rd Street and later with the congregation of the Morgan Park Church of God from 1957 to 1959. In 1959, the church leased space on the second floor of a building at 7439 South Cottage Grove Avenue. With an actual space of its own for worship, Vernon Park's membership began to grow steadily, and Claude Wyatt left his job with the U.S. Post Office to serve as pastor of the church full-time. With the help of a building fund, the church purchased its own edifice in 1966 at 7653 South Maryland where it remained for eighteen years. In 1985, the church moved to 9011 South Stony Island where its membership grew to over one thousand.[17]

The Vernon Park Church of God, true to the Church of God Reformation Movement, was biblically and scripturally rooted in the idea that Christ's followers needed the church for personal and mutual edification and the glorification of God. The social gospel scripture, Luke 4:18–19 guided the Wyatt's ministry:

> The spirit of the Lord is upon me; because he hath anointed me to preach the Gospel to the poor; he hath sent me to heal the broken-hearted, to preach deliverance to the captives, and recovering of sight to the blind, to set at liberty them that are bruised, to preach the acceptable year of the Lord.[18]

Elements of ethical and social conservatism, warning of the dangers of a life of sin, and living a true, clean Christian life, combined with a social justice bent, defined the church's early ministry. As full-time pastor of Vernon Park, Claude also ministered as a counselor to broken families, helped couples struggling in their marriage and welcomed troubled youth and those in economic and social despair. The church became known for its "healing" ministry because of its willingness to work with alcoholics, drug addicts, gang members, and juveniles in order to help them give their lives over to Christ. Claude Wyatt was known as a "street preacher" unafraid to travel to skid row to reach troubled souls, no doubt calling upon his experiences as a community youth leader in Altgeld.[19] Vernon Park's congregation was African American and its members ranged in status from lower-income and impoverished to middle and upper-middle class.

Addie Wyatt was integral to the founding and ultimate success of the Vernon Park Church of God. Over the years she served as co-pastor and occasionally delivered the Sunday sermon. As minister of music she directed the choirs and played the piano during service. Vernon Park was known for its dynamic music ministry and popular musicals. The Wyatts' youngest son, Claude III, followed in his parents footsteps by becoming a gifted gospel musician. Vernon Park's choirs traveled all over Chicago and even internationally to sing and were often featured on television gospel programs like Sid Ordower's "Jubilee Showcase." For a period of time, Addie Wyatt led the church's prison ministry, and she served as the first lady of the church, or the pastor's wife. But much of Wyatt's ministry took place outside of the church, and she was not shy about the fact that she believed God ordained her to do the work that she did on a daily basis in the labor movement on behalf of working people, women, and minorities. As a labor and religious leader, Wyatt saw both spheres as connected: "[W]hile we served different needs, we represented the same people."[20]

The combined visions of the Wyatts contributed to the social activist bent of the Vernon Park Church of God. The Wyatts first became friends of Dr. Martin Luther King Jr. as a result of Addie's work in the UPWA to raise funds for the Montgomery Bus Boycott. As supporters and close friends of King and the southern civil rights movement, Addie went on to become a labor advisor for the SCLC while Claude became the Chicago Director of the Southern Christian Leadership Conference's (SCLC) Ministerial Training Program that provided a backdrop for the formation of Operation Breadbasket in Chicago in 1966, led by Rev. Jesse Jackson. Breadbasket, later Operation PUSH, demanded that businesses operating in black communities hire black employees, stock black products, and utilize black businesses and financial institutions, which many failed or outright refused to do, carrying the dollars of black customers out of rather than into the community. Young ministers like Rev. Jesse Jackson and Rev. Calvin Morris, as well as veteran ministers like Rev. Clay Evans from Fellowship Missionary Baptist Church, Rev. J. L. Thurston of New Covenant Missionary Baptist Church, Rev. A. P. Jackson of Liberty Baptist Church, and Rev. Claude Wyatt Jr. led the organization. Breadbasket had some success with companies including A&P Grocery, High-Low Foods, and Seven-Up.[21]

Women like Addie Wyatt and her close friend and fellow church member Rev. Willie Barrow, who later went on to serve as vice chairman of Operation PUSH, played an important role in Breadbasket. Wyatt and Barrow, both reared in the Church of God, became friends in the 1940s when Barrow and her husband moved to Chicago. Wyatt helped Barrow find employment in meatpacking and the two became best friends. Both incredibly petite and small in stature, the two may have differed in temperament, but they shared a strong commitment to fighting for civil rights, women's rights, and a better way of life. They were often found on the front lines of community demonstrations and protests in Chicago and beyond from the 1950s through the 1990s. According to a mutual friend, Reverend Calvin Morris, Wyatt was known to speak forcefully but quietly, "masking a steely resolve," while Willie Barrow was known to speak her mind "in ways not considered as ladylike."[22] Barrow likewise cast herself and Addie as two women committed to the ministry and to activism, but with very different approaches: "Addie was more mild. She believed what she believed and she had a little more patience than I did. She could wait and see things through. . . . Addie could raise money and I could raise hell."[23] Both women became ordained in the Church of God and influenced one another's religious perspectives and theologies. Barrow, however, never saw herself as a pulpit preacher or sought to lead a congregation in the ways that the Wyatts did. Instead, she saw herself as a more of "preacher-teacher" whose ministry was outside of the walls of the church in the streets and in organizations like Operation PUSH.[24]

Though men dominated the formal leadership of Breadbasket, women like Wyatt and Barrow formed the ground leadership. With her knowledge of labor movement strategies such as picketing and boycotting, Wyatt helped to organize and lead consumer boycotting groups and picketing campaigns comprised of Vernon Park members and community women across faiths and denominations.[25] Rev. Calvin Morris, a former Breadbasket staff member, recalled working with Wyatt and Barrow:

> Addie and Willie were strong symbols for black women. . . . [T]hey were truly trailblazers and they both had to struggle with the recalcitrance and the reluctance of black males to provide them a real place and space at the table. . . . When we were ready to move on a business and boycott, Addie would counsel us on the strategy and how to maximize our efforts. She would caution against acting too brashly or too soon or of losing important allies. Addie was always one to get us to really think about what it was we were doing.[26]

Addie and Claude Wyatt utilized their combined networks and unique skills as ministers within and beyond the walls of the church to build a congregation that was active and invested in the affairs of its community. Addie served in important capacities in the church, but Claude served as its institutional and spiritual leader. Addie's ministry manifested itself more in the organized labor and women's rights movements. Both of their professions infiltrated their home life, for the work of a pastor and a union leader/movement activist is rarely confined to a light or predictable schedule. For much of her marriage, Addie Wyatt had higher earnings and, unlike a more traditional pastor's wife, she had a public persona that was greater than that of her husband despite his leadership in ministerial circles and role as full-time pastor of their church. She appreciated and celebrated being a wife, mother, and grandmother when time permitted, but she equally relished her roles and identities outside of the home as a labor leader, women's rights advocate, and community organizer.

Addie Wyatt seemed pleased with the dynamics of her marriage and the partnership she and Claude built, which was based on respect for one another's talents: "Whatever he needed to be successful in fulfilling his ministry, I've been supportive. . . . And for the many years I was a labor leader and moved around the country, he was always there for me when I needed him."[27] Wyatt was quite vocal about the mutual respect and team ministry within her marriage. In 1981, she remarked: "I've been married to one of the most wonderful men in the world for 41 years. I respect him very dearly and I respect and appreciate his manness. I have been sharing with him these 41 years trying to help God to make a man and he is a very, very good one. He has been working with the Creator trying to help God to make a woman and I think both of us are convinced that she's a pretty good one. The reason why we have been so marvelous in working with each other and sharing is we respect the differences, and have not tried to dominate and change them."[28] Interviews with close friends, family members, and colleagues corroborate the mutual respect and appreciation the Wyatts had for one another. Claude supported Addie in her work in organized labor and other movements while Addie deferred to Claude's authority in the church as its full-time pastor and spiritual leader. Still, the two often crossed over into one another's realms. Claude took labor classes with Addie Wyatt in labor studies at Roosevelt University and participated in labor-community partnerships. Addie occasionally gave sermons at Vernon Park and she and Claude were active members of the National Association of the Church of God.

There were differences between Addie and Claude Wyatt that emerged, particularly around the issue of homosexuality. Rev. Willie Barrow was a member of the Vernon Park Church of God and one of Addie Wyatt's closest friends dating back to the late 1940s. The two were fellow partners in crime in labor, civil rights, feminist, and black political circles. Barrow made Claude and Addie the godparents of her only child, Keith Barrow, who was reared in the Church of God and baptized at Vernon Park. It took ten years for Barrow to conceive and Keith remained her only biological child. He grew up singing gospel music in Chicago but embarked on a secular music career in the late 1970s. He moved to New York and signed a record deal with Columbia Records. Barrow became an R&B sensation, producing three albums from 1977 to 1980. His hits as an artist, songwriter and music producer included, "You Know You Want To Be Loved" and "Turn Me Up." His musical peers and friends included the likes of Patti LaBelle, Ashford and Simpson, and Roberta Flack. Keith was quite close to his mother but also spent quite a bit of time with Addie, and the two shared a great passion for shopping and fashion.[29]

Keith lived an openly gay lifestyle and often had trouble reconciling his homosexuality and Christianity because the church taught that homosexuality was a great sin that took one further away from God rather than closer to him.[30] Willie Barrow was accepting of her son's homosexuality and became an outspoken proponent of gay and lesbian rights, but Keith's openly gay lifestyle caused tension with some of his religious friends and family members, including Claude Wyatt. Sometime in the late 1970s or early 1980s, Keith was diagnosed with HIV/AIDS. According to his friends, he was not ashamed of being gay but was fearful what public perception of the disease might do to harm his family and his career.[31] Keith Barrow's contraction of the disease came in the days before HIV/AIDS Awareness campaigns and nearly a decade prior to basketball great Magic Johnson's public declaration of having contracted the disease. Misconceptions and a lack of knowledge about the disease pervaded the general public as well as the medical community, and the perception of HIV/AIDS as a "gay disease" hampered public health and government intervention. By the summer of 1983, Keith became quite ill and returned to Chicago to live with his mother and father before spending his last days at Michael Reese Hospital. Keith Barrow passed away on October 22, 1983, at the age of twenty-nine. Tensions between Keith's homosexuality and his Christian beliefs came to a head after his death as his friends and family prepared for his homegoing. Keith's funeral was held at the Vernon Park Church of God. A separate memorial tribute "to honor the truth of Keith's life and who he was" was organized by close loved ones Rev. Calvin Morris and Dr. Patricia Carey and took place the night before the funeral at Operation PUSH's headquarters.

Although both the memorial tribute and funeral displayed a love for Keith, there were stark differences in the tone of the two services. Over five hundred people attended the memorial tribute, with some estimates ranging to 1,100. The program featured Keith's friends and peers in the music industry as well as many of his gay friends who remembered Keith fondly. Roberta Flack performed her hit "The First Time Ever I Saw Your Face," and Patti Labelle sent in a taped condolence. Claude and Addie Wyatt were in attendance at the memorial tribute and according to others who attended, Claude was not pleased with the tribute and the open celebration of Keith's gay lifestyle in New York. He loved Keith dearly, but disapproved of his homosexuality.[32] Addie, who was reportedly much closer to Keith than Claude was, gave her own tribute to Keith at the memorial tribute but did not speak at his funeral the next day at Vernon Park.

The dominant theme of the funeral service was Keith's spiritual reconversion to the way of God before his death. Keith struggled with reconciling his homosexuality with his religious beliefs and, according to friends, succumbed to the pressure of religious friends and family within the church who convinced him in his last months that his salvation went hand in hand with denouncing his former life.[33] Yet according to Claude Wyatt and other pastors at the funeral, Keith knew that he had been living a life "away from God" and made his own conscious choice to return his life to the Lord. Claude was glad to see Keith come home and "loved Keith, but did not like the life he lived." And he believed Keith knew he was wrong. Keith's unsanctified friends were blamed for encouraging Keith in living his own way, singing secular music, and living a lifestyle that was not of the Lord. Claude's eulogy, "Jesus Christ, Lord of the Pigpen," depicted Keith as a young man who knew the difference between right and wrong, but chose to live his life in the pigpen where vice, sin, and confusion ruled over him. The pigpen was a metaphor for his life in New York and his homosexuality. Claude believed that it was in the pigpen, when down and out, that Keith remembered his Christian faith and returned to Chicago to seek the salvation of his Lord. Claude argued that everyone had a pigpen and spiritual dark age in his or her life and that everyone had to pass through that dark age in order to truly accept Christ and live the Christian life. The words *gay* and *homosexuality* do not appear to have been used at all during the entire funeral. While Claude preached that God loved Keith just as he loved all sinners, it became clear that homosexuality and Christianity were incompatible and that homosexuality was something that could be discarded and denounced rather than a way of being or an identity that could coexist with a set of Christian beliefs.[34]

A self-described liberal seminarian, Rev. Calvin Morris attended Vernon Park Church of God services and even preached a few sermons at the church prior to Keith's death. Morris's planning of the memorial tribute at PUSH and subsequent speech at the funeral praising Keith's courage to live an open and free life with God's merciful love present throughout all of it, were in stark contrast to Claude's eulogy and precipitated somewhat of a break in Morris's relationship with the church. When asked about Addie Wyatt's reaction to Claude's eulogy, Rev. Morris did not recall seeing any specific visible reaction. He knew the Wyatts well and believed that if Addie disagreed with some of Claude's beliefs, she was never one to show it in public. In the years he attended the church, Addie publicly supported Claude in whatever way he chose to direct the congregation.[35] Any disagreements, debates, or discussions about the direction of the church or even theological beliefs around controversial issues in the church most likely took place behind closed doors within the privacy of their relationship.

Interestingly, Addie Wyatt chose to give a special tribute to Keith at his memorial, but did not speak at his funeral at the church. Was this because her theological views on the subject differed from Claude's and she did not want to challenge his authority within the church? Or did she struggle with Keith's homosexuality and chose to pay tribute to the special relationship that they shared without explicitly engaging or endorsing his life choices and her judgment of those choices? A definitive answer remains elusive. As much as is known about Addie Wyatt's life from her own writings and political voice as well as from friends and colleagues, there are silences that emerge to remind us that not all parts of her life or her beliefs are as clear and open for interpretation, including the inner workings of her marriage and the complicated ways in which she respected her husband's spiritual authority within their church but also created the space for her own spiritual authority.

A PROGRESSIVE FAITH THEOLOGY

As an active woman of faith, Wyatt almost always had to contend with rigid, traditional gender norms that sought to determine her proper "place" in and outside of the church. If there was one role that Addie Wyatt found difficult to navigate early on, it was adjusting to the role of pastor's wife. She penned an article perhaps intended for publication titled "In Honor of the Pastor's Wife," which discussed the need for churches to honor pastor's wives as women, not just extensions of their husbands. In the article, she recalled a conversation with a new member of the church who was floored to learn that Addie Wyatt was in fact the pastor's wife. Wyatt recounted the woman's explanation for her surprise:

> I had no idea that that little woman pumping on that piano was the pastor's wife. I would look and see you sitting in the choir loft praying and rejoicing and noticing everything that was happening, waiting for God to give the directive or the minister to give the signal that something was needed during the service. And I saw you always there available to do what you could do. . . . When we would come on the outside of the church, there you were beautifully dressed in the latest style showing us that Godly women can be beautiful and attractive. I would hear you say, "I will be back to the evening service, and I do not plan to be late, but I am going to work right now." You would be on your way to the community to work and to serve . . . not many pastor's wives work like that.[36]

Wyatt's active participation in service, direction of the music ministry, contemporary fashion sense, and priorities outside of church and home that warranted her dedication set her apart from the more traditional conceptualization of a pastor's wife.

Wyatt believed that given the freedom to break out of the confines of what others expected from the role of the pastor's wife, women would be able to have a more effective ministry of their own within their churches and in society. As a young pastor's wife, she contended with various sets of expectations. Some believed that she should fade into the background and be seen but not heard. This was difficult for her given that she felt compelled to act on her responsibility to God to utilize her talents of organizing people against social and economic injustice. Still, there were other expectations: "There were those who felt that my role was to sit on the front pew and nurse the children. I enjoyed that role and played it to the best of my ability. But that was not my only role. There were some who thought that I should come in looking as though the pastor needed an increase in pay and he did. There were those who were very critical because of my hat, my dress, my coat and many tried to determine whether or not the pastor's wife should wear *that*."[37] Wyatt was one for fashionable clothing, much of which she could have afforded on the basis of her own income, save her husband's earnings as pastor of the church.

Wyatt found the answer to her frustrations in the Bible, in Proverbs 31:10–31, which depicts the portrait of a virtuous woman, attentive to her family and trusted by her husband. This woman worked successfully with her hands to provide income and sustenance for her family, was giving to the poor, and spoke with wisdom. In this virtuous woman, Wyatt saw herself as well as vindication for her roles as a professional working woman and wife of a pastor. She wrote of the scripture: "Exploring this beautiful acoustic poem one observes a woman who was free before Gloria Steinem ever launched her 'Woman's Crusade.' . . . This woman in Proverbs, so distinguished and honored, understood the politics of her time before Harriet Tubman, Sojourner Truth, Eleanor Roosevelt, Shirley Chisholm, Coretta King or Willie Barrow ever appeared on the scene." It was in the Bible that Wyatt found support and authorization for the expansion of women's roles in the church and social justice movements. And it was her belief that Claude and her family benefited from the freedom that she had to develop herself, a freedom bestowed upon her by God.[38]

Rev. Addie Wyatt's sermons and addresses were given before Vernon Park and other congregations, as an Annual Women's Day or guest speaker, and before national religious conventions and conferences across Christian denominations. Regardless of her audience, Wyatt almost always began her religious addresses by acknowledging and thanking her hosts and bringing greetings from Vernon Park and the organized labor movement—her union, the Amalgamated (later the United Food and Commercial Workers), or CLUW. Immediately, Wyatt would convey her commitments to her church and to the labor movement, demonstrating with ease her ability to organize and serve in leadership positions as a woman of faith in male-dominated sacred and secular spaces. Such an orientation allowed Wyatt to begin to acclimate her audiences to her style of ministry, with sermons that were biblically rooted but moved back and forth between the perils and promise of men and women in scripture and the perils and promise of contemporary gender, race, and labor relations in America. Wyatt used her professional credentials and personal experience to relate to women on multiple levels and to demonstrate the authority and power behind her words as a woman chosen by God to put faith into action and action into faith.

In a 1979 speech before the Progressive National Baptist Convention, Wyatt brought greetings from her church and her union but wasted no time in setting up her agenda:

> I hate so very much to take you out of the "garden of prayer" after that beautiful selection by the Women's Chorus, but my sisters and brothers, beyond this beautiful setting of almost 1,000 women filling this dining room of the Fairmont Hotel in New Orleans, Louisiana, is a world that is tossing and turning with unresolved frustrations and problems. . . . Unemployment, immorality, inflation, disease and crime is ravishing almost every community, not to mention the hunger, the nuclear threat, the absence of peace, racism and sex discrimination which has weakened the very fabric of our society. . . . For those of us who pray in faith must be willing to work also with that same faith to bring about the changes that are needed in our world.

Wyatt's understanding of sin went beyond biblical definitions to include societal social problems such as inequality, oppression, poverty, and discrimination. It was not enough for Christians to pray to God for a better life, they had to go out and become active in society—through political action, community organizing, or any other kind of work that would lessen human hurt. For Wyatt, unemployment, a lack of child care and national health care, and oppression on the basis of race and sex were all issues that the church had been silent on for too long.[39] Wyatt was particularly concerned with the fact that the Equal Rights Amendment had not been ratified in Louisiana where the convention took place "because of historical racism and prejudice against women."

The bulk of Wyatt's speech entailed setting the record straight on the issue of women's equality in society as ordained by God. Wyatt did much to dispel the idea that women had a subordinate role to men and that these gender roles had somehow been mandated, sanctioned, and codified in the Bible. Wyatt struck at this assumption by preaching to her audiences that if they believed in women's subordination, then they had misread the Bible beginning with the creation narrative in the Book of Genesis and therefore gravely misunderstood the very foundations of Christian teachings. She stressed the word *them* in Genesis 1:26–28, a passage of scripture she often invoked when discussing the biblical origins of gender equality:

> And God said, Let us make man in our image, after our likeness; and let THEM have dominion over the fish of the sea, and over the fowl of the air, and over the

cattle, and over all the earth, and over every creeping thing that creepeth upon the earth. So God created man in his own image, in the image of God created he Him; male and female created he THEM. And God blessed THEM and God said unto THEM, Be fruitful, and multiply, and replenish the earth, and subdue it; and have dominion over the fish of the sea, and over the fowl of the air, and over every living thing that moveth upon the earth.[40]

She went on to say: "That is what God said unto not him alone, not her alone, but this is what God said onto THEM. His intent is very clear if we read it and emphasize it where the emphasis is needed. When I see the condition of many of our churches, where men and women are playing the game of masculinity and femininity rather than oneness, I can understand why there is so much frustration and confusion in our world when we try to find our right places."[41] She believed that men and women were to be equal partners in the ways of the world with neither man nor woman subordinate.

In a similar address, she quoted the same scripture and then asked:

What has happened to us? Why is the status and role of women one of the most controversial issues of our world today? The sin of historical and traditional discrimination against women and misinterpretations of *God's* word have forced women into inferior roles and ignorance as well as ulterior motives have kept them there.[42]

Wyatt could not understand why the advancement of women in society and their changing status was such a controversial issue when, for Christians, the prescription for male and female gender relations was quite clear if read without the misrepresentation of God's word. She also utilized Galatians 3:28, "There is neither Jew nor Greek there is neither bond nor free there is neither male nor female for ye are all one in Christ," to argue that there were no measurable divisions or hierarchies among Christian men and women before God. Men and women who believed that women were subordinate in the eyes of God and in their roles in society had gotten it wrong and were aiding the sinful ongoing discrimination against women. Wyatt concluded that it was the absence of God among those who sought to curb women's rights that led to discrimination and male chauvinism and that God's people needed to return to His word and faithfully execute His plan.[43] Again, an explicit engagement with gender and women's subordinated status were front and center in many of Wyatt's religious addresses.

Wyatt preached that women should not be subordinate to men, and women should not dominate men, a statement with profound implications that spoke both to prevailing practices in society and in the church. It also spoke to the anxiety and fear of a radical feminist revolution where traditional gender roles and dynamics would be completely turned on head. Wyatt relied on the New Testament as well to support her biblical and social views of gender equality. In addition to the examples of strong women of faith like Esther, Queen Vashti, and Deborah, who played important roles in the Old Testament, Wyatt frequently pointed to examples of women in the New Testament who were acknowledged and used by Jesus Christ to witness His work and word. Speaking at the church of the late Dr. Martin Luther King Jr., the Ebenezer Baptist Church in Atlanta, Wyatt preached:

> Jesus in His attitude toward women clearly illustrated that He considered them worthy and as capable as men of receiving salvation. His acceptance of Mary as she sat at his feet. His acceptance of invitations of conversation with Samaritan women. His acknowledgment of the sick woman who touched the hem of his garment. His forgiveness of the woman caught in adultery and many other examples indicate that Jesus placed great value upon women's intelligence and spiritual worth. He awarded to a woman the honor of being the first witness to His resurrection, even though no woman was an acceptable witness in a Jewish court.[44]

Echoing the cries of feminist theologians, Wyatt questioned how, with such clear examples of women's significance and importance in the eyes of Jesus Christ, could the church continue to so blatantly ignore and, even worse, contribute to women's subordination? Wyatt argued that Jesus Christ did not speak of and emphasize male or female domination but rather the level of one's commitment to God.[45] Despite her ordination, there were many churches that would not allow Wyatt, or any woman, to speak from behind the pulpit. Instead, she would speak from a podium off to the side. Some churches did not believe in women addressing a congregation from a position of spiritual authority and leadership. These churches more than likely did not invite Wyatt to speak, but her provocative theology that indicted the church for sitting silently in the face of women's inequality intended to light a fire under even the most progressive of congregations.

A wife, mother, and a grandmother during this period, Wyatt exalted and respected these roles of women, though she believed in women's prerogatives to not marry or bear children and was an advocate of women's reproductive rights.[46] Wyatt urged that women should involve themselves in the affairs of the world because those affairs, from labor to politics to civil rights and women's rights, affected their work and advancement both within and outside of the home. Women had to do more to contribute to the development of their households, churches, careers, and communities as part of their covenant with God. Moreover, the material circumstances in which many black women found themselves confronting sexism, racism, and poverty necessitated action. In an address titled, "Black Christian Women—More than Conquerors," Wyatt pointed to a long line of black women of faith involved in the freedom struggle who inspired and paved the way for her, including Sojourner Truth, Harriet

Tubman, Fannie Lou Hamer, Rosa Parks, Willie Barrow, Nancy Jones, Shirley Bridges, and others. These are the women that Wyatt actively drew upon in her theology, highlighting the centrality of faith to African American women's individual and collective achievements. More poignantly, she stated:

> I don't know about you, but there are some things I had to *overcome* in order to develop and strengthen my faith and *become*, and what you see standing before you today is the *outcome*!!! God has continued to use me to preach in churches, union halls, in government, in civil rights groups, and various community action programs and causes. . . . In order to become the woman of God that I am today, I had to overcome the chains and shackles of *racism, sexism*, and *economic poverty* and *deprivation*.[47]

Thus it was her experiences with discrimination and oppression that reinforced her belief in God, and it was her faith that enabled her to deal with oppression and discrimination and see beyond the barriers constructed around her.

What Wyatt put forth in her ministry to women was a belief in their equality, dignity, and humanity before God and a need to struggle for their own freedom and liberation from inequality in the church and in society. Her work in the labor movement proved invaluable in fighting for that dignity and equality: "My Christian faith in God, and my personal involvement within the church, strengthened me, and enabled me to cope with the chains of hurt, hate, disappointment and desperation. They also forced me to find the courage to pursue another avenue to relieve the chains that held me captive, and denied me human dignity, self-worth, freedom, justice and equality. Thank God for the union."[48] As a working woman, Wyatt's message potentially resonated with hundreds if not thousands of women whose lives were touched in one way or another by the challenges of unemployment, pay discrimination and glass ceilings, racism on the job, and even inequalities within their interpersonal relationships. The fact that she both articulated and practiced a theology built around experiences born out of the confluence of racism, sexism, and economic inequality appealed to women who sought out her message from the very pulpits and stages they were often denied.

But Wyatt's message was not always welcomed. Her selection as a speaker at the 1980 International Convention of the Church of God on the topic "We Are Christ's Witnesses" generated some controversy from fellow Church of God ministers. In a letter to the Church of God Convention program committee, two male ministers, Richard Draper and David Ball of Kentucky, urged the committee to reconsider its invitation to Wyatt. They cited her feminist activism, vocal support, and campaigning for the ratification of the Equal Rights Amendment, and her association with organizations that openly discussed and in some cases endorsed homosexuality and gay rights, abortion rights, sexual preference teaching, and other issues "that would destroy Christian principles in the home and in the church."[49] They argued that the speakers for the convention "should be above reproach in their Christian teachings." Wyatt was accused of having served on a committee for *Sexual Preference Magazine* and that such an act was out of line with the teachings of the Church of God.[50]

Draper and Ball's charges against Addie Wyatt resonated with a larger spectrum of conservative religious activists and leaders who emerged to protest aspects of the women's movement that they deemed a threat to the traditional structure of the family. As historian Kathleen Berkeley argues, the New Right emerged during this period, fueled by Jerry Falwell's "Moral Majority," Phyllis Schlafly's leadership of the anti-ERA forces, and conservative politicians who cast the family as a sacred entity under the domain of God and Christian teachings. The natural God-given differences between men and women were under assault by the ERA, which they charged would make women equally financially responsible for their households, legalize gay marriage, condone homosexuality, strip women of protective labor legislation, and make women eligible for the draft. For some, it was less the acknowledgment of men and women's equality that inspired opposition toward the ERA than the scope of its application. Still for others, any piece of legislation or campaign for equality that had the possibility of altering gender roles were cast as anti-Christian and targeted by a powerful conservative grassroots constituency. Thus the protection, preservation, and promotion of family values were appropriated and held firmly within the grasp of the Religious Right, not progressive theologians like Addie Wyatt or Pauli Murray—a lawyer, lesbian feminist, and civil rights activist ordained in the Episcopal Church in 1977. Feminism was deemed an anti-Christian threat to the family and it was up to Christians to save America from the feminists. The religiosity of the New Right coincided with a larger set of conservative political views that opposed abortion, busing, affirmative action, certain civil rights measures, and social welfare programs.[51]

Draper and Ball were correct in linking Addie Wyatt with support for the ERA and feminist activism since she had begun campaigning for the amendment in the early 1970s and was one of its most vocal supporters. Because ratification of the amendment took place on a state-by-state basis, ERA activists campaigned primarily in their own states to ensure passage and then targeted other states that had ratified the amendment and later rescinded, as was the case with states like Tennessee and Nebraska, and in states that had yet to ratify the amendment, including Wyatt's home state of Illinois. She worked with groups like National CLUW, the Chicago chapter of CLUW, the National Organization for Women and its Chicago chapter, the League of Black Women, ERA Central, and ERAmerica among others. ERA supporters adopted several strategies to show their support for the amendment, including writing and lobbying political leaders and holding rallies, one of which took place in Springfield, Illinois, in 1976. Over 10,000 gathered in support of the ERA, including Addie Wyatt. Proponents of the amendment also held nationwide fund-raising ERA Walk-A-Thons and boycotted states that failed to ratify the ERA. CLUW relocated its convention from Chicago and Illinois several times due to the state's failure to ratify the ERA. Organizations like the Association of American University Women, the National Business and Professional Women's Foundation, the League of Women Voters, and the National Women's Political Caucus all relocated their meetings and conventions from anti-ERA states like Illinois and Missouri throughout the 1970s. The Chicago Convention and Tourism Bureau reportedly lost upward of 15 million dollars in revenue in 1977 as a result of its failure to ratify the ERA.[52]

Wyatt had firsthand experience with the power of anti-ERA and antifeminist forces as a member of President Jimmy Carter's National Commission on the Observance of International Women's Year (IWY), headed by outspoken New York Congresswoman and feminist Bella Abzug. With federal funding, the Commission planned and held conferences on the problems of women in each of the fifty states and six territories, leading up to a national conference to be held in Houston, Texas, in November of 1977. Wyatt, a national leader among working women, had significant experience working on women's commissions, lobbying for women's rights legislation and leading women's conferences. The ultimate charge of the Commission was to create a National Plan of Action for women's equality based on meeting proceedings at the state and national level that the federal government could endorse and implement in order to improve women's opportunities for advancement. Addie Wyatt participated in state conferences held in Illinois, Nebraska, Kansas, and Delaware and regretted the degree to which pro- and anti-ERA factions dominated the agendas of the gatherings and effectively paralyzed any chances for substantive discussion of the many barriers to women's advancement in society.[53]

The leader of the ERA's opposition was Phyllis Schlafly, who founded STOP ERA in 1972. Raised in a conservative Catholic household in Illinois, Schlafly eventually went on to earn both a master's degree and a law degree while raising six children with her husband. Despite being a professional and educated working woman, Schlafly largely worked on behalf of protecting what she believed were women's proper and most important roles as wives and mothers, even as she ran for political office in Illinois and became a recognizable voice for moral conservatives in the Republican Party. Schlafly founded Eagle Forum, another conservative Christian women's group in 1975. She mobilized both Eagle Forum and STOP ERA against IWY because she believed it to be an instrument of pro-ERA forces. In a March 1977 letter to members of Eagle Forum, Schlafly detailed the developments of the commission and argued that its state coordinating committees had been packed with pro-ERA women and that in order "to counteract the use of these tax dollars to promote women's lib goals," conservative women would need to act swiftly and effectively. Schlafly established an IWY Citizens Review Committee and directed women to find out who was on their state's coordinating committee, whether those representatives were pro-ERA, and then write and phone state legislators to protest the lack of average working women and homemakers on the state committees. Schlafly wrote: "The IWY Coordinating Committees in each state are planning workshops for the state meetings. They will cover women's lib goals such as ERA, abortion, government financed child care, wages for housewives and other antifamily proposals . . . [and] find our when and where your state's IWY conference will be held. Plan to attend and get all your friends to attend. It is URGENT that we send more women than the women libbers do, so we can outvote them."[54]

Conservative women responded to Schlafly's call and their presence at state meetings did not go unnoticed. Members of the state coordinating committees and delegates to the national conference were intended to be representative of female populations within states, including those from women's rights groups, the general public, working women, low-income women, and women from diverse religious and racial groups. In a September 1977 press release, Bella Abzug charged right-wing groups with co-opting meetings in states such as Mississippi and Alabama, where working-class and black women made up a significant percentage of the female population and attended the state meetings but were a vast minority among the women elected as delegates to the national convention. Abzug wrote: "These outcomes seem to be one of the results of a concentrated effort by right-wing groups to discredit IWY through factually inaccurate misrepresentations in the press, and to pack state meetings with people hostile to the legislation's goal of equality for women." The task of IWY was "to identify the barriers that prevent women from participating fully and equally in all aspects of national life, and develop recommendations for means by which such barriers can be removed."[55] These tensions came to a head at the national conference in Houston where 2,000 delegates and about 20,000 attendees gathered to debate what constituted women's equality and inequality in society. The issues that garnered the most vigorous debate were the ERA, abortion, and sexual preference rights. About 20 percent of the conference's delegates and attendees were against the ratification of the ERA and other "anti-family" initiatives. On display throughout the conference was the difficulty of coming up with a unified agenda for women's equality and advancement in society, especially since the very notions of equality and advancement were disagreed upon and open to wide interpretation. Nevertheless, IWY commissioners endorsed a twenty-six plank "National Plan of Action," which included lesbian rights, welfare mother's rights, and the passage of the ERA.[56]

Illinois ERA activists like Addie Wyatt had their hands full lobbying for the ERA and ultimately their efforts were unsuccessful. Despite the efforts of ERA supporters in 1976, the amendment had many opponents whose opposition to the amendment ranged from its perceived disruption of traditional social gender norms to the fear of too much federal jurisdiction of the amendment at the expense of states' rights. Illinois was also the home state of STOP ERA activist and leader Phyllis Schlafly who marshalled anti-ERA factions into a formidable front. Politically, the ERA was a contentious issue with vocal supporters and opponents. The Illinois Senate proved to be the biggest barrier for supporters of the ERA. In 1975, the Illinois Senate adopted a rule requiring that ratification of a constitutional amendment would require a three-fifths majority for approval, when only a simple majority had been required prior to this point.

By the summer of 1976, it was time for the Senate to take an official vote on the ERA. Senator Cecil Partee, the chief Senate sponsor of the bill and one of Wyatt's political allies, stunned supporters when he announced that the ERA would not be called for a vote. Partee argued that supporters just didn't have the votes to pass, stating, "There's no sense in being a loser when you know you are going to lose."[57] Partee assured ERA supporters that he stood by the amendment but believed that more needed to be done by supporters of the amendment to dispel many of the myths, distortions, and fears put out by anti-ERA organizers who were "successful in turning the debate away from the question of discrimination and turning it toward some rather phony issues." According to Partee, only thirty senators were in support of the ERA, still six shy of the number of votes needed for it to pass. Wyatt was frustrated by the turn of the events in the Illinois legislature and stepped up her commitment to the ERA, becoming even more vocal in her support for the amendment and extolling its benefits and virtues in nearly every public address that she gave between 1976 and 1982, regardless of her audience.

The ERA was reintroduced into the Illinois legislature in 1977, and supporters and detractors of the resolution continued to debate the amendment before the legislature and on the national stage. With the backdrop of a larger feminist movement against a growing conservative movement, and more than a few celebrities on the front lines, the ERA and its ratification enjoyed widespread coverage. The ERA became a veritable barometer of the nation's willingness or unwillingness to address the issue of gender equality in society and at a constitutional level. Celebrities like Marlo Thomas, Alan Alda, Jean Stapleton, Lily Tomlin, Phil Donahue, and Esther Rolle were all photographed leading pro-ERA marches and rallies. About 12,000 ERA supporters protested at the 1980 Republican National Convention in Detroit after the party took the ERA out of its platform after more than four decades. Demonstrators held signs that read, "Will the party that freed the slaves become the party that enslaves women?" ERA Walk-A-Thons took place in major cities and small towns from Texas to Michigan, raising millions of dollars for ERA ratification efforts. Rallies took place across the United States, including once again in Springfield, Illinois, in

1981. Wyatt spoke at the rally, alongside actresses Patty Duke Astin and Ester Rolle. In her address, Wyatt argued for viewing the ERA as a human right: "We lobby to loosen them once and for all. We don't want them on ourselves, and we don't want them on our children. They are the chains of racism and sexism."[58]

Still, the three-fifths majority rule put the burden on ERA supporters in Illinois, whereas such a rule did not exist in other states at the time. Supporters saw the rule as specifically designed to kill the ERA, and with powerful opposition in the state legislature to the ERA, the June 20, 1982, deadline came and went without ratification in Illinois or in any additional state. ERA supporters were unable to withstand the forces of opposition against the amendment. What supporters really had to contend with was a deep and entrenched fear (rational or irrational) of the social, political, and economic changes that can accompany mandates for gender equality. For too many men and women, the ERA threatened to take away privileges based on sexual difference and the rewards of patriarchy, even if those privileges and rewards were experienced by only a minority. Black women like Addie Wyatt, Ester Rolle, and Willie Barrow who championed the ERA argued that black women should support the amendment because they were doubly burdened by racism and sexism and often triply burdened by racism, sexism, and poverty. They did not enjoy the "privileges" of womanhood in a society that discriminated against them on the basis of their skin color and their sex. Devalued yet overburdened with responsibility, black women had every cause to support the ERA and any measure that would aid in the betterment of their lives and their families.

Even after the failure of ratification, Wyatt continued to push for support for the ERA, arguing that until women were truly free, men would not be free. She refused to accept that the ERA had no hope for resurrection, resurgence, and ultimately ratification: "The Phyllis Schlaflys of this world cannot stop the progress we have gained. Women will not settle for less than justice."[59] The fact that her home state of Illinois failed to ratify the ERA was a particularly bitter pill for Wyatt to swallow. For over ten years, she campaigned statewide and nationally for ratification of the ERA, testifying before the Illinois Senate and lobbying Illinois legislators. For Wyatt, the ERA was much more than a women's issue—it was a family issue and an important component of the struggle for human equality. The extended deadline for ratification for the Equal Rights Amendment passed on June 30, 1982, still three states shy of ratification. The failure of ERA ratification was a devastating setback for Wyatt and those who supported the amendment, but it would not be the end of Wyatt's quest for greater social, political, and economic empowerment of women.

Addie Wyatt's association with the 1977 International Women's Year Conference, the campaign for the ERA, and her affiliation with numerous feminist organizations no doubt served as fuel for her religious critics in and outside of the Church of God. The planners of the Church of God's 1980 International Conference forwarded Draper and Ball's letter to Wyatt, who then responded directly to the two men. Wyatt chose not to address their direct allegations, but she chastised both men in her response. She believed that they had been misled about her role in society and chided them for the "unchristian manner" in which they attempted to thwart her address. She wrote, "I regret that you are so misled about my role in our society and in our Church that you acted in this unchristian manner. Had you readily followed the steps taught us in Matthew 18:15–17, then perhaps our Christian relationship as a brother and sister in Christ would not be in jeopardy at this very critical time in the Church's historical celebration." The scripture Wyatt referenced, Matthew 18:15–17 instructs Christians to confront one another directly and in private about disagreements before going to the church. If Draper and Ball had an issue with Wyatt, then they should have directed their concerns toward her, before taking them before the convention, so that the two sides should develop an understanding.

Wyatt continued using biblical scripture to craft her response and set the foundations of her work:

> When God speaks to us and we receive His words, it is very difficult to limit ourselves to the little world within our own comfortable setting, but we are much like the disciples in Mark 16:20, and they went forth and preached everywhere, the Lord working with them and confirming the word with signs following. These should be the most exciting times of our Christian career and rather than to spend our precious moments discrediting and destroying one another, that's the enemy's role, to the glory of God we ought to do everything possible to encourage and strengthen one another so that by our demonstrated love and unity, we can best win a lost world to Christ. . . . I firmly believe that one's greatest defense in the hour of criticism is one's production. Therefore, I invite you to observe my work with openness and truth.[60]

Demonstrating a grasp of scripture and the social gospel, Wyatt invited the ministers to bear witness to her ministry before challenging it. She went on to address the convention without incident and bear witness to the problems of racism, sexism and economic poverty in her address, "Witnessing in Difficult Times and Difficult Places." Her address was based on the biblical story of Titus, who was left in Crete, a place infamous for its debauchery, immorality, dishonesty, and strife. The Apostle Paul had the responsibility of sending a believer to Crete to provide witness to Christ's words and minister to the people of Crete. He chose Titus, a man of courage and determination who had stood by Paul's side during difficult times. Titus labored in Crete against what seemed like insurmountable odds. Wyatt likened herself and others who chose to minister in the world at large to Titus and preached that "the church should be grateful and very supportive of those who are called to bear witness of Christ in difficult places."[61] Crete was not some far off, biblical land but anywhere one could look and see economic crisis, poverty, abuse, sickness, war, greed, and discrimination on the basis of race, sex, and age. Crete, in the form of "envy, strife, jealousy, and hatred," existed in the church.

There is no doubt that Wyatt's message was intended to display her knowledge of the Bible and Christian principles, but also how those principles were connected to the day-to-day economic, political, and social problems in the world. It is likely that her message was also colored by and directed toward her critics who viewed her theology and actions as irreconcilable with Christianity. The questions raised about her leadership and moral fitness as a Christian feminist were in many ways indicative of a world behind the times of Rev. Addie Wyatt and the message she sought to convey. Her message was one of gender equality sanctioned by the Bible, including the right and responsibility of women to be active participants and leaders in their religious spaces and in society, and the right and responsibility of black women to actively involve themselves in their liberation from sexism, racism, and economic poverty.

As a figure of religious authority, Addie Wyatt provides a much-needed example of one whose faith and Christian beliefs fell in line with, rather than in opposition to, the women's movement and social justice initiatives. In her own way, Wyatt hoped to wrestle religiosity from the stronghold of those invested in the status quo and spread its message of liberation and equality to the women, minorities, and the poor who bore the brunt of society's hardships and injustice. This mission mirrored her goals of better incorporating working women and minorities in the active membership and leadership of the labor movement. A telling confession of Wyatt's illustrates the depth of her belief in the power of Christianity to serve as the guiding moral force: "It grieves me that if the Church had continued its message of oneness regardless of race, color, creed, or sex we would not have needed the Civil Rights movement of the '60s or the Women's movement of the late '60s and '70s because we could say to them 'look on us.'"[62]

Addie Wyatt, first executive vice president of CLUW, addresses the first convention in Chicago, 1974. Courtesy of the Rev. Addie and Claude Wyatt Photographs, Vivian G. Harsh Research Collection, Chicago Public Library.

A portrait of Wyatt's mother, Maggie Cameron. Courtesy of the Rev. Addie and Claude Wyatt Photographs, Vivian G. Harsh Research Collection, Chicago Public Library.

Wyatt's father, Ambrose Cameron. Courtesy of the Rev. Addie and Claude Wyatt Photographs, Vivian G. Harsh Research Collection, Chicago Public Library.

A gifted gospel pianist, Addie Wyatt frequently accompanied choirs and church services. Wyatt is pictured here playing the piano at the Langley Avenue Church of God in Chicago. Courtesy of the Rev. Addie and Claude Wyatt Photographs, Vivian G. Harsh Research Collection, Chicago Public Library.

Claude and Addie Wyatt in 1944. Claude Wyatt was stationed at the Great Lakes Naval base in North Chicago, Illinois. Courtesy of the Rev. Addie and Claude Wyatt Photographs, Vivian G. Harsh Research Collection, Chicago Public Library.

Claude Wyatt III, Renaldo Wyatt, and Claude Wyatt Jr. preparing for a performance at Langley Avenue Church of God in Chicago. Courtesy of the Rev. Addie and Claude Wyatt Photographs, Vivian G. Harsh Research Collection, Chicago Public Library.

A crowd assembles outside a plant to hear from UPWA representatives. Standing in the foreground are Addie Wyatt and Charles Hayes (second from right). UPWA leaders frequently utilized lunch breaks and shift changes to meet with workers. Courtesy of the Rev. Addie and Claude Wyatt Photographs, Vivian G. Harsh Research Collection, Chicago Public Library.

Addie Wyatt on the speaker's dais at the 1963 March on Washington. Though she did not give a speech, Wyatt represented several different organizations, including the UPWA, the NALC and her church, Vernon Park Church of God. Courtesy of the Rev. Addie and Claude Wyatt Photographs, Vivian G. Harsh Research Collection, Chicago Public Library.

Claude and Addie Wyatt with members of the Wyatt Choral Ensemble, consisting of youth from Altgeld Gardens. Courtesy of the Rev. Addie and Claude Wyatt Photographs, Vivian G. Harsh Research Collection, Chicago Public Library.

Wyatt laughs with two African women trade leaders and their interpreter at her home in the late 1970s. Courtesy of the Rev. Addie and Claude Wyatt Photographs, Vivian G. Harsh Research Collection, Chicago Public Library.

Vernon Park Church of God
Dedication Observance Week
MARCH 24–31, 1985

"GOD HAS BROUGHT US TO THIS PLACE"
9011 Stony Island Avenue

7653 Maryland Av
1966–1985

74th & Cottage Grove
1959–1966

WILDERNESS

THE

THROUGH

JOURNEY

Morgan Park Church of God
1957–1959

Hayes' Basement
1957

Garage 1955–1957

The Vernon Park Church of God was known for its dynamic ministry and steady growth. Courtesy of the Rev. Addie and Claude Wyatt Photographs, Vivian G. Harsh Research Collection, Chicago Public Library.

Wyatt and NOW President, Eleanor Smeal, head a UFCW march in support of ratification of the Equal Rights Amendment, ca.1982. Courtesy of the Rev. Addie and Claude Wyatt Photographs, Vivian G. Harsh Research Collection, Chicago Public Library.

Wyatt leads a press conference on the importance of African American women in Chicago politics. Chicago Alderwoman Dorothy Tillman (L) and Rev. Willie Barrow (second from right) look on, 1985. Lee Bush, photographer. Courtesy of the Rev. Addie and Claude Wyatt Photographs, Vivian G. Harsh Research Collection, Chicago Public Library.

Addie Wyatt, Chicago Mayor Harold Washington, and political organizer Sid Ordower at an event in support of Washington. Courtesy of the Rev. Addie and Claude Wyatt Photographs, Vivian G. Harsh Research Collection, Chicago Public Library.

As a union representative for the UPWA, Wyatt traveled throughout her district to organize, educate, and represent workers in packing industries, 1957. UPWA photographer, JH Kelly. Courtesy of the Rev. Addie and Claude Wyatt Photographs, Vivian G. Harsh Research Collection, Chicago Public Library.

7

UNFINISHED REVOLUTIONS

In June of 1979, Addie Wyatt sat surrounded by both new and familiar faces. Her union, the Amalgamated, had just completed a merger with the Retail Clerks International Union (RCIU) to form the 1.2 million member United Food and Commercial Workers (UFCW). International Vice President and Director of the Civil Rights and Women's Affairs Department Wyatt sat as one of three blacks and one of two women on the union's forty-nine–member executive board. The board was overwhelmingly white and male, unreflective of the union's membership, about half female and 30 percent African American. At the first International Executive Board meeting, International Vice President and Director of Organization Charles Hayes warned the board that the South was where the UFCW needed to devote more of its resources. The UFCW had to organize primarily black and brown unorganized workers in southern poultry, fishing, and retail industries, despite tough right-to-work laws and corporate resistance to unions. Addie Wyatt seconded Hayes's concerns and argued that in addition to organizing the unorganized, UFCW members would be unionized, a statement she often made to emphasize the need for workers to become active participants in the union. Always one to broach the subject of discrimination in the workplace and the union, Wyatt believed that support for her office would be essential to establishing and promoting more aggressive UFCW antidiscrimination programming. Wyatt proposed that the upcoming inaugural UFCW convention include an adequate number of women and minority delegates, as relying on worker seniority alone to choose delegates would leave out newer workers, many of whom were women and minorities. Both she and Hayes made their agendas and strategies for UFCW success known.[1]

Wyatt, Hayes, and other UPWA veterans sought to influence the responsiveness of the union to worker needs, especially the needs of minority and women workers. Similar to the merger of the UPWA and the Amalgamated, the new union hoped its larger membership and increased resources would strengthen its collective bargaining power. Union leadership argued that a merger would increase the union's capacity to organize unorganized workers in the retail and packing industries and increase their political voice both within the AFL-CIO and in the larger political arena.[2] The merger was one of the largest to ever take place in the history of the American labor movement, and the UFCW did indeed become the largest union in the AFL-CIO, barely edging out the American Federation of State, County, and Municipal Employees (AFSCME) and the United Steelworkers of America (USWA).

The formation of the UFCW also coincided with a shift in the AFL-CIO's leadership. George Meany, head of the AFL-CIO since 1955, retired in 1979. Lane Kirkland, Meany's special assistant, assumed leadership of the AFL-CIO. Relatively unknown to labor leaders outside of the AFL-CIO's upper echelons, rank-and-file trade unionists wondered if Kirkland would simply maintain Meany's conservative policies, enacting a laissez-faire approach to race- and sex-based discrimination in organized labor. Labor leaders like Addie Wyatt questioned whether or not the AFL-CIO would respond effectively and decisively against the antiunion policies and the economic, political, and social conservatism of the late 1970s and early 1980s. As it would turn out, Wyatt was right to question the extent to which Kirkland and the AFL-CIO would diversify the body's Executive Council to reflect organized labor's membership. A bitter betrayal would reveal the extent to which black labor leaders' calls for greater representation and leadership in the AFL-CIO would be met only on terms not of their making. Through it all, Wyatt continued to seek out ways to better incorporate labor's growing female and minority base. Navigating the changes and challenges within the UFCW and the AFL-CIO would dominate Wyatt's last years of formal leadership within the labor movement.

More than ever, Wyatt looked to politics, local community empowerment and grassroots worker struggles as crucial to maintaining and winning additional gains for working people, women, and minorities in the workplace and beyond. For Wyatt, building the infrastructure for change necessitated work beyond the labor movement into the world of political organizing. The 1980s may have been the twilight years of Wyatt's formal career in labor leadership and organizing, but her faith in collective action, the power of coalitions, and the righteousness of the struggle for human dignity and equality remained strong. In what has been considered an era of conservatism's stronghold in twentieth-century American politics and society, key late-twentieth-century progressive political and labor victories illustrated that the fight for political representation, economic rights, and human dignity were far from over. Both Harold Washington's stunning election as the first black mayor of the City of

Chicago and struggles for unionism and better working conditions by black workers in the South illustrate that there were chinks in conservatism's perceived impenetrable armor, and that black political and economic insurgency was alive and well in the post–civil rights era. In each struggle, Addie Wyatt was there, helping to marshal financial resources, human capital, and inspiration to support the movements and ensure victory. In both labor and electoral politics, black women like Addie Wyatt were critical architects utilizing their organizing skills, personal and collective experiences, and intellect to achieve greater political and economic power. With varying degrees of success as well as devastating setbacks, Wyatt continued the call for a more inclusive, democratic labor movement and society.

THE UNITED FOOD AND COMMERCIAL WORKERS AND THE END OF AN ERA

While the merger between the Amalgamated and the RCIU would give Addie Wyatt a larger platform through which to push for labor's democratization and diversification, it also made the work that much more difficult, given the bureaucratization of organized labor in the 1970s and 1980s, which exposed a growing rift between rank-and-file trade unionists and union leadership. Wyatt experienced these difficulties in the Amalgamated, but the much larger UFCW membership was even further removed from the UPWA's tradition of interracial social unionism. Considered to be one of the more liberal unions in the AFL-CIO when compared to the more conservative construction and building trades unions, the UFCW in the 1980s was still a far cry from the UPWA in scope, size, structure, leadership, and philosophical orientation. Wyatt, who came into the labor movement through the UPWA and emerged as a leader within that union, continued to try to resuscitate its synergy among a diverse, yet disparate UFCW membership.

Chartered in 1890 under the American Federation of Labor as the Retail Clerks National Protective Association, the RCIU had its roots in the retail employment industry, which for much of the twentieth century refused to hire blacks as retail clerks. The RCIU also failed to adequately represent those blacks who were retail clerks in black commercial districts. Women who entered the retail industry in greater numbers in the 1940s faced discrimination within the industry and in their unions because marriage and pregnancy often required swift resignation from retail employment. The increase of African Americans and other racial minorities into service and retail industries in larger numbers in the 1960s increased the number of black union members in the RCIU. In 1972, black members formed the RCIU's Minority Coalition to help increase opportunities for black employment in the retail industry and to increase the placement of minorities in leadership and policy-making positions at all levels of the union.[3] But the coalition suffered from a small membership and had virtually no institutional backing from the union and its president, William Wynn.

One of the biggest adjustments Wyatt had to make as a staff member of the UFCW was relocating from Chicago to Washington, D.C., the union's new headquarters. The Wyatts discussed the move and any stress it might put on their thirty-nine-year marriage and their family. Even though Wyatt's work in the UPWA and the Amalgamated carried her all over the country and demanded much of her time, Chicago remained her home base. Wyatt made it a priority to attend Sunday services at the Vernon Park Church of God and maintain an active presence in the church. As an involved community member, relocating to the Washington, D.C., area would mean not only distancing herself from her family, but from her spiritual, social, and political roots as well. In the end, the Wyatts determined that it was a worthwhile and necessary move given that Addie believed there was still much more work to do through the union for working people. Furthermore, residing in D.C. would place Wyatt closer to the political epicenter of the nation, making the job of lobbying for better federal labor legislation, civil rights, and women's rights initiatives somewhat more feasible. Addie relocated to the Washington, D.C., area where she maintained a small apartment and kept a hectic schedule flying back to Chicago two to three times a month over the course of her five years with the UFCW. When he was able to get away from his pastoral duties, Claude traveled to see Addie as well.

Wyatt reported directly to William Wynn, former leader of the RCIU and first president of the UFCW, through weekly written reports of her activities and regular departmental reports. As head of Civil Rights and Women's Affairs, Wyatt continued to plan and lead conferences and workshops for workers on the status of working women in the labor movement, the future of organized labor in an age of recession, and the role of minorities and women in the women's movement and civil rights struggles. Wynn frequently appointed Wyatt to represent the union at civil rights and women's meetings when he was unable to attend. Wyatt was also responsible for developing and maintaining relationships with key labor allies in civil rights and women's organizations. She had to put forth an annual budget for her department that included contributions to organizations such as the Martin Luther King Jr. Center for Social Justice, the Southern Christian Leadership Conference, the Coalition of Black Trade Unionists, the Coalition of Labor Union Women, the Democratic National Committee, the National Council of Negro Women, the National Women's Political Caucus, United Way, Women's Equity Action League, and the National Association for the Advancement of Colored People, among others.[4] She was already an active member in a number of these organizations. Wyatt's reputation as someone who could procure financial resources and human capital to the struggle for equality was evident in her UFCW post.

Within the union, Wyatt's department supported affirmative action policies and created aggressive education, training, and work programs that promoted opportunities for women and minorities so they could learn to perform the jobs available. She believed that such efforts could combat race and sex discrimination in hiring and promotions and would ultimately bring more workers into the fold of the organized labor movement, thereby strengthening it. Wyatt saw these affirmative action policies as critical to not only dismantling lily-white and "lily-male" departments and promotions channels, but to the very necessary work of organizing unorganized workers. One of organized labor's lifelines and greatest challenges is to organize unorganized workers, which includes gaining employment for the unemployed, organizing workers without union representation, and keeping those workers who are in unions with jobs. The UFCW could not afford to turn a blind eye to racism and sexism within its ranks if it wanted to organize an increasingly diverse workforce in the growing service-oriented retail and grocery industries.

In the first few years after the merger, the Civil Rights and Women's Affairs Department continued to receive notices of EEOC complaints against employers and the union. After receiving EEOC notifications from the AFL-CIO, Wyatt's department contacted the regions and/or locals involved to ascertain more information about the status of the case and whether or not the charges had already been addressed or dismissed. Once the department received that information, it then forwarded its findings back to the AFL-CIO. The EEOC cases included charges of racism and sexism in hiring, promotions, transfers, and training, sexual harassment, and the failure of UFCW locals to adequately represent worker grievances. Case notes reveal that once some blacks finally had their seniority respected and gained promotion, they were put into new jobs or departments with little to no training by their supervisors and coworkers, only to then be fired for underperformance. Black workers claimed that white workers, even if they were newly hired and lacked seniority, received adequate training. In other cases, women claimed that little had been done by the UFCW to address their grievances of sexual harassment at the hands of their male coworkers and supervisors. Many of the grievances brought by minority and female members cited a lack of fair and equal union representation in grievances as a major problem that the UFCW needed to address.[5]

Charged with building effective civil rights and women's committees on the ground to equip workers with the resources and tools to address discrimination at the local level, Wyatt's department often had to first reclaim and relegitimize the union as an organization for *all* members. Workers would have very little faith in the solidarity premise underlying the union creed if they continued to feel as if the union undermined female and minority workers by aiding in the very discrimination it was supposed to protect them from. In executive meetings, Wyatt frequently called attention to the need to increase the union's financial and organizational support to the needs of women and minority workers. Because of her knowledge of EEOC claims, Wyatt could point to direct evidence of the neglect minority and women workers faced and the problems of representation at the local union level. During her five years in UFCW, Wyatt repeatedly requested the creation of an International Advisory Committee on Sexual Harassment to be housed in her department. The committee would investigate and give locals the tools to properly address sexual harassment. Such a committee was never approved. Despite a membership of over one million, including hundreds of thousands of women and minority workers, the Civil Rights and Women's Affairs Department had a staff of five, including Wyatt as director, plus an assistant director and three research assistants.

In 1980, one of Wyatt's initiatives for addressing the problems of women and minority workers in the union came to fruition with the UFCW's First Women's Affairs and Civil Rights Conference. Thousands of delegates from across the country and Canada attended the two-day conference held in Washington, D.C. The theme of the conference, "Improving Our Lives the Union Way: Collective Bargaining, Social and Political Action," was reflected in the conference workshops. The sessions included workshops on: how to plan local-level women's affairs and civil rights conferences; building coalitions with local community organizations; the impact of recession; health, safety and the woman worker; the continuing fight for equal pay for equal work; and organizing the unorganized and unionizing the organized. Other workshops focused on combating sexual harassment on the job, the proper handling of sex and race-based grievances, ratifying the ERA, child care and women's health concerns as union issues, expanding minority participation in the UFCW, and techniques of effective leadership. To that effect, guest speakers included UFCW President William Wynn; Alexis Herman, director of the Women's Bureau of the U.S. Department of Labor; D.C. Mayor Marion Barry; Coretta Scott King; Gloria Johnson of the International Union of Electrical Workers; Charles Hayes; and Kenneth Young, executive assistant to the president of the AFL-CIO, Lane Kirkland, who could not attend.[6]

A key mission of the conference was to promote the creation of local and regional women's, civil rights, and political affairs committees so that rank-and-file members could have the tools at their disposal to address problems that arose on a daily basis. The Department of Civil Rights and Women's Affairs worked with local and regional UFCW entities to promote the formation of these committees in an effort to increase minority and women's participation in the union as well as to push to the fore the problems of race and sex discrimination. For

Wyatt, the creation of these committees at all levels of the union decentralized its work and helped to further democratize organized labor:

> I see the union body as a circle of people. I see committees as satellites, all connected with that body, taking on special responsibilities for the health of the total body. Women's affairs committees, for example, are composed of men and women who become specialists on women's concerns—dialoging, identifying, interpreting problems, reporting and recommending action. I see many other satellites—committees on political action, health and safety, education—all connected to the main body. Committees are a way to say to each member: "You are welcome here. We need you."[7]

If indeed the union was only as strong as its individual members, Addie Wyatt sought to use her office to ensure that members from the bottom up played a greater role in serving and directing the goals of the union in order to better meet their needs. She believed that conferences and institutional meetings within the union helped give members the tools they needed to build and sustain meaningful committees. In many ways, Wyatt aimed to cultivate the sense of purpose and solidarity in the UFCW that she had witnessed at her very first union meeting in the UPWA. She believed in regular worker education, training, and empowerment to unionize members and believed that the union could be and should be much more than a dues-collecting, bureaucratic organization. The conference was a success and spawned the creation of a number of local civil rights, women's affairs, and political affairs committees. In addition, ten of the UFCW's regional boards across Canada and the United States planned and eventually held their own women's affairs and civil rights conferences annually or biennially.

Democratizing the AFL-CIO Executive Council was a major focus of militant black and female trade unionists. In 1980, Lane Kirkland appointed Joyce Miller, CLUW president, as the first woman to serve on the council. CLUW members had pressured the council for female representation since 1974. At the time of Miller's appointment, there was one black on the AFL-CIO's thirty-five–member board—Frederick O'Neal of the small Associated Actors and Artistes of America union. Both CLUW and CBTU continued to argue for greater representation of blacks and women on the AFL-CIO's top policy-making board as the numbers of blacks and women in organized labor increased. Black labor leaders were especially vocal about the need for greater representation on the council. By 1980, blacks were joining and supporting unions in higher percentages than whites, about 33 percent to 26 percent, respectively.[8] Despite ongoing racism and discrimination in aspects of the labor movement, blacks still believed in the collective bargaining process. Furthermore, blacks sought the protections and benefits that unions could provide, such as increased earnings, compared to nonunionized workers and believed in the progressive economic, political, and social power that unions could potentially harness.[9] Most blacks were concentrated in the service, garment, retail, and public sectors as opposed to the skilled trades, and they represented sizable portions of unions like the UFCW, SEIU, AFSCME, and the UAW. Overall, blacks represented about 17 percent of the AFL-CIO's total membership, but less than 1 percent of its governing council. At the 9th Annual CBTU Convention, during its "Black Women in the Labor Movement" workshop, Addie Wyatt put forth a resolution calling for the expansion of the AFL-CIO Executive Council to include two seats for women of minority groups as vacancies occurred. The resolution passed by a vote of 33 to 1 and Wyatt went on to successfully present the resolution at the 1980 CLUW Convention.[10]

When five vacancies opened up on the council in 1981, AFL-CIO Secretary-Treasurer Thomas Donahue approached Frederick O'Neal and asked him to put together names of blacks who he believed would serve well on the council. O'Neal convened a meeting of 30 to 35 black trade union leaders, many of them affiliated with CBTU, and came up with a short list of names, including: Addie Wyatt of UFCW; Bill Lucy, president of CBTU and vice president of AFSCME; and Leon Lynch, USW vice president; and possibly Charles Hayes.[11] Wyatt was the only woman on the list. But in rather dramatic fashion at the 1981 AFL-CIO International Convention, none of the names put forth by black union leadership were selected. Instead, a virtual unknown among black labor and civil rights circles was selected, a young black woman named Barbara Hutchinson, who was Director of Women's Affairs for the American Federation of Government Employees (AFGE). Hutchinson, a lawyer by trade, had a relatively short career in the labor movement, having joined her union's staff in the late 1970s, and was largely unknown by many in organized labor, including black labor leadership. She was not of the old-line black labor leaders who had years of experience in labor fighting against racism. Nor was she affiliated with the Coalition of Black Trade Unionists.

Hutchinson's selection was a slap in the face to veteran, militant black labor leaders who felt that they had paid their dues to the movement and were in the position to represent their unions and also black workers at the highest level of leadership where policies and decisions were made. These leaders were wedded to the structure of organized labor but critical of its exclusivity. No major union in the AFL-CIO had a black person at its helm and, of its twenty-five largest unions, only two had blacks in second-in-command posts, including Mary Hatwell Futrell of the National Education Association and Bill Lucy of AFSCME. Black trade unionists wanted more positions on the council that were representative of their numbers in organized labor—positions that could be used to provide outspoken, explicit and unapologetic voices against racism and discrimination. In many national unions, and especially in the AFL-CIO, it was difficult for blacks to break into leadership positions because successors were often handpicked and groomed. More often than not, those successors looked just like their white male predecessors. Charles Hayes argued, "You have to force change. Just like any other ruling group those who have power in the trade union movement will not voluntarily relinquish it."[12]

Lane Kirkland favored Barbara Hutchinson for the council's vacant seat and made other council members aware of his decision, including UFCW President William Wynn. Kirkland expected Hutchinson to be nominated and elected without incident. Addie Wyatt soon found herself at the center of the convention's open-seat controversy as one of those expected to be nominated by rank-and-file conference delegates. Wyatt did not feel as if she were personally entitled to the seat as much as she felt that it should go to a black labor leader who had paid his or her dues fighting against racism and discrimination. No one could "vouch" for Hutchinson and she had no proven record of fighting for equality within the larger labor movement. Nor did she have a constituency of supporters behind her, and some wondered if she would simply follow the council's status quo of giving lip service to civil rights and women's rights while failing to sanction discrimination in its affiliates. When Wyatt and Charles Hayes approached William Wynn about Hutchinson's nomination and the lack of input by black labor leaders, Wynn informed them that he would indeed vote for Hutchinson as he had a commitment to Lane Kirkland. Wynn then asked Wyatt to withdraw her name from consideration and the short list, which she ultimately did.[13] It would be virtually impossible given the voting structure of the AFL-CIO for any candidate nominated against Hutchinson to win, as she would have the support of council members and other delegates who would follow the council's vote.

Angry that the wishes of loyal black leaders in the movement had been discarded, and unwilling to stump for someone who had not appeared to pay her dues, Wyatt was even more incensed and hurt by accusations that she posed a threat to the very movement she had devoted her life to. National news media covered the controversy and according to the *New York Times*, Lane Kirkland received and sided with reports from some council members that Wyatt was "too militant, too unpredictable" and therefore not a good fit for the council.[14] The specifics behind these criticisms and any evidence of Wyatt's militancy were not elaborated on, but Wyatt took offense. On hotel letterhead, she penned a response to the *Times* article and other reports that she intended to deliver in a statement before other black labor leaders and members of the convention:

> Now I want you my brothers to know I never have been anxious to be on the council. Especially if I'm not wanted there. I want to be where I'm wanted because

> I want to help and be effective in building and strengthening our movement. If they don't want me on the council, ok. But I will not tolerate anybody discrediting my life's work. Nobody truthfully can say I've been a discredit to the labor movement in my nearly 40 years of being a part of it. Nobody. I represent it in labor circles, political, civil rights, women's religious, government world-wide. And I try to do it proudly. Much of what I've learned I learned in the labor movement. At best I have only a few more years and I don't plan to go out of it bitter.[15]

Addie Wyatt felt that she had always put workers and the labor movement first and that her efforts to increase the participation and opportunities for all within that movement should be seen as a credit to its transformative potential for working people, rather than a threat. She was even more disappointed at the utter lack of support she received from Wynn.

The convention proceedings signaled to militant black labor leaders that although the AFL-CIO was willing to marginally increase the numbers of blacks on its council, it would ultimately be on Kirkland's and the council's terms. Frederick O'Neal later stated in a meeting of black trade unionists that he appreciated that a black woman was now on the council, but objected to the manner in which it was done, "Personally, I'm somewhat weary of persons other than Blacks making decisions for us and telling us in a sense, that 'Father Knows Best.' We don't need this kind of benevolence. It smacks too strongly of paternalism and of the so called 'good old days.'"[16] Still, black leaders did not turn their backs on the organized labor movement despite the feelings of betrayal, frustration, and disappointment bred by the events of the 1981 convention. As far as they were concerned, black trade unionists and the larger labor movement had common enemies—Reaganomics and the flight of industry from the United States. Funding and support for the EEOC, equal opportunity legislation, and affirmative action programs were drastically reduced. Civil rights and voting rights legislation were also weakened. Tax increases for the poor and working class were accompanied by decreased taxes paid by those with much higher incomes. High inflation rates and unemployment along with the flight of manufacturing and industrial work compounded the difficulties faced by working-class laborers. These were all facets of Reaganomics that labor, civil rights, and progressive political activists organized against on a daily basis and in large-scale demonstrations, such as organized labor's 1981 Solidarity Day in which over 250,000 trade unionists protested President Reagan's policies in Washington, D.C.[17]

Black labor leaders recognized the common foe of Reaganomics as a threat to organized labor and gains made by blacks in the civil rights and post–civil rights era. But they refused, especially after the 1981 controversy, to remain silent on the lack of representation and racism in organized labor, which they argued undermined labor's strength and played into the hands of labor's foes. CBTU

President Bill Lucy was especially vocal about the need for organized labor to fully embrace blacks as members and leaders within the movement. Lucy was critical of labor's calls to band together in solidarity against the political currents of the time while racism went unchecked: "[B]efore black union members set their feet to walking, a meeting of the minds needs to take place—their's first, then with whomever they've supposed to be marching with . . . there must be discussion of the status of black workers, the status of black leadership, the role that we play in the trade union movement, and how the institutions of organized labor either serve or impede black progress."[18] Lucy argued that "the media daily conducts a public autopsy of the trade union movement" as good for nothing but making concessions that further weakened workers' bargaining abilities. Yet black workers were joining organized labor in greater numbers. For black workers, the labor movement was not dead. But like Wyatt, Hayes, O'Neal, and other black leaders, Lucy argued that "with the growth of black union membership, the absence of black leadership on all levels of union activity fuels internal fissures and diminishes the credibility of those unions that claim to be opponents of discrimination."[19]

Though she continued to work within the labor movement and the UFCW after the 1981 AFL-CIO convention, Wyatt's years of formal leadership in the labor movement were certainly drawing to an end. Just three years later, in early August of 1984, Wyatt drafted a letter of resignation to William Wynn, effective September 30, 1984. After forty three years in the organized labor movement and thirty years on the staff of her union, Wyatt resigned in a short and concise letter. She did not detail any specific grievances or reasons for her resignation, but offered: "I leave loving my union and still seeing it as the most viable vehicle for the improvement of the lives of working-class people and their families throughout the world. If I had to do it all over again, some things would perhaps be done differently, but I would still choose the labor movement as the place to make my little career contributions." The rest of her letter discussed the administrative aspects of her resignation before closing with: "May God Bless and direct you and each leader of our organization, as you continue to accomplish some of our highest human goals: good jobs, decent wages, safe and healthy working conditions, justice, freedom, equality, and peace."

At the time of her retirement, Addie Wyatt was arguably the most visible and assuredly one of the highest-ranked African American women in the organized labor movement. But what exactly brought her to retire after just five years in the UFCW? Without Wyatt's exact reasoning, we can only speculate. Wyatt may have decided to retire due to her age. She was sixty years old, but much older in activist years. The wear and tear of a life of organizing and activism requires not only extensive travel but an intense emotional, physical, and mental investment. Wyatt battled arthritis and bouts with hypertension as she advanced in age. Keeping up a hectic travel schedule to and from Chicago may have taken its toll and led to her resignation. Wyatt's age, health, and desire to be back in Chicago near her family and church might have factored into her decision.

But several changes in UFCW policies, especially in relation to the Civil Rights and Women's Affairs Department, may shed light on her decision. Wyatt's repeated requests for an International Women's Affairs Advisory Commission to aid the work of her department were consistently dismissed. In 1982, President Wynn announced that EEOC complaints would no longer go through the Department of Civil Rights and Women's Affairs, citing inefficiencies and a need to centralize the process through which such claims were investigated. Austerity budgets limited the scope of the department's annual conferences and the amount of funds the union contributed to allied organizations in political, civil rights, and women's rights organizations. At the same time, Wyatt was given the task of handling the union's retirees without any official programmatic or policy direction from Wynn. It is possible that Wyatt felt too limited by the growing constraints on her department and what may be interpreted as a lack of union investment. Wyatt and Wynn's working relationship was not nearly as strong as Wyatt's relationship with her former supervisors, Charles Hayes and Patrick Gorman. Wynn's lack of support for Wyatt at the 1981 AFL-CIO convention may have also played a role in Wyatt leaving the UFCW after five years.

But yet another explanation is plausible. In the early 1980s, Wyatt became much more involved in electoral politics and political organizing campaigns in Chicago and nationwide. Perhaps it was her increased time stumping and campaigning for Democratic political candidates that led to Wyatt's departure from the UFCW. She played an important role in U.S. Representative Harold Washington's stunning victories in the 1983 and 1987 Chicago mayoral elections. She also devoted energies to campaigning for her friend and fellow activist, Reverend Jesse Jackson, when he ran for president in 1984. When Jackson failed to win the Democratic primary, Wyatt supported the Walter Mondale/Geraldine Ferraro campaign. Wyatt's participation in these campaigns illustrates her belief in the importance of electoral politics in conjunction with social movement activism. Her participation and leadership in the movement to elect Harold Washington as mayor of the city of Chicago perhaps best illustrates her commitment to local community empowerment, coalition building, and the power of women's activism.

HAROLD WASHINGTON: THE PEOPLE'S MAYOR

Scholars, journalists, politicians, and activists have all chronicled the history of black politics in Chicago and Harold Washington's remarkable election as the city's first black mayor.[20] Between 1967 and 1990, the United States witnessed an important shift in the political sphere that included the election of first-time black mayors in major cities across the nation, beginning with Carl Stokes in Cleveland, Ohio, and Richard Gordon Hatcher in Gary, Indiana.[21] This shift coincided with an increase in urban problems like deindustrialization, crime, flight from the city, and budget cuts. Harold Washington's election in 1983 and reelection in 1987 fits neatly within this era of increased local black political power in the post–civil rights era. But within the context of Chicago city politics and the work of longtime political activists like Addie Wyatt, we can gain an even greater understanding of the important transformations in community and municipal politics that took place during Washington's mayoral campaign and subsequent administrations.

Addie Wyatt had a long history of political activism that predated Harold Washington's 1983 mayoral campaign. As early as the 1950s, she engaged in protest politics against Chicago's Democratic machine and supported independent black political candidates. As members of the UPWA actively involved in community politics through the PWCCC, both Wyatt and Hayes were highly critical of William Dawson, their U.S. Congressman from Illinois' First Congressional District and the strongest black in the Cook County Democratic Organization.[22] Dawson was criticized by Hayes, Wyatt, and other black activists due to his silence on civil rights issues like the Trumbull Park riots, the murder of Emmett Till and the Montgomery Bus Boycott. Chicago political activist Bennett Johnson occasionally worked with Wyatt, Hayes, and T. R. M. Howard through an organization of nonpartisan blacks called the Chicago League of Negro Voters. Johnson recalled that blacks in the League were extremely critical of Dawson; they believed he "made concessions to the regular organization and [that] the first Mayor Daley wouldn't have been elected if he hadn't been supported by Bill Dawson. And the problem was that Dawson didn't get enough of that support, he just got approval from on high and didn't get enough jobs, political slating and so forth."[23] In essence, the machine worked for Dawson, but not nearly as well for blacks further removed from the locus of political power.

Black political activists in Chicago were looking to buck the racial conservatism of the machine and Daley's stronghold on Chicago politics. The Cook County Democratic Organization was synonymous with the name Richard J. Daley from the mid-1950s through his death in 1976 and arguably up to the Harold Washington years. According to journalist Mike Royko, Richard J. Daley limited the power around him, making himself a "kingmaker" so that everything and everyone went through him, not only at the local and state level, but nationally as well. Though they continued to vote for him in election after election, blacks in Chicago lamented the ways in which Daley devoted resources to building up Chicago's downtown at the expense of neighborhoods, allowed for police brutality against blacks to go unchecked, and refused to recognize and sanction racial and economic discrimination in employment, housing and education which he attributed to "voluntary segregation."[24] The overwhelming majority of nonwhite political activists and everyday citizens were shut out of the government.

In 1973, black activists formed the Committee for a Black Mayor to explore options for a viable black mayoral candidate that would have support from Chicago's black community as well as wider appeal and electability. The committee included a mix of Chicago's veteran and up-and-coming black political leaders, clergy, and labor and community activists. Charles Hayes served as chairman of the organization with Bennett Johnson as executive director, T. R. M. Howard as treasurer, Tommy Briscoe as fund-raising chair, and James Montgomery, president of the Cook County Bar Association, as chairman of the Interviewing Committee. Others on the committee including Claude and Addie Wyatt, A. A. Rayner, Theresa Fambro Hooks, Leon Finney Jr., Reverend Clay Evans, Leon Davis, Danny Davis, Alderman William Cousins, Arnita Boswell, Timuel Black, Leona Black, Lenora Cartwright, Rev. Jesse Jackson, and Nancy Jefferson. The group operated out of the UPWA's old District One headquarters, the Packinghouse Workers Center at 4859 S. Wabash. The Committee, tired of corruption in city politics, sought a reformed and more inclusive government: "The Committee is dedicated to political empowerment of black, brown, yellow, red and poor people in the City of Chicago. The race for Mayor is only the first part of our program. We want to see a City Council that responds to the needs of people and we are going to get the job done."[25] The committee sought a near-perfect candidate with a clean record of proven integrity, consistent support for civil rights and human rights struggles in Chicago, and an ability to achieve interracial and multiracial support. The committee additionally sought a candidate who was knowledgeable of the political process and able and willing to engage in Chicago's dog-eat-dog politics, essentially a candidate who knew how to handle the Democratic machine. The chosen candidate would also need to possess stellar administrative skills and be willing to stay in the race until the very end.[26]

The Committee for a Black Mayor polled black voters to see whom they would support. Longtime politician and Olympian athlete Ralph Metcalfe polled as the leading candidate, with Harold Washington, Cecil Partee, and several others further down on the list. Metcalfe was one of the senior most blacks in city government, having served as an alderman for the South Side since 1955. In 1970, he won the First Congressional District seat in the U.S. House of Representatives, replacing William Dawson who had retired and died shortly thereafter. Though known in his early career for maintaining loyalty to Daley and the city's Democratic machine, Metcalfe broke with both in the early 1970s over widespread police brutality by Chicago police officers against black citizens and the mayor's reluctance to address the issue, sanction the department, and properly clean house. Two of Metcalfe's own friends were slain by Chicago police officers. Wyatt, who regularly supported and worked with the First Congressional District Citizens Committee in the 1970s, joined Metcalfe on several initiatives, including a task force—Concerned Citizens for Police Reform—that included many prominent black activists in Chicago. With Concerned Citizens for Police Reform, Wyatt served on the Negotiating Committee, which sought to influence the selection and promotion of policemen in the Chicago Police Department to increase police accountability and relations with black communities. She also participated in the highly publicized community hearings held by Metcalfe, which included testimonies from black victims of police brutality.

Metcalfe's new political independence further endeared him to black Chicagoans and independent-minded citizens but it earned him the ire of the regular Democratic organization and the city's machine. Metcalfe was somewhat reluctant to run for mayor in 1975 against the incumbent, Richard J. Daley, boss of the machine. He eventually agreed and made several demands of the Committee for a Black Mayor and his supporters, all of which he believed would increase his chances in the election. According to committee chairman Charles Hayes, these demands included $500,000 in launching funds to support the campaign and public outreach, a broad-based multiracial citizens support committee, and a top public relations firm to market the campaign; an additional demand called for all other possible black candidates to withdraw from the race in hopes of precluding any splitting of the black vote, assuming blacks would back an independent Democratic candidate.[27] The committee was able to partially secure some of the demands, raising about $187,000 for the campaign over the span of a few weeks, mostly from ordinary citizens as opposed to the black community's wealthy elite and politically connected. The committee also secured the services of one of the city's top public relations firms but felt it had no right or authority to ask other possible black candidates to withdraw from the race. However, before the Committee could continue its push forward with the Metcalfe candidacy, Metcalfe announced, in a meeting that took place in the Wyatt's home, that he would not be continuing his run for mayor. Allegedly deterred by threats from other Democratic candidates and the Democratic organization, Metcalfe withdrew.[28]

Wyatt continued to support Metcalfe, who encountered significant machine opposition in his 1976 bid for reelection to U.S. Congress. Wyatt was a member of the steering committee for Women Standing for Metcalfe (also known as STAND for Metcalfe) over the 1976–1977 campaign season. Several First Congressional District groups rallied around their congressman, including those led by Charles Hayes, *Chicago Defender* owner John Sengstacke, and campaign chairman Louis Martin. Metcalfe was ultimately reelected but passed away two years later in 1978. The Committee for a Black Mayor collapsed in 1975, but many from the group would be extremely influential in Harold Washington's unsuccessful mayoral bid in 1977 and later successes in 1983 and 1987. A lawyer by trade, Harold Washington was a protégé of Metcalfe and also represented the First Congressional District. As an alumnus of DuSable High School, Washington had ties to many movers and shakers in Chicago's black political community, including the Wyatts.

Washington gained greater notoriety in Chicago politics after Mayor Richard J. Daley's death in 1976. He was inspired in part to run in the 1977 special mayoral election due to a political fallout on the city council that exposed the machine's racism. African American Alderman Wilson Frost served as president pro tem of the city council and according to the council's constitution, Frost, as the chief executive on the council prior to the mayor's death, should have assumed office. Instead, Daley's political machine blocked Frost and appointed white machine member, Michael Bilandic as Daley's replacement in office.[29] Washington vehemently denounced the machine's treatment of Frost and blatant disregard for the council's constitutional process. He was somewhat of a renegade, unafraid to espouse an independent voice within Illinois' Democratic Party. He departed from the Cook County Democratic machine and the statewide Democratic leadership on key issues, including his support for women's reproductive rights and the Equal Rights Amendment. During his five terms in the state legislature and one term in the state senate, Washington introduced a bill to make Martin Luther King Day a federal holiday in Illinois, called for 10 percent black contractor set-asides, equalized currency exchange fees across neighborhoods, introduced a bill to save ailing Provident Hospital on Chicago's South Side and generally supported policies and programs that would aid Chicago's most disenfranchised citizens.[30] Washington's politics were very much in line with Wyatt's philosophy of social equity, community empowerment, and inclusive democracy.

Progressive and independent-minded activists like Addie Wyatt rallied behind Washington's 1977 bid for mayor. The Committee for Harold Washington included labor organizers and leaders like Charles Hayes and Harold Rogers, who spearheaded the Labor Committee for Washington out of the Packinghouse Center. From the beginning, many black labor activists in the city supported Washington as a political candidate for state legislature, mayor, and U.S. Congress. Women who supported Washington included Addie Wyatt, Nancy Jefferson, Jacqueline Jackson, Dorothy Rivers, and Earline Lindsey. They formed an early women's support group for Washington, who ran in the election as an Independent Progressive Democrat. Wyatt's vocal support of Washington for mayor in 1977 went against that of the larger organized labor movement and the local Democratic Party, both of which toed to the party's mainline machine candidate, Michael Bilandic. Wyatt's open support for Washington even imperiled her chances of being elected to the Democratic National Committee (DNC) in 1978.[31]

In the end, Washington lost the election to Bilandic. He returned to the state legislature and faced stiff opposition from the Democratic organization in his next election because of his ill-fated run for mayor. In Washington's district primary, the party ran three opponents against him, including two who also had the last name Washington, a move clearly crafted to confuse voters and draw votes away from Harold Washington. But Washington held his seat. He was later elected to U.S. Congress in 1980 over a machine-backed nominee and reelected in 1982, where he became a vocal opponent of President Ronald Reagan and the negative impact of Reaganomics.[32] Washington and Wyatt frequented D.C. at the same time, Washington as a U.S. Congressman and Wyatt as labor leader with the UFCW.

The failure to have a black person seriously considered for mayoral office in Chicago in the 1970s was indeed a setback to the movement for greater black political representation and empowerment in the city, but it marked a new beginning rather an end to the struggle. Blacks seemed to be just as marginalized after Daley's death than before it, and far too many black politicians, as well as those representing black communities politically, remained wedded to a machine that failed to aid the city's ailing neighborhood communities, especially the black south and west sides. Jane Byrne, the city's first woman mayor, ran on a reformist platform in 1979, courting much of the black community. Wyatt openly supported Byrne's candidacy believing that she was a reform candidate, as did CBTU, CLUW, and many in organized labor. Wyatt even worked with Byrne's transition committee for a short time. Yet once in office, Byrne turned her back on many of her reform promises and dutifully reported to the city's machine, under the influence of powerful Democratic Alderman Ed Vrydolyak. Byrne disposed of two black Board of Education members and others blacks from the Chicago Housing Authority whom she replaced with whites with questionable racial politics and backgrounds, further divesting blacks of any say in two of the city's entities that largely served black citizens. The city's black community, aided by organizations like Jesse Jackson's People United to Save Humanity (PUSH) and by radio host and activist Lu Palmer, boycotted Byrne's Chicago Fest in the summer of 1982, and got several high-profile black performers to back out on promises to perform at the festival.[33]

The calls for a black mayor again rose—and from several directions—as many scholars of Chicago's black politics and the Harold Washington years have illustrated. Well-documented and recollected are the calls of black nationalists like radio personality Lutrelle "Lu" Palmer, who took to quoting the chant, "We shall see in '83" to trouble the notion that blacks would continue to settle for

neglect and outright exclusion in city politics. Groups like Black Independent
Political Organization (BIPO), Chicago Black United Communities (CBUC),
and the Task Force for Black Political Empowerment were formed to drum up
political sentiment in black communities, register voters, and increase the level
of support for independent black voices like Harold Washington in city government.[34] Washington was a star in black political circles for his willingness
to buck the machine, the issues he supported, and his political acumen. Yet he
somewhat reluctantly agreed to run for mayor in the summer of 1982. Washington enjoyed being in U.S. Congress and was a rising star. Heading back to
Chicago to take on the machine was a risk and an endeavor that would require
the formation of a movement unlike any other in Chicago's history, primarily
among its black citizens but also among those wanting reform in city politics.
As with prior Metcalfe years, Washington made demands on those urging him
to run, including $250,000 in launch funds and 50,000 new registered voters
who would likely support his campaign.

Black business owners like Ed Garner of Soft Sheen would also form a core
part of the constituency supporting Washington, in many cases providing the
capital necessary for voter registration. Civil rights activists and community
groups also played important roles. PUSH, led by Jesse Jackson, played a critical
role in serving as a meeting post and as a major site of voter registration, as did
the Packinghouse Workers Center. Interracial coalitions composed of the city's
black politicians and community activists, Latinos, and independent-minded
whites joined together to back Washington. Latinos like Rudy Lozano, Jesus
"Chuy" Garcia, Luis Guitierrez, and Miguel Del Valle, and whites like Slim
Coleman were key constituents in the campaign as well.

Though much has been written about the Washington coalition and those
representing the movement for reform in city politics, the roles of clergy and
churches, women, and organized labor were integral to Washington's success
but have too often been overlooked. These groups were vital to the Washington
coalition, adding crucial financial resources, human capital, and more expansive
networks. Not by accident, Addie Wyatt was a member of each of these groups,
moving between them to draw greater support for Washington and reform in
city politics. She was as much a staunch believer in the power of diverse coalitions to bring about change as she was a believer in the need for group- or
identity-based empowerment to bring about change. The Washington coalition
provided a unique blend of both.

Among the clergy who supported Washington's campaign and administrations were Chicago religious leaders and political activists, including the Wyatts,
Rev. Willie Barrow, Rev. Jeremiah Wright, Rev. A. P. Jackson, Rev. Eugene Gibson, and Rev. Jesse Cotton. These clergy came together to produce an insight-
ful volume, *The Black Church and the Harold Washington Story*. Many of these

leaders took part in Clergy for Harold Washington, a campaign and election support group. Mixing religion and politics was not anathema to these clergy, many of whom boldly proclaimed their support for Washington even as other black clergy tacitly and explicitly remained wedded to the regular Democratic Organization and its candidates in the 1983 election: incumbent Mayor Jane Byrne and Richard M. Daley (Cook County State's Attorney and son of former Mayor Richard J. Daley). In the fall of 1982 and the winter of 1983, groups of black clergy from various denominations and neighborhoods discussed what kinds of resources they might marshal to promote Washington as an independent black political candidate.

According to Jeremiah Wright, then pastor of Trinity United Church of Christ, members of the clergy endorsed Washington as individuals, rather than as representatives of their congregations, in order to abide by laws regulating political action on the part of churches. Yet even as individuals, these clergy held sway over their congregations, but they were also swayed by their congregations and the growing political momentum behind Washington. They used their roles in churches and communities to engage in outreach toward sectors of the black community too afraid to step away from the machine and endorse Washington, or who believed that a black mayoral candidate could never win. According to Wright, both fear and lack of self-esteem were problems plaguing black Chicagoans. Religious leaders, given their calling and work, had to be able to effect some change in those areas. Wright, who later gained wider recognition as the "controversial" pastor of the Obamas before their public split from Wright and Trinity during the historic 2008 presidential election, acknowledged that even during the Washington years, his congregation was political and "unashamedly black and unapologetically Christian."[35]

The opposition to Washington's campaign was indeed great. If the mainstream media didn't outright ignore Washington's campaign and the groundswell of voter registration and activism in black Chicago, they cast his election in the Democratic primary as virtually impossible. Washington performed well in political debates, often besting his competition. With the white Democratic vote largely split between Byrne and Daley, Washington claimed victory in the primary, in part due to his ability to garner about 85 percent of the black vote. Many white Democrats then jumped ship and voted for the Republican candidate, Bernard Epton, in the general mayoral election. Edward Vrydolyak, 10th Ward alderman and chairman of the Cook County Democratic Party, backed Epton and charged others to do the same, coining the slogan, "Epton, before it's too late." The racism of many white voters showed through bumper stickers, placards, signs, and other literature that urged fellow whites to "vote white, vote right." Racial epithets and derogatory stereotypes were frequently used to refer to Harold Washington. As an aspiring reformist with a record of bucking the machine and growing support in the election, Washington was a clear threat to the machine and the exclusionary spoils system that dominated it. Moreover, Washington proved that he would take "no deals" offered by the machine. He refused to take a deal offered by Eddie Vrydolyak calling for Washington to give up his reformist agenda in exchange for party recognition and support in the election. Instead, Washington argued that without the party's support, he would in return withhold support for party candidates in the larger county elections, threatening patronage and opening the door for suburban Republicans to take control of the Cook County Board.[36] Such demonstrations of fortitude, toughness, and commitment to city government reform and democratization further endeared Washington to those seeking progressive change.

Any analysis of the Harold Washington campaigns would be incomplete without an examination of the efforts of women, especially black women, who were on the front lines of registering and organizing voters, educating their communities, fund-raising, and eventually helping to create policy and programs in the new administration. Everyday women as well as veteran black, white, Latina, and Asian women leaders were as essential to Harold Washington's election victories as any other group. Addie Wyatt was at the heart of women's organizing activities in the Washington coalition. Her contribution to the clergy's volume on the black church and Harold Washington, "The Role of Women in the Harold Washington Story," detailed her role in the Washington campaigns. In the piece, Wyatt recounted an event characteristic of her spiritual sensitivity and movement calling. She wrote that on one Monday in 1982, as she prepared to take an early morning flight back to D.C., she heard the voice of God repeatedly tell her to read the fourth chapter of the Book of Judges. After eventually reading the passage, Wyatt heard the same voice tell her "to go to Harold Washington's office and tell him he is to be the Mayor of Chicago."[37] Unsure of how she would reveal God's words to Washington, Wyatt drove to his office, Bible in hand, and blurted out the revelation. According to Wyatt, Washington laughed and said to her, "Angel, you're the one who should be mayor of the City of Chicago."[38] Wyatt disagreed, convinced that it was to be Washington by virtue of God's revelation. She said to Washington, "God knows that we don't have what it takes to win. God knows that we have no money. But what God is saying to us is that God will go before he and God is going to deliver this city into our hands and we will not be able to take credit for it. We'll have to say, 'Only God did this for us.'" Before leaving his congressional office, Wyatt urged Washington to read the Biblical passage.

In the Bible, Chapter 4 of Judges recounts the story of Deborah and Barak and the deliverance of the fallen children of Israel from the reign of King Jabin and his army general, Sisera. Deborah, a pious, well-respected woman gifted with spiritual wisdom, convinces Barak to fight King Jabin's army, headed by

Sisera. Deborah, with revelatory spiritual insight, ensures Barak that God will give them the victory against a large army with many chariots and warriors to which his smaller forces seemed outmatched. Barak requests Deborah's company into battle, to which she agrees, and Barak and his army are successful at beating back their opponents. Sisera, who flees the battlefield, is welcomed into the home of a sheik by the sheik's wife, Jael. Jael hides Sisera, who believes he will be protected from Barak and his men. However, Jael kills Sisera and later reveals his body to Barak, indeed ensuring a victory against King Jabin for the children of Israel.

A fitting interpretation of this story holds the children of Israel as Chicago's black community in need of deliverance and lacking political power, yet still loyal to the city's Democratic machine. Wyatt, a well-respected and well-known woman revered for her spirituality and commitment to doing God's work in and out of the church, stands in for Deborah as the woman who will work to convince Barak (Harold Washington) of their eventual victory. The exclusionary Democratic machine is Sisera and Jael is perhaps more generally Washington's coalition, or, more specifically, women who would play crucial roles in engineering Washington's win.

Not long after her conversation with Washington, Wyatt was tapped to work with an organization initially deemed Women for Harold Washington, which later became the Women's Network for Washington. As an effective organizer and well-known presence in Chicago women's groups, Wyatt committed herself to pulling together her vast networks and resources, which included memberships and leadership positions in prominent women's organizations such as the Chicago Network, CLUW, the League of Black Women, the National Council of Negro Women, and many other organizations. She assured the predominately male leadership of Washington's campaign, "[I]f I'm permitted to pull together black women, white women, Hispanic women, Asian women, native American, all women together, that it would constitute a winnable coalition. And with that kind of coalition and the direction of God, we can win."[39] Wyatt followed God's word and revelation ensuring victory to guide her work with the Washington campaign. The initial nucleus of the Women's Network for Washington included Wyatt, Rev. Willie Barrow of PUSH, Westside activist Nancy Jefferson, Rebecca Sive-Tomashevsky of the Playboy Foundation and Playboy Enterprises, and Peggy Montes, a Chicago Public Schools educator, civic leader, and political activist. The Women's Network Steering Committee included Wyatt and Sive-Tomashevsky as cochairs, Peggy Montes as coordinator, and Carolyn Phillips as secretary, with Barrow, Jefferson, and Artensa Randolph also on the committee. The expanded leadership council included a wider array of women such as Arnita Boswell of the League of Black Women, Maria Cerda, Barbara Flynn Currie, Clara Day, Theresa Fambro Hooks, and Lupe Lozano. Their goal was to recruit 10,000 women using a captain pyramid system where each captain would recruit 10 women to raise $1,000. The total fund-raising goal was $100,000.

To recruit women, the group planned a press conference to announce their support for Washington and invited one hundred women active in Chicago politics, women's groups, labor, and civic leadership to attend an initial meeting on December 20, 1982. Twice as many women showed up. As one who believed in the power of testimony and sharing experiences with one another as a way of building solidarity, Wyatt shared the story of the revelation of Judges 4 with the women, some of whom readily accepted her witness and others who believed her religious testimony to be out of place in a political meeting. Wyatt stated to the group, "We may not have money. We may not have many things, but I'm not dealing with what we have, I'm dealing with what God has. God is moving with us and on our behalf."[40] That first meeting generated $3,200 in personal donations to produce leaflets, register voters, and get the word out for Harold Washington. Each woman in attendance pledged to bring ten women with her to the next meeting, a women's rally for Harold Washington scheduled for February at Rev. A. P. Jackson's Liberty Baptist Church. Women who had not been invited to the December meeting or heard about it wanted to be involved, many of them everyday women who were not leaders of specific organizations but rank-and-file members of congregations, block clubs, and political groups, and even some who had little history of political activism but were eager to support Harold Washington's candidacy. Thousands of women from across the country, including Shirley Chisholm, Dorothy Height, and Eleanor Mondale, attended the February rally where Harold Washington spoke. More than $40,000 was raised toward the campaign that evening. Fund-raising and efforts to aid the campaign took place in the form of bake sales, parties, church functions, phone centers, envelope stuffing, canvassing and personal donations. Two additional rallies took place at the Charles Hayes Community Center and the Conrad Hilton.

An estimated 12,000 women were eventually involved with the Women's Network for Washington and the group surpassed its fund-raising goal, raising $110,000 for the Washington campaign. They believed that "the Women's Network has been the catalyst that helped turn the campaign around and pick up momentum."[41] Peggy Montes, who lamented the lack of recognition of women's importance to the election, later insisted that "Harold Washington would have never gotten elected had it not been for women."[42] The Women's Network for Washington recognized the incredible organizing and fund-raising potential of women. Likewise, Harold Washington was a male politician who recognized and respected the talents that women could bring to the political process and to government. He acknowledged women and "he reached out to them. He knew that he needed them. . . . He would come to our rallies, come to our meetings, to thank us and share with us. That encouraged us; it inspired us."[43] Looking back on her work with Harold Washington and the Women's Network, Wyatt surmised, "We just had to get busy doing the things that God inspired us to do. And I do mean that God inspired us to do every program that was meaningful toward getting Harold Washington elected. . . . What we promised people he would do, he did that and even more."[44] The Women's Network included women from diverse races, ages, religions, skills, jobs, and neighborhoods, though black women were heavily involved both in and outside of the network in support of Harold Washington.

Beyond the Women's Network for Washington, black women registered voters, engaged in community organizing and took their political work to new heights. Brenda Little, a black Baptist minister who worked closely with clergy-women for Harold Washington, supported him because

> for many women he represented a strong black male image. A man that was not afraid to take a stand for what he believed was right. A man that could not be bought. A man that loved family, a man that showed character and strength. And then a man who was concerned about the rights of women. He was concerned about us as a sex being put into positions and being paid less, not being given positions because we were female. He demonstrated that in hiring women, we should not limit them to positions that are reserved just for women, but they should be placed in positions that required knowledge; positions where women can make important decisions, sit on boards, function as managers and organizers.[45]

Washington cultivated not only the leadership of seasoned feminists and women's rights activists but capitalized upon black women's abilities to organize their neighborhoods, churches, and social civic centers. Washington's eagerness to accept and recognize the contributions of women within his campaign was not lost on women who believed they had so much to offer his administration and their communities. Katie Jordan, a member of CBTU and CLUW, recalled how she was inspired to get actively involved in Harold Washington's campaign: "I knew him because he was my congressman. That was my first time signing up to be a voter registrar; I was going to go out there and register some people to vote. With the union, when Harold ran in the primary, my union did not endorse him, but the rank and file voted for him anyway. Then when Harold won the primary, the union got out there working for him. When he became mayor, he was a reachable person."[46] As such, women leaders in the network expected to make a stamp not only on the campaign, but on Washington's mayoralty. They expected to work with him to construct a viable women's political agenda and program in the city. Washington vowed that he would put more women in his administration than any mayor in Chicago's history.

When Harold Washington claimed victory in the election on April 12, 1983, by a slim 3 percent margin over the Republican candidate, Bernard Epton, he became the city's first black mayor. By many accounts, Washington's tenure as mayor of the city of Chicago revealed the complex possibilities and limits of political change in a city long dominated by an exclusive and in many ways corrupt city machine. Scholar Larry Bennett argues that "at the height of the Reagan era, Washington built a political coalition and led a big-city administration whose programmatic agenda explicitly sought to advance social and racial justice. . . . [H]e emphasized the plight of Chicago's most disadvantaged residents and sought to assemble a policymaking team that would creatively use municipal authority and resources to meet the needs of the city's poorest residents and most deteriorated neighborhoods."[47] Washington remained committed to reforming city government, even in spite of the debilitating and vehement opposition he faced with the infamous Council Wars in which the Vrydolyak 29, composed of a bloc of twenty-nine aldermen and city council members, systematically blocked many of Washington's initiatives and appointments, resulting in a government stalemate for much of his first term as mayor.

Washington's twenty-one aldermen included all sixteen black aldermen on the council as well as a few white liberals and Latinos willing to go against the Vrydolyak 29. Washington's opponents waged a bitter battle, complete with mainstream media coverage that charged him as an incompetent, ineffective, and divisive leader. According to research done by Washington's Transition Committee, he had some one hundred board vacancies to fill on commissions, task forces, and committees devoted to economic development, health and human services, housing, zoning, transportation, and education—vacancies that would remain unfilled throughout the majority of his first term in office.[48] Incensed at the Vrydolyak 29, Washington was determined to make progress "despite the desperate opposition of a declining majority who scrambled to salvage what was left of their preserves of patronage . . . old-style politicians who admitted publicly that their strategy was to plunge Chicago into a depression of stagnated programs, rather than let this mayor and his administration take credit for a New Spirit of Chicago."[49]

Despite the Council Wars, Washington was able to make some important changes. He began a Political Education Project (PEP) to continue the work of voter education and registration to support Washington and his political allies, including other black and Latino politicians. Washington's endorsements of political candidates held a significant amount of weight in certain sections of the city, including his old congressional district. In the 1983 election for his vacated U.S. Congressional seat, Washington endorsed his friend and Labor for Harold Washington leader, Charles Hayes, among a field of thirteen other candidates, including other members of the Washington coalition like Al Raby and

Lu Palmer. Addie Wyatt, whom some believed Washington would tap to take his seat, supported her longtime friend and labor comrade, Hayes, as a member of Women for Hayes, otherwise known as "Charlie's Angels." She was honorary cochair of Women for Hayes with Peggy Montes as campaign cochair. Others supporting Hayes were Clara Day, Jackie Vaughn, Barbara Flynn Currie, Toni Preckwinkle, Zenobia Black, and Carol Moseley Braun.[50] It is no coincidence that many of these women had been heavily involved in the Women's Network for Harold Washington.

As Chicago's most noted black labor leader, Hayes had considerable visibility within Chicago's strong black labor sector. As Katie Jordan observed, rank-and-file trade unionists supported Washington before the larger labor movement did. Hayes, Wyatt, and Jordan, although not leaders in Chicago's Federation of Labor or the Illinois Federation of Labor, used their influence within their unions and Chicago's labor community to drum up support for Washington. Washington no doubt recognized the centrality of Chicago's black and progressive labor community to his victory. They were a powerful voting bloc and, along with Hayes's proven ability to serve as a leader, could lead Hayes to victory. Hayes received about 45 percent of the vote in the primary and went on to soundly defeat his Republican opponent, Diane Preacely. As the first trade unionist elected to U.S. Congress, Hayes pushed for full employment legislation, full national health insurance, increases in federal school funding, job training programs, and public works projects. He served on the House Committee on Small Business, the House Committee on Education and Labor, and the House Committee on the Post Office and Civil Service. During his ten years in Congress, Hayes was the only member to have a 100 percent voting record on labor issues.[51] For activists like Wyatt, the elections of Washington and Hayes illustrated the power of local community organizing and coalitions to secure concrete political gains and representation.

Aside from PEP, Washington created a Tenant's Bill of Rights for Chicago renters, upheld the Freedom of Information Act that would make city government more transparent for its citizens, ordered better and a more timely distribution of city services like garbage collection and street sanitation, and broke up the city's taxi monopoly to provide more competitive fares and options for riders. Washington cut his own salary by 20 percent, ended the designated limousine service for mayor, put a $1,500 cap on campaign contributions by companies doing business with the city and cut the city payroll by 700 employees to deal with the fiscal crisis facing Chicago.[52] Washington also went to greater lengths than any other mayor to involve everyday citizens and neighborhoods in the governing process by ensuring that relevant budget hearings would take place in local neighborhoods as opposed to downtown.

Eugene Gibson, head of the Roseland Church Association and a Washington supporter, witnessed the greater transparency in city government after Washington's election. Gibson stated that prior to Washington's election, those out-side of the city's group of political insiders, which included a large percentage of blacks, didn't know whom to talk to or whom to see for help with certain problems. They did not have access to the machine or to city government in ways that others did. Black churches registered and organized voters, prayed, and raised funds to get Harold Washington into office and they were proud of him for challenging the white power structure and winning: "We were not just putting a man in place because he was Black. He was not just a Black mayor; he was a mayor who happened to be black. He knew about finance; he knew about the economic structure; he knew the business structure; he knew the educational structure. He was a politician who knew how to politick."[53]

A major breakthrough occurred near the end of Washington's first term in 1986 that aided in creating a more demographically diverse city government. Years prior, black activists filed a suit charging that the city council was redraw-ing election maps and racial gerrymandering. A federal court agreed with the activists and issued an order requiring special aldermanic elections in four Latino and three African American wards. The resulting elections in March of 1986 tipped the scales of the city council to an even balance with a 25/25 split between pro- and anti-Washington factions. With neither side at a majority, Washington as mayor would cast the deciding vote in matters before the coun-cil, effectively allowing him to finally govern the city nearly four years into his administration. Washington was able to push through his nominations for city appointments, which included an appointment for Addie Wyatt to the city's Personnel Board. Over the course of the Washington years, white full-time city government employment decreased from 68.4 percent to 60.6 percent while black full-time employment increased from 27.1 percent to 32.3 percent and La-tino full-time employment increased from 3.6 percent to 5.7 percent. The latter irked some Latino activists who had campaigned for Washington and wanted to see more Latinos in city government.[54] Washington also won a court deci-sion against Mayor Richard J. Daley's patronage system and hiring practices that prohibited the hiring and firing of employees based on political support of sponsorship. While there were obvious benefits for those wanting to break into city government who had otherwise been kept out, the ruling also hampered Washington from being able to dole out patronage jobs that were expected by his constituents.[55] Still, he was able to bring many more women and minorities into city government than ever before.

One of the starkest transformations of city government under Harold Wash-ington included his commitment to creating a broader arena for women in lead-ership positions, more contracts with women-owned businesses, commissions dedicated toward women's issues, and greater numbers of women employed by the city. Washington created a Women's Affairs Policy Task Force led by Nancy

Jefferson and Rebecca Sive-Tomashevsky in 1983. Many of its members were pulled from the Women's Network for Washington, including Addie Wyatt. The goals of Washington and the task force were to create an official office of women's affairs, to make the Chicago Council on Human Relations address discrimination, to promote affirmative action in city government, and to expand existing human rights ordinances. The task force also hoped to establish direct links between City Hall, women, and women's organizations in Chicago. Furthermore, the task force sought to realign programs geared toward servicing women and women's issues so that they actually did so, for example, agencies like the CHA, which governed public housing—of which 80 percent of the households were headed by women—and health and human service agencies, which had no services for victims of rape and domestic violence.[56] Addie Wyatt also sat on Washington's Oversight Committee of fifty-seven business, religious, academic, and community leaders who looked at labor issues, employment, health care, public safety, housing, education, cultural diversity, affirmative action, neighborhood development, transportation, and women's affairs.

In 1984, Washington issued Executive Order 84-1, which created the city's first Commission on Women's Affairs. Although the movement to create women's affairs commissions in government began after President Kennedy's Commission on the Status of Women and gained steam during the women's movement throughout the 1960s and 1970s, Chicago was slow to join the movement and institute such a commission to explore the ways in which the city interacted with and met the social, political, and economic needs of women. The Chicago Commission on Women's Affairs created by Washington and led by prominent female activists and women-centered organizations, included committees on health and human services, employment, and affirmative action. Washington eventually created a Mayor's Commission on Women's Affairs, which was chaired by Women's Network for Washington coordinator, Peggy Montes, in 1986.

Affirmative action and the opening up of economic opportunities for all of Chicago's citizens was a major item on Washington's agenda. He created a cabinet-level Affirmative Action Officer position and even pushed for the creation of an Affirmative Action Advisory Council to implement and monitor affirmative action plans. Washington backed quotas like the one instituted under his Executive Order 85-2 in 1985, which mandated that 5 percent of the city's contracts go to women-owned businesses. As a result, city purchases of supplies and services from women-owned businesses increased from 1 percent in 1982 to 4.2 percent in 1985, amounting to a total of about $14.4 million in city contracts to women in 1985.[57] Washington boasted that contracts at O'Hare airport illustrated the city's new commitment to affirmative action because 26 percent of construction contracts went to black-owned firms, 9 percent to Hispanic firms, 8.8 percent to

Asian firms and 3 percent to women-owned firms.[58] Not only did Washington increase the numbers of blacks and Latinos in city government (in the case of the latter only marginally), he made good on his promise to hire more women in city government than any of his predecessors. Even more significantly, Washington placed many of these women in active leadership posts. Some 175 women were appointed to boards and commissions by Mayor Washington. Prior to Washington's tenure, women held about 12 percent of top-level staff positions as mayoral assistants, senior staff, and advisers. Under Washington, that proportion increased to 39 percent.[59] Further encouraging to many of his labor and female supporters, Washington also signed the city's first collective bargaining contract, which covered 7,500 of the city's clerical, technical, paraprofessional, and professional jobs predominantly held by women. Through the collective bargaining process about 3,500 employees, predominantly women, received an additional 5 percent increase in pay as restitution for past pay and gender-based discrimination stemming from court cases and legal claims against the Jane Byrne administration for discrimination against women.[60]

Washington was by no means a perfect mayor, but his commitment to diversifying city government and making citizens feel as if they had a say in governing when so many had felt isolated before, was indeed remarkable, and resembled Wyatt's efforts to empower women and minorities in the labor movement. Washington was reelected in 1987 having won 54 percent of the total vote. He garnered 92 percent of the black vote, about 53 to 60 percent of the Latino vote and 80 percent of the Asian vote. The 575,000 votes Washington received in the February election was the highest vote total any Democratic nominee had received within the last forty-five years. He won by a nearly 80,000-vote margin and with greater support along the lakefront and in demographically diverse wards.[61] He still maintained the support of groups like the Women's Network as well as Labor for Harold Washington, both of which included Addie Wyatt.

Addie Wyatt's revelation from Chapter 4 of the Book of Judges did indeed come true. Harold Washington became mayor of the city in the face of formidable opposition. But just like the Israelites in the Book of Judges, black Chicagoans would soon find themselves again in turmoil and in need of new direction. On Thanksgiving eve 1987, Harold Washington suffered a massive heart attack and died. His second term in office lasted only eight months. Wyatt had honored Washington just days before his death at an event sponsored by the Committee to Defend the Bill of Rights, an event which she and fellow comrades later christened, following Washington's death, "the last supper."

The city mourned Washington, and the city council scrambled to find an interim mayor to take his place, a powerful post given Washington's reformist agenda. Washington biographer, Gary Rivlin posited that among blacks in the Washington coalition, three different ideological bents existed: Chicago machine

Democrats who were loyal to Washington because of his ability to garner the black rank and file, the progressives who were civil rights activists and anti-machinists in the past, and the nationalists who cornered the market on black cultural and community representation.[62] The machine Democrats resisted some of the reformist principles of other members of the coalition, the nationalists sought to use city government to increase and solidify African American power, and the progressives appeared to lie somewhere in the fray as well. Washington's death fractured his coalition, not only among various ideological sectors of the black community but also between the very fragile coalition that existed between blacks and Latinos. Long-standing black machine politicians who had allied with Washington suddenly appeared not to be so in line with Washington and the reform agenda after his death.[63] Regular machine politicians, whites, and opponents of Washington hoped to engineer the selection of an interim black mayor of the machine's choosing.[64]

The machine's pick for mayor was Eugene Sawyer. Sawyer was the 6th Ward's alderman and a former chemist and engineer for the city. He began his career as an alderman in 1971 and was the first black alderman to endorse Harold Washington for mayor. Sawyer had the backing of the old white machine guard, including Cook County Democratic Chairman George W. Dunne. For this reason, as well as questions about his loyalty to Washington's reformist agenda, Sawyer faced immense criticism and pressure from a large portion of Chicago's black community. The other major candidate for interim mayor was Tim Evans. Evans, first elected as an alderman in 1973, was tapped by Washington to serve as the city council's floor leader and chairman of its finance committee. Black aldermen like Danny Davis, Jackie Grimshaw, William Beavers, William C. Henry, and Bobby Rush saw Evans as a true reformer and supported him over Sawyer.[65]

According to Addie and Claude Wyatt, they initially backed Tim Evans for interim mayor, believing that he was most in line with Washington's reformist agenda. But Sawyer had more support and potential votes on the city council. The Wyatts "realized that he [Sawyer] was the only black who could get the [city council] support to the hold position." They would rather see Sawyer maintain hold of city government than have it revert back into the hands of the city's machine leaders. So they threw their support to Sawyer and counseled him during the turbulent city council session where he was eventually sworn in as mayor.[66] Sawyer was also a dear friend of the Wyatts and a member of the Vernon Park Church of God, and Claude Wyatt was his spiritual advisor. So much controversy and debate ensued over Sawyer's appointment as interim mayor that his supporters released a pamphlet, "Answers to the 12 Most Asked Questions about the Election of Eugene Sawyer as Mayor," to quell any negative assumptions about Sawyer as the "machine's candidate." Sawyer supporters argued that he did not actively campaign against Evans, but simply had the majority of votes behind him that Evans failed to garner, despite the detraction of some black aldermen who, after threats of physical violence, backed out of supporting Sawyer. Supporters also argued that no meetings or deals took place between Sawyer and aldermen Burke and Vrydolyak. Instead, they argued that at the time of the so-called meeting on November 30th, Sawyer was at a meeting of Clergy United for Washington with 150 ministers. They also argued that Sawyer was his own man and not a puppet of the machinists.

In office, Sawyer supported Washington's reforms, won council approval for Washington's 1988 budget, and expanded some of Washington's programs, including the dream ticket that defeated Vrydolyak in favor of Aurelia Pucinski, Carol Moseley Braun, and Joe Gardner. In addition, Sawyer kept most of Washington's appointments during his administration while making sure that city upkeep continued in the neighborhoods. It was difficult for Sawyer to be seen as a mayor with the support of the people. As one writer argued, "Sawyer is viewed as a mayor without a constituency" who lacked the fire power and strength evident in his predecessor.[67]

The Wyatts played major roles in Sawyer's election campaign through the Mayor Sawyer Fund, Clergy for Sawyer, and Women for Sawyer. Clergy for Sawyer argued that it considered the other Democratic mayoral candidates in 1989, Tim Evans and Richard M. Daley, but ultimately believed Sawyer to be the best candidate. "In one of the other two major candidates, we found a serious lack of leadership and an inability to control adversity and stand up for peace and justice. In the other we found the threat of returning to the past: government by the few, for the few." They went on to argue that in Sawyer's short time as mayor, the CHA had a new executive director who was producing results, the city had a balanced budget, and senior citizen centers and nutrition and health programs were on the rise and readily available in neighborhoods.[68] Sawyer also had the support of a significant group of labor leaders, including Addie Wyatt, Charles Hayes, Robert Simpson of Teamsters and Lou Montenegro of ILGWU, and Mollie West of the Chicago Typographical Union. Sawyer, a lifetime member of Local 150 of Operating Engineers, had maintained union contracts with city workers, gaining him the respect and support of key progressive labor leaders who were longtime backers of Washington. However, big labor threw its support to Daley.[69]

Under Sawyer, the Mayor's Advisory Commission on Women's Affairs became a permanent fixture and the Chicago Commission on Women and the city police instituted a new SMART program allowing for the indexing of information on previous sex crimes and convicted sex offenders. Wyatt served as cochair for a reception of the Mayor Sawyer Fund in 1988 and sent a personal letter out to invitees and donors, stating, "In my judgment, Mayor Sawyer is making every effort, with considerable skill, to implement the Harold Washington Legacy and the people's agenda, and I believe he deserves the opportunity to succeed."[70] Just as her support of Harold Washington resulted in an appointment on the city's Personnel Board, Wyatt's support of Eugene Sawyer garnered her a position on the Regional Transportation Authority's Board (RTA) in 1988, a position she would hold until her retirement from the board in 2008.

Sawyer lost the 1989 election and Richard M. Daley, son of Richard J. Daley, won, eventually surpassing his father as the longest-serving mayor in the history of the city, serving from 1989 to 2011. He would go on to defeat many black and Latino candidates unable to unify the black and Latino bases. He beat Sawyer by 100,000 votes and Evans by 150,000 votes, in the process courting the Latino vote, promising to appoint minorities to city government, and courting the lakefront liberals, an emulation of Washington's strategies.[71] For true supporters of Washington and members of his coalition, what amounted in city government and politics upon his death, was an unfinished revolution. Washington was the leader, or the focal point of movement, but the synergy of it ultimately belonged to the individuals, groups, and networks of activists and leaders who made up the movement. Their inability to keep that synergy in the aftermath of Washington's death was just as tragic as the loss of the people's mayor and resulted in an unfinished revolution.

Wyatt's support of progressive political candidates continued after the mayoral reigns of Washington and Sawyer. Most notably, Wyatt threw her support behind the 1992 historical campaign of Carol Moseley Braun, who successfully became the first U.S. female senator from Illinois and the one and only black woman senator to date. As a founder of the National Political Congress of Black Women in 1984 (now the National Congress of Black Women), Wyatt utilized the Congress as well as her previous networks to rally mass support for Moseley Braun. Wyatt remained active in not only political campaigns in local, state, and national arenas but in efforts among workers to organize and protest inhumane treatment.

AN UPRISING IN THE DELTA

Addie Wyatt's retirement from the UFCW signaled an end to her formal career in the labor movement, but it by no means ended her support of worker struggles to achieve collective action, better working conditions, better wages, and dignity on the job. No longer on the front lines, Wyatt frequently served as an advisor, advocate, and inspirational voice to younger generations of workers seeking support and success in their efforts to organize. Given that Wyatt was no longer a director in the UFCW—which required regular records of her schedule, travels, outcomes of her work investigating grievances, planning conferences, and promoting the establishment of antidiscrimination committees at all levels of the union—the details of her work in the labor movement are less clear after 1984. However, by the 1990s, programs and correspondence indicate that Wyatt maintained a presence and active advisory role in CBTU, CLUW (especially its Chicago chapter), and new organizations like the National Interfaith Committee for Worker Justice, later Interfaith Worker Justice.

Less frequent were Wyatt's trips across the country to organize workers and stump for workplace justice. More often than not, Wyatt was sought after for her legendary speeches and ability to inspire workers with her own testimony about the importance of solidarity and collective action through the union. Likely Wyatt's last trip to her birth state, Mississippi, occurred in 1990, when she and a group of labor and civil rights activists traveled to Indianola in the heart of the Mississippi Delta's famed Sunflower County, the home of both staunch segregationist James Eastland and civil rights activist Fannie Lou Hamer. In the Delta, Wyatt and others would encourage workers on strike at Delta Pride, a large catfish-processing plant where black women comprised 90 percent of the workforce. Many were young single mothers in their twenties and thirties struggling to make a living in the Delta where about 40 percent of all blacks fell below the federal poverty line. The jobs available to them in the multimillion-dollar, low-wage, service-sector, food-processing industries failed to provide an adequate living wage. As Charles Hayes had predicted, the South—with its substantial number of black and brown workers in the service and food-processing industries—would be the next great battleground for union organizing. After years of poor working conditions, insufficient wages, racism, and sexual harassment on the job, Delta Pride workers voted for unionization with the UFCW in 1986, only to go on strike in 1990. Their highly publicized strike, the largest by workers in Mississippi history, would ultimately be successful.

Commercial catfish production began in the Delta region in the 1960s and exploded in the 1970s. Within ten years, Delta catfishing farms produced more than half of the nation's farm-raised catfish.[72] Cooperatively owned by 180 Delta farmers (none of whom were African American), these farms "grew" catfish under controlled conditions in a process defined as aquaculture. Those who owned a stake in Delta Pride literally had been handed down former plantation lands and farms through which to venture into aquaculture and build up a new system of inequitable labor relations and racial discrimination.[73] Delta Pride, the largest of these catfish farms in the United States, produced $144 million of catfish by 1990, about 35 percent of the catfish market, which included national grocery store chains and fast-food restaurants. Yet workers were paid about $3.80 per hour on average, just above the federal minimum wage—a salary that was anything but living wage. Some workers who had been at the plant for years made $4.50 and had received raises of less than seven cents per year.[74] The industry relied upon black labor, predominantly black female labor, to process the catfish. Given that management and ownership of Delta Pride was predominantly white and its underpaid, poorly treated workforce largely black, conditions within the plants were deemed as little more than new-age plantations with walls.[75]

The push for unionization at Delta Pride in the mid-1980s grew out of worker grievances around unsanitary and unsafe working conditions, limited access to medical and health care, sexual harassment and inhumane plant practices, low wages, and discrimination. Workers were at the mercy of plant management and an unpredictable catfish processing schedule. They had to report to work early, but if there were no catfish available for processing until later in the day, they would have to sit for hours waiting until the catfish arrived, at which point they might work a twelve- or thirteen-hour shift. They were unpaid for the time they waited.[76] Workers would stand for hours on end in ankle-deep water filled with blood and fish entrails. A sewage line with no drain covers ran off in the plant and workers often fell into the drains, twisting their ankles and injuring themselves because of the slippery floors. High levels of ammonia in the plant's water system led workers to complain of chronic eye, throat, and stomach irritation. Others got bad skin rashes on their faces and arms made worse by the plant rule that they were not allowed to go to the bathroom to wash the refuse of the line and fish parts off of their bodies.[77]

The pace of the line was fast and workers were often clocked, meaning that a supervisor would stand behind a worker on the line timing how many catfish they could skin and clean. Despite low wages and lack of raises, workers were expected to skin anywhere from 15 (low end) to 28 (high end) catfish per minute. They were expected to scale as many as 50 catfish per minute, amounting to 24,000 catfish scaled over the course of an eight-hour day, even though many workers worked much longer than eight hours a day.[78] The fast-paced, repetitive nature of skinning and scaling catfish resulted in high levels of carpal tunnel syndrome among workers and complaints of chronic joint pains. When workers complained of aches and carpal tunnel syndrome, they were given aspirin by the company nurse and told to report back to the floor. The company nurse, an LPN or licensed nurse practitioner, did not have authority or credentials to prescribe medication or give much more than first aid to workers. Medical benefits were nonexistent, and taking time off to tend to children, family, and other needs was at best discouraged and at worst could result in the loss of one's job. Sarah White, a worker-organizer at the plant, stated, "We feared for our livelihood, but also for our lives. . . . But what does a job mean when you can get fired for wanting to take your baby to the doctor or refusing to let a supervisor run his hands up your thigh?"[79] Workers complained of being called dumb, stupid, lazy, and cotton pickers by their supervisors. Black women were frequently told by supervisors and managers that they were nothing but baby machines.[80]

Sexual harassment in the form of propositions, threats, and even groping placed black women at the mercy of their white male supervisors, a dynamic that again drew references to the plantation-style relations between the company's black workforce and white management. Women's grievances also revolved around an archaic, inhumane bathroom policy in which male supervisors followed women into the bathrooms where the doors had been removed from the stalls. The supervisors argued that the women took too long and too frequent bathroom breaks that cut into their overall production and the company's profit margin. In order to gain some semblance of privacy and protection, women would journey into the bathroom in twos, one shielding the other as she tended to her bodily needs. To make matters worse, whether or not a woman could take a bathroom break was up to her supervisor and bathroom breaks were strictly monitored. Older women who couldn't wait for a restroom break or feared using the restrooms without door stalls would wear adult diapers to spare themselves the public humiliation of wetting their pants in public. The experience was dehumanizing and humiliating.

For too many of Delta Pride's workers, the catfish plants represented the old-style plantation politics of racial and economic exploitation. Sarah White, a Delta native, first began working at a Con-Agra plant skinning catfish in the early 1980s. By 1983, she was at the main Delta Pride catfish plant in Indianola, Mississippi, and would soon become of the lead organizers in the workers' struggle for unionization, better working conditions, and higher wages. White initially made $3.40 an hour, about five cents more than the minimum wage in 1983. She often worked thirteen-hour days to support her young son. At the time, the only holiday that Delta Pride workers were given off from work was Christmas Day.[81] Company representatives argued that if they could afford to give workers higher wages, they would. They argued that the catfish industry was still near its infancy and thus needed to protect its bottom line as much as possible. Scholar Kristal Zook reported, "At Delta Pride, executives often argue that the catfish industry is a strong generator of jobs, and that poor blacks should be grateful for this. Delta Pride is therefore excused from the responsibility of paying higher wages or improving factory conditions because it is, after all, providing workers with a reliable income."[82] But as workers argued, they received no discounts for groceries, gas, utilities, and medical services. They paid the same price as others and they were struggling to make ends meet. Most full-time Delta Pride workers had qualified for and relied on food stamps, Medicaid, and other government assistance programs to make ends meet.[83] As scholar Laurie Green argues, "the catfish industry was subsidized by the state of Mississippi."[84]

White quickly became acquainted with the culture of Delta Pride: "We were told: if you want to keep your job, you keep your mouth shut and do the work. It seemed like they had control of our minds, that nobody really understood that there was an avenue we could go down to break through to a better place. It's what we call the 'plantation mentality.'"[85] White and another woman, Mary Young, were contacted by UFCW organizers and the organizing campaign began shortly thereafter. Young and White, along with Margaret Hollins and Rose Turner, became lead organizers, quietly meeting with workers at lunchtime and outside of the job to talk about the benefits of unionization. The lead organizers relied upon local politics and local history as a source of inspiration. The women were fueled by local events to fight for their own rights in the plant, including a successful campaign to have a black school superintendent over the predominantly black local school system.[86] Just as with that campaign, the issue in the plants was surely one of a lack of adequate representation for the predominantly black workforce. In terms of local history, one of the most famed women to come out of the Mississippi Delta was civil rights and political activist Fannie Lou Hamer, a resident of nearby Ruleville. As scholar Jacqueline Grant writes, Hamer epitomized the struggle against racism, sexism, and classism that black women dealt with, even often within the very movements they aided and fueled to ease their burdens. Hamer's "affirmation of humanity through political empowerment, interconnectedness, self-determination and self-definition"[87] held critical theoretical and practical relevance for White and others struggling for dignity, respect, and equity in the plants and in their communities. The history of the Delta and the activism of a woman like Hamer provided real intellectual, spiritual, and practical guidance for the women at Delta Pride who sought ways to validate themselves while demanding fair treatment and wages as well as dignity and respect on the job.

Delta Pride's response to the unionization campaign included pulling out all of the stops to persuade workers that unionization would be disastrous for them. Delta Pride had a deep presence in the community. Many who owned stock in the company and the catfish processing industry lived locally in the Delta. Delta Pride's lawyer, Bob Winstead, was even the mayor of Indianola.[88] So workers were not just going against the company, they were in some ways challenging their wider community. One of the most startling efforts of the company to dissuade workers from voting for union representation with the UFCW included hiring Charles Evers, brother of slain civil rights activist Medgar Evers, to talk to workers and convince them that Delta Pride's management was on their side and that they were supportive and fair. He argued that it was talk of a union that created problems that didn't exist. With stunning paternalism, the company attempted to utilize the history of the civil rights movement and Mississippi racial politics in their favor.[89]

On the day of the vote, September 10, 1986, the company posted pictures of plant closings to put fear into workers that unionization would mean the loss of their jobs. Delta Pride officials also posted signage and warned workers that now they would have to pay union dues, which would only take more money out of their pockets. These union dues, they argued, would only go to the union bosses so that they could drive their fancy cars and live the good life at the expense of their members.[90] Many of these tactics were the same tactics used by companies in the 1950s and 1960s organizing campaigns that Addie Wyatt led. The final vote at Delta Pride was 489 in favor of the union to 349 against it and UFCW Local 1529 was born. Eventually, UFCW Local 1529 would represent more than 5,000 workers, including 1,000 workers at Delta Pride's main facility where the organizing drive originated. Sarah White recalled, "When the union came in, I finally felt like I was somebody. The union made me respect myself. The union taught me how to stand up and be proud, and showed us that we don't have to take abuse."[91]

But this was not the end of the workers' struggle, only the beginning. Delta Pride workers were largely absent from the contract negotiating process that followed official representation by the UFCW. Because the very women and men who had been on the ground organizing, who had firsthand knowledge of the horrendous conditions at Delta Pride, were not at the decision-making table, their absence as well as the recalcitrance of company officials showed in the workers' first contract. The contract included a structured grievance process, doors on the bathroom stalls, and a clause against sexual harassment, but it did not include medical leave, sick time, or maternity leave, all of which were extremely important given the predominantly female workforce of Delta Pride and the high percentage of women who were single mothers. Ultimately, the women of Delta Pride and the new UFCW Local 1529 felt as if the union reps did not adequately and fully represent them. Progress in the plants was aggravatingly slow, while worker grievances and management harassment of employees persisted. When it was time to negotiate with Delta Pride for a new contract, the workers vowed to make sure that all of their demands would be brought to the negotiating table. The workers' contract demands included an extra holiday, unlimited bathroom privileges, a wage increase, medical and doctor choice (as opposed to only being allowed to see the company's physician), a limit on how many departments one would have to work in, and several other demands. In response, the company offered no extra holiday, only a six-cent raise, and bathroom breaks only at lunch. About 500 workers, nearly half of Delta Pride's workforce, went on strike on September 12, 1990.[92]

Some Delta Pride employees sought work in nearby unionized plants like Con-Agra while others remained off work and participated in the two strike lines outside of the plant, where tensions soon flared up. The company brought in armored trucks and guards to preside over the picket line and even touted money in wheelbarrows in front of the strikers to remind them of the money they were losing on the picket line and to try and entice others to return to work.[93] On September 17th, shots were fired at picketers on the Delta South line. The following day, several strikers were arrested in the Delta Main parking lot. On September 19th, another ten picketers were arrested and a Delta Pride picketer, Mary Green, was beaten by a policeman. The incidents only fueled national outrage at the events in Indianola as the strike itself was already highly publicized in local and national news media. On September 22nd, the NAACP called for a national boycott of Delta Pride catfish, which at the time was one of the largest national farm-raised catfish producers in the nation.[94]

Shortly after the start of the boycott, a rally was held on September 27th at a local church, St. Benedict the Moor, to galvanize Delta Pride workers and show support for their efforts. The rally featured UFCW leaders and religious, civil rights, and political activists. Addie Wyatt was among them. From afar in Chicago, Wyatt and other Mississippi natives organized clothing and food drives and solicited donations for the striking workers at Delta Pride. She also supported the boycott against Delta Pride. All too aware of the difficulties of going on strike while trying to provide for families and keep spirits up, Wyatt readily accepted an invitation to address workers at the rally. But decades of organizing and galvanizing resources in the fight for human equality had taken their toll on Wyatt. At the age of sixty-six she required a cane, which she called her "stick of honor and distinction," to get around and needed help climbing up to the podium to address the hundreds of workers present. She received a standing ovation. Wyatt began by stating how moved she was by the many letters and calls she had received from workers and labor activists about the situation at Delta Pride and how good it was to be "in the midst of this great struggle."

The workers were captivated by Wyatt's telling of her own story in the labor movement. She drew upon local knowledge and embraced Fannie Lou Hamer by stating that she too was "sick and tired of being sick and tired." She recalled how the union became the mechanism through which she sought change and protection from discrimination, harassment, and misuse. Wyatt told the workers about being barred from Armour's front offices and recalled her first union meeting, lauding the UPWA and the ability of working people to come together for a better way of life. She argued that the "union makes the difference in the lives of working people" and that collective bargaining, political action, and social action were the trinity through which working people could empower themselves to bring about positive change. She asked, "where in the world can you find people coming together to talk about those great concerns than in the union?" For those in the crowd who were skeptical of the union and its ability to improve working people's lives or who were afraid to take a stand and strike, Wyatt admonished them. She reminded them that they were standing on a bridge built by those who came before them in labor and in civil rights and who had given their lives so that they could have the right to talk about what they don't like on the job and organize for change. She encouraged them to "stretch back, throw your heads up" and bask in the "dignity, respect and fellowship of one another."

Applause, amens, and other affirmations peppered Wyatt's remarks as the preacher in her became ever more evident. "God helps us when we are doing what is right for ourselves and our cause," she urged. Recalling the advice of her mother that guided her life, Wyatt told the workers that if they wanted a better life, it was up to them to make it so, and collective action and solidarity would surely help them to get there, because there is no running from oppression. She had put in her years of organizing and working through the union for change and it was not easy. She argued that the union had its problems and was far from perfect, but that the union was not about the staff alone, but about the people and the members that comprise it. Therefore, it was up to the members to direct the course of the union. She ended her speech by advising the workers to stay strong through the strike and to not let anyone or anything, including the company, break their spirit and the bonds they shared with one another as members of the union and workers engaged in collective struggle. As she did with many of her audiences, she asked the audience to join hands with one another, shouting that together they could gain their freedom with the help of God and their own determination not to give up in the fight for a better way of life. Reciting some of the labor tune, "Solidarity Forever," Wyatt finished with shouting, "Solidarity forever, for the union makes us strong."[95] Several media outlets, including the *Chicago Tribune*, covered Wyatt's speech at the rally.

According to Sarah White, Addie Wyatt was specifically sought out by the UFCW who wanted to bring in someone who could provide support for the Delta Pride workers and who knew something about their struggle. Addie Wyatt could speak from the perspective of a worker and a black female trade unionist because she had been one for many years. Though many of the Delta Pride women were not familiar with Wyatt's vast legacy in the labor movement, they came to view her as a heroine and as one who had spent many years, "fighting, maneuvering, and demanding justice." She challenged them to take the torch and carry on for justice and dignity on the job, a challenge that the Delta Pride workers had already accepted, and she inspired them to keep going. For White, just hearing Addie Wyatt speak instilled in her a fire to do better and to make an impact. Much more than just a rhetorician, Wyatt was a black woman who had walked in their shoes. She imparted a sense of a broader struggle that these women were a part of, a struggle that was ongoing and one in which they had to take part to improve their lives.[96]

After the rally, Sarah White, Mary Green, Margaret Hollins, and others traveled to Washington, D.C., to testify before the Congressional Black Caucus Labor

Braintrust about the conditions at Delta Pride and the struggle of its workers. To provide teeth to—and hopefully fuel support for—the boycott, Delta Pride workers traveled across the South picketing grocery stores that sold Delta Pride products and educating local townspeople about their cause. In October, workers traveled across Mississippi from Greenville to Jackson and far as Atlanta, Georgia, picketing restaurants like Captain D's and grocery stores like Winn Dixie that served and carried Delta Pride catfish. The boycott garnered nationwide attention from Houston to St. Louis to Chicago to Atlanta as well as support from organizations like the NAACP, the SCLC, and PUSH. In early November, the AFL-CIO voted to provide $250,000 in strike aid for Delta Pride workers, which added to the strike assistance given to workers from the UFCW in the form of weekly checks. Workers received about $60 per week and a bag of groceries from the union and formed a strike committee to help dole out additional monies on a case-by-case application basis to help striking workers with rent, mortgages, car payments, utilities, and other essential bills.[97]

UFCW locals contributed about $112,000 to support the strike efforts at Delta Pride. Delta Pride did its best to break the strike. The company brought in workers from neighboring communities who were desperate for work. According to White and others, the new workers, despite company musings that they were working out just fine, couldn't produce at the same level as the veteran workers on strike. In addition, the company saw high turnover among the strikebreakers as many failed to return after experiencing firsthand the conditions in the plants. In late October, the National Labor Relations Board found Delta Pride guilty of coercing workers to quit the union. Delta Pride was also fined $32,000 by OSHA in 1990 for the poor working conditions within the plant and the failure of the company "to take effective action to prevent and provide proper treatment for repetitive motion injuries—the first catfish processor OSHA ever cited."[98] Despite a company appeal, the ruling and the fines remained. A Delta Pride stockholder and his son were also indicted for threatening and attempting to bribe striker Dorothy Kimbrough into using her influence to end the strike.[99]

The difficulties of these workers, the nationwide attention brought to the strike, mounting support for the boycott, and the company's inability to meet all of its contracts ultimately led to Delta Pride being willing to negotiate.[100] After three months on the picket lines, the workers won the strike and a contract that included an average raise of $1.50 per hour over the course of three years, an extra holiday, more vacation time, the creation of a joint labor/management safety committee, improved grievance procedures, a clause prohibiting sexual harassment, and unlimited bathroom privileges. While these wages were still nowhere near enough to pull catfish workers out of poverty, they did amount to more income for workers and could at least ease some financial barriers.[101] White believed that the value of the struggle of Delta Pride was about more than the strike: "Even more, it's more about how to make a change in the mind, in how workers think about themselves and what they can do."[102]

After several years of working in an improved but far from perfect Delta Pride, Sarah White became a full-time staff member of UFCW Local 1529 in 1996 and worked for the union for several years before retiring in the early 2000s. Like Addie Wyatt, when she first became a union representative and organizer in the 1950s, White's duties went beyond her local as she organized workers in catfish and poultry processing, nursing homes, and warehouses across Mississippi, Alabama, Arkansas, and North Carolina.[103] After the contract negotiations in the 1990s, the demographics of workers in the catfish industry in the Mississippi Delta began to change. Companies like Delta Pride and others, capitalizing on the South's rapidly growing Hispanic population, began hiring Hispanic workers, some of whom were undocumented and "willing to work for lower wages and fewer benefits." The company divided Spanish-speaking workers from other workers by providing exclusive company housing for these workers, sometimes on company property. Sarah White estimated that about 30 percent of the 5,000 catfish workers in the Delta were Hispanic in the late 1990s and early 2000s. Unfortunately, only one was a member of UFCW Local 1529. One of White's biggest charges was appealing to and providing outreach to Hispanic workers: "We try to tell the Hispanic workers about the unions. But mostly they're afraid and desperate and will do whatever to keep food on their table. Just like us."[104] White appealed to the UFCW with little success for Spanish-speaking union organizers to help organize immigrant and undocumented workers. In addition, Mississippi is an open-shop and right-to-work state. Open-shop states do not require workers to be a part of the union or a dues-paying member in order to reap the benefits of representation. As with many unions, the UFCW faced a greater number of concessions-based contracts that included giving up many of its hard-won improvements in wages, working conditions, and benefits in order to stay competitive as a union. An unfinished revolution, indeed.

Addie Wyatt's role in the events at Delta Pride may have been fleeting, but her legacy in the UFCW and in the minds of the predominantly young black women who took inspiration from her life in the labor movement was not. Likewise, the events at Delta Pride must have signaled to Wyatt that fight for fairness and justice in the workplace was ongoing and that black women would continue to be on the forefront of that struggle. At a time when many rank-and-file workers were further and further removed from unions and contract negotiations, these predominantly female workers were on the front lines of the process, demanding fair wages, better treatment, and dignity and respect from the company and their union.

But just as with the struggles for adequate representation on the AFL-CIO Executive Council and political empowerment in Chicago, the struggle for economic rights, dignity, and respect in the Delta remains an unfinished revo-lution. In many ways, these struggles speak to the possibilities and the limits of racial, economic, gender, and political equality in America. They also speak to the possibilities and the limits of black collective action and coalition politics as well as the complex matrix of race, class, and gender that continues to impact black women's quest for equality. What connects these struggles beyond these factors is Addie Wyatt and her unshakable belief in the equality, dignity, and humanity of all people. Wyatt refused to see poverty, racism, sexism, and dis-crimination as immutable structural forces. According to Wyatt, it would take solidarity in collective action to move these forces, whether through the union, the church, grass roots, or electoral politics. Wyatt attempted change in all of these realms. A believer and a fighter for collective empowerment, Wyatt's choice of movement struggles and organizations reveals just how important it was to continue to motivate, educate, and organize against inequality. Even when she was not at the heart or the center of the organizing, it was important for Wyatt to continue to motivate and educate others about their individual potential as agents of social change but ultimately about the power of solidarity in collective action.

ALL THINGS ARE CONNECTED

We tell stories for many reasons. We tell them to pass the time and to communicate events and memories that have special significance. But we all tell stories to educate and to pass on pieces of our personal and collective histories that we do not want to become lost. Life histories and biographies fall into this category and the story of Addie Wyatt's remarkable life is no different.

Over the course of the 1990s and early 2000s, Addie Wyatt's speaking engagements and public appearances diminished, but she remained a celebrated figure in Chicago and a nationally known labor, civil rights, and women's activist. She gave numerous oral histories and interviews from her home on Chicago's South Side. She remained a member of the Regional Transportation Authority board, an appointment she received by former Mayor Eugene Sawyer. In the late 1990s, the Wyatts turned the pastoral duties of their church over to their nephew-in-law, Reverend Jerald January. Claude had begun to exhibit early signs of Alzheimer's and his health, along with the couple's age, led them to step down after leading the Vernon Park Church of God for forty-five years. In the early 2000s, Addie Wyatt suffered a serious stroke, which, along with her arthritis, resulted in her being confined to a wheelchair and in need of constant care. Her years of service in the labor movement and various appointments, along with Claude's retirement income and a bevy of close family members and friends, allowed the couple to receive the care that they needed on a daily basis. Tragedy struck when the Wyatts lost their eldest son, Renaldo, in 2006. As Claude's Alzheimer's progressed and he lost his motor skills, including his ability to speak words, Addie Wyatt always wanted him nearby, never too far away so that she could see him and still be near to him. On April 11, 2010, Claude Wyatt passed away. Two years later, on March 28, 2012, Addie Wyatt passed away at the age of 88. The Wyatt's youngest son, Claude "DeDe" Wyatt III passed on in 2014.

Throughout her life, Addie Wyatt sought to take social movements outside of themselves in order to reach and influence greater numbers of people, aided by her ability to traverse the boundaries of these movements. She practiced an expansive ministry and philosophy of equality that operated both within and outside of the walls of the church and which sought to take social justice movements outside of themselves and to a broader audience and base of power. In her church and before religious audiences, she represented the organized labor movement and the struggles of working people; she addressed racial inequalities and disparities in health, education, and employment; and she urged men and women to join in the fight for gender equality. In the labor movement, she fought for workers but recognized that the union's strength was in its membership. A membership susceptible to race and gender discrimination and hierarchies could never have the strength to adequately fight for a better way of life for working people. In black civic, political, and labor organizations Addie Wyatt represented the perspectives and problems of black women but refused to be the only black female voice present at the decision-making table and on the front lines. Similarly, she argued for the perspectives and voices of working-class women and women of color in the organizations and mission of the women's movement. Her goal in supporting social justice movements included calling into question their exclusivity and the limitations of their philosophical and tactical approaches to political, social, and economic equity and equality. Not always the loudest voice, hers was the most persistent and consistent voice for greater inclusion and representation across the organized labor, civil rights, women's rights, and religious movements of the twentieth century.

For Addie Wyatt, the philosophical thread that held together her participation in the organized labor, civil rights, women's rights, and religious movements was the desire for equality and a better way of life. What began as an individual journey to break away from poverty became a commitment to a collective struggle against economic, racial, and gender inequalities. She was not born an activist and a leader. She grew into these roles as a result of specific experiences in her life and a spiritual faith that refused to see poverty, racism, sexism, and discrimination as immutable structural forces. Before Addie Wyatt's family knew abject poverty, they had some semblance of economic stability and comfort. She grew up in the Church of God (Anderson, Indiana) rooted in interracial and male and female leadership and worship before segregation and gender discrimination came to determine its congregational structure. She raised her own family in the Altgeld Gardens public housing project, which served as a site of semiautonomous black community organizing, neighborhood pride, and a source of affordable, decent housing before it became synonymous with race and class pathologies and the breakdown of community and family structures. In the UPWA, she became inspired by a true multicultural coalition of workers, and organized women workers who openly discussed the ways in which racism, sexism, and discrimination weakened the strength of all workers. The Church of God, Altgeld Gardens, and the UPWA were by no means perfect, but they all illustrated to Addie Wyatt that there was strength, power, and promise in the collective possibilities of a different, better way of life. As a result of these experiences and struggles, she became a believer and a fighter for collective empowerment.

At every step of the way, Addie Wyatt faced opposition to her beliefs and questions about her fitness as a representative and leader in the church and the secular movements for social justice that she embraced. While she may have seen her beliefs and work connected, others called into question her loyalty to a labor movement that saw the problems of working women and racial minorities as miniscule, often times actively participating in their degradation. Fellow workers whom she sought to organize and represent spit in her face and doubted her ability to fight for them at the bargaining table because she was a black woman. Ultimately, her own history of pushing for minority and women's participation and leadership cast her as a militant threat to the new guard of labor leadership and unfit to represent the movement. Others questioned how she as a pastor's wife could spend so much time out in the rough-and-tumble men's world of labor and politics when her role as pastor's wife called for her to be seen and not heard. Still yet, her fitness as a Christian and as a member in the Church of God was called into question because of her support of the ERA, women's movement, and other organizations that "threatened the Christian family." It is striking that these criticisms came from within the very movements and organizations she was a part of rather than from outside. Still, Addie Wyatt refused to let these criticisms define her career or dissuade her from a belief in the equality of all people. In fact, such criticisms reinforced her belief in the need for greater collective solidarity against racism, sexism, and poverty from within as well as outside of the church, the labor movement, the women's movement, and the civil rights movement.

In Addie Wyatt's life work and in criticisms of her work, we see connections between social movements and their ideologies, achievements, and limitations that have previously been discussed in the abstract rather than viewed from experiences of one who lived through and left indelible imprints on them. By the standards of many, the ideologies, achievements, lessons, and limitations of the organized labor, civil rights, women's rights, and religious movements are already well known, and thus their possibilities remain fixed in our collective American past. But Wyatt's life challenges many of these fixed assumptions and beliefs and opens up the possibility for a more expansive understanding of the possibilities and limits of social movements and those who operate among them.

In our own highly political times, debates surrounding unions, women's rights, civil rights, and the place of religion in social discourse looms large. The ongoing quests for racial, gender, and economic equality, among numerous other calls for an end to various injustices, illustrate that the meanings of freedom, dignity, fairness, justice, and equality are still very much up for debate. At many stages of my research and writing over the past six years, I could not help but be struck by the strong parallels between Wyatt's time as an activist and leader and my own. Attacks on collective bargaining rights for public employees in Wisconsin, Ohio, and other states dominated the media as antiunionism gained political traction as a solution for state budget crises. The organized labor movement, unions and workers, antilabor politicians argued, stood as barriers to overcoming the great recession in 2008. If unions, and by proxy their workers, could sacrifice for the good of the whole, then the country could move forward. Prolonged lockouts in the National Basketball Association and the National Football League that pitted millionaire professional athletes against millionaire league owners, appeared at times to garner more debate and emotions than did the precarious plight of public employees and the unemployed. Both the Occupy movement in 2011 and the fast-food workers strikes that began in 2012 illustrate just how much we as a society continue to struggle politically and ideologically with growing economic inequality and the plight of the working poor.

The women's movement and its lasting legacy on American society continues to come under attack. Reproductive rights and women's bodies have taken center stage as states and employers move to constrict (much less frequently, expand) women's access to birth control and fertility care. Many of these decisions disproportionately affect poor women and women of color who rely upon state-funded and federally funded women's health-care facilities as well as their employer benefits for adequate care. And though the wage gap between men and women is shrinking, that it still exists reveals just how tangible women's economic inequality remains. Everything from gay marriage to radical feminist Girl Scouts is pitted against the future and safety of the American family and gender norms, even as we fail as a society to adequately and consistently criminalize sexual assault. Finally, Barack Obama's presidential election by a young and multiracial coalition has come to signify for some the long-overdue manifestation of the gains of the civil rights movement and America's entrée into a postracial era. Yet questions about President Barack Obama's religious and racial heritage in relation to his fitness to represent and lead the American people plague his presidency and illuminate to the world America's reluctance to come to terms with its racial and religious past, present, and future.

This is by no means an exhaustive discussion of American economic, gender, and race relations. I reference them because they are important to understanding the relevance of Addie Wyatt and social movement activism to our current world. Some might argue that the persistence of discrimination and inequality in our present means that Wyatt, the civil rights movement, the women's movement, and the labor movement failed. I disagree. To be sure, Wyatt, these movements, and the activists who led them were not perfect. Indeed, much of Wyatt's life work is a testament to the need to eradicate injustices within these movements before they can even be effective at bringing greater equity and fairness. I argue that we must see Wyatt, these movements, and the activists who led them as fighters in struggles that both preceded and outlived them. I believe that Addie Wyatt was acutely aware of her own place within a greater struggle, understood the power of faith in the struggle, and inspired others to take part in the struggle for human freedom and equality.

Though Addie Wyatt was in many ways a movement activist, her faith, belief, and philosophy of equality and diversity ultimately transcended the movements she was a part of and are emblematic of a progressive struggle for social justice. She possessed a dogged determination to improve the quality of life for people. This was the barometer through which she measured the potential and power of a movement. Beyond freedom from oppression, poverty, and discrimination, she believed in the equality of all people and as such the connectedness, or universal humanity, of all. Wyatt's philosophy of equality and her story create a blueprint, a framework for the ongoing struggle for human dignity, freedom, solidarity, and equality. In difficult times, Wyatt often repeated to herself this biblical message: "The race is not given to the swift nor to the slow, but to the one that endureth to the end." Wyatt's ability to endure and to maintain faith in the struggle is one of the greatest lessons that her life gives. For that, she deserves a place in our collective history.

NOTES

INTRODUCTION: TELL THE STORY

1. *TIME*'s Women of the Year included: First Lady Betty Ford; Carla Hills, cabinet member and HUD director; Ella Grasso, governor of Connecticut; Democratic Rep. Barbara Jordan; Chief Justice of North Carolina's state supreme court, Susie Sharp; Jill Ker Conway, first woman president of Smith College; Billie Jean King, tennis champion; author Susan Brownmiller; Addie Wyatt; Kathleen Beverly, Navy lieutenant commander; Carol Sutton, first woman managing editor of a major U.S. newspaper; and Alison Cheek, first woman to celebrate communion at a U.S. Episcopal church and priest at Washington's Church of St. Stephen and the Incarnation.

2. Patricia O'Brien, "Addie Wyatt's Blend of Authority, Femininity Achieves Labor Clout," *Oregonian*, January 15, 1976.

3. Diane Bartley, "Woman of the Year Wyatt—Now She's a Doctor," *Anderson Sunday Herald*, June 20, 1976. Addie Wyatt was interviewed about the problems of working women and the role of the women in the union but was unaware that the interview was for *TIME*'s Twelve Women of the Year. None of the women who were interviewed and ultimately selected as Women of the Year were aware of the honor at the outset.

4. Mike LaVelle, "She's Proud of Her Union Label," *Chicago Tribune*, January 20, 1976.

5. "Women of the Year: Great Changes, New Chances, Tough Choices," *TIME*, 107, 1 (January 5, 1976): 6.

6. Ibid.

7. Kenneth Silverman, "Biography and Pseudobiography," *Common-Place* 3, 2 (January 2003).

8. David Nasaw, Introduction to AHR Roundtable: Historians and Biography, *American Historical Review* (June 2009).

9. Hebrews 11:1, KJV.

10. Patricia Hill Collins, *Black Feminist Thought* (New York: Routledge, 2000), 138. Kimberle Crenshaw initially coined the term in the 1970s and articulated the theory

further in "Mapping the Margins: Intersectionality, Identity Politics and Violence against Women of Color," *Stanford Law Review* 43 (1991): 1241–1299; bell hooks, *Feminist Theory: From Margin to Center* (Cambridge, Mass.: South End Press, 1984).

11. See Alan Anderson and George Pickering, *Confronting the Color Line: The Broken Promise of the Civil Rights Movement in Chicago* (Athens: University of Georgia Press, 1986); Diane Pinderhughes, *Race and Ethnicity in Chicago Politics* (Urbana: University of Illinois Press, 1987); David Garrow, *Chicago 1966: Open Housing Marches, Summit Negotiations, and Operation Breadbasket* (Sandy, Utah: Carlson Publishing, 1989); William Grimshaw, *Bitter Fruit: Black Politics and the Chicago Machine, 1931–1991* (Chicago: University of Chicago, 1992); James Ralph, *Northern Protest: Martin Luther King, Jr., Chicago and the Civil Rights Movement* (Cambridge: Harvard University Press, 1993); Christopher Reed, *The Chicago NAACP and the Rise of Black Professional Leadership, 1910–1966* (Bloomington: Indiana University Press, 1997); Wallace Best, *Passionately Human, No Less Divine: Religion and Culture in Black Chicago* (Princeton: Princeton University Press, 2005); Adam Green, *Selling the Race: Culture, Community and Black Chicago, 1940–1955* (Chicago: University of Chicago Press, 2007); Davarian Baldwin, *Chicago's New Negroes: Modernity, the Great Migration and Black Urban Life* (Chapel Hill: University of North Carolina Press, 2007); Jeffrey Helgeson, *Crucibles of Black Empowerment* (Chicago: University of Chicago Press, 2014).

12. The Introduction of Helgeson's *Crucibles of Black Empowerment* explores Wyatt as an activist and leader emblematic of Black Chicago. Two journal articles focus substantially on Rev. Wyatt: an interview conducted by Rick Halpern and Roger Horowitz as part of the Wisconsin Historical Society's UPWA Oral History Project printed as "Lost Visions of Equality: The Labor Origins of the Next Women's Movement" in *Labor's Heritage* 12 (Winter/Spring 2003): 26–33, and Bruce Fehn, "African American Women and the Struggle for Equality in the Meatpacking Industry, 1940–1960," *Journal of Women's History* 10, 1 (Spring 1998): 45–69. A number of short biographical pieces have appeared in reference books, magazines, and newspapers.

CHAPTER 1. A CHILD OF THE GREAT MIGRATION

1. James Cobb, *The Most Southern Place on Earth: The Mississippi Delta and the Roots of Regional Identity* (New York: Oxford University Press, 1962).

2. Julius E. Thompson, *Black Life in Mississippi—Essays on Political, Social and Cultural Studies in a Deep South State* (New York: University Press of America, 2001), 57, 62.

3. Durr Walker Jr., *Lincoln County: A Pictorial History* (Marceline, Mo.: Walsworth Publishing Co., 1998).

4. *Semi-Weekly Leader* (hereafter *SWL*), June 25, 1919.

5. Ibid.

6. Ancestry.com. 1910 U.S. Federal Census [database online]. Provo, Utah, USA: Ancestry.com Operations Inc., 2006. See specifically 1910, Beat 1, Lincoln County, Mississippi, roll T624_749, page 5B, enumeration district 0081, Image 640. While the 1910, 1920, and 1930 federal census records consistently list the birthplace of all the Camerons as Mississippi, Ambrose Cameron listed Louisiana as his birthplace on the birth records of his three children born in Chicago after 1930. Additionally, Addie Wyatt stated in a video oral history with The HistoryMakers that her father and paternal grandmother

were from Louisiana, though she had no idea of where in the state or the reason for their departure. Also, Laura is listed as a boarder in the census but, according to family members of Addie Wyatt, was a sibling of Ambrose Cameron.

7. Gilbert Hoffman, *Dummy Lines through the Long Leaf: A History of the Sawmills and Logging Railroads of Southwest Mississippi* (Brookhaven, Miss.: Quentin Press, 1999), xi.

8. Ancestry.com. 1910 U.S. Federal Census [database online]. Provo, Utah, USA: Ancestry.com Operations Inc, 2006. See specifically 1910, Beat 1, Lincoln County, Mississippi, roll T624_749, page 5B, enumeration district 0081, Image 640.

9. Brookhaven, Mississippi City Directory, Volume 2, 1914–1915.

10. Centennial Historical Program, Commemorating the Incorporation of the City of Brookhaven in 1858–1859 and More than 100 Years of Progress as a Community (Brookhaven Centennial, Inc., 1859–1959), Mississippi Department of Archives and History (hereafter, MDAH).

11. Sam Jones, Interview with Bob and Betsy Jones, Lincoln-Lawrence-Franklin Regional Library Oral Histories, February 18, 1989. www.llf.lib.ms.us/LLF/Oral%20Histories/SJones.htm (accessed December 14, 2009).

12. Educable Children, Lincoln County, Mississippi, 1916, MDAH.

13. Addie Wyatt, Interview with Elizabeth Balanoff, Oral History Project in Labor History, Roosevelt University, 1977, Chicago, Ill. (hereafter, Balanoff Interview).

14. Addie Wyatt, The HistoryMakers A2002.096, Interview by Julieanna Richardson, June 1, 2002, The HistoryMakers Digital Archive (hereafter, The HistoryMakers), session 1, tape 2, story 2, Addie Wyatt shares memories from her family life. http://thmdigital.thehistorymakers.com/iCoreClient.html#/&i=15933 (accessed October 28, 2015). See also Balanoff Interview, 1977; Ron Wilson, "Life Can Be Better, Addie," Rev. Addie Wyatt and Rev. Claude Wyatt Papers, Box 18, Folder 39, Vivian G. Harsh Research Collection of Afro-American History and Literature, Chicago Public Library (hereafter Wyatt Papers, Harsh).

15. Maggie often used a number of surnames: her mother's maiden name, Green; her stepfather's surname, Stubbs, and the surname Nolan, which may have been the surname of her birth father.

16. The HistoryMakers, session 1, tape 1, story 6; Addie Wyatt recounts her family history. http://thmdigital.thehistorymakers.com/iCoreClient.html#/&i=15929 (accessed October 28, 2015).

17. *SWL*, January 1, 1930. See also Mrs. Eva Harris, Interview with Mrs. Kay Calcote, Lincoln-Lawrence-Franklin Regional Library Oral Histories, July 1987.

18. U.S. Federal Census, 1930.

19. Two of the most detailed and illuminating recounts of Wyatt's childhood include the 1977 interview with Elizabeth Balanoff as part of Roosevelt University's Oral History Project in Labor History and the 2002 interview with The HistoryMakers, an African American oral history project.

20. The HistoryMakers, session 1, tape 1, story 7; Addie Wyatt describes the sights, sounds and smells of Brookhaven, Mississippi, her childhood home. http://thmdigital.thehistorymakers.com/iCoreClient.html#/&i=15930 (accessed October 28, 2015).

21. The HistoryMakers, session 1, tape 2, story 2; Addie Wyatt shares memories from her family life. http://thmdigital.thehistorymakers.com/iCoreClient.html#/&i=15933 (accessed October 28, 2015).

22. The HistoryMakers, session 1, tape 1, story 5; Addie Wyatt shares her earliest childhood memory. http://thmdigital.thehistorymakers.com/iCoreClient.html#/&i=15928 (accessed October 28, 2015). See also Balanoff Interview; Wilson, "Life Can Be Better, Addie." References to Addie's dark skin color did strike a chord within her. Her mother, older brother, and eventually her other siblings were all fairer in complexion than she was; Addie took after her father who had darker brown skin. While she would again reference colorism years later as part of the discriminatory practices of employers in the meatpacking industry, she appears to remain silent on the issue and its effect on her as a young woman aside from stating that a lot of love and discussions with her mother helped her to see her beauty; see also Oral Histories of Women Civil Rights Activists, 1940s-1960s, Videotape, William Rainey Harper College, Women's History Week, 1991.

23. The HistoryMakers, session 1, tape 1, story 7; Addie Wyatt describes the sights, sounds and smells of Brookhaven, Mississippi, her childhood home. http://thmdigital.thehistorymakers.com/iCoreClient.html#/&i=15930 (accessed October 28, 2015).

24. The HistoryMakers, session 1, tape 2, story 2; Addie Wyatt shares memories from her family life. http://thmdigital.thehistorymakers.com/iCoreClient.html#/&i=15933 (accessed October 28, 2015).

25. The HistoryMakers, session 1, tape 2, story 3; Addie Wyatt discusses her awareness of racism as a child. http://thmdigital.thehistorymakers.com/iCoreClient.html#/&i=15934 (accessed October 28, 2015).

26. Seven recorded lynchings took place in the Brookhaven area between 1891 and 1928. See Thompson, *Black Life in Mississippi*, 192.

27. *SWL*, June 30, 1928.

28. For studies of lynchings and mob violence against blacks during this period, see Scott Ellsworth, *Death in a Promised Land: The Tulsa Race Riot of 1921* (Baton Rouge: University of Louisiana Press, 1992); Jacqueline Jones Royster, ed., *Southern Horrors and Other Writings: The Anti-Lynching Campaign of Ida B. Wells, 1892–2000* (Boston: Bedford/St. Martins, 1997); James Allen, *Without Sanctuary: Lynching Photography in America* (Santa Fe, N.M.: Twin Palms Publishers, 2000); Thompson, *Black Life in Mississippi*; James Hirsch, *Riot and Remembrance: The Tulsa Race War and Its Legacy* (New York: Houghton Mifflin Harcourt, 2002); Jacqueline Goldsby, *A Spectacular Secret: Lynching in American Life and Literature* (Chicago: University of Chicago Press, 2006); Paula Giddings, *Ida: A Sword among Lions* (New York: Amistad, 2008); Amy Louise Wood, *Lynching and Spectacle: Witnessing Racial Violence in America, 1890–1940* (Chapel Hill: University of North Carolina Press, 2009).

29. The HistoryMakers, session 1, tape 2, story 5; Addie Wyatt discusses her family's migration to Chicago. http://thmdigital.thehistorymakers.com/iCoreClient.html#/&i=15936 (accessed October 28, 2015).

30. Addie L. Wyatt, Interview by Joan McGann Morris, Working Women's History Project, December 14, 2002, Chicago, Ill. http://wwhpchicago.org/rev-addie-wyatt/. Transcribed by Helen Ramirez-Odell; accessed May 5, 2004 (hereafter McGann Morris Interview, 2002).

31. St. Clair Drake and Horace Cayton, *Black Metropolis* (Chicago: University of Chicago Press, 1993), 8.

32. "Introduction by Richard Wright," in Drake and Cayton, *Black Metropolis: A Study of Negro Life in a Northern City*, xvii. Other works on the first wave of Chicago's Great Migration in particular include Timuel D. Black, *Bridges of Memory: Chicago's First Wave of the Great Migration, Vol. 1* (Evanston: Northwestern University Press, 2003); James Grossman, *Land of Hope: Chicago, Black Southerners and the Great Migration* (Chicago: University of Chicago Press, 1989); Richard Wright, *12 Million Black Voices* (New York: Thunder's Mouth Press, 1941).

33. Grossman, *Land of Hope*; James Gregory, *The Southern Diaspora: How the Great Migrations of Black and White Southerners Transformed America* (Chapel Hill: University of North Carolina Press, 2007). See also the interviews of Fred Smith, Lillie Lodge Brantley, Juanita Tucker, and George Johnson in Timuel D. Black's collection of oral histories, *Bridges of Memory*.

34. Nicholas Lemann, *The Promised Land: The Great Black Migration and How It Shaped America* (New York: A. A. Knopf, 1991), 63. See also Beryl Satter, *Family Properties: How the Struggle over Race and Real Estate Transformed Chicago and Urban America* (New York: Picador, 2010).

35. Lionel Kimble, "Combating the City of Neighborhoods: Housing, Employment and Civil Rights in Chicago, 1935–1955," PhD Dissertation, University of Iowa, 2004, 41.

36. Harold Gosnell, *Negro Politicians: The Rise of Negro Politics in Chicago* (Chicago: University of Chicago Press, 1967), 20.

37. Drake and Cayton, *Black Metropolis*, 379.

38. Ibid., 203.

39. Kimble, "Combating the City of Neighborhoods," 70, 77.

40. Balanoff Interview, 1977.

41. Black, *Bridges of Memory*, 27.

42. Balanoff Interview, 1977.

43. Ibid.

44. Addie Wyatt, "The Included Ones," June 1984, Wyatt Papers, Box 8, Folder 14, Harsh.

45. Wallace Best, *Passionately Human, No Less Divine: Religion and Culture in Black Chicago, 1915–1952* (Princeton: Princeton University Press, 2005), 63.

46. Ibid., 9.

47. The HistoryMakers, session 1, tape 2, story 6; Addie Wyatt discusses her school life in Chicago. http://thmdigital.thehistorymakers.com/iCoreClient.html#/&i=15937 (accessed October 28, 2015).

48. Addie Wyatt, "Look for the Best, Addie," *Guideposts* 31 (October 1976): 33.

49. Drake and Cayton, *Black Metropolis*, 203.

50. The HistoryMakers, session 1, tape 2, story 7; Addie Wyatt remembers her family's financial struggles—Part I. http://thmdigital.thehistorymakers.com/iCoreClient.html#/&i=15938 (accessed October 28, 2015).

51. Judy Nicol, "How Many Hats Can She Wear?" *Chicago Sun-Times Family Magazine*, June 27, 1970, Wyatt Papers, Box 257, Folder 1, Harsh.

52. The HistoryMakers, session 1, tape 3, story 1; Addie Wyatt remembers her family's financial struggles—Part II. http://thmdigital.thehistorymakers.com/iCoreClient.html#/&i=15939 (accessed October 28, 2015).

53. Ibid.

54. Balanoff Interview, 1977.

55. Addie Wyatt, "Where Are the Children?" Program #3916. First air date February 18, 1996. http://www.csec.org/csec/sermon/wyatt_3916.htm (accessed November 7, 2009).

56. There is a Church of God based in Anderson, Indiana, and another separate Church of God based out of Tennessee. Wyatt was a lifelong member of the Church of God in Anderson.

57. Mac Spence, ed., *Mississippi Church of God History* (Wolfe, Tex.: Henington Publishing Co., 1980), 2. Viewed at the Anderson University Archives, Church of God Reformation Movement Archives, Anderson, Indiana.

58. James Earl Massey, *African Americans and the Church of God, Anderson, Indiana: Aspects of a Social History* (Anderson: Anderson University Press, 2005), 19.

59. "The History of the Langley Avenue Church of God," accessed from www.langleycog.org/PDF%20File/Langley%20history.PDF (hereafter, "History of Langley"; accessed October 28, 2015).

60. See Katie R. Davis, Zion's Hill at West Middlesex in David Alden Telfer, "A Study of the Relationship between Negro and Caucasian Church of God Congregations in Metropolitan Chicago," Thesis, Chicago Theological Seminary, 1968, 28–30, Church of God Archives, Anderson, Ind.

61. Ibid.

62. Marcus H. Morgan, "The Negro Church of God," unpublished paper, May 21, 1951, 9, Church of God Archives, Anderson, Ind.

63. Sarah Joneane Anderson. "A Study of Leadership Roles of Six Selected Ordained Women Ministers in the Church of God in Anderson, IN," Thesis, Anderson College, June 1980, 20, Church of God Archives, Anderson; see also Best, *Passionately Human, No Less Divine*, for a broader perspective of women's pastoral leadership.

64. "History of the Langley." The church eventually relocated to 6159 South Langley Avenue.

65. Telfer, "Study of the Relationship," 45.

66. "History of the Langley."

67. Oral Histories of Women Civil Rights Activists, 1940s-1960s, Videotape, William Rainey Harper College, Women's History Week, 1991. See also Balanoff Interview, 1977.

68. Best, *Passionately Human, No Less Divine*, 149.

69. Susie Staley, "Women Evangelists in the Church of God at the Beginning of the Twentieth Century," in *Called to Minister . . . Empowered to Serve*, ed. Juanita Evans Leonard (Anderson, Ind.: Warner Press, 1989), 37. See also Nancy Hardesty and others, "Women in the Holiness Movement: Feminism in the Evangelical Tradition," in *Women of Spirit: Female Leadership in the Jewish and Christian Traditions*, ed. by Rosemary Reuther and Eleanor McLaughlin (New York: Simon and Schuster, 1979), 241–243.

70. Acts 2: 17–18, KJV.

71. Hardesty, *Women of Spirit*, 244, 247.

72. Balanoff Interview, 1977.

73. Ibid.

74. Ibid., 1977.

75. The HistoryMakers, session 1, tape 2, story 6; Addie Wyatt discusses her school life in Chicago. http://thmdigital.thehistorymakers.com/iCoreClient.html#/&i=15937 (accessed October 28, 2015). Addie states that she had gotten several "doubles" or promotions in school and was able to attend high school at a young age.

76. Lillie Lodge Brantley, Interview with Tim Black, *Bridges of Memory*, 55.

77. 1937 DuSable High School Yearbook; *DuSable Recorder* 19, 10, March 17, 1937, Harsh.

78. McGann Morris Interview, 2002.

79. Morris Ellis, Interview with Tim Black, *Bridges of Memory*, 181.

80. Lillie Lodge Brantley, Interview with Tim Black, *Bridges of Memory*, 60; see also Commander Milton Deas Jr., Interview with Tim Black, *Bridges of Memory*, 410.

81. Tim Black, Interview by author, February 2009, Chicago, Ill.

82. Claude Wyatt Jr., "Outline for The Eagle and the Swan," Wyatt Papers, Box 3, Folder 4, Harsh.

83. Ibid.

84. In the 1960s and 1970s, the Wyatts received awards from the Association of Mannequins for being among the most fashionable black men and women in Chicago.

85. Jerry Thornton, "Couple Harvest Full Lives from Seeds of Faith," *Chicago Tribune* (pre-1997 fulltext), May 26, 1995, 11.

86. Balanoff Interview, 1977.

87. McGann Morris Interview, 2002.

88. Balanoff Interview, 1977.

89. Ibid.

CHAPTER 2. IN SEARCH OF WORK AND COMMUNITY

1. Addie Wyatt, "The Included Ones," 1984, Wyatt Papers, Box 8, Folder 14, Harsh.

2. Judy Nicol, "How Many Hats Can She Wear?" *Chicago Sun-Times' Family Magazine*, June 27, 1970, Wyatt Papers, Box 257, Folder 1, Harsh.

3. A host of sources exist on the employment discrimination of black women in clerical or "pink-collar" employment at white-owned companies prior to the post–Civil Rights era. See Thomas Wright, *Human Relations in Chicago*. Mayor's Relation on Human Relations (Chicago, Ill., 1946), 12, 18. See also Jacqueline Jones, *American Work: Four Centuries of Black and White Labor* (New York: W. W. Norton and Company, 1998), 320.

4. Roger Horowitz, *Negro and White Unite and Fight: A Social History of Industrial Unionism in Meatpacking, 1930–90* (Urbana: University of Illinois Press, 1997), 6; Rick Halpern, "Race and Radicalism in the Chicago Stockyards: The Rise of the Chicago Packinghouse Workers Organizing Committee," in *Unionizing the Jungles: Labor and Community in the Twentieth-century Meatpacking Industry*, ed. by Shelton Stromquist and Marvin Bergman (Iowa City: University of Iowa Press, 1997), 82.

5. Christopher Reed, *The Chicago NAACP and the Rise of Black Professional Leadership, 1910–1966* (Bloomington: Indiana University Press, 1997), 119.

6. Rick Halpern and Roger Horowitz, *Meatpackers: An Oral History of Black Workers and Their Struggle for Racial and Economic Equality* (New York: Monthly Review Press, 1999), 2.

7. Dennis Deslippe, *Rights Not Roses: Unions and the Rise of Working Class Feminism, 1945–1980* (Urbana: University of Illinois Press, 2000), 36.

8. Leslie Orear and Stephen Diamond, *Out of the Jungle: The Packinghouse Workers Fight for Justice and Equality* (Chicago: Hyde Park Press, 1968); Halpern, "Race and Radicalism," 75.

9. For more on the Stockyard Labor Council, the PWOC and organizing in meatpacking in the 1930s, see Alma Herbst, *The Negro in the Slaughtering and Meat-Packing Industry in Chicago* (Boston: Houghton Mifflin, 1932); Horace Cayton and George S. Mitchell, *Black Workers and the New Unions* (Chapel Hill: University of North Carolina Press, 1939); Catherine Elizabeth Lewis, "Trade Union Policies in Regard to the Negro Worker in the Slaughtering and Meatpacking Industry of Chicago," Master's Thesis, University of Chicago, 1945; James Grossman, *Land of Hope: Chicago, Black Southerners, and the Great Migration* (Chicago: University of Chicago Press, 1989); Stromquist and Bergman, *Unionizing the Jungles*; Horowitz, *Negro and White Unite and Fight*.

10. For a history of the AFL, see Andrew Kersten, *Labor's Home Front: The American Federation of Labor during World War II* (New York: New York University Press, 2006).

11. For histories of the CIO, see Nelson Lichtenstein, *Labor's War at Home: The CIO in World War II* (Philadelphia: Temple University Press, 2003); Robert Zieger, *The CIO: 1935–1955* (Chapel Hill: University of North Carolina Press, 1997).

12. Orear and Diamond, *Out of the Jungle*.

13. Halpern, "Race and Radicalism," 76–77.

14. Ibid. See also Paul Street, "The Swift Difference: Workers, Managers, Militants, and Welfare Capitalism in Chicago's Stockyards, 1917–1942," in Stromquist and Bergman, *Unionizing the Jungles*, 16–50.

15. Addie Wyatt, Interview by author, February 21, 2008, Chicago, Ill., tape recorded. Wyatt also recounts the story of her being hired at Armour in several other interviews and articles, including Addie Wyatt, Interview by Rick Halpern and Roger Horowitz, State Historical Society of Wisconsin UPWA Oral History Project, January 30, 1986, tapes 54–56, printed as "Lost Visions of Equality: The Labor Origins of the Next Women's Movement" in *Labor's Heritage* 12 (Winter/Spring 2003): 26; Balanoff Interview, 1977; McGann Morris Interview, 2002; Diane Bartley, "Woman of the Year Wyatt: Now She's a Doctor," *Anderson Sunday Herald* June 20, 1976, 9; Wilson, "Life Can Be Better, Addie," Wyatt Papers, Harsh.

16. Lionel Kimble Jr., "I Too Serve America: African American Women War Workers in Chicago, 1940–1945," *Journal of the Illinois State Historical Society* 93, 4 (Winter 2000/2001): 421–422.

17. Halpern and Horowitz, *Meatpackers*, 7–10; see also Bruce Fehn, "African American Women and the Struggle for Equality in the Meatpacking Industry, 1940–1960," *Journal of Women's History* 10, 1 (Spring 1998).

18. Excerpts from Oral History of Ada Tredwell, a Waterloo, Iowa, UPWA Local 46 member who began working at Rath as a janitor in 1941. See Halpern and Horowitz, *Meatpackers*, 132–133.

19. Halpern and Horowitz, "Lost Visions of Equality," 26.

20. McGann Morris Interview, 2002.

21. Fehn, "African American Women," 49–54. See also McGann Morris Interview, 2002.

22. Ibid. Charles Hayes of the UPWA remarked that front-office grievance procedures represented one of the first times that white men had to sit and listen to black women speak their voice. Large numbers of black women handled grievances for black, white, and Hispanic men and women. See *Paving the Way*, Filmmaker's Library, 1995, videocassette.

23. McGann Morris Interview, 2002; *Paving the Way*; Halpern and Horowitz, "Lost Visions of Equality," 27.

24. Fehn, "African American Women," 50.

25. Roger Horowitz, "This Community of Our Union: Shopfloor Power and Social Unionism in the Postwar UPWA," in Stromquist and Bergman, *Unionizing the Jungles*, 110–111.

26. Excerpts from oral history of Mary Salinas in Halpern and Horowitz, *Meatpackers*, 105.

27. The United Auto Workers (UAW) was another industrial union with a strong female presence and a record of organizing on behalf of women's issues such as pregnancy leave, promotion and seniority, job protection, and sexual harassment. The UAW developed the first full-scale union women's department in the nation in 1944, but working women struggled to overcome discrimination and stigmas as a result of their working, marital, and pregnancy status. For more, see Nancy Gabin, *Feminism in the Labor Movement: Women and the United Auto Workers, 1935–1975* (Ithaca: Cornell University Press, 1990).

28. The HistoryMakers, session 1, tape 3, story 3; Addie Wyatt talks about her first job and her involvement in labor union policies. http://thmdigital.thehistorymakers.com/iCoreClient.html#/&i=15941 (accessed October 28, 2015).

29. Ibid.

30. For more on black women's wartime and postwar employment, see Deslippe, *Rights Not Roses*; Karen Tucker Anderson, "Last Hired, First Fired: Black Women Workers during World War II," *Journal of American History* 69, 1 (June 1982); Jacqueline Jones, *Labor of Love, Labor of Sorrow* (New York: Vintage Press, 1986).

31. Balanoff Interview, 1977.

32. Sarah Anderson, "A Study of Leadership Roles of Six Selected Ordained Women Ministers in the Church of God in Anderson, IN," Thesis, Anderson University, June 1980, 42, Church of God Archives, Anderson.

33. Ibid.

34. Balanoff Interview, 1977.

35. Ibid.

36. Ibid., 1977.

37. Ibid.

38. Ibid., 1977.

39. Ibid.

40. The HistoryMakers, session 1, tape 4, story 6; Addie Wyatt describes managing work and home life after the death of her mother. http://thmdigital.thehistorymakers.com/iCoreClient.html#/&i=15941 (accessed October 28, 2015).

41. Balanoff Interview, 1977.

42. Lionel Kimble, "Combating the City of Neighborhoods: Housing, Employment and Civil Rights in Chicago, 1935–1955," PhD Dissertation, University of Iowa, 2004, 19–20.

43. Devereux Bowly, *The Poorhouse: Subsidized Housing in Chicago, 1895–1976* (Carbondale: Southern Illinois University Press, 1978), 18.

44. Kimble, "Combating the City of Neighborhoods," 156, 159.

45. For more on the problem of housing in Chicago in the 1940s and the advent of public housing, see J. S. Fuerst, *When Public Housing Was Paradise* (Urbana: University of Illinois Press, 2005); Arnold Hirsch, *Making the Second Ghetto: Race and Housing in Chicago, 1940–1950* (Chicago: University of Chicago Press, 1998); D. Bradford Hunt, *Blueprint for Disaster: The Unraveling of Chicago Public Housing* (Chicago: University of Chicago Press, 2009); Martin Meyerson and Edward Banfield, *Politics, Planning and the Public Interest: The Case of Public Housing in Chicago* (Glencoe, Ill.: The Free Press, 1955).

46. Kimble, "Combating the City of Neighborhoods," 163–165.

47. Philip M. Hauser and Evelyn M. Kitagawa, eds. *Local Community Fact-book for Chicago, 1950* (Chicago Community Inventory: University of Chicago, 1953), 222.

48. Ibid.

49. Bowly, *The Poorhouse*, 42–43.

50. Altgeld Gardens Dedication Program and First Annual Festival Program Book, August 19–26, 1945, Chicago History Museum.

51. The CHA gained sole control and ownership of Altgeld Gardens in 1956.

52. Bowly, *The Poorhouse*, 42–43.

53. "Altgeld Housing Project to Have Child Care Unit," *Chicago Tribune*, June 17, 1944, 16.

54. Fuerst, *When Public Housing Was Paradise*, 153.

55. Ibid.

56. Ibid., 57–58.

57. Ibid., 114.

58. Ibid., 115.

59. Willie McShane, "My Personal View of Altgeld Gardens," Altgeld-Carver Alumni Association, *History of Altgeld Gardens, 1944–1960* (Dallas, Tex.: Taylor Publishing, 1993), 40.

60. *History of Altgeld Gardens*, 40. Plans for a privately owned commercial center for Altgeld Gardens to be located at 131st St. and Ellis were planned as early as June of 1944. See "Plan Private Shops in CHA Home Project," *Chicago Daily Tribune*, June 25, 1944, 15.

61. *The Altgeld Beacon* 5, 1 (August 1953), Harsh.

62. *Altgeld Gardens Fifth Annual Festival Program Book*, 1949, Chicago History Museum.

63. Fuerst, *When Public Housing Was Paradise*, 137.

64. *History of Altgeld Gardens*, 42; "Joe Louis Will Attend Teen-Age Talent Show," *Chicago Daily Tribune*, September 5, 1948, S.3.

65. *The Altgeld Beacon* 3, 8 (August 1951), Harsh.

66. Ibid.

67. *History of Altgeld Gardens*, 42.

68. Fuerst, *When Public Housing Was Paradise*, 153.

69. Bowly, *The Poorhouse*, 76.

70. "500 New Homes Ordered Built at Altgeld Site: $4,878,500 Contract Opens CHA," *Chicago Tribune*, January 9, 1952, 19.

71. Fuerst, *When Public Housing Was Paradise*, 154.

72. Bowly, *The Poorhouse*, 76.

73. Ibid., 77.

74. "Five Families Tell of Home Search—Two Ordered Evicted Leave Project," *Chicago Daily Tribune* (1923–1963), April 13, 1950; Proquest Historical Newspapers; Chicago Tribune (1849–1986), S-83.

75. Fuerst, *When Public Housing Was Paradise*, 154.

76. Ibid., 154–155.

77. *History of Altgeld Gardens*, 41.

78. Ibid. For more on People for Community Recovery, see www.peopleforcommunityrecovery.org (accessed November 12, 2010); John Elson, "Dumping on the Poor," *TIME*, August 13, 1990; Leslie Ansley, "Homesick from the Fumes," *Banger Daily News*, April 17, 1992, 17–19; Josh Getlin, "Fighting Her Good Fight," *Los Angeles Times*, February 18, 1993; Robert Ballard, *Unequal Protection* (San Francisco: Sierra Club Books, 1994); Jim Motavalli, "Toxic Targets," *E: The Environmental Magazine*, June 30, 1998; Margaret Ramirez, "Hazel M. Johnson: 1935–2011: Mother of Environmental Justice," *Chicago Tribune*, January 17, 2011, 1.22.

79. *Chicago Daily Tribune*, August 12, 1951.

80. Fuerst, *When Public Housing Was Paradise*, 160–161.

81. Ibid., 190.

82. "Rev. E. R. Williams, South Side Pastor," *Chicago Sun-Times*, obituary section, January 25, 1997, 38.

83. For more on gospel music in Chicago during this era, see Wallace Best, *Passionately Human, No Less Divine* (Princeton: Princeton University Press, 2005); Adam Green, *Selling the Race: Culture, Community and Black Chicago* (Chicago: University of Chicago Press, 2007); Bernice Johnson Reagon, *We'll Understand It Better By and By* (Washington, D.C.: Smithsonian Institution Press, 1992); Bernice Johnson Reagon, *If You Don't Go, Don't Hinder Me* (Lincoln: University of Nebraska Press, 2001).

84. Ibid.

85. The *Altgeld Beacon* 3, 8 (August 1951), Harsh.

86. Rev. Addie Wyatt, Address at Calvary Baptist Church's Annual Women's Day, 1981, Wyatt Papers, Box 314, AV 050, Harsh.

87. Fuerst, *When Public Housing Was Paradise*, 152. See also Balanoff Interview, 1977.

88. Balanoff Interview, 1977.

89. Fuerst, *When Public Housing Was Paradise*, 155.

90. Rev. Addie Wyatt, "The Included Ones," 1984, Wyatt Papers, Box 8, Folder 14, p. 11, Harsh. Neither of the Wyatts were ordained or held ministerial credentials while at Altgeld.

91. Fuerst, *When Public Housing Was Paradise*, 159.

92. Ibid.

93. Rev. Addie Wyatt, "The Included Ones," 1984, Wyatt Papers, Box 8, Folder 14, Harsh.

94. The *Altgeld Beacon* 3, 8 (August 1951), Harsh.

95. Fuerst, *When Public Housing Was Paradise*, 153.

96. Charles Hayes (The HistoryMakers A1993.002), Interview by Julieanna Richardson, January 1, 1993, The HistoryMakers Digital Archive, Session 1, tape 1, story 6, Charles Hayes lists several prominent Chicagoans who've influenced his career. http://thmdigital .thehistorymakers.com/iCoreClient.html#/&i=8195 (accessed October 28, 2015).

CHAPTER 3. FOR THE UNION MAKES US STRONG

1. "Anti-Discrimination Conference, 1953," UPWA Papers, Box 349, Folder 5, Wisconsin Historical Society (hereafter WHS).

2. McGann-Morris Interview.

3. Addie Wyatt, Interview by Rick Halpern and Roger Horowitz, Tape 54, Side 2, January 30, 1986, UPWA Oral History Project, WHS.

4. Balanoff Interview, 1977.

5. Leslie Orear and Stephen Diamond, *Out of the Jungle: The Packinghouse Workers Fight for Justice and Equality* (Chicago: Hyde Park Press, 1968).

6. Cyril Robinson, *Marching with Dr. King: Ralph Helstein and the United Packinghouse Workers of America* (Santa Barbara, Calif.: Praeger SB, 2011), 62–63.

7. Bruce Fehn, "The Only Hope We Had": United Packinghouse Workers Local 46 and the Struggle for Racial Equality in Waterloo, Iowa, 1948–1960" in Shelton Stromquist and Marvin Bergman, eds., *Unionizing the Jungles: Labor and Community in the Twentieth-century Meatpacking Industry* (Iowa City: University of Iowa Press, 1997), 165.

8. Ibid.

9. Addie Wyatt, Interview by Rick Halpern and Roger Horowitz, UPWA Oral History Project, Tape 55, Side 2, January 30, 1986,WHS.

10. Fehn, "The Only Hope We Had," 166; Robinson, *Marching with Dr. King*, 78.

11. UPWA Papers, "Anti-Discrimination Fisk U. Survey correspondence, 1950," Box 342, Folder 8, WHS; Fehn, "The Only Hope We Had," 167.

12. Bruce Fehn, "African American Women in Meatpacking, 1940–1960," *Journal of Women's History* 10, 1 (1998): 53–54; "Memo, 1951," UPWA Papers, Box 342, Folder 10, WHS.

13. Ibid.

14. Dennis Deslippe, *Rights Not Roses: Unions and the Rise of Working Class Feminism, 1945–1980* (Urbana: University of Illinois Press, 2000), 80.

15. Seventh Constitutional Convention of the UPWA Proceedings, Minnesota, May 25–28, 1950.

16. Addie Wyatt, Interview by author, February 21, 2008, Chicago, Ill., tape recorded.

17. Balanoff Interview, 1977; see also Rick Halpern and Roger Horowitz, "Lost Visions of Equality: The Labor Origins of the Next Women's Movement" in *Labor's Heritage* 12 (Winter/Spring 2003): 28; McGann Morris Interview, 2002.

18. Scholar Cheryl Townsend Gilkes argues for seeing black women's community work outside of the home as labor and indicative of the kinds of social action and political culture evident in communities where black women are active participants and leaders. See Gilkes, "If It Wasn't for the Women . . . African American Women, Community Work, and Social Change," in Maxine Baca Zinn and Bonnie Thornton Dill, eds, *Women of Color in U.S. Society* (Philadelphia: Temple University Press, 1994), 229.

19. Glenda Gilmore, *Gender and Jim Crow: Women and the Politics of White Supremacy in North Carolina, 1896–1920* (Chapel Hill: University of North Carolina Press, 1996); Evelyn Brooks Higginbotham, *Righteous Discontent: The Women's Movement in the Black Baptist Church, 1880–1920* (Cambridge: Harvard University Press, 1993).

20. Dee Myles, "Black Union Leaders Continue to Make History," http://www.peoples world.org/black-union-leaders-continue-to-make-history (accessed April 13, 2007).

21. Ron Wilson, "Life Can Be Better Addie," Wyatt Papers, Box 18, Folder 39, Harsh.

22. Myles, "Black Union Leaders."

23. A lengthy debate at the 1954 and 1955 UPWA Constitutional Convention between male and female unionists revealed the tension around women's leadership opportunities in the union.

24. McGann Morris Interview, 2002.

25. Maude McKay and Claude Wyatt III, Interview by author, May 13, 2010, Chicago, Ill.

26. Addie Wyatt, "Look for the Best, Addie," *Guideposts* 31 (October 1976): 33.

27. Ibid., 34.

28. Balanoff Interview, 1977.

29. Roger Horowitz, "This Community of Our Union: Shopfloor Power and Social Unionism in the Postwar UPWA," in Stromquist and Bergman, *Unionizing the Jungles*, 98, 117; UPWA, *Officers Report and Proceedings*, Sioux City, Iowa, May 3–7, 1954, 68–72; see controversy over Women's Activities Committee push for single seniority as opposed to sex-segregated seniority in UPWA, *Proceedings of Tenth Constitutional Convention*, Cincinnati, Ohio, June 18–21, 1956, 119–175, 272–285.

30. UPWA, *Officer's Report and Proceedings, 1954 Constitutional Convention*, Sioux City, Iowa, May 3–7, 1954, 120–139.

31. Addie Wyatt, Interview by Rick Halpern and Roger Horowitz, Tape 54, Side 2, January 30, 1986, UPWA Oral History Project, WHS.

32. UPWA, *Officer's Report and Proceedings, 1954 Constitutional Convention*, Sioux City, Iowa, May 3–7, 1954, 120–139.

33. Ibid.

34. Fehn, "African American Women in Meatpacking," 55–56.

35. Rick Halpern and Roger Horowitz, *Meatpackers: An Oral History of Black Workers and Their Struggle for Racial and Economic Equality* (New York: Monthly Review Press, 1999), 104.

36. Addie Wyatt, Interview by Rick Halpern and Roger Horowitz, Tape 55, Side 1, January 30, 1986, UPWA Oral History Project, WHS.

37. UPWA, *Twelfth Constitutional Convention Officer's Reports and Proceedings*, May 23–27, 1960, xxxxvi.

38. *District One Champion*, March 1963, Vol. 11, No. 7, Charles Hayes Papers, Box 1, Folder 20, Harsh.

39. Halpern and Horowitz, "Lost Visions of Equality," 30.

40. Myles, "Black Union Leaders."

41. Biographical Statements, Charles Hayes Papers, Box 4, Folder 8, Harsh.

42. "How One Union Makes Democracy a Reality," *Atlanta Daily World*, July 4, 1954, 7.

43. Addie Wyatt once stated that there were no more than seven women in the UPWA-CIO who served as international representatives throughout the 1950s and 1960s. See Judy Nicol, "How Many Hats Can She Wear?" *Chicago Sun Times Family Magazine*, June 27, 1970, Wyatt Papers, Box 257, Folder 1, Harsh.

44. The number of international field representatives in each district varied by the size of the district. Some districts had as few as two or three field representatives, while it was not uncommon for large districts like District One to maintain an average of six to seven representatives between 1954 and 1968.

45. *Paving the Way*, Filmmaker's Library, 1995, videocassette.

46. Balanoff Interview, 1977.

47. Ibid.

48. Balanoff Interview, 1977.

49. Brown received a leave from the UPWA in 1954 to serve in the military, and Wyatt informally (later formally) assumed his duties as district program coordinator, taking direction from Charles Hayes and national program coordinator Richard Durham. Durham was one of the most famous black disc jockeys of the late 1940s and early 1950s, writing and producing "Democracy U.S.A." and "Destination Freedom." Many racially progressive artists and actors outside of meatpacking took positions working in the UPWA because it was a progressive union that provided stable employment but allowed them to still participate in and shape important civil rights and antidiscrimination initiatives.

50. Addie Wyatt, Interview by Roger Horowitz and Rick Halpern, UPWA Oral History Project, Tape 55, Side 2, WHS.

51. "District One," UPWA Papers, Box 384, Folder 1, WHS.

52. *District One Champion*, Vol. 9, No. 2, March 1956, UPWA Papers, Box 364, Folder 6, WHS.

53. Addie Wyatt, Interview by Roger Horowitz and Rick Halpern, UPWA Oral History Project, Tape 55, Side 2, WHS.

54. Lionel Kimble Jr., "I Too Serve America: African American Women War Workers in Chicago, 1940–1945," *Journal of the Illinois State Historical Society* 93, 4 (Winter 2000/2001): 421–422. See also Ruth Rothstein, Interview by Emily Freidman, August 20, 2008, Chicago, Ill., Hospital Administration Oral History Collection, American Hospital Association, http://www.aha.org/research/rc/chhah/Rothstein--FINALFINAL--013109.pdf (accessed January 11, 2010).

55. *District One Champion*, Vol. 8, No. 2, April 1955, Wyatt Papers, Box 234, Folder 1, Harsh.

56. Patricia O'Brien, *The Oregonian*, Chicago Daily News Service, January 15, 1976.

57. Balanoff Interview, 1977.

58. Nicol, "How Many Hats?"; Balanoff Interview, 1977.

59. Ibid.

CHAPTER 4. CIVIL RIGHTS AND WOMEN'S RIGHTS UNIONISM

1. For greater detail of the city's housing riots and the violence at Trumbull Park, see Arnold Hirsch, *Making the Second Ghetto: Race & Housing in Chicago, 1940–1960* (Chicago: University of Chicago Press, 1998); Adam Green, *Selling the Race: Culture, Community, and Black Chicago, 1940–1955* (Chicago: University of Chicago Press, 2007); D. Bradford Hunt, *Blueprint for Disaster: The Unraveling of Chicago Public Housing* (Chicago: University of Chicago Press, 2009); Frank London Brown, *Trumbull Park* (Chicago: Regency, 1959); Lionel Kimble Jr., "Combating the City of Neighborhoods: Housing, Employment and Civil Rights in Chicago, 1935–1955," PhD Dissertation, University of Iowa, 2004; Devereux Bowly Jr., *The Poorhouse: Subsidized Housing in Chicago, 1895–1976* (Carbondale: Southern Illinois University Press, 1978).

2. "Minutes of Meeting of District One Staff and Trumbull Park families, June 20, 1954," UPWA Papers, Box 353, Folder 12, WHS.

3. Ibid.

4. Bruce Fehn, "African American Women and the Struggle for Equality in the Meatpacking Industry, 1940–1960," *Journal of Women's History* 10, 1 (1998): 47.

5. "Minutes of Meeting of District One Staff and Trumbull Park families," June 20, 1954, UPWA Papers, Box 353, Folder 12, WHS.

6. Rick Halpern and Roger Horowitz, *Meatpackers: An Oral History of Black Workers and Their Struggle for Racial and Economic Equality* (New York: Monthly Review Press, 1999), 3.

7. *District One Champion*, Vol. 8, No. 2, April 1955, Wyatt Papers, Box 234, Folder 1, Harsh.

8. Letter from Patrick Gorman to Charles Hayes, April 22, 1954, UPWA Papers, Box 113, Folder 8, WHS.

9. "Chicago Hospitals Are Letting Negroes Die rather than Admit Them," UPWA Papers, Box 364, Folder 5, WHS.

10. Telegram from Ralph Helstein to The Honorable William G. Stratton, July 1, 1955, UPWA Papers, Box 114, Folder 9, WHS.

11. Christopher Reed, *The Chicago NAACP and the Rise of Black Professional Leadership, 1910–1966* (Bloomington: Indiana University Press, 1997), 161–167.

12. Mass Rally and Negro History Week Demonstration flyer, 1956, UPWA Papers, Box 373, Folder 6, WHS.

13. Adam Green, *Selling the Race: Culture, Community and Black Chicago, 1940–1955* (Chicago: University of Chicago Press, 2007).

14. *The Packinghouse Worker*, September 1955, UPWA Papers, Box 369, Folder 7, WHS.

15. Memo from Charles Hayes, September 3, 1955, UPWA Papers, Box 369, Folder 7, WHS.

16. Ibid.

17. In this sense, the UPWA and its alliances with progressive civil rights, community organizations, and religious institutions fit into a larger historiographical narrative in which scholars point to indigenous northern civil rights movements and struggles that predated the southern civil rights movement and attacked racism and discrimination in employment, housing, education, and politics. See Martha Biondi, *To Stand and Fight: The Struggle for Civil Rights in Postwar New York City* (Cambridge: Harvard University Press, 2006); Angela Dillard, *Faith in the City: Preaching Radical Social Change in Detroit* (Ann Arbor: University of Michigan Press, 2007); Robert Self, *American Babylon: Race and the Struggle for Postwar Oakland* (Princeton: Princeton University Press, 2005); Thomas Sugrue, *Sweet Land of Liberty: The Forgotten Struggle for Civil Rights in the North* (New York: Random House, 2008); Jeanine Theoharris and Komozi Woodward, eds., *Freedom North: Black Freedom Struggles outside of the South, 1940–1980* (New York: Palgrave MacMillan, 2003).

18. *Paving the Way*, Filmmaker's Library, 1995, videocassette.

19. Ibid.

20. Wyatt argued that the support of organized labor and workers helped lend credibility to the civil rights movement. See Addie Wyatt, Interview by author, February 21, 2008, Chicago, Ill.

21. Proceedings of the Montgomery, Alabama, Bus Boycott Conference, February 13, 1956, UPWA Papers, Box 373, Folder 6, WHS.

22. Roger Horowitz, *Negro and White, Unite and Fight: A Social History of Industrial Unionism in Meatpacking, 1930–1990* (Urbana: University of Illinois Press, 1997), 97.

23. McGann Morris Interview, 2002.

24. Addie Wyatt, Speech given at the Tenth Birthday Observance for Dr. Martin Luther King Jr. at Ebenezer Baptist Church, Atlanta, Georgia, January 14, 1978, Wyatt Papers, Box 5, Folder 52, Harsh.

25. For literature on the Chicago Freedom Movement, see Alan Anderson and George Pickering; *Confronting the Color Line: The Broken Promise of the Civil Rights Movement in Chicago* (Athens: University of Georgia Press, 1986); David Garrow, *Bearing the Cross: Martin Luther King Jr. and the Southern Christian Leadership Conference* (New York: W. Marrow, 1986); Adam Fairclough, *To Redeem the Soul of America: The Southern Christian Leadership Conference and Martin Luther King Jr.* (Athens: University of Georgia Press, 1987): David Garrow, *Chicago 1966: Open Housing Marches, Summit Negotiations and Operation Breadbasket* (Brooklyn: Carlson Publishing, 1989); James Ralph, *Northern Protest: Martin Luther King, Jr., Chicago, and the Civil Rights Movement* (Cambridge: Harvard University Press, 1993); Adam Cohen and Elizabeth Taylor, *American Pharaoh: Mayor Richard J. Daley and His Battle for Chicago and the Nation* (Boston: Little, Brown, 2000); Taylor Branch, *At Canaan's Edge: America in the King Years, 1965–1968* (New York: Simon and Schuster, 2006).

26. McGann Morris Interview, 2002.

27. Addie Wyatt, "My Sojourn to Selma," 1965, Wyatt Papers, Box 5, Folder 2, Harsh.

28. Addie Wyatt, Interview by Rick Halpern and Roger Horowitz, Tape 54, Side 2, January 30, 1986, UPWA Oral History Project, WHS.

29. Robert Zieger, *The CIO, 1935–1955* (Chapel Hill: University of North Carolina Press, 1995), 277–293.

30. Letter from A. T. Stephens to George Meany, January 19, 1960, UPWA Papers, Box 287, Folder 2, WHS.

31. Letter from Ralph Helstein to Francis E. Walter, HUAC Chairman, May 1, 1959, UPWA Papers, Box 287, Folder 1, WHS.

32. Letter from Theodore A. Jones to Congressman Francis Walter, May 1, 1959, UPWA Papers, Box 287, Folder 1, WHS.

33. Back of the Yards Neighborhood Council Press Release, UPWA Papers, Box 287, Folder 1, WHS.

34. Cyril Robinson, *Marching with Dr. King: Ralph Helstein and the United Packinghouse Workers of America* (Santa Barbara, Calif.: Praeger SB, 2011), 88.

35. Addie Wyatt, Interview by Rick Halpern and Roger Horowitz, Tape 54, Side 2, January 30, 1986, UPWA Oral History Project, WHS.

36. In *The New Left and Labor in the 1960s* (Urbana: University of Illinois Press, 1994), Peter Levy argues that AFL-CIO's Committee on Political Education (COPE) sent funds to the Student Nonviolent Coordinating Committee (SNCC) and that progressive unions like the UPWA and United Auto Workers (UAW) raised funds for SNCC from 1961 through 1963. However, more radical elements of the civil rights movement received little funds from labor and white liberal supporters. In "Organized Labor and the Civil Rights Movement of the 1960s: The Case of the Maryland Freedom Union," *Labor History* 31, 3 (1990), 322–346, Michael Flug argues that civil rights organizations like the NAACP, SCLC, SNCC, and CORE made demands on organized labor that ranged from "financial, legislative and political support" to demands to enforce antidiscriminatory hiring and employment practices and to organize unorganized workers. Flug further argues that little financial support was given to the civil rights movement (aside from the UPWA's and UAW's support for the Montgomery Bus Boycott) after 1955 from organized labor.

37. Founding Convention Program, Negro American Labor Council, May 27–29, 1960, Detroit, Mich., Timuel Black Papers, Box 126, Folder 1, Harsh.

38. Herbert Hill, "Racism within Organized Labor: A Report of Five Years of the AFL-CIO, 1955–1960," Labor Department, NAACP, January 3, 1961, New York.

39. "NALC Fact Sheet" (1963) and "Letter from Alice Armstrong, Women's Day Chairman to Chicago Area Chapter N.A.L.C," Timuel Black Papers, Box 127, Folder 1, Harsh.

40. See David Garrow, *Bearing the Cross: Martin Luther King, Jr., and the Southern Christian Leadership Conference* (New York: Perennial, 2004), 165–166; Sugrue, *Sweet Land of Liberty*, 302; Stewart Burns, *To the Mountaintop: Martin Luther King Jr.'s Mission to Save America, 1955–1968* (New York: Harper Collins, 2004), 131, 144.

41. Timuel Black, Interview by author, January 12, 2010, Chicago, Ill.

42. Addie Wyatt, Interview by author, February 21, 2008, Chicago, Ill.

43. A long list of prominent activists and organizations were represented at NALC conventions, including Dorothy Height of the National Council of Negro Women (NCNW); Dr. Martin Luther King of the SCLC; Herbert Hill of the NAACP; Mrs. Daisy Bates, advisor to the Little Rock Nine; James Farmer of CORE; Walter Reuther of the UAW; Ralph Helstein of the UPWA; and eventually George Meany, president of the AFL-CIO. See NALC Convention Programs to the First, Second, and Third Annual NALC Conventions, Timuel Black Papers, Boxes 126 and 127, Harsh.

44. Timuel Black, Interview by author, January 12, 2010, Chicago, Ill.

45. Addie Wyatt, Interview by Rick Halpern and Roger Horowitz, Tape 55, Side 1, January 30, 1986, UPWA Oral History Project, WHS.

46. Dorothy Sue Cobble, *The Other Women's Movement: Workplace Justice and Social Rights in Modern America* (Princeton: Princeton University Press, 2004). Cobble argues that labor feminists emerged over the course of the 1930s, 1940s and 1950s with the aim of eliminating sex-based disadvantages.

47. Ibid., 7–8.

48. Ibid., 159, 225; Dennis Deslippe, *Rights Not Roses: Unions and the Rise of Working Class Feminism, 1945–1980* (Urbana: University of Illinois Press, 2000), 29.

49. Ralph Helstein's name surfaced on the list of sought-after members for the Committee on Protective Labor Legislation. However, by the date of the first meeting of the committee on June 6, 1962, Addie Wyatt had taken his place. It is likely that Helstein was unable to participate or perhaps felt that Wyatt would be a better fit for the committee. Wyatt's invitation to serve on the committee was so last-minute that she was contacted via telephone just days before the first meeting in Washington, D.C., to confirm her participation. Given her relationship to other labor feminists at the time, her name may have also been suggested to Helstein as a possible replacement. See Esther Peterson Papers, Box 45, Folder 908, Arthur and Elizabeth Schlesinger Library on the History of Women in America, and Wyatt Papers, Box 34, Folder 72, Harsh.

50. Papers of the President's Commission on the Status of Women (hereafter PCSW Papers), *American Women*, 1963, 76, Wyatt Papers, Box 117, Folder 5, Harsh.

51. "Commission Meeting," February 12–13, 1962, PCSW Papers, Box 1, Folder 1, Schlesinger Library.

52. "Commission meetings," October 1–2, 1962, PCSW Papers, Box 1, Folder 4, Schlesinger Library. For a lengthier discussion of the equality versus difference debate in relation to working women, see Cobble, *The Other Women's Movement*; Deslippe, *Rights Not Roses*; Nancy Gabin, *Feminism in the Labor Movement: Women and the United Auto Workers, 1935–1975* (Ithaca: Cornell University Press, 1990); and Karen Pastorello, *A Power among Them: Bessie Abramowitz Hillman and the Making of the Amalgamated Clothing Workers of America* (Urbana: University of Illinois Press), 2008.

53. "Possible Adaptation of Protective Labor Legislation to Changing Conditions," February 12–13, 1962, PCSW Papers, Box 1, Folder 1, Schlesinger Library.

54. "USDL/PCSW" Background, March–June 1961, Esther Peterson Papers, Box 45, Folder 833, Schlesinger Library.

55. Margaret Mealey was chairman of the Committee on Protective Labor Legislation. Other committee members included Margaret Ackroyd, chief of the Rhode Island State Department of Labor's Division of Women and Children; Doris Boyle, professor of economics at Loyola College-Baltimore; Mary E. Callahan, commission member; Henry David, commission member; Bessie Hillman, vice president of Amalgamated Clothing Workers of America; Mrs. Paul McClellan Jones, vice president of the national board of the YWCA of the U.S.A.; Mary Dublin Keyserling, associate director of the Conference on Economic Progress; Carl A. McPeak, AFL-CIO special representative on state legislation; Clarence Thornbrough, commissioner of the Arkansas State Department of Labor; S. A. Wesolowski, assistant to the president of Brookshire Knitting Mills, Inc.;

and Addie Wyatt, field representative of the United Packinghouse, Food and Allied Workers.

56. Transcript of meeting minutes, Committee on Protective Labor Legislation, June 6, 1962, 115–116, PCSW Papers, Box 5, Folder 30, Schlesinger Library.

57. Transcript of meeting minutes, Committee on Protective Labor Legislation, June 6, 1962, 101, PCSW Papers, Box 5, Folder 30, Schlesinger Library.

58. Ibid.

59. Pastorello, *A Power among Them*, 168–169.

60. Letter from Addie Wyatt to Russell Lasley, November 5, 1962, UPWA Papers, Box 397, Folder 14, WHS.

61. Transcript of meeting minutes, Committee on Protective Labor Legislation, June 6, 1962, 113–114, PCSW Papers, Box 5, Folder 30, Schlesinger Library.

62. *American Woman*, "Report of the Committee on Protective Labor Legislation," Wyatt Papers, Box 117, Folder 8, Harsh.

63. Deslippe, *Rights Not Roses*, 65.

64. "American Woman Points to Inequalities," *District One Champion*, November 1963, Vol. 11, No. 9, Leon Beverly Papers, Box 1, Folder 5, WHS.

65. "State 'Protective Laws' Still Needed for Women," *District One Champion*, Vol. 12, No. 4, July 1967, UPWA Papers, Box 472, Folder 1, WHS.

66. *Step by Step: Building a Feminist Movement*, Videotape, dir. by Joyce Follet (New York City: Women Make Movies, 1998).

CHAPTER 5. CHALLENGES IN THE HOUSE OF LABOR

1. Toni Anthony, "Chicago Leaders Mobilize Woman Power," *Chicago Daily Defender (Daily Edition) (1960–1973)*, July 20, 1971, 18. ProQuest Historical Newspapers Database: Chicago Defender.

2. See Kim Moody, *An Injury to All: The Decline of American Unionism* (Brooklyn: Verso Press, 1988); Paul Buhle, *Taking Care of Business: Samuel Gompers, George Meany, Lane Kirkland, and the Tragedy of American Labor* (New York: Monthly Review Press, 1999); Aaron Brenner, Robert Brenner, and Cal Winslow, eds., *Rebel Rank and File: Labor Militancy and Revolt from Below during the Long 1970s* (Brooklyn: Verso, 2010); Philip Dray, *There Is Power in a Union: The Epic Story of Labor in America* (New York: Anchor, 2011); Nelson Liechtenstein, *State of the Union*, rev. ed. (Princeton: Princeton University Press, 2013); Robert Zieger, Timothy Minchin, and Gilbert Gall, *American Workers, American Unions*, 4th ed. (Baltimore: John Hopkins University Press, 2014).

3. "A History of the Amalgamated," Wyatt Papers, Box 43, Folder 9, Harsh.

4. Cyril Robinson, *Marching with Dr. King: Ralph Helstein and the United Packinghouse Workers of America* (Santa Barbara, Calif.: Praeger SB, 2011), 147.

5. Thomas Sugrue, *The Origins of the Urban Crisis: Race and Inequality in Postwar Detroit* (Princeton: Princeton University Press, 1996), 130.

6. Olga Madar, "Statement before the U.S. Senate Judiciary Committee in Washington, D.C. in Support of the ERA," Wyatt Papers, Box 16, Folder 53, Harsh.

7. Les Orear, Interview by author, December 2, 2009, Chicago, Ill.

8. Robinson, *Marching with Dr. King*, 148.

9. Ibid. See also "A History of the Amalgamated Meat Cutters and Butcher Workmen," Wyatt Papers, Box 43, Folder 9, Harsh.

10. Merger Agreement between the United Packing, Food and Allied Workers of America and the Amalgamated Meat Cutters and Butcher Workmen of North America, 1968, ii, Wyatt Papers, Box 41, Folder 8, Harsh.

11. Robinson, *Marching with Dr. King*, 199.

12. "Minutes of the Meeting of the Wives of Breadbasket, VPCOG, June 19," c. 1966–1967, Wyatt Papers, Box 148, Folder 15, Harsh.

13. Letter from Patrick Gorman to Addie Wyatt, July 24, 1972, Wyatt Papers, Box 45, Folder 11, Harsh.

14. Ibid.

15. Gorman Report to 1976 International Convention of the Amalgamated, Wyatt Papers, Box 46, Folder 4, Harsh.

16. Letter from Patrick Gorman to Addie Wyatt, July 24, 1972, Wyatt Papers, Box 45, Folder 11, Harsh.

17. Ibid.

18. Ibid.

19. Letter from Charles Hayes to Patrick Gorman, September 22, 1972, Wyatt Papers, Box 45, Folder 11, Harsh.

20. Ibid.

21. While Wyatt did receive copies of EEOC complaints by Amalgamated members, there is no evidence that suggests she directly handled or investigated such complaints or played a major role in that dimension of the Civil Rights Department. Harry Alston performed the bulk of this work.

22. Letter from Addie Wyatt to Patrick Gorman, October 9, 1972, Wyatt Papers, Box 45, Folder 11, Harsh.

23. Ibid.

24. Study of Unions with Women's Affairs Departments, Wyatt Papers, Box 53, Folder 10, Harsh.

25. Report of Women's Affairs to the 24th Amalgamated Convention, June 1976, Wyatt Papers, Box 56, Folder 5, Harsh.

26. Women's Affairs Department Projections for 1977, January 3, 1977, Wyatt Papers, Box 56, Folder 8, Harsh.

27. Addie Wyatt—Patrick Gorman Correspondence, April 11, 1975, Wyatt Papers, Box 46, Folder 1, Harsh.

28. Letter from Patrick Gorman to Akiva Eger, November 7, 1975, Wyatt Papers, Box 46, Folder 3, Harsh.

29. Letter from Eugene Utecht to Patrick Gorman, January 28, 1974, Wyatt Papers, Box 45, Folder 13, Harsh.

30. "Women's Affairs Director: Addie Wyatt," *The Butcher Workman*, May 1975, Wyatt Papers, Box 227, Folder 8, Harsh.

31. Civil Rights and Women's Affairs Department Report, January–May 1979, Wyatt Papers, Box 44, Folder 9, Harsh.

32. CBTU Convention Report, Conference of Black Trade Unionists, Chicago, Ill., September 23–24, 1972, Wyatt Papers, Box 103, Folder 8, Harsh.

33. Taylor Dark, *The Unions and the Democrats: An Enduring Alliance* (Ithaca: Cornell University Press, 1999), 87–89.

34. Speech by William Lucy at Conference of Black Trade Unionists, September 23–24, 1972, Wyatt Papers, Box 16, Folder 47, Harsh.

35. "Numbers, but No Clout: Minorities in the Chicago Labor Movement," *Chicago Reporter*, Vol. 3, No. 11, November 1974, Wyatt Papers, Box 45, Folder 13, Harsh.

36. Harold Rogers, Interview by author, December 21, 2009, Chicago, Ill.

37. Jervis Anderson, *A. Philip Randolph: A Biographical Portrait* (Berkeley: University of California Press, 1986), 305.

38. Ibid.

39. Ibid., 309–311.

40. CBTU Convention Proceedings, speech by Congressman Ralph Metcalfe, Coalition of Black Trade Unionists Conference, Chicago, Ill., September 23–24, 1972, Wyatt Papers, Box 103, Folder 8, Harsh.

41. Rev. Calvin Morris, Interview by author, February 3, 2010, Chicago, Ill. .

42. CBTU Convention Report, September 23–24, 1972, Wyatt Papers, Box 103, Folder 8, Harsh.

43. Addie Wyatt, "Women Workers and Affirmative Action," Wyatt Papers, Box 5, Folder 20, Harsh.

44. Ibid.

45. Panel discussion on the early role of CBTU in Chicago, January 19, 2010.

46. CBTU Convention Proceedings, CBTU Resolutions, Chicago, Ill., September 23–24, 1972, Wyatt Papers, Box 103, Folder 8, Harsh.

47. Letter from Bayard Rustin to William "Bill" Lucy, April 7, 1976, Cleveland Robinson Papers, Box 9, Folder 12, Tamiment Library and Robert F. Wagner Archives.

48. Letter from William "Bill" Lucy to Bayard Rustin, April 29, 1976, Cleveland Robinson Papers, Box 9, Folder 12, Tamiment Library and Robert F. Wagner Archives.

49. Philip Foner, *Organized Labor and the Black Worker, 1619–1981* (New York: International Publishers, 1981), 425.

50. Addie Wyatt, Interview by author, February 21, 2008, Chicago, Ill. .

51. Ibid.

52. Panel discussion on the early role of CBTU in Chicago, January 19, 2010.

53. Harold Rogers, Interview by author, December 21, 2009, Chicago, Ill.

54. McGann Morris Interview, 2002.

55. Balanoff Interview, 1977.

56. Midwest Conference Trade Union Women Leaders Proceedings, June 1973, CLUW Papers, Box 2, Folder 3, Walter Reuther Library Archives of Labor and Urban Affairs, Wayne State University.

57. Addie Wyatt, Speech at the New York Trade Union Meeting, June 1973, Wyatt Papers, Box 5, Folder 21, Harsh.

58. Philip Foner, *Women and the American Labor Movement: From the First Trade Union to the Present* (New York: The Free Press, 1982), 439; Diane Balser, *Sisterhood & Solidarity: Feminism and Labor in Modern Times* (Brooklyn: South End Press, 1987), 153–156.

59. Balanoff Interview, 1977.

60. Foner, *Women and the American Labor Movement*, 442.

61. Silke Roth, *Building Movement Bridges: The Coalition of Labor Union Women* (London: Praeger, 2003), 5.

62. Foner, *Women and the American Labor Movement*, 454; Roth, *Building Movement Bridges*, 113; Balser, *Sisterhood and Solidarity*, 133, 156–188; Annemarie Troger, "Coalition of Labor Union Women: Strategic Hope, Tactical Despair," *Radical America* 9 (1975): 85–110.

63. Balanoff Interview, 1977.

64. Ceil Poirier, Report of the First CLUW Conference, 1974, CLUW Papers, Box 2, Folder 6, Walter Reuther Library.

65. Ibid.

66. Addie Wyatt, Statement before the Illinois Senate Executive Committee, April 4, 1973, Wyatt Papers, Box 5, Folder 18, Harsh.

67. Addie Wyatt, "Women, It's Your Fight Too," Wyatt Papers, Box 6, Folder 7, Harsh.

68. For more on trade union women and the ERA, see Alice Cook, "Women and American Trade Unions," *Annals of the American Academy of Political and Social Science*, Vol. 375, 1968, 124–132; Dorothy Sue Cobble, "A Spontaneous Loss of Enthusiasm: Workplace Feminism and the Transformation of Women's Service Jobs in the 1970s," *International Labor and Working-Class History* 56 (Fall 1999): 23–44; Verta Taylor, "Social Movement Continuity: The Women's Movement in Abeyance," *American Sociological Review* 54 (October 1989): 761–775.

69. Olga Madar, Statement in Support of the ERA before the U.S. Senate Judiciary Committee, September 9, 1970, Wyatt Papers, Box 16, Folder 53, Harsh.

70. Congress, Senate Commission on Judiciary, *Equal Rights 1970: Hearing before the Committee on the Judiciary*, 91st Congress, 2nd session, September 9, 10, 11, and 15, 1970 (Washington, D.C.: U.S. Government Printing Office, 1970) taken from http://historymatters.gmu.edu/d/7018 (accessed November 21, 2011). "Do We Discard Protective Legislation for Women?" Two Labor Union Officials Voice Opposition to the ERA" (accessed November 21, 2011).

71. Addie Wyatt, "Statement on ERA Amendment," Spring 1975, Wyatt Papers, Box 5, Folder 31, Harsh.

72. Balanoff Interview, 1977.

73. Dee Myles, "Black Union Leaders Continue to Make History," http://www.peoplesworld.org/black-union-leaders-continue-to-make-history (accessed April 13, 2007).

74. Panel discussion on the early role of CBTU in Chicago; see also Katie Jordan, Interview by author, February 4, 2010, Chicago, Ill.

75. Mary Crayton, Interview by author, May 14, 2010, Chicago, Ill.

76. Ibid.

77. Ibid.

CHAPTER 6. A BLACK CHRISTIAN FEMINIST

1. Sarah Anderson, "A Study of Leadership Roles of Six Selected Ordained Women Ministers in the Church of God in Anderson, Indiana," Master's Thesis, Anderson University Archives, June 1980, 45, Church of God Archives, Anderson.

2. The number of women ordained and leading Church of God congregations declined by over half from 1925 to 1975 from 32 percent to 3 percent. See Juanita Evans Leonard, ed., *Called to Minister, Empowered to Serve* (Anderson, Ind.: Warner Press, 1989), 175; Nancy Hardesty, Lucille Sider Dayton, and Donald Dayton, "Women in the Holiness Movement: Feminism in the Evangelical Tradition," in *Women of Spirit: Female Leadership in the Jewish and Christian Traditions*, Rosemary Ruether and Eleanor McLaughlin, eds. (New York: Simon and Schuster, 1979).

3. Chanta Haywood, *Prophesying Daughters: Black Women Preachers and the Word, 1823–1913* (Columbia, Mo.: University of Missouri Press, 2003), 20; Jacquelyn Grant, "Black Women and the Church," in Gloria Hull, et al., *All the Women Are White, All the Blacks Are Men, but Some of Us Are Brave: Black Women's Studies* (New York: The Feminist Press, 1982), 141–143.

4. My use of theology most closely follows the definition provided by Jacquelyn Grant in *White Women's Christ and Black Women's Jesus: Feminist Christology and Womanist Response* (Atlanta: Scholars Press, 1989) taken from Sheila Collins, *A Different Heaven and Earth* (Valley Forge, Pa.: Judson Press, 1974), 14, where theology is a systematized body of knowledge about God, derived from cultural contexts.

5. Anderson, "A Study of Leadership Roles," 44.

6. Charles Payne, "Men Led, but Women Organized: Movement Participation of Women in the Mississippi Delta," in Rhoda Luis Blumberg and Guida West, *Women and Social Protest* (Oxford: Oxford University Press, 1990), 161.

7. Rosetta Ross, *Witnessing and Testifying: Black Women, Religion and Civil Rights* (Minneapolis: Fortress Press, 2003), 91, 112.

8. Ibid., 184, 189–190.

9. Evelyn Brooks Higginbotham, *Righteous Discontent: The Women's Movement in the Black Baptist Church, 1880–1920* (Cambridge: Harvard University Press, 1993); Marla Fredrick, *Between Sundays: Black Women and Everyday Struggles of Faith* (Berkeley: University of California Press, 2003); Wallace Best, *Passionately Human, No Less Divine: Religion and Culture in Black Chicago, 1915–1952* (Princeton: Princeton University Press, 2005); and Bettye Collier-Thomas, *Jesus, Jobs and Justice: African American Women and Religion* (New York: Knopf, 2010) have all served to expand and deepen historical understandings of black women's Christian religiosity and faith within recent years.

10. For a lengthier and more complete discussion of liberation theology's emergence, see Gustavo Gutierrez, et al., *A Theology of Liberation: History, Politics and Salvation* (New York: Orbis, 1998); Phillip Berryman, *Liberation Theology* (Philadelphia: Temple University Press, 1987); Christian Smith, *The Emergence of Liberation Theology: Radical Religion and Social Movement Theory* (Chicago: University of Chicago Press, 1991).

11. James Cone, *A Black Theology of Liberation*, 2nd ed. (Maryknoll, N.Y.: Orbis Books, 1986), 5.

12. For more on black liberation theology, see James Cone, *For My People: Black Theology and the Black Church* (New York: Orbis Books, 1984); James Cone, *Black Theology and Black Power* (New York: Seabury Press, 1969); Gayraud Wilmore and James Cone, eds., *Black Theology: A Documentary History, 1966–1979* (Maryknoll, N. Y.: Orbis Books, 1979); Dwight Hopkins, *Introducing Black Theology of Liberation* (New York:

Orbis Books, 1999); Dwight Hopkins, *Black Faith and Public Talk: Critical Essays on James H. Cone's Black Theology and Black Power* (New York: Orbis Books, 1999).

13. Grant, *White Women's Christ*, 5.

14. Some of the major works on Christian feminist and feminist theology include Rosemary Ruether, ed., *Religion and Sexism: Images of Women in Jewish and Christian Traditions* (New York: Simon and Schuster, 1974); Mary Daly, *The Church and the Second Sex* (New York: Harper and Row, 1968); Letty Russell, *Human Liberation in a Feminist Perspective—A Theology* (Louisville, Ky.: Westminster John Knox Press, 1974).

15. A number of black women theologians appropriated the term "womanism" from writer Alice Walker's *In Search of Our Mother's Garden: Womanist Prose* (New York: Harcourt Brace, 1983). Womanism referred to black feminists or feminists of color and their experiences and responses to the world around them. According to Walker, womanism included black women's courage, willfulness, audacious behavior and grown-up, in-charge demeanor; loving other women sexually or nonsexually; loving oneself, nature, and humanity; and concluded with the analogy "womanist is to feminist as purple is to lavender."

16. The field of womanist and black Christian feminist scholarship is broad. See Katie Cannon, *Black Womanist Ethics* (Oxford: Oxford University Press, 1988); Grant, *White Women's Christ*; Delores Williams, *Sisters in the Wilderness: The Challenge of Womanist God-Talk* (New York: Orbis, 1993); Cheryl Townsend Gilkes, *If It Wasn't for the Women: Black Women's Experience and Womanist Culture in Church and Community* (New York: Orbis Books, 2000); Stephanie Mitchem, *Introducing Womanist Theology* (New York: Orbis Books, 2002).

17. "History of the Vernon Park Church of God" and "A Journey through the Wilderness," Wyatt Papers, Box 76, Folders 1–3, Harsh.

18. Luke 4:18–19, KJV. This scripture is often proclaimed as one of several social justice scriptures embraced by liberation theology advocates and believers in the social gospel roots of Christianity.

19. Rev. Claude Wyatt Jr. Biographical Sketch, Wyatt Papers, Box 2, Folder 11, Harsh. See also Interview with Everett Jackson in J. S. Fuerst, *When Public Housing Was Paradise* (Westport, Conn.: Praeger, 2003), 153–158.

20. Addie Wyatt, Address at Ebenezer Baptist Church, July 20, 1980, Wyatt Papers, Box 9, Folder 42, Harsh.

21. Operation Breadbasket organizational files, Wyatt Papers, Box 148, Folder 15, and Box 149, Folder 11, Harsh.

22. Rev. Calvin Morris, Interview by author, February 3, 2010, Chicago, Ill.

23. Anderson, "A Study of Leadership Roles," 57.

24. Rev. Willie Barrow, Interview by author, March 15, 2010, Chicago, Ill.

25. Rev. Calvin Morris, Interview by author, February 3, 2010, Chicago, Ill.

26. Ibid.

27. Jerry Thornton, "Couple Harvest Full Lives from Seeds of Faith," *Chicago Tribune*, May 26, 1995, 11. Interviews with colleagues and friends—including Harold Rogers, Timuel Black, Rev. Calvin Morris, and Rev. Willie Barrow—corroborate the Wyatt's public displays of mutual respect for another's work.

28. Addie Wyatt, Speech before the National Education Association, Washington, D.C., 1981.

29. Rev. Calvin Morris, Interview by author, February 3, 2010, Chicago, Ill.

30. See Renee Hill, "Who Are We for Each Other? Sexism, Sexuality and Womanist Theology," in Cone and Wilmore, *Black Theology*, 345–351; Elias Farajaje-Jones, "Breaking Silence: Toward an In-the-Life Theology," in Cone and Wilmore, *Black Theology*, 139–159; Cathy Cohen, *The Boundaries of Blackness: AIDS and the Breakdown of Black Politics* (Chicago: University of Chicago Press, 1999); Kelly Brown Douglas, *Sexuality and the Black Church: A Womanist Perspective* (New York: Orbis Books, 1999); Neela Banerjee, "For Some Black Pastors, Accepting Gay Members Means Losing Others," *New York Times*, March 27, 2007; Roger Sneed, *Representation of Homosexuality: Black Liberation Theology and Cultural Criticism* (New York: Palgrave MacMillan, 2010).

31. Calvin Morris, Interview by author, February 3, 2010, Chicago, Ill; Albert Williams, "Musician Keith Barrow Remembered," *Gaylife—The Midwest New Weekly* 9, 22 (December 1, 1983).

32. Albert Williams, "Musician Keith Barrow Remembered," *Gaylife—The Midwest New Weekly* 9, 22 (December 1983); Calvin Morris, Interview by author, February 3, 2010, Chicago, Ill.

33. Ibid.

34. Keith Barrow Funeral Service, 1983, audio recording, Wyatt Papers, Box 314, AV 065–066, Harsh.

35. Rev. Calvin Morris, Interview by author, February 3, 2010, Chicago, Ill.

36. Addie Wyatt, "In Honor of the Pastor's Wife," 1972, Wyatt Papers, Box 5, Folder 12, Harsh.

37. Ibid.

38. Balanoff Interview, 1977.

39. Addie Wyatt, Speech at Progressive National Baptist Convention, 1979, Wyatt Papers, Box 5, Folder 64, Harsh.

40. Genesis 1:26–28, KJV.

41. Addie Wyatt, Speech at Progressive National Baptist Convention, 1979, Wyatt Papers, Box 5, Folder 64, Harsh.

42. Addie Wyatt, "Critical Issues for Concerned Christians—Women's Roles in Today's Society," 1970, Wyatt Papers, Box 6, Folder 4, Harsh.

43. Addie Wyatt, "Who Am I God? What Are My Horizons?" Wyatt Papers, Box 9, Folder 19, Harsh.

44. Addie Wyatt, Address at Ebenezer Baptist Church (Atlanta, Ga.), July 20, 1980, Wyatt Papers, Box 9, Folder 42, Harsh.

45. Addie Wyatt, "Women in the Bible," Wyatt Papers, Box 9, Folder 21, Harsh.

46. Wyatt was pro-choice and believed that abortion was a personal matter best left up to the individual. See Diane Bartley, "Woman of the Year Wyatt: Now She's a Doctor," *Anderson Sunday Herald*, June 20, 1976.

47. Addie Wyatt, "Black Christian Women—More than Conquerors," Wyatt Papers, Box 9, Folder 52, Harsh.

48. Ibid.

49. Letter from Laura Withrow to Addie Wyatt, 1980, Wyatt Papers, Box 308, Folder 74, Harsh.

50. A search for *Sexual Preference Magazine* yielded no results, and whether or not Wyatt endorsed the magazine and served on one of its committees is unknown.

51. Kathleen Berkeley, *The Women's Movement in America* (Westport, Conn.: Greenwood Press, 1999), 88–89. See also Jonathan Schoenwald, *A Time for Choosing: The Rise of Modern American Conservatism* (Oxford: Oxford University Press, 2001); Rick Perstein, *Before the Storm: Barry Goldwater and the Unmaking of the American Consensus* (New York: Hill and Wang, 2001); Donald Critchlow, *Phyllis Schlafly and Grassroots Conservatism* (Princeton: Princeton University Press, 2005); Donald Critchlow and Nancy MacLean, *Debating the American Conservative Movement: From 1945 to the Present* (Lanham, Md.: Rowman and Littefield Publishers, 2009).

52. *Dallas Times Herald*, October 24, 1977.

53. Balanoff Interview, 1977.

54. Letter from Phyllis Schlafly to Eagle Forum Members, March 1977, Wyatt Papers, Box 141, Folder 5, Harsh.

55. International Women's Year Press Release, President's National Commission on the Observance of International Women's Year, September 1977, Wyatt Papers, Box 140, Folder 6, Harsh.

56. Berkeley, *The Women's Movement in America*, xxii.

57. Ed McManus, "Two-Year Fight Ends for ERA," *Equal Rights Monitor* 2, 9 (August 1976): 12, National Organization for Women, Dallas County Chapter Archives, Box 90, Briscoe Center for American History, University of Texas–Austin.

58. *National Organization for Women Magazine*, NOW, Dallas County Chapter Archives, Box 92, Briscoe Center for American History, University of Texas–Austin.

59. Addie Wyatt, Statement on the ERA, July 14, 1982, Wyatt Papers, Box 7, Folder 3, Harsh.

60. Letter from Laura Withrow to Addie Wyatt, 1980, Wyatt Papers, Box 308, Folder 74, Harsh.

61. Addie Wyatt, "Witnessing in Difficult Times and Places," June 26, 1980, Wyatt Papers, Box 6, Folder 10, Harsh.

62. Sarah Anderson, "A Study of Leadership Roles," 65.

CHAPTER 7. UNFINISHED REVOLUTIONS

1. UFCW International Executive Board Meeting Minutes, 1979, Wyatt Papers, Box 78, Folder 11, Harsh.

2. James Strong, "Meat Cutters, Retail Clerks Plan Biggest Union Merger in History," *Chicago Tribune*, November 15, 1978, Section 1, Wyatt Papers, Box 258, Folder 29, Harsh.

3. UFCW Minority Coalition Report, 1979, Wyatt Papers, Box 82, Folder 24, Harsh.

4. Civil Rights and Women's Affairs Annual Reports, 1981–1983, Wyatt Papers, Box 62, Folders 10–12, Harsh.

5. UFCW, EEOC Complaints, Wyatt Papers, Box 77, Folders 6–39, Harsh.

6. Report of the First Women's Affairs, Civil Rights Conference, 1980, Wyatt Papers, Box 64, Folder 1, Harsh.

7. Ibid.

8. Warren Brown, "A Basic Change: Blacks Surpass Whites in Unions," *Washington Post*, December 28, 1980, Wyatt Papers, Box 257, Folder 12, Harsh.

9. Ibid.

10. 1980s Convention Proceedings, CBTU Collection, Series 1, Box 2, Folder 31, Reuther Library.

11. Steve Askin, "Turmoil in the Ranks," *Black Enterprise* 13, 2 (September 1982): 62.

12. Ibid.

13. Addie Wyatt, Remarks before Black Caucus of AFL-CIO at 1981 Convention on the Executive Council Election, Wyatt Papers, Box 9, Folder 46, Harsh.

14. William Serrin, "Kirkland's Influence on the AFL-CIO," *New York Times*, November 21, 1981.

15. Ibid.

16. "Summary Minutes of the Black Trade Unionists Leadership Meeting, March 14, 1982, Detroit Michigan," Wyatt Papers, Box 118, Folder 13, Harsh.

17. For more on Reaganomics, see Gary Wills, *Reagan's America* (New York: Penguin, 1988); Steve Fraser and Gary Gerstle, *The Rise and Fall of the New Deal Order, 1930–1980* (Princeton: Princeton University Press, 1990); Thomas Edsall and Mary Edsall, *Chain Reaction: The Impact of Race, Rights and Taxes on American Politics* (New York: W. W. Norton and Company, 1992); Andrew Busch, *Reagan's Victory: The Presidential Election of 1980 and the Rise of the Right* (Lawrence: University of Kansas Press, 2005); Jules Tygiel, *Ronald Reagan and the Triumph of American Conservatism, 2nd ed.* (New York: Longman, 2006); Joseph McCartin, *Collision Course: Ronald Reagan, the Air Traffic Controllers, and the Strike that Changed America* (Oxford: Oxford University Press, 2011).

18. William Lucy, "The Crossroad for the American Trade Union Movement: Black Leadership," Black Trade Unionists Leadership Meeting, March 14, 1982, Detroit, Michigan, Wyatt Papers, Box 118, Folder 13, Harsh.

19. Ibid.

20. See Paul Kleppner, *Chicago Divided: The Making of a Black Mayor* (Dekalb: Northern Illinois University Press, 1985); Dempsey Travis, *An Autobiography of Black Politics* (Chicago: Urban Research Press, 1987); Abdul Alkalimat and Doug Gills, *Harold Washington and the Crisis of Black Power in Chicago* (Chicago: Twenty First Century Books and Publications, 1989); Alton Miller, *Harold Washington: The Mayor, the Man* (Chicago: Bonus Books, 1989); William Grimshaw, *Bitter Fruit: Black Politics and the Chicago Machine, 1931–1991* (Chicago: University of Chicago Press, 1992); Gary Rivlin, *Fire on the Prairie: Chicago's Harold Washington and the Politics of Race* (New York: Henry Holt and Co., 1992); Salim Muwakkil, *Harold! Photographs from the Harold Washington Years* (Evanston: Northwestern University Press, 2007).

21. David Colburn and Jeffrey Adler, eds., *African American Mayors: Race, Politics and the American City* (Urbana: University of Illinois Press, 2005); J. Philip Thompson III, *Double Trouble: Black Mayors, Black Communities and the Call for a Deep Democracy* (Oxford: Oxford University Press, 2005).

22. David T. Beito and Linda Royster Beito, *Black Maverick: T. R. M. Howard's Fight for Civil Rights and Economic Power* (Urbana: University of Illinois, 2009), 182; Bennett Johnson, Interview by author, March 25, 2010, Chicago, Ill.

23. Bennett Johnson, Interview by author, March 25, 2010, Chicago, Ill.

24. Mike Royko, *Boss: Richard J. Daley of Chicago* (New York: Plume Book, 1976).

25. Committee for a Black Mayor, "Criteria—Candidate for Black Mayor," Wyatt Papers, Box 118, Folder 1, Harsh.

26. Ibid.

27. Charles Hayes, Statement of the Committee for a Black Mayor, December 3, 1974, Wyatt Papers, Box 118, Folder 11, Harsh.

28. Bennett Johnson, Interview by author, 25 March 2010, Chicago, Ill.

29. Muwakkil, *Harold!* 2; D. C. Coleman, "Harold Washington as a Role Model for Black Youth," in Henry Young, ed., *The Black Church and the Harold Washington Story* (Lima, Ohio: Wyndham Hall Press, 1988), 149–150; Stephen Alexander, "Equity Policies and Practices of the Harold Washington Administration: Lessons for Progressive Cities," in Michael Bennett and Robert Giloth, eds., *Economic Development in American Cities: The Pursuit of an Equity Agenda* (New York: SUNY Press, 2007), 53.

30. Building an Illinois Legislative Lobby (B.I.L.L.) files, Wyatt Papers, Box 93, Folder 6, Harsh.

31. Letter from Mary Lou Hedlin to Addie Wyatt, July 19, 1977, Wyatt Papers, Box 122, Folder 6, Harsh. Wyatt was ultimately elected to the DNC.

32. Colburn and Adler, *African American Mayors*, 111.

33. Willie Barrow; "The Black Church as Agent of Social Change: The Harold Washington Story," in Young, *The Black Church*; Muwakkil, *Harold!*.

34. Rivlin, *Fire on the Prairie*, 35, 131–137; Muwakkil, *Harold!*.

35. Jeremiah Wright, "Church Growth and Political Empowerment—The Significance of Harold Washington," in Young, *The Black Church*, 1–9.

36. Muwakkil, *Harold!* 102.

37. Addie Wyatt, "The Role of Women in the Harold Washington Story," in Young, *The Black Church*, 95.

38. Ibid., 96.

39. Ibid.

40. Ibid., 97.

41. Ibid., 102.

42. La Risa Lynch, "Women Played Pivotal Role in Washington's Election, Administration." *Hyde Park Citizen*, November 23, 2005, 6.

43. Ibid.

44. Ibid.

45. Brenda Little, "The Significance of the Harold Washington Story for Black Women in Ministry," in Young, *The Black Church*, 145.

46. Dee Myles, "Black Union Leaders Continue to Make History," http://www.peoples world.org/black-union-leaders-continue-to-make-history (accessed April 13, 2007.

47. Larry Bennett, "Harold Washington and the Black Urban Regime," *Urban Affairs Quarterly* 28, 3 (March 1993): 423–424.

48. The Washington Papers, Wyatt Papers, Box 102, Folder 1, Harsh.

49. Harold Washington, "State of the City, 1986," Wyatt Papers, Box 102, Folder 5, Harsh.

50. The Washington Papers, Wyatt Papers, Box 129, Folder 6, Harsh.

51. Committee to Re-Elect Congressman Charles Hayes, "Charles Hayes: A Working Man's Story," Wyatt Papers, Box 129, Folder 16, Harsh; U.S. House of Representatives, "Black Americans in Congress," 1870–2007. Hayes did suffer from some negative blots on his congressional record, specifically investigations into monetary practices and fiscal use during his campaign in 1983 and in his last term of Congress, which ultimately cost him in the 1992 election. The former involved Wyatt and several others who endorsed a loan for Hayes that extended the personal financial contributions allowed per campaign. Hayes was later cleared of any wrongdoing in the latter incident. Hayes passed away from lung cancer in 1997.

52. Colburn and Adler, *African American Mayors*, 118.

53. Eugene Gibson, "Where Do We Go from Here? Harold Washington and the Future," in Young, *The Black Church*, 21.

54. Bennett, "Harold Washington," 435; Figures from "Annual Report to the Equal Employment Opportunity Commission on the Employment of Minorities and Women in City Government," 1983, 1985, 1987, 1989, by City of Chicago Municipal Reference Library based on City of Chicago Department of Personnel.

55. Bennett and Giloth, eds. *Economic Development in American Cities*, 54–55.

56. The Washington Papers, Wyatt Papers, Box 102, Folder 1, Harsh.

57. "Women in Chicago Government," 1986, Wyatt Papers, Box 102, Folder 5, Harsh.

58. Ibid.

59. Ibid.

60. Ibid.

61. "An Analysis of the Mayoral Primary Election," 1987, Wyatt Papers, Box 176, Folder 7, Harsh.

62. Rivlin, *Fire on the Prairie*. See also Bennett, "Harold Washington," 434; Colburn and Adler, *African American Mayors*, 123–124.

63. Colburn and Adler, *African American Mayors*, 120–121.

64. Ibid., 123.

65. *Chicago Sun Times* Special Memorial Section, November 25–30, 1987.

66. Michael Hirsley, "Churches Are Sources of Power—Congregations Form Hub of Existence in Community," *Chicago Tribune*, Proquest (pre-1997 fulltext), Chicago, Illinois, February 5, 1992, 6, North Sports Final Edition.

67. R. Bruce Dold, "Sawyer Leans on Outsiders for His Support," Final Edition, Section C of the *Chicago Tribune*, June 19, 1988, 1, Proquest database (pre-1997 fulltext).

68. Clergy for Sawyer, Wyatt Papers, Box 172, Folder 9, Harsh.

69. "Mayor Sawyer Receives Labor Support for Re-Election," 1989, Wyatt Papers, Box 172, Folder 10, Harsh.

70. Letter from Addie Wyatt, March 18, 1988, Wyatt Papers, Box 172, Folder 11, Harsh.

71. Colburn and Adler, *African American Mayors*, 124.

72. Dawn Turner Trice, "Immigration Issues Real in the Delta: Struggle to Hold on to What We Have," June 20, 2006, *A Katrina Reader*, katrinareader.org/immigration-issues-real-delta-struggle-hold-what-we-have (accessed January 31, 2014).

73. *This Far by Faith*, Videocassette, dir. by Patrice O'Neil (Berkeley: California Working, 1991); Candace Ellis, "Pickets in the Land of Catfish": The African American Labor Rights Struggle in the Catfish Industry in the Mississippi Delta, 1965–1990," Masters Thesis, University of Florida, 2012, 9; Kristal Brent Zook, *Black Women's Lives: Stories of Power and Pain* (New York: Nation Books, 2006), 163; "Women's Pride at Delta Pride," *CLUW News* 17, 1 (January-February 1991).

74. Trice, "Immigration Issues Real in the Delta."

75. "Women's Pride at Delta Pride."

76. Sarah White, Interview by author, June 11, 2010, Indianola, Miss.

77. Sarah White and Margaret Hollins, Interview with Michael Flug, Tape 5, Side 2, April 1995, Transcript, Sarah White Papers, Harsh.

78. "Women's Pride at Delta Pride"; Zook, *Black Women's Lives*, 162; Ellis, "Pickets in the Land," 47.

79. Trice, "Immigration Issues Real in the Delta."

80. Zook, *Black Women's Lives*, 163.

81. Ibid.

82. Ellis, "Pickets in the Land," 59–60.

83. *This Far by Faith*; "Delta Pride Workers on Strike," *UFCW Action* (January–February 1991), 4.

84. Laurie Green, "A Struggle of the Mind": Black Working-Class Women's Organizing in Memphis and the Mississippi Delta, 1960s to 1990s," in Marguerite Waller and Jennifer Rycenga, eds., *Frontline Feminisms: Women, War and Resistance* (New York: Routledge, 2001), 412.

85. Sarah White, "Change in a Closed Little Town," *Southern Exposure* (Fall/Winter 1997), 45.

86. Michael Flug, "Sarah White," in Henry Louis Gates Jr. and Evelyn Brooks-Higginbotham, eds., *African American National Biography* (Oxford: Oxford University Press, 2008), 257–258.

87. Jacqueline Grant, "Civil Rights Women: A Source for Doing Womanist Theology," in Darlene Clark Hine, ed., *Black Women in U.S. History* (New York: Carlson Publishing Series, 1990), 43–44.

88. Ibid.

89. Ellis, "Pickets in the Land," 57; Sarah White, Interview by author, June 11, 2010, Indianola, Miss.

90. Sarah White, Interview by author, June 11, 2010, Indianola, Miss.

91. "Delta Pride Workers on Strike."

92. Trice, "Immigration Issues Real in the Delta"; Margaret Hollins Interview by Michael Flug, Tape 6, Side 2, April 1995, Transcript, Sarah White papers, Harsh.

93. Ellis, "Pickets in the Land," 63.

94. "1990 Strike, 9/12/90–12/14/90," Sarah White Papers, Harsh.

95. UFCW Delta Pride Strike Rally, 1990, videotape, Wyatt Papers, Box 219, AV 076, Harsh.

96. Sarah White, Interview by author, June 11, 2010, Indianola, Miss.

97. Sarah White and Margaret Hollins, Interview with Michael Flug, Tape 7, Side 1, April 1995, Transcript, Sarah White Papers, Harsh; *This Far by Faith*.

98. Ibid.

99. "Delta Pride Workers on Strike."

100. Sarah White and Margaret Hollins, Interview with Michael Flug, Tape 7, Side 2, April 1995, Transcript, Sarah White Papers, Harsh.

101. "Women's Pride at Delta Pride"; Trice, "Immigration Issues Real in the Delta."

102. White, "Change in a Closed Little Town," 46.

103. Flug, "Sarah White," 258.

104. Trice, "Immigration Issues Real in the Delta."

SELECTED BIBLIOGRAPHY

ARCHIVAL REPOSITORIES AND COLLECTIONS

Anderson University Archives, Anderson, Indiana
   Church of God Reformation Movement Collection
Arthur & Elizabeth Schlesinger Library on the History of Women in America, Radcliffe
   College, Harvard University, Boston, Massachusetts
   Esther Peterson Papers
   President's Commission on the Status of Women Papers
   National Organization for Women Records
Chicago History Museum, Chicago, Illinois
   Altgeld Gardens Public Housing Project Materials
Dolph Briscoe Center for American History, University of Texas–Austin, Austin, Texas
   National Organization for Women Records–Dallas County Chapter
   National Organization for Women Records–Austin Chapter
King Center, Atlanta, Georgia
   Papers of the Southern Christian Leadership Conference
   Papers of Martin Luther King Jr.
Mississippi Department of Archives and History, Jackson, Mississippi
   Lincoln County Subject Files
   Educable Children Database
Robert W. Woodruff Library, Morehouse College, Atlanta, Georgia
   Martin Luther King Jr. Collection
Schomburg Center for Research in Black Culture, New York, New York
   A. Philip Randolph Collection
   Coalition of Black Trade Unionists Collection
   Dupree African-American Pentecostal and Holiness Collection
   Frank Crosswaithe Papers
   Richard Parrish Papers

Tamiment Library, New York University, New York, New York
  Betsy Wade Papers
  Cleveland Robinson Papers
Walter Reuther Labor Library, Wayne State University, Detroit, Mississippi
  Coalition of Black Trade Unionists Papers
  Coalition of Labor Union Women Papers
Wisconsin Historical Society, Madison, Wisconsin
  Amalgamated Meat Cutters and Butcher Workmen of North America Collection
  Herbert March Papers
  Leon Beverly Papers
  United Packinghouse Workers of America (UPWA) Collection
  UPWA Oral History Project
Vivian G. Harsh Research Collection, Carter G. Woodson Branch–Chicago Public Library, Chicago, Illinois
  Rev. Addie and Rev. Claude Wyatt Papers
  Charles Hayes Papers
  Coalition of Black Trade Unionists, Chicago Chapter Archives
  Illinois Writers Project/Negro in Illinois Papers
  Lucy Smith Collier Papers
  Timuel Black Papers
  Sarah White Papers

INTERVIEWS BY AUTHOR

Addie Wyatt
Les Orear
Harold Rogers
Timuel Black
Bennett Johnson
Sarah White
Mary Crayton
Katie Jordan
Rev. Willie Barrow
Maude McKay
Claude Wyatt, III
Rev. Calvin Morris

INTERVIEWS BY OTHERS

Harris, Eva. Interview by Mrs. Kay Calcote, Lincoln-Lawrence-Franklin Regional Library Oral Histories, July 1987.
Hayes, Charles. The HistoryMakers, Interview by Julieanna Richardson, January 1, 1993. Chicago, Illinois. The HistoryMakers Digital Archive.
Jones, Sam. Interview by Bob and Betsy Jones, Lincoln-Lawrence-Franklin Regional Library Oral Histories, February 18, 1989.

Rothstein, Ruth. Interview by Emily Freidman, August 20, 2008, Chicago, Illinois, Hospital Administration Oral History Collection, American Hospital Association.

Wyatt, Addie. Interview by Elizabeth Balanoff, March 16, 1977. Transcribed through Oral History Project in Labor History, Roosevelt University, Chicago, Illinois, 2001.

Wyatt, Addie. Interview by Joan McGann Morris, December 14, 2002, Chicago, Illinois. Working Women's History Project, UIC Chicago Labor Education Program.

Wyatt, Addie. Interview by Rick Halpern and Roger Horowitz, January 30, 1986. State Historical Society of Wisconsin UPWA Oral History Project, tapes 54–56. Printed as "Lost Visions of Equality: The Labor Origins of the Next Women's Movement" in *Labor's Heritage* 12 (Winter/Spring 2003): 26.

Wyatt, Addie. The HistoryMakers, Interview by Julieanna Richardson, June 1, 2002, Chicago, Illinois. The HistoryMakers Digital Archive.

INDEX

MARCIA WALKER-MCWILLIAMS holds a doctorate in American history from the University of Chicago.

The University of Illinois Press
is a founding member of the
Association of American University Presses.

—————————————————————————

Composed in 10.5/13 Adobe Minion Pro
by Lisa Connery
at the University of Illinois Press
Manufactured by Sheridan Books, Inc.

University of Illinois Press
1325 South Oak Street
Champaign, IL 61820-6903
www.press.uillinois.edu